The Geography of the Canadian North

Issues and Challenges

Second Edition

Robert M. Bone

OXFORD
UNIVERSITY PRESS

OXFORD
UNIVERSITY PRESS

70 Wynford Drive, Don Mills, Ontario M3C 1J9
www.oup.com/ca

Oxford University Press is a department of the University of Oxford.
It furthers the University's objective of excellence in research, scholarship,
and education by publishing worldwide in

Oxford New York

Auckland Bangkok Buenos Aires Cape Town Chennai

Dar es Salaam Delhi Hong Kong Istanbul Karachi Kolkata

Kuala Lumpur Madrid Melbourne Mexico City Mumbai Nairobi

São Paulo Shanghai Singapore Taipei Tokyo Toronto

with an associated company in Berlin

Oxford is a trade mark of Oxford University Press
in the UK and in certain other countries

Published in Canada by Oxford University Press

Copyright © Oxford University Press Canada 2003

The moral rights of the author have been asserted

Database right Oxford University Press (maker)

First published 2003

National Library of Canada Cataloguing in Publication Data

Bone, Robert M
The geography of the Canadian north : issues and challenges/
Robert M. Bone.—2nd ed.

Includes bibliographical references and index.
ISBN 0-19-541820-4

1. Canada, Northern—Geography.
2. Canada, Northern—Economic conditions.
3. Natural resources—Canada, Northern.
4. Indians of North America—Canada, Northern. I. Title

HC117.N5B65 2003   917.19   C2003-901085-6

Cover design: Brett Miller
Text design: Valentino Sanna, Ignition Design and Communications

1 2 3 4 - 06 05 04 03
This book is printed on permanent (acid-free) paper ⊖.
Printed in Canada

Contents

LIST OF FIGURES

Preface

The North is a fascinating region of Canada. I hope that the students reading this book will not only agree, but also become familiar with its unique character and challenges. Over the last 50 years, profound changes have taken place in the Canadian North, including the emergence of the resource industry as the dominant factor in the economy, the rise of Aboriginal political power, and the recognition of industrial pollution as a serious threat to the northern environment and its peoples. Megaprojects define the nature of the resource industry and the scope of impact on the environment and Aboriginal peoples. These projects are not distributed evenly across the North, but are concentrated in the Subarctic. The hidden costs of resource development, especially its effect on the land, are now recognized in the much more stringent environmental impact assessment procedure. Prior to the 1970s, many resource projects damaged the northern environment, and to this day abandoned mine sites often contain toxic wastes.

As we move forward in the twenty-first century, Aboriginal peoples have ceased to be marginal players in the process of economic development and have become major players. Aboriginal participation in megaprojects—whether as partners in the proposed Mackenzie Valley pipeline project, as owners of vast northern property as a result of land claim agreements, or as active participants in environmental impact assessments—has changed the way of doing business in the North. Still, Aboriginal workers hold relatively few jobs in the northern economy. This low rate of participation is a complex subject worthy of a much fuller discussion than found in this book. Nevertheless, geography and culture play a role. Most Native settlements, for example, are both small in size and remote in location. As a result, they are ill-suited for economic development, thereby stranding their residents from job opportunities. An economy based on huge projects to extract resources from the environment is not part of Aboriginal culture, which stresses collectivism and respect for the environment. Yet the flexible nature of Aboriginal culture is coming to grips with resource development in different ways.

The readers of this book will note that resource development is perceived differently by northerners and southerners. The first group sees the North as a homeland. They look at resource development from two perspectives: What benefits do northerners receive? And what effect does it have on the environment, especially wildlife? Southerners regard the North as a frontier where resource development translates into profits.

The first edition of this book was published in 1992. While I had planned to revise this book much earlier, serious work did not begin until 2002. The staff at Oxford University Press, but particularly Laura Macleod and Phyllis Wilson, and the copy editor, Richard Tallman, were instrumental in guiding this work through its final stages. Gerald Weinstein and an anonymous reader selected by Oxford University Press, both of whom made a number of constructive suggestions and brought a number of issues into focus, deserve special mention.

Finally, a special note of appreciation goes to my wife, Karen, for her support and willingness to shoulder so many of my family responsibilities.

CHAPTER 1

Northern Perceptions

The North is a unique region within Canada. Canadians have several images of the North. While most Canadians have never visited the North, this region holds a special place in their minds and hearts. In many ways, the challenges and issues facing northerners symbolize the nation's sense of purpose and suggest the course of its future development. Yet, what exactly is the North? For most, the North represents the colder lands of North America where winters are extremely long and dark, where permafrost abounds, and where few people live. Canadians also perceive of this cold and diverse environment in two ways: either as a frontier or as a homeland. For the indigenous peoples who first occupied these lands many thousands of years ago, the Canadian North is their homeland. Others accept the frontier version of the North, which implies building communities and an economy similar to those found in southern Canada. While the vision of the frontier dominates the overall direction of northern development, the homeland theme surfaces in areas where Native people comprise the majority of the population and where they hold Aboriginal rights to the land. The economic and political forces shaping the North of tomorrow swing back and forth between these two visions. The fundamental question is: will the North of tomorrow replicate the course of development found in southern Canada or will it break away from that template? Already, there are signs of a different course. Nunavut, for example, represents a political divergence from the other two territories and the 10 provinces, and it represents an Inuit response to the northern homeland question. Another example is the effort of the Aboriginal Pipeline Group to obtain a one-third ownership in the proposed $4 billion Mackenzie Valley natural gas pipeline, reflecting both a desire on the part of northern Aboriginal peoples to participate in resource development and recognition by corporate Canada that Aboriginal participation is necessary for business in the North (see Vignette 1.1).

DEFINING THE NORTH

The North is both easy and difficult to define. Some see the North as a place of great wealth—a kind of northern Eldorado.[1] Many focus on its cold environment, perhaps picturing the North as a frozen land where permafrost is commonly found, where ice covers the Arctic Ocean for most of the year, and where winter nights are long and cold.

Vignette 1.1 What Is Development?

The concept of development is a process of long-term change in society. As such, development is concerned with economic, social, and political factors shaping society. It includes not only the notion of economic growth but also social and political changes that involve people's health, education, housing, security, civil rights, and other social characteristics. Seen in this light, development is a normative concept, involving Western values, goals, and beliefs. It follows that development in the Canadian North occurs within the market economy and is supported by the Canadian political system. Until recently, the place of Aboriginal peoples within the Canadian version of development was often ignored or dismissed. Since then, the legal validation of Aboriginal rights, the establishment of modern land claims negotiation processes, and the participation of Aboriginal groups in the market economy mark the inclusion of Aboriginal peoples within the development process.

Others subscribe to a homeland definition where those born and raised in the North have a special, deeper commitment to that place. Louis-Edmond Hamelin (1979: 9) described this feeling as 'a trait as deeply anchored as a European's attachment to the site of his hamlet or his valley'. In this single statement, Hamelin has captured the geographer's notion of a sense of place and the parallel idea of regional consciousness.[2] In this text, these three images of the North—as a northern Eldorado, as a cold environment, and as a homeland—are taken into account, but the North as a geographic area is defined as consisting of two biomes, the Arctic and Subarctic (Figure 1.1). These biomes extend over a vast area—nearly 80 per cent of Canada—that includes the three territories and reaches into the territories of seven provinces. The southern boundary of the North is marked by the places where the northern coniferous forest of the Subarctic gives way to other natural vegetation zones such as the grasslands of the Canadian Prairies. Often, this boundary corresponds to the southern limit of permafrost, indicating the interrelationship between natural features of the environment (Figure 1.2). The Arctic exists in the three territories and four of the provinces (Quebec, Newfoundland/Labrador, Ontario, and Manitoba), while the Subarctic occurs in all seven provinces with a northern landscape (British Columbia, Alberta, Saskatchewan, Manitoba, Ontario, Quebec, and Newfoundland/Labrador) and two territories (Northwest Territories and Yukon). Each biome is described in detail in Chapter 2. Yet, what are often missed in such images and definitions are the North's extremely varied cultural and biological environments. The richness and diversity of its physical geography are captured in the next chapter, 'The Physical Base', while its cultural/historical geography is the focus of Chapter 3, 'The Historical Background'.

SENSE OF ISOLATION

The North is a different region from the rest of Canada. Many northern communities are small and some are beyond the national highway system. Southern Canadians now living in such remote centres are confronted by a sense of isolation from the rest of

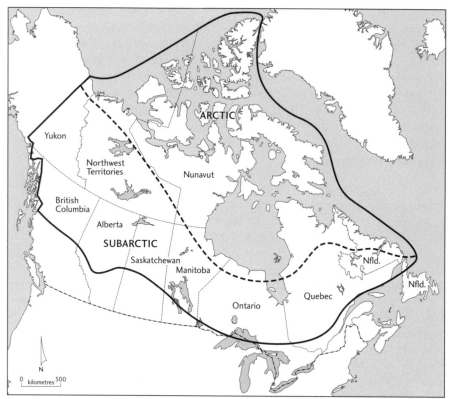

FIGURE 1.1 The Canadian North
The Canadian North consists of the three territories (Yukon, Northwest Territories, and Nunavut) and the northern areas of seven provinces (British Columbia, Alberta, Saskatchewan, Manitoba, Ontario, Quebec, and Newfoundland/Labrador). The North is also divided into two natural biomes: the Arctic and Subarctic. The southern boundary of the Canadian North corresponds with the southern limit of the northern coniferous forest.

Canada. This psychological barrier affects the lives of its newly arrived residents, who live in communities where air transportation represents the only means of reaching southern Canada. Such communities are found in the three territories and, with the exception of British Columbia, in all seven provinces with northern areas. This sense of isolation has a negative effect on recruiting skilled workers and professional people, and partially accounts for the high job turnover and out-migration. Companies and governments often employ incentives to attract workers to live in remote centres. Northerners, for example, receive a special income tax deduction for living in the North (Northern Residents Deduction), but this deduction varies by tax region. In the more northerly (less accessible) tax region the deduction is pegged at 100 per cent, while in the less northerly (somewhat more accessible) tax region the deduction falls to 50 per cent. By reducing the amount of taxable income, northerners are able to reduce their personal income tax. Because the geographic definition of these two regions determines the amount of the Northern Residents Deduction and of northern living allowances for many federal employees, Statistics Canada has joined in the search for a working definition of the North (McNiven and Puderer, 2000). A permanent definition of the North is complicated by two factors: (1) improvements in the national transportation system that create greater accessibility to northern communities; and (2) population increases of northern urban centres that lead to the availability of more public and private services. This dynamic element to northern boundaries is discussed further in this chapter under the subsection 'Nordicity'.

THE POLITICAL NORTH

Political structure poses an additional challenge to defining the North. Federal and provincial jurisdictions make for a political divide. Ottawa continues to play a key role in territorial affairs and provides the territories with most of their budgets. Each province treats its northern areas as a provincial hinterland that parallels the core/periphery model discussed later in this chapter. Provinces, unlike territories, have total control over resource developments within their respective boundaries. Provinces also benefit from the taxation of these developments. Accordingly, provincial governments wish to open their hinterlands to resource development by constructing highways and railways from southern cities into their northern areas. The strategy is simple: by lowering the cost of transporting such resources to world markets, hinterland development becomes possible. British Columbia provides one example of this strategy. The provincial government built and operates BC Rail (formerly the Pacific Great Eastern Railway), which connects the northern interior of British Columbia with the port of North Vancouver. As a result, the forest and other resources of the northern interior of British Columbia were exploited and their products exported to southern markets by means of BC Rail.

The North's political structure also creates a mental divide for many Canadians, who believe that the three territories represent Canada's North. Margaret Johnston (1994: 1) correctly observed that 'there has been a tendency to view much of this [provincial] part of the north in Canada as less northern than Yukon and the Northwest Territories, and consequently it has received considerably less attention as a northern region.' Indeed, Coates and Morrison (1992) describe the northern areas of seven provinces as 'the forgotten north'. In this text, as noted earlier, the North includes the three territories and the cold lands found in the northern sectors of seven provinces. The political division between territories and provinces warrants identifying the three territories as the 'Territorial North' and the northern parts of the seven provinces as the 'Provincial Norths'.

DUALISM IN THE NORTH

Northern Canada's peoples, Aboriginal and non-Aboriginal, have distinct economic systems deeply rooted in their cultural aspirations, goals, and values. These two economies may be described as the resource/service economy and the mixed economy. The resource sector produces most of the wealth while the service sector accounts for most employment. The resource sector produces primary products for export to world markets. Multinational companies and Crown corporations play a leading role in this resource-based economy because vast sums of capital are required. The service sector is dominated by governments and small businesses. The mixed or Native economy has evolved from a subsistence hunting economy. In this mixed economy wage employment, transfer payments, and trapping generate the cash income, while hunting and fishing provide country food. While the mixed economy is unable to match the high incomes associated with the resource economy, it does encompass Aboriginal traditional activities and values. For many Aboriginal peoples, the mixed economy satisfies their needs and wants. However, some have chosen to participate in the resource/service economy. This trend is especially noticeable among younger and more educated Indians, Métis, and Inuit, many of whom are employed by governments. The government of Nunavut, for instance, employs more Inuit than any other sector of the Nunavut economy.

SIZE OF THE NORTH

The North accounts for 78 per cent of Canada's geographic area. This area is almost equally divided between the Territorial North and the Provincial Norths (Table 1.1). While most Canadians realize that the three territories occupy a vast area of Canada, the sheer size of the northern area found in the seven provinces is surprising to many people. A second surprise comes from the realization that by whatever standard of measurement we use—cultural, economic, ecological, or climatological—at least half of the total area of five provinces is in the North (Table 1.1). Of all the provinces, Quebec has the largest 'northern' area, making up 81 per cent of the province. Newfoundland and Manitoba are next with 74 per cent of their territory classified as 'northern'. Northern lands make up 65 per cent of Ontario and 50 per cent of Saskatchewan. Alberta and British Columbia trail behind, with 47 and 40 per cent respectively.

COMMON CHARACTERISTICS

Even though the geographic extent of the Canadian North is vast, this region has many common characteristics (Table 1.2). A cold environment, sparse population, and extensive wilderness areas with enormous biological diversity represent but three common characteristics. Another characteristic is the high percentage of Aboriginal peoples in the northern population. Unlike southern Canada, where the Aboriginal population forms a very small proportion of the total population, Aboriginal peoples comprise a large portion of the northern population. In some areas, they form a majority of the local population. In Nunavut, for example, the Inuit make up around 85 per cent of the territory's population. Like other hinterlands within the core/periphery structure of the world economy, the North has a resource economy. While forestry and mining activities account for most of the value of economic production in the North, these industries employ relatively few workers. In fact, the vast majority are employed by public agencies. In the next pages, the North's winter, the concept of nordicity, and the core/periphery model are explored.

TABLE 1.1 Geographic Size of the Canadian North by Province/Territory (000 km² and per cent)

Province or Territory	Total Area	Northern Area	North (%)	Canada (%)
Newfoundland/Labrador	405	300	74	3.0
Alberta	662	310	47	3.2
Saskatchewan	651	325	50	3.3
British Columbia	945	375	40	3.8
Manitoba	648	480	74	4.9
Ontario	1,076	700	65	7.1
Quebec	1,542	1,250	81	12.7
Provinces	**5,929**	**3,740**	**63**	**38.0**
Yukon	482	482	100	4.9
Northwest Territories	1,346	1,346	100	13.7
Nunavut	2,093	2,093	100	21.2
Territorial North	**3,921**	**3,921**	**100**	**39.8**
Canada	**9,850**	**7,661**		**77.8**

SOURCE: Adapted from Statistics Canada, Land and Freshwater Area, available at: <www.statca/english/PGdb/Land/Geography/phys01.htm>.

TABLE 1.2 Common Characteristics of the North

Physical Characteristics	Human Characteristics
Cold environment	Sparse population
Biological diversity	Population stabilization
Wilderness	High cost of living
Remote	Few highways
Permafrost	Aboriginal population
Vast geographic area	Settling of land claims
Fragile environment	Financial dependency
Slow biological growth	Resource economy
Importance of wildlife	Reliance on imported foods
Global warming	Country food
Continental climate	Economic hinterland

NORTHERN WINTERS

Winter, its length and intensity, is one measure of a cold environment (Vignette 1.2). Canadians living in the North are confronted by one of the longest and coldest winters in the world. The key physical element controlling Canada's cold environment is the low quantity of solar energy received in Canada's high latitudes that roughly translates into the mean annual air temperature isotherms shown in Figure 1.2. The moderating influence of the warm Pacific Ocean breaks the latitudinal pattern of winter as measured by these isotherms. For example, the direction of the five-degree isotherm runs in a north/south direction along the coastal area of British Columbia while the same isotherm takes an east/west direction as it enters the interior of British Columbia where the influence of the Pacific Ocean diminishes.

Vignette 1.2 Long Winter Nights

The longest winter nights occur at the winter solstice (21 December). The Arctic Circle marks the area of the earth where one winter night lasts for 24 hours. The Arctic Circle is an imaginary line that circles the globe at 66° 33'N, the northward limit of the sun's rays at the time of the winter solstice. At this latitude, the sun does not rise above the horizon for one day of the year. However, the polar night does not begin immediately because twilight occurs for a short period of time when the sun is just below the horizon (Burn, 1995:70). Beyond the Arctic Circle, considerable variation occurs in the number of days in which the sun is not visible. At Alert (82° 29') there are nearly five months of 'polar night', while at Inuvik (68° 21') there is just over one month of total darkness.

The cold environment is also associated with extremely long winter nights. For example, the sun does not rise above the horizon in areas north of the Arctic Circle (65° 30'N). The Arctic Circle is shown in Figure 1.2. This phenomenon of darkness increases towards the North Pole. Twilight does occur when the sun is just below the horizon (Burn, 1995: 70). Otherwise the sky is dark. Northerners living at the Arctic Circle are subjected to this 'darkness' phenomenon for at least one day a year while those living in higher latitudes are subject to an even longer period without seeing the sun. Within this 'zone of winter darkness', the number of days in which the sun does not rise above the horizon varies. At Alert (82° 29'N) there are nearly five months of continuous darkness, while at Inuvik (68° 21') there is just over one month of continuous darkness. The reverse conditions occur in the summer: Alert has nearly five months of continuous sunlight and Inuvik has just over one month of continuous sunlight—providing there is no cloudy weather.

There are economic, social, and psychological implications of this 'darkness' phenomenon for southern Canadians in the North, who are unacclimatized to the lack of light (and the lack of darkness) for long periods of time. For those living in high latitudes, the continuous darkness of the Arctic winter imposes severe restrictions on outdoor work and recreational activities. Even more important, the combination of darkness and a reduction of normal activities may adversely affect the emotional

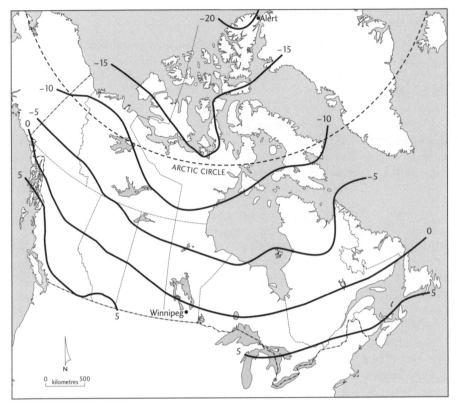

FIGURE 1.2 The Cold Environment
A measure of the North's cold environment is provided by mean annual air temperatures in degrees Celsius. Each of the six isotherms indicates that the mean annual air temperature becomes progressively lower as latitudes increase. The energy deficit zone lies north of the zero degree isotherm that also closely approximates the southern boundary of permafrost.

equilibrium and motivation of southern Canadians living in high latitudes. This phenomenon is commonly called 'bushed'. The reappearance of the sun on the horizon usually provokes a favourable response from 'transplanted' Canadians. In Inuvik, residents celebrate the return of the sun with a 'Sunrise Festival' featuring a huge bonfire and variety of community events to celebrate the sun's return.

While the North has a cold environment, this environment varies from place to place (Slocombe, 1995: 161). The human landscape also varies. 'Nordicity' is a term that attempts to mix human and physical factors and then to measure the degree of 'northernness' at specific places.

NORDICITY

Created by a Canadian geographer, Louis-Edmond Hamelin (1979), nordicity provides a quantitative measure of 'northernness' for any place based on 10 selected variables that attempt to represent all facets of the North. These variables, called polar units, are a combination of physical and human elements. The North Pole has a nordicity value of 1,000 polar units, which is the maximum value possible. The southern limit of areas in Hamelin's classification system occurs at 200 polar units.

The physical elements measure 'coldness' while the human elements measure development (see Appendix 1 for the complete list of variables, the assigned values, and the method of calculating nordicity). This approach permits the classification of the North into three regions (Middle North, Far North, and Extreme North) as shown in Figure 1.3. It also provides a dynamic quality that may change the nordicity rating of a place. For example, some of the variables determining the level of nordicity reflect human activities such as population size and transportation accessibility. If such variables change, then a place may acquire a lower or higher rating of nordicity (Vignette 1.3). Table 1.3 indicates the nordicity rating of selected Canadian cities.

Vignette 1.3 The Dynamic Nature of Nordicity

The design of nordicity incorporates change, that is, the value for a particular place can change over time. Hamelin (1979: 35) stated that, in 1881, Saskatoon had a polar value of over 200. Over the next 75 years, Saskatoon grew in size and formed a transportation hub in western Canada. Consequently, by 1975, its nordicity rating fell to 116, placing the city in a 'southern' location. Similarly, Hamelin described the evolution of nordicity at Chibougamau, Quebec. In the 1880s, by this classification, its nordicity was around 400 on a scale of 1,000, but in 1979 he gave it a value of 151. At that time, he speculated that, given the role Chibougamau was expected to play in the James Bay Project, its nordicity could drop below 100.

TABLE 1.3 Nordicity Values for Selected Canadian Centres*

Centres in Southern Canada	Polar Units	Centres in Northern Canada	Polar Units
Halifax	43	Thompson	258
Montreal	45	Fort Nelson	282
Timmins	67	Whitehorse	283
Calgary	94	Schefferville	295
Winnipeg	111	Uranium City	396
St John's	115	Kuujjuarapik	414
Edmonton	125	Aklavik	511
Chibougamau	151	Iqaluit	584
The Pas	185	Old Crow	624
Grande Prairie	198	Sachs Harbour	764

*Centres with 200 or more polar units are defined as 'northern'.

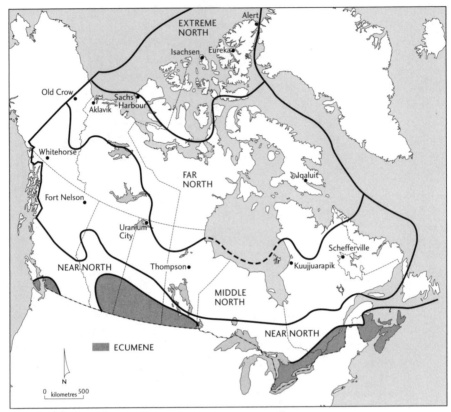

FIGURE 1.3 Canadian Nordicity
Nordicity permits the creation of three northern regions: the Middle North, the Far North, and the Extreme North. The southern limit of nordicity is marked by the 200 polar unit line.
SOURCE: Adapted from Hamelin (1979: 150).

Hamelin is describing the North from a 'southern' perspective that reflects attitudes, beliefs, and values held by people residing in that part of Canada. An underlying assumption of such an ethnocentric viewpoint is that 'development' of the North reduces its nordicity and therefore makes it more like southern Canada. Another assumption is that the North is viewed as a hinterland of southern Canada. Southern Canadians see the North quite differently from those living in the North. For instance, each descriptive label—Middle, Far, and Extreme Norths—may seem strange and out of place to a Canadian born north of the 60th parallel. A northerner, for example, might have a different mental map of Canada with the North described as the 'centre' and southern Canada as the 'distant land'. Furthermore, place names are a critical reflection of a region's cultural and historical experience. Ludger Müller-Wille (2001: 33) describes this importance:

> In Canada, as elsewhere, toponymy mirrors the country's cultural history and socio-economic and political structures, and it represents the various aspirations and goals of

the different components that have shaped this particular spatial entity. The Canadian toponymic landscape, along with its glossary, is continuously evolving and thus also functions as a barometer for rapid changes that have occurred throughout the Canadian territory. Since the 1960s, these changes relate predominantly to the assertion of cultural and territorial rights by either Aboriginal or Québécois populations, using, among other elements, toponyms as strong cultural and political symbols to express distinctness.

Yet, Hamelin's scheme for determining nordicity, with its southern perspective, has a practical use. The federal and territorial governments have used this concept to determine isolation allowances for their employees, including administrators, nurses, and teachers. Back in the 1970s, the vast majority of these employees had come from southern Canada. For them, living in the North, but especially in a small community, represented a sacrifice warranting additional pay and staff housing. For the government, these allowances remain a necessary means of luring skilled and professional workers to relocate in isolated northern communities.

CORE/PERIPHERY MODEL

Northern development takes place within a global economy. The core/periphery model best describes the economic relationship between the two abstract regions: resource hinterlands and industrial cores. Friedmann's version of the core/periphery model constructed three hypothetical hinterlands (Friedmann, 1966: 76–98; Bone, 2002: 20–2). One, known as the resource frontier, is far from the industrial world. Its remote location and small population limit economic development and diversification. For our purposes, the North is a resource frontier periphery, and the rest of Canada and the world are the core. Companies in the industrial core dominate the economy in the resource hinterland and control the hinterland's pace of resource development. Put differently, much of the economic destiny of resource hinterlands is controlled by external forces. However, resource development is extremely sensitive to fluctuations in world commodity prices. These fluctuations magnify the boom/bust economic cycle found in the global economy. For this reason alone, government intervention in the marketplace is warranted to shelter those living in resource hinterlands.

The hinterlands of the world are remote areas with limited transportation networks. These networks are designed to provide access to resources and to facilitate their export to world markets. The Canadian North is no exception. Its transportation network is not only limited in its geographic extent but it has two principal characteristics. The most striking is the heavy reliance on air transportation. All communities are served by air transportation but only a few by roads and even fewer by railways. For example, Nunavut is not connected to the rest of Canada by surface transportation but air service is available to all 26 communities. A second characteristic is the north/south orientation of the North's transportation system. Unlike southern Canada, which has an east/west transportation axis, northern Canada has a 'feeder' system that allows resources to flow from the North to Canada's main transportation system. As well, the movement of supplies and food to northern communities and mining sites takes place on these north/south routes. This transportation system, whereby supplies go north and resources go south but the North rarely if ever serves as a midpoint, is common in resource hinterlands around the world and is another indicator of the core/periphery spatial structure found in Canada's North.

The core/periphery model says little about the potential for diversification of the periphery. Harold Innis (1930) took a Canadian perspective of the core/periphery model by examining the economic history of resource (staple) development in Canada. Innis saw regional development occurring as a consequence of resource exploitation because it triggered a series of related economic activities that eventually led to regional economic diversification. In the case of the Canadian North, economic diversification is difficult for three reasons: small population, great distance from major markets, and high level of economic leakage. Ottawa, in conjunction with the provincial and territorial governments, may have to intervene in the marketplace to ensure that the process of diversification does not stall.

CRITICAL ISSUES

Within the two visions of the North lie several conflicting issues. Over the past 30 years, the balance of power between three key variables in the northern development equation has shifted (Table 1.4). The first change saw resource companies forced to take into consideration Aboriginal cultural and environmental concerns.[3] The second change revolves around some Aboriginal groups taking an active role in the market economy, especially those groups that have negotiated comprehensive land claim agreements. Furthermore, the link between comprehensive land claim agreements and self-government became more transparent with the Nunavut Land Claims Agreement because it included a commitment by Ottawa to create the Territory of Nunavut.[4] Third, respect for the environment is now more widespread within Canadian society, various governments, and resource companies.[5] Along with the recognition of the importance of the environment to our future world, a growing number of regulations have made resource companies much more conscious of the need to minimize damage to the land and waters within their development site. These three power shifts have profound implications for the shape of northern development in the twenty-first century and may well lead to a greater diversification of the economy.

In spite of progress, the North still faces many issues and challenges related to the interaction between resource development and the place of Aboriginal groups in resource development and Canadian society. In broad terms, all of these challenges relate to the effect of the resource economy on the northern environment and peoples. In particular, three issues are central:

• Can the resource economy be a driving force for diversification of the northern economy?
• What is the place for Aboriginal peoples in the resource economy and Canadian society?
• How can government ensure that the resource industry limits its impact on the environment?

TABLE 1.4 Timetable of Social Change

Year	Megaproject	Aboriginal Issues	Environment Issues
1949–1954	Iron Ore Company of Canada constructed a resource town, a railway, mine, power plant, and extensive port facilities at Sept-Îles.	Ignored	Ignored
1971–1975	A 1973 court ruling forced Hydro-Québec to negotiate with the Cree and Inuit of northern Quebec over Aboriginal title before completing the construction of the first phase of the James Bay Project.	James Bay and Northern Quebec Agreement, 1975	Linked to the JBNQA
1974–1977	Mackenzie Valley Pipeline Inquiry brought the environment and social costs of this project to the attention of the Canadian public.	Raised but no agreement	Formal inquiry
1969–1984	Three factors caused the Inuvialuit to seek the first comprehensive land claims agreement. One was the discovery of oil at Prudhoe Bay in 1969, a second was the settlement of the Alaskan Native Claims in 1971, and the third was the discovery of vast petroleum deposits in the Beaufort Sea.	Inuvialuit Final Agreement, 1984	Formal inquiry

Since these issues are interrelated and are sometimes at cross-purposes, the search for solutions becomes extremely complex and inevitably must result in compromises. The linkage of these critical issues forms the crux of this book. Given the physical nature of the North, questions of economic diversification and Aboriginal self-determination may be resolved differently in the Subarctic than in the Arctic. For example, in comparison with the Subarctic, the Arctic has few resources that warrant commercial development. Similarly, given the federal jurisdiction and the differing political cultures in the Territorial North, these issues may be approached differently in the territories than in the provinces.

The next two chapters outline the physical and historical geography of the North. This background information equips the reader to better understand the physical limitations imposed on the resource economy, the historical process of northern development, and contemporary economic issues facing northerners. Northern development and its impact on Aboriginal peoples and the fragile environment form the main thrust of the remainder of this text. To be sure, past human activities have damaged the northern environment and the road to economic diversification is far from assured. We will see that the Aboriginal peoples of northern Canada face an uphill (but not impossible) struggle to find a place within Canada.

NOTES

1. Eldorado is a mythical place abounding in great wealth. This word is derived from the Spanish *el dorado*, meaning 'the gilded'. In the sixteenth century, Spanish explorers believed that a city of gold existed in the Americas. They named this fabled city El Dorado.

2. 'Sense of place' is a term used by geographers to denote the special and often emotional feelings that people have for the region in which they live. These feelings are derived from a variety of personal and group experiences; some are due to natural factors, such as climate, while others result from cultural factors, such as the economy, language, and religion. Whatever its origin, a sense of place is a powerful psychological bond between people and their region.

3. The erosion of resource companies' power over the nature of development resulted from the loss of public support and the ensuing change in government policy. A new paradigm for northern development emerged along with a rethinking of the costs/benefits of megaprojects. Major resource projects were no longer automatically approved by Ottawa and provincial governments but had to run the gauntlet of public scrutiny. One result has been the emergence of corporate social responsibility to ensure that more benefits flow to the North; another has been a shift in power from Ottawa to the North, especially through the territorial governments and land claim agreements. Essentially, this process of social change results in a devolution of control, management, and ownership of the land and its resources from the centre (resource companies and Ottawa) to the hinterland (provincial and territorial governments and Aboriginal peoples).

4. Aboriginal issues reached national attention some 20 years later when, in 1969, Ottawa proposed to 'enable the Indian people to be free—free to develop Indian cultures in an environment of legal, social and economic equality with other Canadians' (*Statement of the Government of Canada on Indian Policy*, 1969: 3). This so-called 'White Paper', which called for the abolishment of the Department of Indian Affairs, the elimination of legal distinction between Indians and other Canadians through the amendment of the Indian Act, and the rejection of the legal validity of Aboriginal rights caused a storm of protest from Indian leaders. Their reaction centred on the proposed loss of special rights embedded in the treaties and prompted Harold Cardinal to write his book, *The Unjust Society: The Tragedy of Canada's Indians.*

   Unlike other areas of Canada, Aboriginal peoples often form a sizable minority or a majority in different areas of the North. This demographic fact adds considerable political weight to the Aboriginal position in resolving these contentious issues. Northern solutions are tempered somewhat by the limitations of the region's geography, which encourages people to work together, and by the realization that change through negotiations is already underway. The Territory of Nunavut represents a major political realignment within Canada while a series of comprehensive land claim agreements have altered the political geography of the North. Both provide hope for economic and social gains by Aboriginal northerners within Canadian society (see Chapter 8 for more details). In turn, such events have affected Canadian society, making it more aware of minority issues and the social cost of resource development.

5. Hidden costs of development became more apparent in the post-World War II period. By the 1950s, the environmental movement emerged in the United States and it quickly spread to Canada. One of the first signs that Canadians were paying attention to environmental issues took place in 1958 when the Resources for Tomorrow Conference brought together administrators, developers, and scientists to discuss the management of resources. From that point on, non-governmental organizations (NGOs) mobilized public opinion against plans for resource development.

REFERENCES AND SELECTED READINGS

Bone, Robert M. 2002. *The Regional Geography of Canada,* 2nd edn. Toronto: Oxford University Press.

Burn, Chris. 1995. 'Where Does the Polar Night Begin?', *The Canadian Geographer* 39, 1: 68–74.

Canada. 1969. *Statement of the Government of Canada on Indian Policy.* Ottawa: Queen's Printer.

Cardinal, Harold. 1969. *The Unjust Society: The Tragedy of Canada's Indians.* Edmonton: Hurtig.

Coates, Ken, and William Morrison. 1992. *The Forgotten North: A History of Canada's Provincial Norths.* Toronto: James Lorimer.

Francis, Daniel. 1997. *National Dreams: Myth, Memory and Canadian History.* Vancouver: Arsenal Pulp Press.

Friedmann, John. 1966. *Regional Development Policy: A Case Study of Venezuela.* Cambridge, Mass.: MIT Press.

Hamelin, Louis-Edmond. 1979. *Canadian Nordicity: It's Your North, Too,* trans. William Barr. Montreal: Harvest House.

Innis, Harold A. 1930. *The Fur Trade in Canada.* Toronto: University of Toronto Press.

Johnston, Margaret E., ed. 1994. *Geographic Perspectives on the Provincial Norths,* vol. 3, Centre for Northern Studies, Lakehead University. Mississauga, Ont.: Copp Clark.

McNiven, Chuck, and Henry Puderer. 2000. *Delineation of Canada's North: An Examination of the North-South Relationship in Canada,* Geography Working Paper Series No. 2000–3. Ottawa: Statistics Canada.

Müller-Wille, Ludger. 2001. 'Shaping Modern Inuit Territorial Perception and Identity in the Quebec-Labrador Peninsula', in Colin H. Scott, ed., *Aboriginal Autonomy and Development in Northern Quebec and Labrador.* Vancouver: University of British Columbia Press, 33–40.

Slocombe, D. Scott. 1995. 'Understanding Regions: A Framework for Description and Analysis', *Canadian Journal of Regional Science* 18, 2: 161–78.

CHAPTER 2

The Physical Base

The physical geography of the Canadian North provides the essential background information necessary to appreciate the relationship between the North's physical base and economic development. Of all the regions of Canada, the North has the narrowest range of natural resources and the most demanding physical environment for settlement and resource development. Global warming, if it occurs, would have a greater impact on Canada's high latitudes than its middle latitudes, perhaps causing permafrost to retreat and glaciers to melt. Across the northern half of North America, two natural areas—the Arctic and Subarctic biomes—exist (Figure 2.1). These two biomes provide a regional context for discussing the physical geography of the North. But first we must consider the essential physical characteristics of the North.

The North's natural character is dominated by its polar climate. With such a short growing season, natural vegetation, soils, and wildlife have had to adapt. The particular seasonal rhythm of the North is reflected in many natural phenomena, including the spring migration of the caribou herds to the tundra, the extreme variation in amount of daylight from summer to winter, and the dramatic release of water from ice-locked lakes and rivers every spring. But the North's physical geography was also affected by past climates. Some 16,000 to 25,000 years ago, extremely low world temperatures associated with the Late Wisconsin ice advance dramatically altered the North's physical geography by freezing the ground, thus creating permafrost; by covering land with a continental ice sheet that depressed the earth's crust; and, as the ice sheet advanced, by eroding landforms beneath the ice sheet. Unique natural features abound in the North, such as pattern ground, pingos, and pack ice.

From the perspective of global energy balance, the North is an energy deficit area (Vignette 2.1). The length and intensity of winter in the North are indicative of its energy deficit. While Canadians are familiar with winter, those living in the North face a much longer and colder winter. The principal factor is the low amount of solar energy received in high latitudes compared to that received in middle latitudes. Williams (1986: 6–7) defines a cold environment as having a negative annual heat balance due to a greater amount of long-wave radiation emitted to outer space than the amount of incoming short-wave radiation and energy transfer by global winds and ocean currents. Mean annual air temperature, defined as the total of daily mean temperatures for the year at one place divided by 365 days, provides one measure of the negative annual heat balance. Those areas with annual mean air temperatures of less than zero

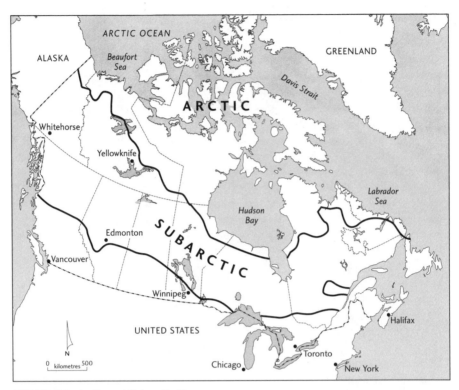

FIGURE 2.1 Arctic and Subarctic Biomes
The natural division of the Canadian North into the Arctic and Subarctic biomes has biological, economic, and cultural implications. These implications focus on biodiversity and ecozones, the impact of resource companies on the environment, and the concept of traditional homelands for Indians and Inuit.

Celsius have a negative heat balance. With the exception of a small area of the boreal forest that extends into the middle latitudes of Ontario and Quebec, the Canadian North has a negative energy balance (Figure 1.2).

The North's cold environment has a direct bearing on the human landscape. Unlike the continuous settlement pattern found in southern Canada, the North consists of many small, often isolated communities. Like the oasis pattern of settlements found in deserts, each northern centre is separated from other centres by vast areas of unoccupied lands. In Nunavut, for example, its 26 communities and two mine sites occupy only a small fraction of the total area of Nunavut. The rugged Canadian Shield makes highway construction extremely expensive. This fact and the great distances between communities explain why Nunavut has no highway system and why its residents must travel by air to reach other centres. Similarly, extraction and transport of natural resources are made more difficult by the cold environment, though a few advantages do exist, such as winter ice roads that allow trucks to bring supplies and fuel to remote mining sites at a fraction of the cost of air transportation.

Vignette 2.1 The Global Energy Balance

The sun is the primary source of energy for the earth. The flow of energy from sun to earth and then into our atmosphere is an extremely complex process. Most solar energy reaches low latitude areas while high latitude areas like the Canadian North receive much less energy. The former are described as having an energy surplus while the latter have an energy deficit. Fortunately, the global circulation system transfers heat from low to high latitudes. This spatial differentiation in solar energy and the resulting global circulation system form the basis of world climates.

Three processes—radiation, energy storage, and energy movement—account for the variation in annual mean surface temperatures across the earth's surface. Solar energy (short-wave radiation) heats the earth's surface and, in turn, the earth emits long-wave radiation into our atmosphere. The atmosphere is warmed mainly by long-wave radiation. Some long-wave radiation is lost because it passes through our atmosphere to outer space. Solar energy received at different latitudes on the earth's surface varies because of the angle of the sun's rays. The angle of these rays striking the earth's surface ranges from right-angle (intense energy) at the equator to zero at the North and South poles for half of the year (no energy) and at a low angle for the rest of the year (low energy). As a result, more solar energy is received in equatorial areas (low latitude areas) than in polar areas (high latitude areas). This differential heating results in an energy surplus in equatorial areas and an energy deficit in polar areas. In low latitude areas, storage of energy occurs in the oceans and atmosphere. The global circulation system is comprised of atmospheric winds and ocean currents. These winds and currents transfer surplus energy to high latitude areas. However, because of the global pattern of atmospheric winds and ocean currents, this transfer is uneven, with more being received in the high latitudes of the west coasts of North America and Europe.

The northern environment is often described as fragile, meaning that the risk of anthropogenic damage is much higher in the North than in other regions of Canada. The primary reason for this regional variation is due to the much greater length of time required for nature to repair a northern environment compared to the time required in more temperate regions of the world. One illustration of the delicate nature of this cold environment is revealed by the relationship of temperature and precipitation to plant growth (Figure 2.2). Such regions have a limited capacity to support a human population, and overpopulation leads to greater pressure on the natural environment, which can result in a deterioration of the environment and damage both its ecosystems and biodiversity. Geographers refer to this relationship between a human population and their environment as carrying capacity (Vignette 2.2). In our global world, the demand for resources places a similar pressure on the environment and the North's ecosystems and biodiversity are more threatened by the ever-increasing resource development than by population growth.

The basis of understanding the impact of human activities on the environment lies in the nature and meaning of ecology and ecosystems. Ecosystems are comprised of

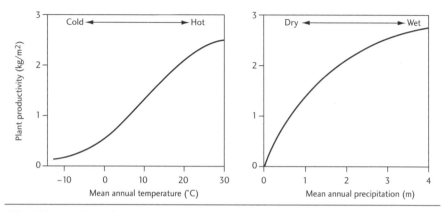

FIGURE 2.2 Biological Growth in a Cold Environment
Plant growth varies with temperature and precipitation. A combination of low temperatures and meagre precipitation results in very low levels of plant growth, and hence limited soil development and biological life. The Arctic, for example, has a colder environment than the Subarctic and hence the Subarctic has a higher level of plant growth.

biological communities interacting with one another within a particular geographic area. Biodiversity, defined as the number of species inhabiting a particular geographic area or habitat, has become one of the major environmental issues of our times. While the Arctic has a narrower range of species than the Subarctic, resource development has had a greater impact on the Subarctic and has destroyed habitats and, in impacted areas, threatened biodiversity. Large-scale land-use changes to the environment, such as clear-cut logging and major hydroelectric projects, affect ecosystems, eliminate wildlife habitat, and otherwise affect the biological life in the impact area.

Vignette 2.2 The Concept of Carrying Capacity

The biological concept of carrying capacity suggests that a population cannot increase its size indefinitely and that there is a point at which a 'ceiling' is reached. When applying this concept to human population, the technological level of a society can alter its ability to produce food and other products from the region that it inhabits. For example, in the same geographic area, a hunting society would have a more limited food production than an agricultural society. The result would be a low population density for the hunting society compared to the density of an agricultural society. In short, carrying capacity is the relationship between population size and food supply. Among human societies, however, the concept of carrying capacity is much more complex and involves many more factors than just food supply. Still, carrying capacity refers to the number of people a specific area can support at a given time. In this sense, carrying capacity involves the environment. The assumption is that humans must have a sustainable economy that protects the natural environment. Otherwise the natural environment will deteriorate, thus reducing the area's carrying capacity.

NORTHERN BIOMES

The North occupies over three-quarters of the land mass of Canada. The division of the region into two biomes—Arctic and Subarctic—allows the reader to grasp more easily the physical complexity of such a vast area. A biome is a broad, regional type of ecosystem characterized by distinctive climate and soil conditions and a distinctive kind of biological community adapted to those physical conditions. Natural vegetation serves to distinguish the Arctic and Subarctic biomes, though the biological complexity of each biome goes well beyond natural vegetation (Vignette 2.3). Tundra is the natural vegetation found in the Arctic while the boreal forest covers the lands of the Subarctic biome.

Since the warming of the world's climate some 15,000 years ago that led to the melting of the last ice sheet covering much of Canada and a small part of the United States, natural processes but especially milder climatic conditions led to the formation of the Arctic and Subarctic biomes. These continental-size zones have distinct climates, natural vegetation, soils, and biological life. Because natural vegetation provides a visible record of the geographic extent of biomes, geographers often determine the spatial extent of each biome by its natural vegetation. The two northern biomes also represent cultural regions. Over a long time, Indian and Inuit peoples developed material cultures and technologies suitable for living as hunters and gatherers in each natural region. More recently, each northern environment poses a different set of physical challenges to resource developers. Much of this challenge is related to the fragile nature of the northern environment. Slow biological response means that polar lands and seas take much longer to recover from industrial accidents, such as an oil spill, than do more temperate places. Permafrost and frozen seas add to the fragile nature of the North and complicate efforts to repair a damaged environment.

Vignette 2.3 Ecology and Ecosystems

Ecology is the study of the interactions of living organisms with one another and their physical environment. One of the characteristics of biological life is its high degree of complexity and interrelationship. For example, a group of individuals of the same species living and interacting in the same geographic area is defined as a population. Many populations may exist in the same geographic area or habitat and, collectively, these populations form a biological community. Ecozones are one way of expressing the spatial extent of this complexity and interrelationship. In Canada, there are 15 terrestrial and five marine ecozones. Additional information about Canada's ecozones can be obtained at Environment Canada's Web site <www.ec.gc.ca> while a report by Thomas Clair, *Climatic Change and Ecosystem Research in Canada's North*, is available at <www.atl.ec.gc.ca/nei/pdf/summary.pdf>. A map of Canada's terrestrial ecozones produced by the Atlas of Canada is available at <http://atlas.gc.ca>. A report on the cumulative impacts that threaten sustainable use of the boreal forest system can also be found at the Atlas of Canada Web site.

THE ARCTIC

Lying north of the treeline, the Arctic is the coldest region in Canada. The Arctic is found primarily in Nunavut and the Northwest Territories, but large areas exist in Quebec, Newfoundland and Labrador, Ontario, Yukon, and Manitoba. It is characterized by a very cold climate where the warmest month has a mean monthly temperature of less than 10°C. Under such climatic conditions, normal tree growth and soil formation are not possible. Instead, tundra vegetation and thin soils known as cryosols (soils formed in areas of permafrost that have a shallow active layer in the summer) are found in the Arctic. Even when summer air temperatures thaw the top few centimetres of the ground, the presence of permafrost beneath this thin active layer acts not only as a cooling agent but also as a barrier to water. Under these conditions, soil-forming processes work extremely slowly because soil temperatures are often just above the freezing point. Not surprisingly, rock and unconsolidated gravels and sands commonly form the ground surface.

Arctic vegetation is divided into two subzones—Low Arctic and High Arctic. The Low Arctic occupies the mainland while the High Arctic is found in parts of Keewatin and the Arctic Archipelago. The Low Arctic is characterized by nearly complete plant cover, including many shrubs, sedges, and scrub trees such as birch and willow. Tussock sedge and low tundra shrubs are the summer grazing grounds of barren ground caribou, which are still a major source of food for Aboriginal peoples. Heath, herbs, and lichen are the typical plants. While trees such as willows do grow, they reach a height of only a few centimetres. The High Arctic zone, by contrast, has little vegetation. Most of its surface consists of rock and unconsolidated material. Lichen grows on rocks. Such barren Arctic lowlands are called polar deserts (Vignette 2.4).

Vignette 2.4 Polar Desert

Polar desert exists in Arctic Lands where extremely cold, arid conditions occur throughout the year. Low summer temperatures combined with permanently frozen ground greatly limit biological activities. For that reason, little vegetation is found in polar deserts. These severe growing conditions are essentially an extreme form of fellfield, with vegetation cover, at least of higher plants, reduced to near zero. Lichens are by far the most important group of primitive plants found in polar deserts. Since the principal geomorphic process is a freeze/thaw cycle, a sterile, barren-looking landscape consisting of shattered bedrock, pattern ground, and unconsolidated materials prevails.

SOURCE: Young (1989: 198).

The treeline serves as the boundary between the Arctic and the Subarctic. Ecologically, the treeline represents a major break between the two regions, though in fact the break is a gradual one consisting of wooded tundra (Vignette 2.5). The proportion of tundra to forest varies, but towards the Arctic zone only a few stunted trees are found in the more protected areas of river valleys. Spruce and larch are the predominant species found in the wooded tundra. This transition zone also represents a biological and cultural boundary. Many Subarctic animals, including beaver and moose, are not found in the Arctic.

Vignette 2.5 The Treeline

The treeline represents a dividing zone between the Arctic and Subarctic regions. It closely corresponds to the 10°C monthly mean temperature for July. Other natural factors, such as the depth of the active layer of permafrost, protection from wind, south-slope radiation, and well-drained land, may result in patches of trees growing north of this isotherm, or conversely, tundra occurring south of it. Then, too, weather varies from year to year, causing the annual position of the isotherm to fluctuate somewhat. During the relatively warm decade of the 1990s, for instance, summer temperatures were much higher in high latitudes than in most previous decades. All of these factors have produced a transition zone of wooded tundra between the Arctic and Subarctic regions.

Three centres close to this imaginary line are Aklavik (68° 12'N), Churchill (58° 48'N), and Cartwright (53° 36'N). Aklavik, located on a deltaic island at the mouth of the Mackenzie River, has a warmest-month average mean temperature of 14°C; Churchill, situated near the shore of Hudson Bay, has an average July temperature of 11.8°C; and Cartwright, lying along the Labrador coast, has a mean July figure of 12°. About 250 km inland from the coast, temperatures are much higher: at Happy Valley-Goose Bay the mean July temperature is 15.8°. The continental effect of this large land mass coupled with the summer cooling caused by the ocean waters of Hudson Bay have resulted in a northwest to southeast trend to the 'treeline'.

THE SUBARCTIC

The Subarctic is the largest natural region in North America. Its boreal forest extends in a continuous belt from the Rocky Mountains to Labrador. Its summers are short but warm, allowing for a much richer vegetation cover than that found in the Arctic. Coniferous trees predominate. Variation in the size and density of forest cover allows for the identification of four subzones: wooded tundra, lichen woodland, closed boreal forest, and forest parkland. The wooded tundra, as noted above, forms the transition zone between the Arctic and Subarctic. Patches of spruce and larch are found in sheltered, low-lying areas while high, more exposed lands are treeless. The lichen woodland consists of a thick groundcover of lichens under stands of spruce and pine. The closed boreal forest, a dense forest of fir, spruce, and pine, is found in southern Yukon, a small part of the Northwest Territories (principally the upper Mackenzie Valley), and the northern areas of the seven provinces. Within this huge zone, the forest cover is broken by a variety of wetlands, including muskeg and peat bogs. In this wet environment, black spruce and larch are the most common species. On well-drained land, species of spruce, fir, pine, and larch are common along with stands of poplar and birch. Towards its southern limits, broadleaf trees, particularly aspen and birch, are found. The forest parkland, a narrow transition area adjacent to the Canadian Prairies, is a combination of forest and mid-latitude grasslands. Small bushes, including blueberries, and grasses form the floor cover.

Podzolic soils are common in the Subarctic. These thin, acidic soils are best formed under cool, wet growing conditions where the principal vegetative litter is derived from a coniferous forest. A low evaporation rate, immature drainage, and permafrost ensure an excess of ground moisture, resulting in severely leached soils and the widespread occurrence of marsh and bogs. Yet, the longer summer temperatures in the Subarctic allow the ground to thaw to a depth of several metres, promoting biological activity, plant growth, and chemical action.

POLAR CLIMATE

In the classification of climates throughout the world, the polar climate represents the coldest climatic type. The polar climate is divided into four climatic subtypes: the Arctic, Subarctic, mountain, and ice cap climates. In this text, however, the mountainous area of northern British Columbia, Yukon, and Northwest Territories is treated as part of the Subarctic (Vignette 2.6). Similarly, the ice cap climatic type is merged with the Arctic climatic type. The ice cap climate is associated with glaciers found on Baffin, Devon, and Ellesmere islands. This climate has a mean temperature below freezing for all months. Those small areas covered by glaciers are considered part of the Arctic climate.

Vignette 2.6 The Subarctic Climate in the Cordillera

Many factors, such as latitude, topography, the proximity of bodies of water, and the nature of the underlying surface, control climate. In Yukon, due to its mountainous nature, topography becomes very important. The territory benefits from Pacific airflows from the west, while high mountain ranges block Arctic air masses from the north. The mountain ranges also affect atmospheric circulation patterns, the amount, frequency, and type of precipitation, winds, atmospheric pressure, and the local radiation regime. Elevation in particular plays a major role in determining temperature. During the winter, a strong surface-based inversion develops in Yukon due to the net negative radiation balance. Thus, temperatures tend to increase with height, especially in the bottom 1,500 metres of the atmosphere.

SOURCE: Adapted from Etkin (1989: 12).

Unlike other climatic types, the polar climate is characterized by extreme seasonal variations in the amount of solar energy. Summer days, for example, are long while winter days receive little to no sunlight. The Arctic Circle marks the latitude where the sun remains above the horizon for one summer day (June 21, the summer solstice) each year and it remains below the horizon for one winter day (December 21, the winter solstice) each year. At latitudes well beyond the Arctic Circle, summer days and winter nights can last for months. At the North Pole, the sun is above the horizon for six months and below the horizon for the rest of the year. A day of continuous darkness is referred to as a 'polar night' (Vignette 2.7).

Vignette 2.7 The Polar Night

The polar night is a period of continuous winter darkness. Twilight does not occur. Polar nights take place north of 72° 33'N, well beyond the Arctic Circle (66° 33'N). Why is this? We know that the sun does not rise above the horizon at the Arctic Circle during the winter solstice. Yet there are not 24 hours of continuous darkness because diffused light from the sky is caused by the sun's rays being reflected from a position below the horizon onto the atmosphere and then back down to the earth. Twilight may last for an hour or more at the time when the sun is below but less than 6° below the horizon, thus providing at that time sufficient light for outdoor activities. On 21 December, the latitude of 72° 33'N, not the Arctic Circle, marks the geographic point where 24 hours of continuous winter darkness occurs.

SOURCES: Burn (1995, 1996).

Monthly receipts of solar energy vary widely throughout the year (Vignette 2.1). On a yearly average, the earth's poles receive 40 per cent less radiation than the equator (Lawford, 1988: 144). Within the Canadian North, the major dividing line, the Arctic Circle, marks the point where solar radiation is reduced to zero for one day (21 December) and, at higher latitudes, for longer periods of time. Such low levels of radiation result in continuous cooling of the land and the buildup of masses of frigid arctic air, which are associated with daily high temperatures of –40°C or lower and strong surface winds. In fact, the Arctic coast is one of Canada's windiest places with annual average wind speeds exceeding 20 km/hr. Cold polar air is often associated with extreme wind-chill conditions that will freeze exposed flesh in a matter of seconds. Arctic winds drive frigid air masses southward, causing stormy and sometimes blizzard conditions in the Canadian Prairies, sub-zero temperatures in eastern Canada, and freezing temperatures in the southern United States. In the spring, solar radiation increases but much of its effect is lost due to snow-covered surface. In fact, up to 80 per cent of the spring solar radiation is reflected into space by the snow-covered ground. Once the snow is gone, winter's grip is quickly broken. Temperatures recover rapidly and the ensuing warm weather quickly melts the ice from lakes, rivers, and the ocean. By early July, sea ice has disappeared from Hudson Bay and, a few weeks later, from along the edge of the Arctic coast. The polar pack, no longer attached to the coastline, drifts around the Arctic Ocean. During the long summer days, massive amounts of solar radiation reach the northern lands, warming the ground. In response, plants quickly appear and flower. Daily summer temperatures in the Mackenzie Valley and southern Yukon can reach into the low thirties Celsius. By late August, however, summer is over. Within another month, ice has formed on lakes and rivers, marking a return to a frozen landscape.

The sharp seasonal shift of air temperatures is illustrated in Figure 2.3. The winter regime has low mean monthly temperatures. The coldest January temperatures are found in two places—the northern extremes of Ellesmere and Axel Heiberg islands and just south of Boothia Peninsula. On the other hand, the mean daily temperature for July demonstrates both the warming effect of the northern land mass and the cooling

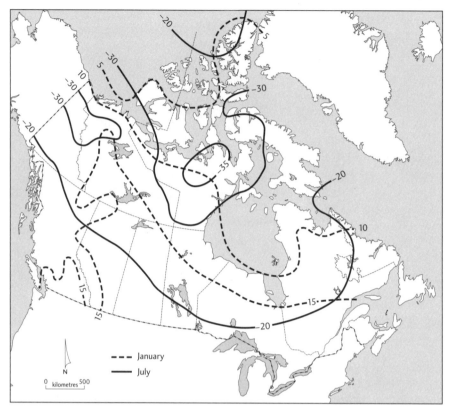

FIGURE 2.3 Mean Daily Temperatures in Degrees Celsius, January and July
July isotherms indicate a northwest-southeast trend, with a warm corridor extending into the
Mackenzie River Valley. The 15°C July isotherm reaches beyond 60 degrees North in the inte-
rior of the Northwest Territories, indicating a continental warming effect. The reverse situation
occurs in the winter, as demonstrated by the −20°C January isotherm that reaches nearly 50
degrees North in Ontario while the same isotherm is north of the 60th parallel in Yukon and
Nunavut, indicating the temperature-modifying influence of the Pacific and Atlantic oceans.
SOURCE: After Hare and Thomas (1979: 37).

effect of the Arctic Ocean, Hudson Bay, and the North Atlantic. A distinct northwest
to southeast direction to the July isotherms exists. As well, a warm 'corridor' extends
down the Mackenzie Valley to Norman Wells, where July temperatures are similar to
those experienced in the Canadian Prairies.

Precipitation in the North is generally light, with the least amount falling in the
Arctic due to the inability of Arctic air masses to absorb moisture from cold bodies of
water (Figure 2.4). The lowest annual precipitation occurs in the ice-locked islands situated in the Arctic Archipelago (Vignette 2.8). Victoria Island, for example, has such
scant rain and snowfall (often less than 140 mm annually) that the island is described
as an 'Arctic desert'. Towards the northern edge of the Subarctic, annual precipitation
increases. At Yellowknife, the annual precipitation is around 250 mm. The Subarctic, on

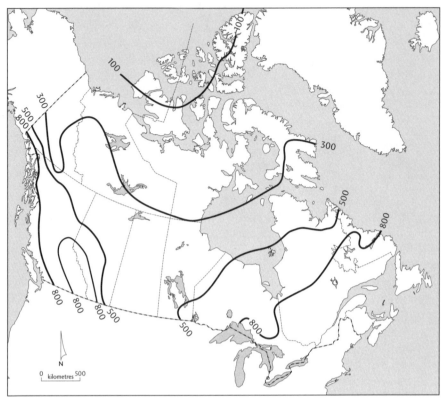

FIGURE 2.4 Mean Annual Precipitation in Millimetres
Air masses originating over the Atlantic and Pacific oceans bring most moisture to the North. Air masses forming over the cold Arctic Ocean usually contain little moisture. As a result, the highest levels of annual precipitation are found along the western and eastern edges of the North while the Arctic Archipelago is extremely dry, causing scientists to refer to this area as having a polar desert (Vignette 2.4).
SOURCE: After Hare and Thomas (1979: 41).

Vignette 2.8 Arctic Archipelago

The Canadian Arctic Archipelago is a group of islands in the Arctic Ocean. Stretching over 1.3 million km^2, they form the largest group of islands in the world. The largest islands are Baffin Island (507,451 km^2), Victoria Island (217,290 km^2), and Ellesmere Island (196,236 km^2). Most islands have elevations below 200 metres and few topographic features. Elevations do rise above 2,000 metres in the eastern islands of the Arctic Archipelago. Mount Barbeau on Ellesmere Island, for example, reaches an elevation of 2,616 metres. At these high elevations, glaciers exist. The geological history of the Arctic Archipelago began some 3 billion years ago and Precambrian rock exists at the surface on Baffin, Devon, and Ellesmere islands. Most of the Arctic islands were formed much later and contain sedimentary rocks. Within these sedimentary rocks, vast oil and gas deposits exist.

the other hand, generally receives more precipitation, usually over 300 mm annually. Precipitation does vary, however. The greatest amount of precipitation occurs in the Cordillera and along the Atlantic coast. In these two areas, the high terrain results in orographic precipitation (rain or snow caused when warm, moisture-laden air is forced to rise over hills or mountains and is cooled in the process). The south coast of Baffin Island receives around 400 mm annually while the figures for the southern coast of Labrador and northern Quebec exceed 800 mm. Most precipitation falls as snow. In the spring, the runoff peaks when melting snow and ice flow into the streams and rivers. Some communities along the Mackenzie River are subject to spring flooding. Fort Simpson, situated on an island at the confluence of the Liard and Mackenzie rivers, has been inundated a number of times, and Aklavik, located in the delta of the Mackenzie River, is threatened by flood waters almost every spring. The occurrence of spring flooding at Aklavik is so regular that, in the late 1950s, the federal government decided to create the new town of Inuvik rather than expand the community of Aklavik.

The Arctic climate is defined as one in which the average mean temperature for the warmest month is less than 10°C. It has extremely long winters and a brief, cool summer. The Arctic climate lies north of the treeline and includes all of the Arctic Archipelago, the coastal zone stretching from the Beaufort Sea to the coast of Labrador, and much of the interior of the northern territories, known as the 'Barren Lands'. While the Arctic climate is normally associated with high latitudes, it does reach into the middle latitudes along the Labrador coast. Here, the chilling effect of the cold Labrador Current keeps summer temperatures along the east coast of Canada low, allowing the Arctic climate to extend down the Labrador coast to the northern tip of Newfoundland. Resolute and Iqaluit have Arctic climates and their mean monthly temperature regimes are shown in Table 2.1.

Unlike its Arctic counterpart, the Subarctic climate has a distinct but short, warm summer. Normally, this climate is found in continental or inland locations and is characterized by a wide range in seasonal and daily temperatures. This continental effect results in record daily cold temperatures being set in Yukon rather than in the Arctic Archipelago. The coldest temperature recorded in Canada (−62.8°C) was at Snag, Yukon. In contrast to the cold winter temperatures, a number of 'hot' summer days can occur. In the summer of 1989, for example, during a 'heat wave' in the Mackenzie Valley, Norman Wells recorded an all-time daily high of 35°C. The climatic regions for all of Canada are shown in Figure 2.5.

Winter is the dominant season, and although an occasional summer day may be extremely hot, summers in the Subarctic are short, usually less than three months. Freezing temperatures can occur at any time. By late August, cool fall-like weather is common and there is an impending sense of winter. By November, the land, lakes, and rivers are frozen and winter, lasting until late April or May, has set in. During the winter, the warming influence of the Pacific keeps temperatures of the western Subarctic relatively high while the frozen Hudson Bay reinforces the cold continental effect on the winter temperatures of the eastern Subarctic. The average January temperatures for Prince George and Chibougamau reflect these differing climatic influences (Table 2.1). The reverse situation occurs in the summer, when Chibougamau has higher average monthly temperatures than Prince George.

TABLE 2.1 Mean Monthly Temperatures for Chibougamau, Prince George, Iqaluit, and Resolute

Centre	Latitude	Jan.	Feb.	Mar.	Apr.	May
Chibougamau	49° 55'	−18.4	−10.5	−1.0	6.4	13.3
Prince George	53° 53'	−9.6	−5.4	−0.3	5.2	9.9
Iqaluit	63° 45'	−25.6	−25.9	−22.7	−14.3	−3.2
Resolute	74° 43'	−32.4	−33.1	−30.7	−22.8	−10.9

SOURCE: Environment Canada (2002).

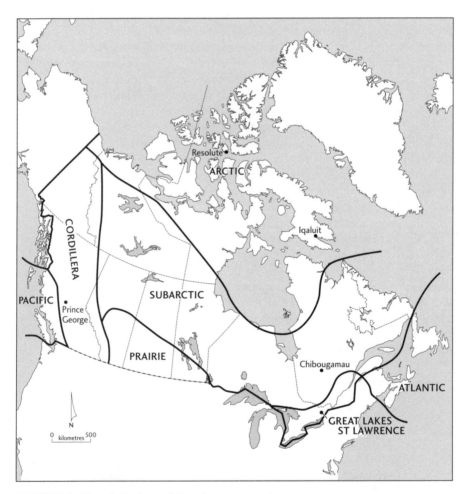

FIGURE 2.5 Climatic Regions of Canada
Three climatic regions—the Cordillera, the Subarctic, and the Arctic—are found in the Canadian North.
SOURCE: After Hare and Thomas (1979: 17).

TABLE 2.1 (cont.)

June	July	Aug.	Sept.	Oct.	Nov.	Dec.	Year
15.8	15.8	14.1	9.1	2.6	−4.7	−15.9	−0.8
13.3	15.5	14.8	10.1	4.6	−2.9	−7.8	4.0
3.4	7.6	6.9	2.4	−5.0	−13.0	−21.8	−9.3
−0.1	4.3	1.5	−4.7	−14.9	−23.6	−29.2	−16.4

CLIMATE CHANGE: REAL OR IMAGINED?

Global warming is occurring—or is it? Most climatologists believe that global warming is underway. Certainly, world surface air temperatures have increased in recent years, but do these relatively minor variations fall within the range of 'normal' world temperature fluctuations or are they the forerunners of a dramatic rise in global temperatures? Confirmation that global warming is taking place would require an increase in global surface air temperatures of over 1°C, but by then the world's climate as we know it would have changed dramatically.

Those scientists who warn of global warming predict that a dramatic increase in global surface air temperatures will occur over a relatively short time span in the twenty-first century. They further predict that local and regional habitats throughout the world but especially in high latitudes will be severely altered, causing the loss of some species. Accordingly, by 2050, Canada will be faced with major environment and land-use changes (Cohen, 1997; Bouchard, 2001). As a result of such global warming, Mireille Bouchard predicts five major environmental changes will occur in Canada: the warming of the Canadian climates; an increase in aridity in the Canadian Prairies; a northward shift of biomes; a reduction in the extent of permafrost; and a rise in sea level. While not denying the potential impact of global warming on the landscape, geographers point out that human activities and human-constructed landscapes have already significantly altered the natural environment: by replacing forests with agricultural lands; by polluting the atmosphere, such as the brown haze over much of southern and southeast Asia; and by dumping sewage and other waste products into our oceans. In the same vein, Olav Slaymaker (2001: 76) recognizes that climate change is but 'one of the two main drivers of environmental change, the other being human activities'. He argues that 'It seems highly probable that the environmental changes caused by land use change far exceed those generated by climate change over both short and very long time scales' (ibid., 71). Slaymaker (74) adds that 'In spite of the overwhelming importance of climate change at the national scale, it is common knowledge that at the scale of a mining site (Gardner, 1986) or an urban construction site (Gertler and Crowley, 1977), land use change far exceeds the potential influence of climate change.'

What evidence and theory are behind the concept of global warming? A prominent scientific body, the Intergovernmental Panel on Climatic Change, reported that the global average surface temperature has increased by 0.6°C since the late nineteenth century and that the 1990s was the warmest decade and 1998 the warmest year since

1861 (Houghton et al., 2001: 26). The same research group predicts rapid increases in world temperatures over the next 100 years, with increases in the range of 1.7°C to 4.2°C (ibid., 70). The main cause is the addition of greenhouse gases to the atmosphere through the burning of fossil fuels. Theoretically, those who argue the case for global warming have a very strong case based on the greenhouse effect hypothesis (as the percentage of greenhouse gases in the atmosphere increases, the capacity of the atmosphere to absorb solar energy also increases, thus causing air temperatures to rise); predictions made by computer simulations of the atmosphere called general circulation models (GCMs); and by recorded increases in world temperatures over the past three decades. Scientists know that our industrial world is adding more and more greenhouse gases to the atmosphere. Fossil fuels provide most energy needed by our industrial world, yet the burning of coal, natural gas, and oil produces greenhouse gases (gases that absorb solar energy). In doing so, fossil fuels increase the atmospheric capacity to absorb solar energy and thereby increase air temperatures. World leaders are concerned about possible climatic change caused by the burning of fossil fuels. At the 2002 Earth Summit in Johannesburg, Canada announced that it would sign the Kyoto Protocol, thus joining many other nations promising to reduce the production of greenhouse gases (Vignette 2.9). In December 2002, Ottawa ratified the Kyoto Protocol.

Vignette 2.9 Energy Needs, Global Warming, and the Kyoto Protocol

The central technological breakthrough of the Industrial Revolution was the utilization of fossil fuels to drive machinery. However, the burning of fossil fuels launches harmful chemicals into the earth's atmosphere, causing air pollution and adding greenhouse gases, such as carbon dioxide, to the atmosphere. Greenhouse gases are believed to be the source of rising global temperatures and, possibly, of climate change. Since the 1992 Earth Summit in Rio de Janeiro, the international community has been seeking a way to strike a balance between expanding the pace of economic development and protecting the environment. At the 1997 Earth Summit in Japan, the participants announced the Kyoto Protocol. This agreement-in-principle aims to cut greenhouse gas emissions from developed countries by 5 per cent from their 1990 levels by 2012. At the 2002 Earth Summit in Johannesburg, Prime Minister Jean Chrétien announced that Canada would sign the Kyoto Protocol that would commit Canada to reduce its greenhouse gas emissions by 6 per cent within 10 years. Reaching this goal will be made more difficult because Canada's North American economic partner, the United States, has decided not to sign this agreement because of its potential negative impacts on the American economy. The integrated nature of the North American economy could cause conflicts between the two countries. For example, if Canadian energy developments, such as those projects planned for the Alberta oil sands, were delayed to meet Ottawa's international commitments to lower its greenhouse gas omissions, would the United States' goal to secure a North American supply of oil be affected?

Dramatic climatic changes have occurred in the geological past, but normally a climate maintains its temperature and precipitation characteristics for a long time—often for thousands of years. During that time, fluctuations in temperature and precipitation do occur, and these fluctuations are more severe in higher latitudes due to the albedo effect (Vignette 2.10). The Medieval Climatic Optimum represents a short period (900 to 1300) of warmer world surface air temperatures and much warmer temperatures in higher latitudes. But the Medieval Climatic Optimum was not a climate switch, that is, a total change in its long-term average temperature and precipitation characteristics, but rather a minor variation of just less than 1°C (Ahrens, 1994: 481). The cause of the Medieval Climatic Optimum is unknown, but the temperature change during this period pales in comparison with the change during the last Ice Age, when world temperatures may have declined from present levels by as much as 10°C. Climate, like weather, is a complex natural phenomenon that makes forecasting very difficult because so many variables affect climate. For example, perhaps the last Ice Age (the Late Wisconsin) was caused by a reduction in solar energy received by the earth's atmosphere.

Vignette 2.10 The Albedo Effect

If the climate warmed, why would the average annual temperatures in the North increase more than in the South? The answer lies in the albedo effect (the proportion of solar radiation reflected from the earth's surface). Under the global warming model, snow cover disappears more quickly and for a longer period. Under those conditions, the darker surface of the earth is able to absorb more solar energy. In turn, the warmed earth then re-radiates heat to the lower portion of the atmosphere. The reverse process took place during the Little Ice Age.

What do we know about past climatic shifts? A number of scholars have looked at this intriguing question, and Marsh (1987: 160) places it within a geological perspective that another ice advance (and cooler world temperatures) is inevitable. About two million years ago, the climate cooled again and the most recent Ice Age began. This period has been marked by several dramatic expansions and contractions of the world's ice volume, thus altering the sea level. Over the past million years, global temperatures may have fluctuated as much as 10°C. For example, about 16,000 years ago, the ice-age climate grew warmer until 4000 BC. Since then the climate has generally cooled, but the cooling trend has been interrupted by oscillations of about 2°C every 2,000 years. Geologists generally agree that the earth is still in the last Ice Age, probably in a warm period between major glaciations, called an interglacial period. While geologists are not refuting the possibility of global warming, they place it within a much longer time frame of an interglacial period.

What do we know about past climatic fluctuations that took place over hundreds if not thousands of years? The Little Ice Age[1] (c. 1450–1850) represents a recent cool period when the world surface air temperatures were perhaps nearly 1°C cooler than the present levels. The Little Ice Age is therefore considered a minor fluctuation in our present climate rather than a major climatic shift, as occurred at the time of the last great ice advance (Late Wisconsin). Historic records provide evidence that this cooler period took place. From these descriptive accounts of crop failures and the freezing of water bodies, temperatures in the northern hemisphere probably declined around 1450 and began to increase after 1850. Some argue that Viking settlement on the southern tip of Greenland disappeared during the Little Ice Age because its agricultural economy failed; and the Thule culture based on harvesting of bowhead whales collapsed during this cold spell.

GEOMORPHIC REGIONS

Across the Canadian North, the surficial geology forms the basis of major geomorphic regions.[2] Such regions must have three major characteristics—they cover a large, contiguous area with similar relief features; they have experienced similar geomorphic processes that shaped their terrain; and they have had a similar geological history and therefore possess a common geological structure. These geomorphic regions are seen easily from a high-flying aircraft or from satellite photographs.

Five geomorphic regions—the Canadian Shield, the Interior Plains, the Cordillera, the Hudson Bay Lowland, and the Arctic Lands—are found in the North (Figure 2.6). The Late Wisconsin ice sheet modified the surface of these geomorphic regions either directly by glacial erosion or deposition, or indirectly by the formation of glacial lakes and the invasion of depressed land by seawater.

The Canadian Shield, stretching from Labrador to the Northwest Territories, is the largest geomorphic region in the Canadian North. It is the geological core of the northern landscape. Its Precambrian rocks are more than 2.5 billion years old and are found under most of the more recently formed strata, such as the Interior Plains and the Hudson Bay Lowland.

Over most of the northern areas of Manitoba, Ontario, Quebec, Labrador, the northern half of Saskatchewan, the northeast corner of Alberta, and about half of the Northwest Territories, the Canadian Shield is exposed at the earth's surface. Shaped like a saucer, its highest elevations are found around its outer limits while the central area lies beneath the waters of Hudson Bay. Much of the exposed Canadian Shield consists of a rough, rolling upland. Along the east coast from Labrador to Baffin Island, the Shield has been strongly uplifted. Glaciers moving down slope to the sea deeply scoured valleys and created fjords, giving the coast spectacular scenery.

The Interior Plains, flat to gently rolling landscape, lie between the Cordillera and the Canadian Shield. Their sedimentary rocks were formed after the end of the Precambrian era (some half-billion years ago) and include Cretaceous-age rocks formed some 100 million years ago. Within these Cretaceous-age rocks, vast oil and gas deposits exist (Vignette 2.11). At the end of the last glacial advance, a mantle of glacially deposited debris covered these sedimentary rocks. In places, glacial lakes were formed. Silts and clays were deposited. Later, when the ice front no longer served as a barrier, the lakes drained, leaving glacial spillways and outwash plains to mark this geological event. The Mackenzie River and its tributaries created a river valley system that extends to the Arctic Ocean. Two huge deltaic landforms exist. One is at the western end of Lake Athabasca where the Peace and Athabasca rivers deposit their silt. The other is the Mackenzie Delta, located at the mouth of the Mackenzie River.

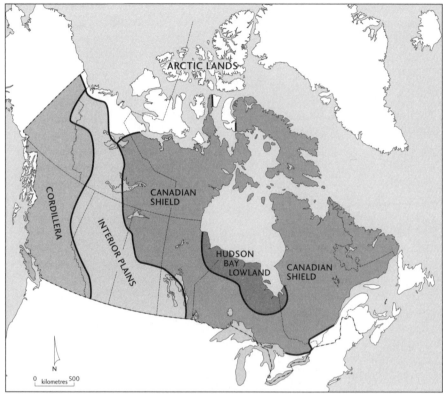

FIGURE 2.6 Geomorphic Regions of Canada
Five geomorphic regions are found in the Canadian North.
SOURCE: After Bird (1972) and Slaymaker (1988).

Vignette 2.11 Oil and Gas in the Beaufort Sea and Mackenzie Delta

Within the sedimentary rocks in the Mackenzie Delta and in the shallow continental shelf waters of the Beaufort Sea, geologists have already found vast quantities of oil and natural gas. Petroleum exploration began in the mid-1960s. Nearly 200 exploration wells have been drilled in the region, resulting in the discovery of nearly 60 oil and gas fields. The largest discoveries in the Mackenzie Delta include the Taglu and Parsons Lake natural gas fields. The Amauligak oil field represents the largest offshore discovery. The petroleum reserves of the Beaufort Sea and Mackenzie Delta amount to over 10 per cent of Canada's petroleum reserves. With the exception of local gas production for the town of Inuvik, these petroleum deposits still await commercial development. Such development would require a pipeline to markets in the United States. In 2001, companies again expressed an interest in developing these resources because of rising energy prices and the desire by the United States to promote a continental energy system.

The Cordillera, a complex mountainous region, occupies much of British Columbia, Yukon, and a small portion of southern Alberta and the Northwest Territories west of the Mackenzie River. The Canadian Cordillera begins at the 49th parallel. The Cordillera is about 800 km wide and extends to the Alaska border. The Cordillera contains a variety of mountainous terrain as well as plateaus, valleys, and plains. It also contains glaciers and icefields. This geomorphic region has majestic mountains, including the world famous Rocky Mountains. These mountains were formed by severe folding and faulting of sedimentary rocks. The highest mountain in Canada, Mount Logan, has an elevation of nearly 6,000 metres and is part of the St Elias Mountains in the southwest corner of Yukon.

During the Wisconsin ice age, the Cordillera was glaciated. Alpine glaciers created arêtes, cirques, and U-shaped valleys. Over most of the Cordillera, the land became ice-free some 10,000 years ago and in this postglacial period, river terraces, alluvial fans, flood plains, and deltas were formed. While today many glaciers are retreating, some glaciers are still active, though their rate of movement is relatively slow.

The Hudson Bay Lowland is a low, flat coastal plain that has recently emerged from the Tyrrell Sea, which was an inland extension of Hudson Bay some 8,000 years ago. The surface of this lowland consists of recently deposited marine sediments combined with reworked glacial till. These deposits accumulated in the postglacial period when the lowland was beneath the Atlantic Ocean (part of a much larger Hudson Bay). With the retreat of the ice sheet some 7,500 years ago, the process of isostatic rebound came into play. Gradually, more and more of the seabed became land, creating a distinct geomorphic region known as the Hudson Bay Lowland. Its underlying Precambrian bedrock is masked entirely by glacial and marine sediments. The inland boundary of this region is marked by elevations of around 180 metres, which indicate that, with the removal of the weight of the ice sheet, the earth's crust began to regain its former shape. This phenomenon is called isostatic uplift. Since isostatic uplift is continuing at a rate of around 70 to 130 cm/100 years, William Barr speculated that the Hudson Bay Lowland will increase in size at the expense of shallow waters of Hudson Bay. Within 12,000 years, Hudson Bay could become a fraction of its present size (Barr, 1972). Barr raised another intriguing idea—that within 1,000 years the Northwest Passage would shrink so much that ships could no longer pass through Simpson Strait between King William Island and Adelaide Peninsula (Barr, 1986).

The Arctic Lands are a complex geomorphic area centred on the Arctic Archipelago. Here, geological events and geomorphic processes have created lowlands, hilly terrain, and mountains. The cold, dry climate results in many periglacial features that provide a distinctive appearance to the land. Rock-scattered bedrock and patterned ground are widespread in the lowlands, while alpine glaciers occur in the more mountainous landscapes. Rolling to hilly terrain underlain by permafrost is affected by slumping, caused by solifluction or gelifluction: 'soil flow' down a sloping frozen surface (Trenhaile, 1998: 84–5). Hilly and mountainous landforms are found in the Queen Elizabeth Islands, although lowlands occupy much of Banks Island and Victoria Island. Most of Canada's glaciers are found in this region.

GLACIATION

Glaciation involves the formation, movement, and recession of glaciers. Over the past 25,000 years, the most recent phase of glaciation affected most landforms in Canada. Glacial formation took place as the climate cooled, causing snow to accumulate and eventually forming glaciers. Glacial recession commenced when the climate began to warm, causing the front of the continental glaciers to melt. As the glaciers melt and recede, material contained in the ice is deposited on the ground. Glacial movement involves the advance of massive ice sheets, causing the erosion of the landforms. In the Canadian North, unglaciated terrain is limited to a small area of Yukon. Here, there was not enough precipitation to nourish the expansion of glaciers.

Over the last two million years, the earth has known several ice ages (Vignette 2.12). The last one, the Late Wisconsin, began some 25,000 years ago. During the Late Wisconsin ice age, two huge ice sheets, the Laurentide and the Cordillera, covered most of North America. These ice sheets reached a maximum thickness of 4,000 and 2,000 metres thick, respectively. In comparison, the largest Canadian glaciers are found on Ellesmere Island, having a thickness of nearly 1,000 metres. Some time around 18,000 years ago, as the climate warmed, these huge ice sheets began to retreat. By 14,000 years ago, an ice-free corridor appeared along the eastern edge of the Cordillera ice sheet, connecting the unglaciated areas in Yukon with the rest of ice-free North America. By about 10,000 years ago, most of these two ice sheets had melted.

During this process of advance and retreat, two geomorphic processes took place. First, the advancing ice sheet caused glacial erosion; later, the retreating ice sheet deposited debris on the land. Glacial erosion took various forms, such as scraping off the unconsolidated material and plucking out huge chunks of bedrock. Where the bedrock was highly resistant, the rock was scraped and scoured. In the mountains, alpine glaciers moved quickly down slope and had a much greater erosional effect than did continental glaciers. Evidence of such massive erosion is found in U-shaped valleys in the Cordillera and the fjord coastline of Labrador and Baffin Island. Glacial features of deposition consist of water-sorted deposits and unsorted deposits. As the ice sheets melted, some of the material contained in the ice was discharged into running melt water and glacial lakes. The debris held in the ice sheets was deposited on the land; in some cases, glacial melt waters sorted the debris or till into eskers and outwash plains. Eskers—long, narrow ridges of sorted sands and gravel—were deposited from melt streams within the decaying ice sheet. Some eskers are over 100 kilometres in length. The most common glacial deposit is ground moraine. Ground moraine or till is unsorted material deposited by a melting ice sheet or glacier. Till extends over large areas while drumlins appear as clusters of low hills, shaped by the flow of the ice. Most drumlins are believed to have formed a short distance behind the ice margin just prior to deglaciation and therefore record the final direction of ice movements. As the massive ice sheets melted, enormous quantities of water were released. These melt waters either overtaxed the existing southern-flowing drainage system or formed glacial lakes. Often, these glacial lakes were created when the northward-flowing rivers were still blocked from reaching the sea by the remaining ice sheet. The largest glacial lake, Lake Agassiz, occupied much of Manitoba.

Vignette 2.12 Contemporary Glaciers

Over the past two million years, at least four distinct ice ages have covered Canada with huge ice sheets. Each ice age is associated with many ice advances and retreats. The latest ice advance, the Late Wisconsin, began about 25,000 years ago. Today, ice remnants of the huge Laurentide and Cordillera ice sheets exist in two areas of the Canadian North, the Cordillera and the Arctic Islands. Large masses of ice called glaciers, icefields, and ice caps are the remnants of the Late Wisconsin ice cover, which consisted of the Cordillera and Laurentide ice sheets. In the Canadian North, there are around 200,000 km^2 of land covered by glaciers. Approximately 75 per cent of the area occupied by glaciers is found in the Arctic Archipelago, 15 per cent on Baffin Island, and 10 per cent in Yukon.

The distinction between the types of ice masses is generally as follows: ice caps flow outwards in several directions and submerge most or all of the underlying land, while a glacier flows in one direction and is normally confined to a valley. Icefields consist of a number of ice caps that have coalesced. Today, these ice masses are located in the St Elias Mountains and the adjacent mountain ranges of southwest Yukon and British Columbia, and on Baffin Island (Penny and Barnes ice caps), Devon Island (Devon Ice Cap), Axel Heiberg Island (Franz Muller Ice Cap), and Ellesmere Island (Prince of Wales, Sydkapand, and Agassiz ice caps and an unnamed one). These ice caps and glaciers occupy less than 5 per cent of the Arctic while those in the Cordillera form less than 1 per cent of the Subarctic. The Cordillera also contains rock glaciers: glaciers that have been covered by debris from rock fall and from movement of glacier debris to the ice surface. There are two types of rock glaciers: those with cores of glacial ice and those with interstitial ice (Johnson, 1988: 277). When glaciers receive a thick and complete cover of debris, their rate of melting is slowed.

Glaciation has created landforms that have both positive and negative impacts for resource development. In particular, glaciation has affected road-building. For example, the scraping of the Canadian Shield in northern Saskatchewan has created a northeast-southwest alignment of the Precambrian rock outcrops. Since highways from the south tend to head north or northwest, this requires building roads against the 'grain' of the land. On the other hand, eskers and other sorted glacial deposits are a much-valued source of sand and gravel for highway construction in northern Saskatchewan.

PERIGLACIAL FEATURES

Periglacial landforms are widespread in Arctic Lands. The most distinctive periglacial landforms, such as tundra polygons and ice-cored hills known as pingos, are associated with permafrost and a cold, dry Arctic climate where frost action (the freezing-and-thawing cycle) is the dominant geomorphic process. During the Late Wisconsin glacial period, these conditions were associated with the southern edge of the Laurentide and Cordillera ice sheets. As these ice sheets retreated, more periglacial features were formed. Hugh French (1996: 5) has described this process:

During the cold periods of the Pleistocene, large areas of the now-temperate middle latitudes experienced intense frost action and reduced temperatures because of their proximity to the ice sheets. Permafrost may have formed, only to have degraded during a later climatic amelioration.

French estimates that periglacial features are found over one-fifth of the earth's surface. Today, relic periglacial features exist great distances from Canada's cold, dry Arctic climate, but the formation of new patterned ground and other periglacial features continues to take place in Arctic Lands where unconsolidated material forms the ground surface. Patterned ground refers to symmetrical forms, usually polygons, caused by intense frost action over a long period of time. Patterned ground includes frost-sorted circles of polygon patterns of stones and pebbles. The general process of frost heave causes coarse stones to move to the surface and outwards. Another even more dramatic periglacial feature, though not a common one, is the pingo. This ice-core hill occurs in lowlands where continuous permafrost exists. A pingo occurs when an ice lens in permanently frozen ground is nourished by extraneous water. Over time, the ice lens grows and pushes itself upwards, forming a mound and eventually a hill.

PERMAFROST

Permafrost, perennially frozen ground, is found in almost all of the Canadian North. It is defined as ground remaining at or below the freezing point for at least two years. Permafrost reaches its maximum depth in high latitudes where its frozen state extends to several hundred metres or more into the ground; at more southerly sites its depth may be less than 10 metres. The greatest recorded thicknesses in Canada are over 1,000 metres on Baffin and Ellesmere islands.

Permafrost has existed for thousands of years in the Canadian North. The upper layer of permafrost (called the active layer) thaws each summer. The thickness of the active layer varies from a few centimetres in the Arctic to several metres in the Subarctic. The southern extent of permafrost is associated with the mean annual air temperature isotherm of 0°C (Williams, 1986: 3).

Since permafrost varies in its depth and geographic extent, it is divided into four types—continuous, discontinuous, sporadic, and alpine permafrost (Figure 2.7). An area is classified as having continuous permafrost when over 80 per cent of the ground is permanently frozen; for discontinuous permafrost, 30–80 per cent must be frozen; and for sporadic permafrost, less than 30 per cent. The sporadic permafrost zone represents a transition area between permanently frozen and unfrozen ground. Alpine permafrost is not defined by the percentage of permanently frozen ground but by its presence in a mountainous setting. Such permafrost is found in British Columbia and Alberta. In terms of geographic distribution, continuous permafrost is found where the mean annual temperature is around –7°C while discontinuous permafrost lies between –5°C and –7°C (Figure 1.2). Sporadic permafrost is often found between 0°C and -5°C.

Permafrost affects the land surface by slowing the growth of vegetation, impeding surface drainage, and creating periglacial landforms such as pingos and thermokarst features. While permafrost and periglacial landforms are often found in the same

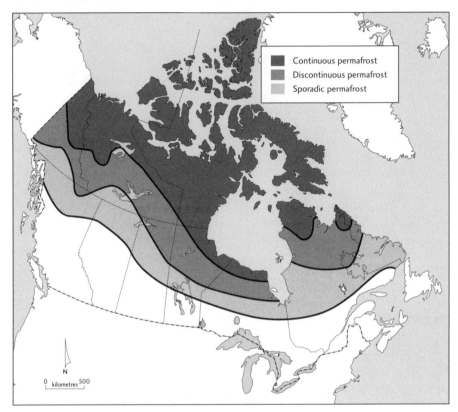

FIGURE 2.7 Permafrost Zones in the Canadian North
The three permafrost zones extend across the Canadian North. In addition, occurrences of permafrost are found at higher elevations in the Cordillera.
SOURCE: After The Atlas of Canada <http://atlas.gc.ca>.

geographic area, permafrost refers to permanently frozen ground while periglacial features are created by freeze-thaw action. Permafrost has only become a problem since efforts have been made to develop the North by building roads, pipelines, and towns. The design of these human-made features must take into account the presence of permafrost. Exposure of ice-rich ground during construction can result in retrogressive thaw slumps (Burn and Lewkowicz, 1990) and such slumps can prove costly. Permafrost has made northern construction 'a matter of geotechnical science and engineering' (Williams, 1986: 27).

NORTHERN HYDROLOGY

The hydrological cycle has two phases—active and inactive. The annual cycle is most active in the spring due to the release of water stored as snow and ice. As well, most precipitation falls during the spring. With such a rush of water, flooding often occurs. For the rest of the year, the cycle is inactive, that is, the flow of water is well within the

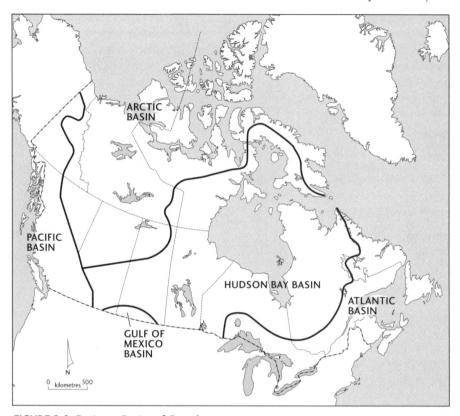

FIGURE 2.8 Drainage Basins of Canada
Canada has four major river basins and one minor basin whose waters flow to the Gulf of Mexico.
A more detail account of river basins is shown in The Atlas of Canada.
SOURCE: After The Atlas of Canada <http://atlas.gc.ca>.

capacity of streams and rivers. Though annual precipitation in the North is low, water resources in the North make up the bulk of Canada's water reserves. These resources are found in four drainage basins—the Arctic, Hudson Bay, Atlantic, and Pacific (Figure 2.8). The river systems found in each drainage basin empty their waters into the three oceans surrounding Canada. The Arctic and Hudson Bay drainage basins form nearly 75 per cent of the area of Canada and, despite relatively low precipitation over much of this area, these two basins account for almost 50 per cent of the stream flow (Table 2.2).

In terms of runoff volume, the Mackenzie River is the most important river in the North. Since most of its headwaters are located in British Columbia, Alberta, and Saskatchewan, spring melting first occurs south of 60°N while the lower reaches of the Mackenzie River are still frozen. Ice jams frequently occur, causing widespread flooding. Northern rivers, such as the La Grande, Mackenzie, and Churchill rivers, empty vast quantities of fresh water into the sea. One impact of this fresh water is to stratify the ocean waters, that is, river water tends to overlie the colder and denser ocean

TABLE 2.2 The Drainage Basins of Canada and Their Streamflows

Drainage Basin	Area (million km²)	Streamflow (m³)
Hudson Bay	3.8	30,594
Arctic	3.6	20,491
Atlantic	1.6	21,890
Pacific	1.0	24,951
Total	10.0	105,135*

*The Gulf of Mexico accounts for 7,209m³ of streamflow.

waters. This stratification of ocean waters results in surface layers having a lower salt content. Another effect of these fresh waters is to provide a suitable estuarial habitat for marine life, such as bowhead whales.

NORTHERN SEAS

The seas of the Canadian North extend from the Beaufort Sea to the Labrador Sea and include the waters of Hudson Bay. These cold water bodies have less impact on the northern hydrological cycle than might be expected. The reasons for their limited impact are twofold: (1) cold seas have a lower evaporation rate than warm seas; and (2) ice-covered seas have low evaporation rates similar to those found on equally cold land bodies. The Arctic Ocean has a permanent ice cover known as the polar pack ice (ice that has not melted for at least two years and is not attached to land and therefore moves in a clockwise motion within the Arctic Ocean). Pack ice is much thicker than other ice cover, making navigation by ship most difficult.

On the Canadian side of the Arctic Ocean, cold surface water flows from the Arctic Basin into the Atlantic Ocean around Baffin Bay, where it mixes with the warmer Atlantic waters, forming Subarctic water. Baffin Bay is connected to the Arctic Ocean through Nares Strait and Jones and Lancaster sounds, and to the Labrador Sea through Davis Strait. Most icebergs are formed from the Greenland Ice Sheet. The Labrador Current carries them to the waters off Newfoundland, where they represent a hazard to both ocean shipping and offshore drilling rigs. During winter when there is extensive ice cover, a polynya or open-water area (called 'North Water') exists in the northern part of Baffin Bay. The scientific explanation for the natural factors that create open water in a frigid environment still eludes physical scientists (Vignette 2.13).

HUMAN IMPACT ON THE ENVIRONMENT

The North's physical geography poses a different set of physical challenges to settlement and resource development from those found in temperate Canada. Much of this challenge is related to the delicate nature of the northern environment. The slow rate of biological growth and the wide extent of permafrost mean that polar lands and seas take much longer to recover from damage caused by industrial activities than do

Vignette 2.13 Polynyas

The Arctic Ocean has a thick cover of ice, but a dozen or more areas of open water do occur each winter. Many recur each winter. The largest recurring open water lies between Baffin Island and Greenland. Such open water is known as a polynya, which is a derivation of the Russian word for open water surrounded by ice. The explanation remains unresolved but most hydrographers believe that the basic mechanism involves various combinations of tides, currents, ocean-bottom upwellings, and winds that keep the surface waters moving and thus prevent them from freezing. Polynyas may be as small as 50 metres across or as large as the famous North Water polynya, which often extends over 130,000 km^2. These biological 'hot spots' serve as Arctic oases where marine animals, polar bears, and birds congregate. Not surprisingly, archaeologists have uncovered Thule settlement sites near the North Water.

more temperate places. The accelerating pace of resource development has placed wilderness habitats and the North's biodiversity at risk. A basic understanding of the North's physical geography and its fragile nature alerts the reader to two of the grand themes in geography:

- Does the physical environment shape the range of human activities?
- Are human activities, but especially those related to resource development, necessarily damaging to the northern environment?

NOTES

1. The Little Ice Age represents a relatively short-term cooling of the northern climate for some 400 years between 1450 and 1850. The Little Ice Age is considered a minor change in the global climate. However, during this period, the impact on human beings living in the Arctic was dramatic. The Viking settlement on Greenland ended during the Little Ice Age and the Thule lost their main source of food—the Bowhead whales ceased to enter the Arctic Ocean because ice cover was more extensive. As a result, the Thule had to adjust their hunting economy to focus more on seal and caribou. Archaeologists believe that the Inuit are the descendants of the Thule.
2. In a recent article in *The Canadian Geographer*, Sauderson, Smith, and Woo (2000) summarize recent developments in Canadian geomorphology. Much of their discussion deals with research advances in geomorphology occurring in northern Canada.

REFERENCES AND SELECTED READINGS

Ahrens, C. Donald. 1994. *Meteorology Today: An Introduction to Weather, Climate, and the Environment*, 5th edn. New York: West Publishing Company.

Barr, William. 1972. 'Hudson Bay: The shape of things to come', *The Musk-Ox Journal* 11: 64.

———. 1986. 'Glacio-Isostatic Rebound and the Changing Face of the Northwest Passage', paper presented to the joint meeting of the Hakluyt Society and the Society for the History of Discoveries, Brown University, Providence, RI.

Bird, J.B. 1972. 'The Physical Characteristics of Northern Canada', in William C. Wonders, ed., *The North: Studies in Canadian Geography*. Toronto: University of Toronto Press.

Bone, Robert M., S. Long, and P. McPherson. 1997. 'Settlements in the Mackenzie Basin: Now and in the Future 2050', in Stewart J. Cohen, ed., *Mackenzie Basin Impact Study Final Report*. Downsview, Ont.: Environment Canada, 265–75.

Bouchard, Mireillle. 2001. 'Un défi environnemental complexe du XXIe siècle au Canada: l'identification et la compréhension de la réponse des environnements face aux changements climatiques globaux', *The Canadian Geographer* 45, 1: 54-70.

Burn, Chris R. 1995. 'Where Does the Polar Night Begin?', *The Canadian Geographer* 39, 1: 68–74.

———. 1996. *The Polar Night*. Scientific Report No. 4. Inuvik: Aurora Research Institute, Aurora College.

——— and A.G. Lewkowicz. 1990. 'Retrogressive Thaw Slumps', *The Canadian Geographer* 34, 3: 273–6.

Clair, Thomas. 1999. *Issue Scan: Climate Change and Ecosystem Research in Canada's North*. Available at: <http://www.atl.ec.gc.ca/nei/pdf/summary.pdf>.

Cohen, J. Stewart. 1997. *Mackenzie Basin Impact Study Final Report*. Downsview, Ont.: Environment Canada.

Draper, Dianne. 2002. *Our Environment: A Canadian Perspective*, 2nd edn. Toronto: Nelson.

Environment Canada. 2002. Canada Climate Normals 1971–2000. Available at: <http://www.msc-smc.ec.gc.ca/climate/climate_normals/index_e.cfm>.

Etkin, Dave. 1989. 'Elevation as a Climate Control in Yukon', *Inversion: The Newsletter of Arctic Climate* 2: 12–14.

French, Hugh M. 1996. *The Periglacial Environment*, 2nd edn. London: Longman.

——— and Olav Slaymaker, eds. 1993. *Canada's Cold Environments*. Montreal and Kingston: McGill-Queen's University Press.

Gardner, J.S. 1986. 'Snow as a resource and hazard in early 20th century mining, Selkirk Mountains', *The Canadian Geographer* 30, 2: 217–28.

Gertler, L.O., and R.W. Crowley. 1977. *Changing Canadian Cities: The Next Twenty-Five Years*. Toronto: McClelland & Stewart.

Haggett, Peter. 1983. *Geography: A Modern Synthesis*. London: Harper & Row.

Hare, F. Kenneth, and Morley K. Thomas. 1979. *Climate Canada*, 2nd edn. Toronto: Wiley.

Houghton, J.T., Y. Ding, D.J. Griggs, M. Noguer, P.J. van der Linden, X. Dai, K. Maskell, and C.A. Johnson. 2001. *Climate Change 2001: The Scientific Basis*. Contribution of Working Group I to the Third Assessment Report of the Intergovernmental Panel on Climate Change. Cambridge: Cambridge University Press. See <http://www.ipcc.ch/pub/reports.htm>.

Johnson, Peter G. 1988. 'Rock glaciers, Southwest Yukon', *The Canadian Geographer* 32, 3: 277–80.

Lawford, R.G. 1988. 'Climatic Variability and the Hydrological Cycle in the Canadian North: Knowns and Unknowns', *Proceedings of the Third Meeting on Northern Climate*, Canadian Climate Program. Ottawa: Minister of Supply and Services, 143–62.

Marsh, William M. 1987. Earthscape: *A Physical Geography*. Toronto: Wiley.

——— and John Grossa, Jr. 2002. *Environmental Geography: Science, Land Use, and Earth Systems*, 2nd edn. Toronto: Wiley.

Norton, William. 2002. *Human Geography*, 4th edn. Toronto: Oxford University Press.

Sauderson, Houston C., Dan J. Smith, and Ming-Ko Woo. 2000. 'Progress in Canadian geomorphology and hydrology', *The Canadian Geographer* 44, 1: 56–66.

Slaymaker, Olav. 1988. 'Physiographic Regions', in James H. Marsh, *The Canadian Encyclopedia*, 2nd edn. Edmonton: Hurtig, vol. 3, 1671.

———. 2001. 'Why so much concern about climate change and so little attention to landuse change?', *The Canadian Geographer* 45, 1: 71–8.

Trenhaile, Alan S. 1998. *Geomorphology: A Canadian Perspective.* Toronto: Oxford University Press.

Williams, Peter J. 1986. *Pipelines and Permafrost: Science in a Cold Climate.* Ottawa: Carleton University Press.

——— and Michael W. Smith. 1991. *The Frozen Earth: Fundamentals of Geocryology.* Cambridge: Cambridge University Press.

Young, Steven B. 1989. *To the Arctic: An Introduction to the Far Northern World.* New York: Wiley.

CHAPTER 3

The Historical Background

History is essential for an understanding of present events taking place in Canada's North. While the story of Canada's North began some 30,000 years ago when the first Old World hunters entered Alaska and then Yukon, the post-contact history is examined in more detail here because it provides insights into the changing relationship between Canada's first peoples and the newcomers—first, the European explorers, traders, and settlers, and later, Canadians who have come from practically every place in the world. To simplify matters, the North's history is set into three historic phases:

- the pre-contact and early contact period;
- the fur trade era;
- the modern period of resource development.

Some 12,000 years ago, Old World hunters passed quickly through the ice-free corridor into the heartland of North America. Once the Laurentide Ice Sheet had melted, Paleo-Indians began to occupy these lands. The Arctic remained uninhabited until 5,000 years ago when the first wave of migrants from the Bering Strait area, the Paleo-Eskimos, began to spread across the Arctic coastline of Canada. At the time of contact, the Indian and Inuit peoples of the Canadian North numbered close to 60,000. First contact, though a fleeting one, was with the Vikings. More continuous contact began in the sixteenth century when explorers landed on the east coast of Canada and Basque fishers established summer fish-processing camps on the island of Newfoundland.

The second phase, characterized by much greater interaction with European fur traders, brought many changes to Aboriginal cultures and economies. The fur trade brought great riches to the Hudson's Bay Company (HBC) based in London and to the North West Company in Montreal. The fur trade reached its zenith in the eighteenth century when Native peoples across the Subarctic were engaged in trapping beaver and trading beaver pelts for European goods. At first, Indians brought their furs to the HBC posts along Hudson and James bays, but by the end of the eighteenth century both companies had established fur posts in the rich fur country of the Mackenzie Basin. With the amalgamation of the two companies in 1821, the Montreal fur trade route was abandoned in favour of the more economical Hudson Bay route. By the late nineteenth century, the Hudson's Bay Company made use of American and later Canadian rail service to transport its trade goods and fur bales. The fur trade exposed Native peoples not only to Western goods but also to another culture. In the early days of the fur trade, the relationship between the trappers and the fur traders was more of a partnership, but gradually the relationship saw the Indian trappers grow more and more dependent on the traders and eventually the federal government. At the beginning of the twentieth century, the Arctic white fox pelt was highly prized in the European fur market, and the HBC opened fur trading posts in the Arctic, thereby bringing the Inuit into the fur economy.

The last historical phase begins when Canada gained political control over its northern territories in 1870 (the HBC lands, known as Rupert's Land) and 1880 (Arctic Archipelago). While the fur economy continue to hold sway, the late nineteenth century saw the emergence of resource development. In 1896, the discovery of gold in the Klondike transformed Yukon from a fur-trapping economy to a resource economy. While other natural resources were exploited in the following years, none approach the magnitude of the Klondike gold rush until World War II. Seeking secure supplies of oil and the reliable transport of men and materiel, the US Army financed several large-scale development projects, including the building of the Alaska Highway from Dawson Creek, BC, to Fairbanks, Alaska, the expansion of oil production at Norman Wells, and the construction of the Canol Pipeline from Norman Wells to Whitehorse and then to Fairbanks. After World War II, the resource boom continued in response to American demand for energy and raw materials, transforming the North into a resource hinterland for the world economy. At the same time, great social changes were taking place among the Aboriginal community. Basic to the economic and social changes occurring in the North is the place of Aboriginal peoples in northern resource development.

THE FIRST PHASE: PRE-CONTACT

Old World hunters who crossed the Beringia land bridge into Alaska were the first people to set foot in North America (Vignette 3.1). But just when these paleolithic people reached Alaska and then the heartland of North America remains in doubt. Archaeological evidence confirms that Paleo-Indians occupied what is today the southwest United States some 11,000 years ago, suggesting that their ancestors migrated along the ice-free corridor between the Cordillera and Laurentide ice sheets some 12,000 years ago (Vignette 3.2).

Yet, there is a nagging feeling that Old World hunters may have reached the interior of North America at an earlier time, perhaps 12,000 years ago (Bonnichsen and Turnmire, 1999). New archaeological evidence suggests humans arrived in Yukon before the last ice advance—some 25,000 to 30,000 years ago. Archaeological findings such as those at Bluefish Caves near Old Crow in Yukon support this hypothesis, although the dating of the Bluefish Caves artifacts remains controversial (Cinq-Mars and Morlan, 1999).

One theory espoused by Wright (1995) suggests that two major migrations from Siberia to the temperate areas of North America took place—one before the last ice advance (25,000 years ago or more), the other when the ice sheets began to retreat (12,000 to 15,000 years ago).[1]

Vignette 3.1 Beringia

During part of the last ice age, a land bridge some 1,500 km in length joined Asia to North America. This land is called Beringia. Now submerged some 100 metres below sea level, the land bridge allowed Old World hunters to move into Alaska. Around 18,000 years ago, the ice sheets reached their maximum extent. At that time, huge quantities of water were locked into the ice sheets, causing the sea level to drop by as much as 150 metres. Later, as the climate began to warm, two major physical events took place. The ocean waters rose, covering the land bridge once again, and an ice-free corridor appeared between the Laurentide Ice Sheet and the Cordillera Ice Sheet. This corridor made it possible for the Old World hunters to migrate southward along the eastern slope of the Rocky Mountains.

Occupying Northern Canada

Once south of the ice sheet, the Old World hunters gradually spread across America (Vignette 3.2). Their main source of food remained the woolly mammoth and other big-game animals. Around 10,000 years ago, the woolly mammoth became extinct and its hunters, now described as Paleo-Indians, had to adjust to new circumstances. At the same time, the Laurentide and Cordillera ice sheets had retreated, allowing the people to occupy these new hunting grounds. The archaeological record for this period is very sketchy, leaving no clear picture of the pattern of occupancy by various Paleo-Indian groups until contact.

Vignette 3.2 The Clovis Theory: The Original Paradigm

Since the 1930s, the Clovis theory has served as the central paradigm for archaeologists studying the peopling of the Americas. According to the Clovis theory, some 12,000 years ago, Old World hunters from Alaska and Yukon found an ice-free corridor through the vast ice sheet to the unglaciated areas of the New World. Armed with spears that had a distinctive fluted projectile point, these Paleo-Indians quickly spread across North and South America. Archaeological evidence clearly demonstrates that Paleo-Indians were hunting the woolly mammoth and other big-game animals in the Great Plains and the Southwest of what is today the United States as early as 11,000 years ago. Within 2,000 years, descendants of these primitive hunters had reached the southern tip of South America. The empirical support for the Clovis theory is based on archaeological finds of flaked-stone projectile points. These distinctive spear points were first unearthed in 1932 at a New Mexico mammoth kill site near Clovis, New Mexico. Since then, similar finds dated to the same early period have been made in other parts of North America. However, more recent archaeological findings, especially the Monte Verde site in Chile, which apparently dates to 12,500 years ago, suggest that Old World hunters reached South America well before the Clovis people. Does this mean that the original paradigm is no longer valid?

SOURCES: Adapted from Thomas (1999); Bonnichsen and Turnmire (1999: 1–26).

Roughly a thousand years later, a second wave of Old World hunters, the Paleo-Eskimos, crossed the Bering Strait from Siberia to Alaska. By this time, ice sheets had retreated from the Arctic coast, allowing the sea-based hunting economy of the Paleo-Eskimos to flourish. These early migrants are named Denbigh after an important archaeological site in Alaska. Their culture, the Arctic Small Tool Tradition, was based on the use of flint to shape bone and ivory into harpoons and other tools. As sea hunters, they occupied Arctic coastal lowlands and eventually reached the coast of Labrador and Newfoundland. Over time, the culture of these people either evolved or was replaced by a new wave of Paleo-Eskimo migrants—the Dorset—who in turn were replaced by the Thule. While the archaeological story is incomplete, two major cultural changes have been identified. The first one saw the Denbigh culture evolve into or replaced by the Dorset culture. The Dorset lived in semi-permanent houses built of snow and turf, heating them with soapstone oil lamps.

Around AD 1000, the Thule culture appeared. The Thule originated in Alaska and gradually spread across Arctic Canada, replacing the Dorset inhabitants. In the open waters around the Arctic coast of Alaska, the Thule hunters had developed the technology and skills necessary to hunt the large bowhead whales. They migrated eastward, perhaps driven by population pressures or encouraged by a warming of the Arctic climate that resulted in an increase in open water in the Arctic Ocean. In any case, the Thule spread across the Canadian Arctic using their innovative transportation system of skin boats (kayak and umiak) and dogsleds to harvest seal, walrus, caribou, and the bowhead whale. By the fifteenth century the Thule reached Greenland, where they probably encountered the Vikings.

After AD 1200, the climate began to cool, making ice cover more extensive. The climate continued to cool and the period between 1450 and 1850 is referred to as 'the Little Ice Age'. Ice cover became more extensive, thereby limiting sea areas suitable for the bowhead whale. Unable to secure food from their favourite source, the bowhead whale, a shift in Thule hunting strategy was necessary. In this new hunting regime, the Thule became more mobile and formed smaller groups to hunt the seal and caribou. About this time, Europeans, such as the English explorer, Martin Frobisher, came into contact with these people. Their descendants are the present-day Inuit.

Terra Nullis

The New World was not, as Europeans believed, terra nullis—empty lands. Dickason (2002: 11) describes this pre-contact world:

> When Europeans arrived, the whole of the New World was populated not only in all its different landscape and with varying degrees of density, but also with a rich cultural kaleidoscope of something like 2,000 or more different societies.

Exactly how many lived in Canada, let alone northern Canada, in these early days is unknown.[2] Unlike the more populated lands to the south, the North must have had a small population spread over a vast territory. One estimate suggests that some 50,000 Indians and Inuit occupied the Subarctic and Arctic areas of Canada at the time of contact (Crowe, 1974: 20), while Mooney (1928) and Kroeber (1939) estimated a slightly higher figure of 56,000, with 16,000 Inuit in the Arctic and 40,000 Indians in the Subarctic (Vignette 3.3). Such numbers show a population density of 130 km^2 per person, indicating that the hunting economy could only support a relatively small population due to the limited availability of game and its seasonal nature. In fact, the Arctic and Subarctic, as might be expected, had the lowest population density of all the Aboriginal cultural regions in North America, suggesting lower carrying capacity (Vignette 2.2).

In 1857, the first comprehensive estimate of the Indian and Inuit population of British North America was made by Sir George Simpson for the Special Committee of the British House of Commons on the affairs of the Hudson's Bay Company (*Census of Canada*, 1876, vol. 4: ix–xiv). Simpson's figure of nearly 139,000 for British North America was based on reports made by local Hudson's Bay Company officials on the number of Indians trading at their posts. Approximately 61,000 Indians were reported as trading at posts in the Subarctic. Added to these numbers was Simpson's guess that 4,000 Eskimos occupied the Arctic. In 1881, the census indicated about 108,000 Indians, Métis, and Inuit residing in the provinces and territories of Canada (Table 3.1).

TABLE 3.1 Indian Population, 1881

	Indian Population	Canada's Population	Indian Percentage of Total Population
Prince Edward Island	281	108,891	0.3
Nova Scotia	2,125	440,572	0.5
New Brunswick	1,401	321,233	0.4
Quebec*	7,515	1,359,027	0.6
Ontario*	15,325	1,923,228	0.8
Manitoba*	6,767	49,459	10.3
British Columbia	25,661	49,459	51.9
North-West Territories	49,472	56,446	87.6
Canada	108,547	4,324,810	2.5

* In 1881, the geographic size of Quebec, Ontario, and Manitoba was smaller than today. After 1881, these three provinces obtained land from the North-West Territories. In 1905, the provinces of Alberta and Saskatchewan were formed and the North-West Territories became the Northwest Territories.

Where did Aboriginal peoples live? The geography of Aboriginal people at the time of contact is based on the diaries and accounts of early explorers, fur traders, and missionaries. The broad pattern involves a threefold geographic division, with the Algonkian Indians living in the eastern Subarctic while the Athapaskan Indians occupied the western Subarctic. To their north lived the Inuit. This same broad geographic settlement pattern exists today.

Determining the geographic location of individual tribes is much more problematic, but these peoples likely had occupied the territory shown in Figure 3.1 for some

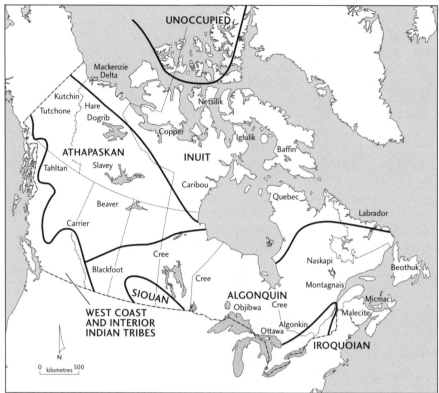

FIGURE 3.1 Geographic Areas Occupied by Aboriginal Peoples at Contact
Indians and Inuit had spread across northern Canada well before contact with Europeans. The geographic arrangement of these peoples at the time of contact has been reconstructed by anthropologists and ethnographers.
SOURCE: After Harris (1987: Plate 11).

time, perhaps centuries. The geographic stability of the pre-contact hunting societies can only be guessed at because archaeological evidence is so limited. Only in the Arctic is there evidence of the replacement of one group by another—the Dorset by the Thule, who were the ancestors of the Inuit.

These small but highly mobile Indian and Inuit hunting groups had become finely tuned to harvesting the particular food resources in their geographic territory. Within that territory, hunters followed a seasonal rhythm of movement as they sought wild game. Through this seasonal movement, they exerted a form of political control over the territory. The main source of food was big game. For many, caribou was the preferred food; whale blubber and seal meat were common food sources for the Inuit. These hunting people moved according to the seasonal migrations of wild animals. Such a migratory hunting strategy is a form of sustainable resource use because the necessity of moving from one area to another limits the pressure on local resources. Limited weapon technology and cultural taboos also reduced the possibilities of overhunting or overfishing.

The pre-contact hunting economy had many attractions but it also contained an element of risk. For example, an unforeseen reduction in game, such as a shift in the annual migration route of caribou, could expose hunters and their dependants to severe shortages of food and perhaps starvation. As Ray (1984: 1) observed, 'opinions are divided whether hunting, fishing, and gathering societies generally faced a problem of chronic starvation—the more traditional viewpoint, or whether they were the original affluent societies.' Key to resolving this puzzle is reliability of food sources and the size of the population. Some geographic areas had a more readily available source of food than other areas. The west coast of British Columbia, for example, had abundant fish stocks, which permitted relatively dense pre-contact Indian populations (Harris, 1997: 30). Caribou hunters, who were dependent on the seasonal migration patterns of caribou, had to deal with a more problematic food source. Over the long run, archaeological evidence suggests that the population in each cultural region attained a size that was in balance with its food sources, but short-term food shortages occurred.

The Arrival of Europeans

The first Europeans to land on North American soil were the Vikings. During the tenth century, the Vikings regularly travelled from Greenland to Ellesmere and Baffin islands to trade with either the Dorset or Thule peoples. They also attempted to establish settlements along the coast of Labrador and Newfoundland. The first authentic Norse site found is located at L'Anse aux Meadows on the northern tip of Newfoundland's Great Northern Peninsula.

Some 500 years later, the Viking discoveries were all but forgotten, leaving Europe's geographic knowledge of the New World scanty at best. European explorers sought to reach the rich spice lands of Cathay by sail across the Atlantic Ocean but reached North America. Reports of the new land's great riches, based on information obtained from local Indians, may have been misinterpreted or embellished in hopes of securing financial support for later voyages. In 1536, Jacques Cartier returned to France with a report of a golden 'Kingdom of Saguenay' (Trudel, 1988: 368). This report was based on information supplied by Indians and supported by the Iroquois chief Donnacona, whom Cartier had captured and taken back to France. Cartier thought that he had discovered diamonds and gold from this mythical kingdom. These riches, upon careful examination in France, turned out to be quartz and iron pyrites—'fool's gold'.

In a similar vein, Martin Frobisher, under orders from Queen Elizabeth I, set sail from England to find the Northwest Passage to the Orient. Instead, he discovered Baffin Island and the promise of great mineral wealth—gold. Like the Spaniards, the English sought gold and silver from this New World. Would Frobisher's discovery give England a source of gold to rival Spain's New World gold mines? Over 1,200 tonnes of rock from Baffin Island were transported to England, but this rock was found to contain not an ounce of gold! Nevertheless, Frobisher's two sea voyages in 1576 and 1577 mark the beginning of British exploration of Arctic Canada. As with most early voyages, contact with the local peoples was established and trade often followed. However, contact between these two very different peoples did not always end on a friendly note. For instance, after landing on the shore of Baffin Island in 1576, five of Frobisher's crew were captured by local Inuit during a skirmish and were never seen again (Cooke and

Holland, 1978: 22–3). The following year, Frobisher lured an Inuk in his kayak to come near his ship. Captured and taken to England, the Inuk's skills at handling his kayak while hunting the royal swans were observed by the Queen (Crowe, 1974: 65). After a few years, he died of natural causes in England.

During the remainder of the sixteenth century and in the early seventeenth century, many explorers, including Davis, Hudson, and Button, continued to search for a route to the Orient. In the course of this search they explored the waters of Baffin Bay and Hudson Bay. These explorers failed to find a route to the Orient but the 'casual' trade with Indians for furs marked the beginnings of a highly profitable enterprise and led to the formation of an English fur-trading company—the Hudson's Bay Company.

THE SECOND PHASE: THE FUR TRADE

The story of the fur trade in Canada began with the Basque fishers who traded with Indians along the shores of Newfoundland. From these humble beginnings, the fur trade became the centrepiece of New France's economy and then the most profitable enterprise of the Hudson's Bay Company. As early as the sixteenth century, French fur traders located along the St Lawrence River recognized that the best furs came from the Subarctic, where the long, cold winter resulted in long-haired fur pelts. Geography provided easy access to these northern Indians by means of southward-flowing rivers, such as the St Maurice and Saguenay.[3] Late in the next century, the British established a series of trading posts on the shore of Hudson and James bays. For over a century, the French and English competed for the highly prized furs of the northern Indians, and by 1760 the fur trade was certainly the dominant economic activity in New France and Rupert's Land (Figure 3.2). Even when French Canada fell to the British in 1763, two centres, London and Montreal, continued to compete for northern furs (Figure 3.3). Montreal fur traders of the North West Company, now a blending of French-Canadian and Scottish traders, were forced to establish posts on the Saskatchewan River in order to intercept Indians on their way to trade at the Bay posts (Vignette 3.3). After decades of fierce and sometimes bloody competition, the two companies merged in 1821 (Figure 3.4). Over the next 100 years or so, the Hudson's Bay Company dominated the Canadian fur economy.

The Hudson's Bay Company

Like all colonial powers, Britain and France looked to their colonies for riches. Wealth often took the form of gold and silver, but in the case of Canada's North, wealth took the form of beaver pelts. The fur trade drew Canada's North and its Indian inhabitants into the European market, where the demand for furs was dependent on the European fashion industry (Vignette 3.4). The political implications of the fur economy are far-reaching and they take the form of a core/periphery relationship within a mercantile economic system. In this historical period, the core nations were Britain and France while the North served as the hinterland.

For over 300 years, the HBC dominated the Canadian fur trade. This British company was the most powerful economic, social, and political force in the Canadian

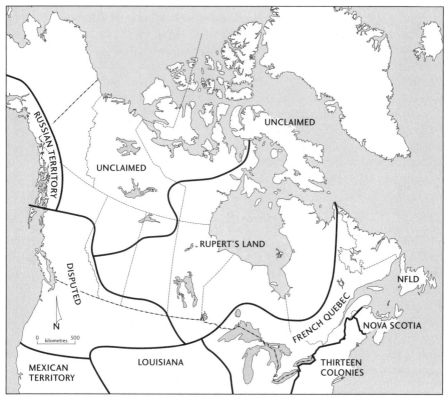

FIGURE 3.2 European Spheres of Influence, *circa* **1760**
The struggle to gain control over lands in North America is part of the much larger story of European colonization of the world. By 1760, most of North America had been claimed by Britain, France, Russia, and Spain.

Vignette 3.3 York Factory: Rise and Fall

In 1684, the Hudson's Bay Company established York Factory. It soon became the key trading post along the coast of Hudson Bay. Located on a marshy peninsula bounded by the estuaries of the Hayes and Nelson rivers, York Factory had the advantages of easy access to the fur riches of the western interior through the Hayes River. York Factory also served as the gateway for furs shipped to London and supplies coming from England for the many inland trading posts. Both the French and British realized the geographic significance of this site. In 1694, the French captured York Factory and named their prize Fort Bourbon. For 20 years, the French controlled the trade with Indians in the western interior of Canada. With the signing of the Treaty of Utrecht in 1714, this fort was returned to Britain. In 1782, a French naval force attacked and destroyed York Factory by burning its wooden buildings. The Hudson's Bay Company quickly rebuilt the fort, which soon became the headquarters of its operations in western Canada. By 1860, the fort comprised over 50 buildings, including an Anglican church, school, hospital, and a blacksmith shop. An Indian village was just south of the fort. At about the same time, a revolution in transportation took away York Factory's advantage of shipping furs and goods along the Hayes River. Substantial savings could be achieved by using American railways. By 1874, furs and trading goods from Canada's western interior were transported by rail from St Paul to New York. York Factory was left with coastal trade. In 1957, the coastal fur economy could no longer support this trading post and the Hudson's Bay Company abandoned it.

North. Within the British mercantile system the HBC was an instrument of its foreign policy and a means of acquiring wealth. Thus, the role of the company was twofold: to function as a commercial enterprise and to exert British sovereignty

Vignette 3.4 Beaver Hats

For several centuries, the fur trade was based on the beaver skin, highly valued in Europe for hats. This demand, driven by fashion, was both the strength and weakness of the fur trade. Prices of beaver and other furs were subject to sharp fluctuations and these changes could greatly alter the number of furs required for European goods. The beaver was sought not for its pelt but for fur-wool, the layer of soft, curly hair growing next to the skin, which had to be separated from the pelt and from the layer of longer and stiffer guard hairs. This fur-wool was then felted for cloth or hats. The use of beaver fur-wool for hats became especially important. In England, for example, Spanish and Dutch immigrants popularized the habit of wearing hats in place of woollen caps early in the sixteenth century. Thereafter, no amount of sumptuary legislation could stem the decline of cap-making. Wearing caps became a hallmark of the lower classes. For those of higher status, shape and type of hat became a barometer of political allegiance. The Stuarts and their followers favoured the high-crowned, broad-brimmed, and square 'Spanish beaver'. Only in the early nineteenth century did the beaver hat go out of fashion, in favour of hats made of silk and other materials.

SOURCE: Wolfe (1982: 159–60).

Ironically, the British did not conceive of a northern sea route to the rich fur lands of Canada's North through Hudson Bay. Such a route would outflank the French route to the south and, in the context of British/French rivalry, strike an economic blow against their enemy. The idea of a northern route came from two French traders, Medard des Groseilliers and Pierre Radisson. After failing to gain support from French officials, Groseilliers and Radisson approached the British and convinced Prince Rupert that a great deal of money could be made by trading furs with Indians along

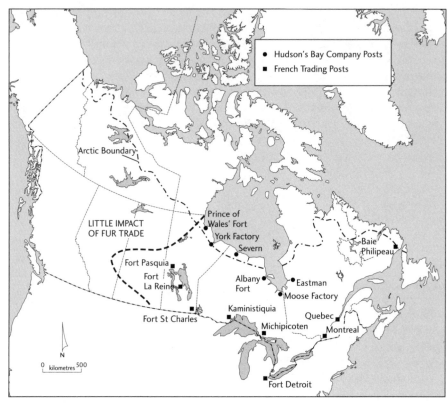

FIGURE 3.3 Fur Trade Posts, *circa* 1760
British and French control over the land in northern Canada was determined by the fur trade. Fur-trading posts operated by subjects of these two countries marked the limits of their colonial empires.

the Hudson Bay coast. These northern Indians currently traded their furs with the French, who were based on the St Lawrence. Groseilliers and Radisson knew that ships anchored near important northern rivers would soon attract local Indians and trade would ensue. Prince Rupert persuaded his cousin, Charles II of England, and some merchants and nobles to back the venture. In 1670, the King granted wide powers to the 'Governor and Company of Adventurers' of the Hudson's Bay Company and Rupert became the Company's first governor. These powers included exclusive trading rights to all the lands whose rivers drain into the Hudson Bay. These lands were named Rupert's Land.

At first, the company sent ships to trade with the Indians who gathered at the mouths of rivers draining into Hudson Bay. Once the trade was completed, the ships returned to England. The Hudson's Bay Company soon established permanent trading posts, encouraging Indians living in the interior of the country to trade there. By locating at the mouths of rivers draining western Canada, the HBC extended its control over lands far into the interior, thereby increasing the number of Indians involved

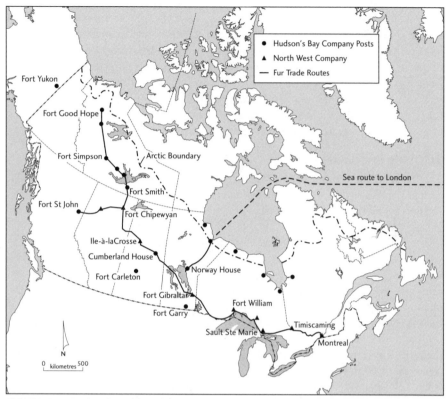

FIGURE 3.4 Fur Trade Posts and Main River Routes, *circa* 1820
Just before the Hudson's Bay Company and the North West Company amalgamated, each had its own river routes to supply their trading posts and to ship fur pelts.

in trapping and, of course, maximizing the number of furs received. The HBC was a great commercial success from the start. It was also a political success, for its Bay forts provided an important foothold for the British.

The harsh climate around Hudson Bay prevented the fur traders from supplementing their food supply with agricultural products. They turned to local Indians to supply them with game and with other useful products of Aboriginal technology, such as snowshoes and canoes. These Indians who maintained permanent camps near the HBC forts became known as the Homeguard. Indian middlemen became traders who exchanged European goods for furs with inland Indians. This arrangement provided great profits to the middlemen and allowed them to control the inland Indians. Often the middlemen Indians would not even permit other Indians to travel to the coastal trading posts.

The trading posts along the coast of Hudson Bay and James Bay all followed the same pattern, being established at the estuaries of the major rivers draining the interior of the forested lands of what are now Manitoba, Saskatchewan, Quebec, and

Ontario. The most important of these trading posts was York Factory. Situated at the mouth of the Hayes River, it offered the easiest river access to the rich fur lands of the interior. This post, because of its access to the river network leading into the interior of the Subarctic, soon began drawing furs from Indians as far distant as the Mackenzie River Basin (Zaslow, 1984: 6). By the early eighteenth century, then, the HBC's fur hinterland extended into the 'unclaimed' territories indicated in Figure 3.2. A similar case may be made for the Russian fur trade zone because Indians in the Yukon Basin may have made their way to the Pacific coast trading posts.

The Time of Competition

The Hudson's Bay Company's hold on the fur trade in the western interior remained firm until French traders established inland posts on the Saskatchewan River. By 1750, French competition had caused a sharp decline in the number of pelts reaching York Factory. After the fall of New France in 1763, Montreal became the strategic headquarters for a number of fur traders, first known as the 'Pedlars' and, in 1784, as the North West Company. In spite of a long supply route from Montreal to the western interior of Canada, these Montreal fur traders were determined to intercept Indians on their way to trade furs at the HBC posts on the shores of Hudson Bay and thus to obtain the highly prized furs from Canada's Northwest. The strategy of the Montreal traders was simple—reduce the distance Indian fur trappers had to travel to reach a trading post. The North West Company built a number of fur posts and connected them by its two main fur brigades. The Montreal brigade would bring supplies from Montreal to Grand Portage (later Fort William), which served as the supply depot, where trade goods were shipped for later distribution to its inland posts; the northern brigade originated at Fort Chipewyan, bringing fur bales to Grand Portage that would be taken to Montreal by the Montreal brigade (Vignette 3.5).

Vignette 3.5 Geographic Advantages of Fort Chipewyan

In 1788, the North West Company established a fort on the shore of Lake Athabasca. It was named Fort Chipewyan after the Indians who hunted in the area. Fort Chipewyan was an ideal place for the furthermost post on a fur-trading route. Not only was the fort located in prime beaver country where the pelts were of the highest quality, but its location allowed the northern brigade to leave Fort Chipewyan at breakup, reach Grand Portage, and return to Fort Chipewyan with a new supply of trade goods before freeze-up. From the east, the Montreal brigade brought a new supply of trade goods to Grand Portage and returned to Montreal with fur bales. Another geographic advantage of Fort Chipewyan's location was its ready access to the Athabasca River, which breaks up in the spring a month before the lake. This gave the western fur brigade an extra month for their canoe trips to rendezvous with their eastern counterparts.

SOURCE: Donaldson (1989: 10).

The strategy of permanent inland posts, however, had one serious problem—provisioning. The North West Company solved this problem by supplying its inland posts with pemmican, a food made by Plains Indians, and by having its Métis employees and Indian trappers supply the post with country food. Pemmican was light and nutritious and, most importantly, would not spoil. It consisted of dried meat (usually buffalo) pounded into a coarse powder and then mixed with melted fat and possibly dried Saskatoon berries. In this way, the fur trade of the late eighteenth century became dependent on food supplies from another natural region, the grasslands of the Canadian Prairies. This arrangement indirectly involved the buffalo-hunting Plains Indians and Métis in the fur trade.

The success of the Nor'Westers' inland trading posts forced the Hudson's Bay Company to meet the competition by moving inland. In 1774, the English company established its first inland post at Cumberland House on the Saskatchewan River. This action caused the Montreal traders to move further west, and in 1776 Louis Primeau established a post on the Churchill River near the present-day settlement of Île-à-la-Crosse (Cooke and Holland, 1978: 95). In 1787, the remaining individual traders either joined forces with the now powerful North West Company or left the country. Competition between the North West Company and the HBC intensified, leading to the strategy of 'matching' trading posts, i.e., if one company established a post in a new area, the other company built one nearby.

For the Indians, there were several consequences of this competition. First of all, the new posts allowed inland Indians direct access to traders. Second, it weakened the power base of the Cree, who lost their role as middlemen. The role of middlemen passed to the Chipewyans who traded with the northern Indians, namely, the Yellowknife and Dogrib Indians. Lastly, the competition between trading companies drew local Indians more fully into the fur trade and so made them more dependent on trade goods.

AMALGAMATION: A TIME OF MONOPOLY

The next phase in the fur trade saw a return to a monopolistic situation. With profits down and frequent bitter struggles between rival fur traders, the British Colonial Office wanted the North West Company and the Hudson's Bay Company to settle their feuding. In 1821, a parliamentary Act of the British government attempted to placate both parties by devising a coalition. The British government authorized that the name, charter, and privileges of the HBC would be assigned to the new firm but that its fur traders would include those of both the North West Company and the Hudson's Bay Company.

Under the direction of George Simpson, the 'new' Hudson's Bay Company began a rationalization of its trading posts. Posts were abandoned, staff reduced, and prices increased. Soon profits rose, reaching unimagined levels. The Company controlled not only Rupert's Land but also the North-Western Territory. Trade again flowed through its forts on the shores of Hudson Bay.

While his main objective was to increase the profits of the Company, Simpson realized that such profits could only be achieved if the Indian way of life also 'prospered', i.e., if Indians devoted most of their time to trapping. He supported the concept of supplying Indians with food when country food—fish and game—was in short supply. Short supply was a product of the fur trade, largely because the demand for more game to meet the needs of fur traders resulted in overexploitation around fur posts and because trappers, faced with depleted game stocks in the more accessible areas, had less time for hunting in their traditional hunting grounds.

A new challenge to the Bay route appeared by the late 1850s when an American railway company extended rail service from New York to St Paul on the Mississippi River. In 1859, the Mississippi steamboat, the *Anson Northrup*, arrived at Fort Garry (Winnipeg). By 1872, the English River (now named the Churchill River) and Athabaska brigades abandoned the Hayes River route to York Factory. Fur brigades now followed a southern route to Fort Garry. From there, the fur bales were shipped south by steamboat to St Paul and transferred by train to New York. The last stage in the journey to London, England, was by transatlantic steamer. Later, when the Canadian Pacific Railway was completed, the furs were shipped along this Canadian railway to Montreal and then on to London.

Impact on Indians

The fur trade, by introducing European goods, institutions, and values to the Aboriginal people, caused many changes to the traditional Aboriginal way of life and rearranged the geographic distribution of many Indian tribes. Traditional Aboriginal material culture was greatly diminished by substituting European goods for those produced from the local environment. Indian women found an iron needle much easier than a bone needle for sewing skins. Similarly, iron kettles and copper cooking pots replaced the traditional wooden and bone ones, making domestic life easier, and wool Hudson's Bay blankets[4] became a popular trade item among the Native peoples themselves. European firearms, iron knives, and axes were in great demand, replacing traditional weapons such as bows and arrows. Such an advance in weaponry often tipped the balance of power between those Indian tribes with muskets and those with bows and arrows. The fur trade had implications, therefore, for tribal relations, control of territory, and access to fur-trading posts.

In a similar fashion, Europeans challenged the Aboriginal customs and spiritual beliefs. Most spiritual changes occurred when missionaries brought Christian beliefs into the North. These missionaries accelerated the process of cultural change. By the middle of the nineteenth century, Anglican and Roman Catholic missionaries had established themselves throughout the North. Usually, Anglican and Roman Catholic priests located their missions adjacent to the fur posts. Their objective was simple— to convert the Indian peoples to their version of Christianity. It was not long before the shamans/medicine men no longer held a central position in Aboriginal society. In the nineteenth century the introduction of boarding-school 'European-style' education by the two churches was an important step towards assimilation and the erosion of traditional Aboriginal beliefs and languages. Until the post-World War II years, the federal government encouraged the Anglican and Roman Catholic missions to educate Aboriginal children. The languages of instruction were English and French and the children were not allowed to speak their own language. Regardless of the 'good intentions' of the missionaries, their efforts further weakened the confidence of Aboriginal peoples in their own cultures, causing them to be more dependent on but at the same time not part of Western culture.

The fur trade drew the Indians and, much later, the Inuit into a new pattern of social and economic relations. Yet the degree of involvement of Aboriginal people varied over time and space. While the exchange of furs for trade goods provided the Indians and Inuit with access to European technology, the main impact was on those Aboriginal people involved in direct trading with Europeans. Others, more distant from the fur traders, were only marginally involved. Relations between trappers and traders were not constant over time. Whenever trapping and/or hunting was unable to satisfy the needs of Aboriginals, they turned to their fur trader for help. In this way, a rather balanced, mutually advantageous relation in which each partner was more or less equal and certainly in need of the other changed into an unbalanced dependency, with Aboriginals trapped into bartering for Western tools and weapons now essential for hunting, fishing, and trapping. Goods were also needed to run the household. This dependency culminated in an Aboriginal welfare society, which Ray (1984) has argued was not a sudden event associated with the decline of the fur trade but rather was rooted in the early fur trade and the role of the Hudson's Bay Company:

> The Hudson's Bay Company was partly responsible for limiting the ability of Indians to adjust to the new economic circumstances at the beginning of this century. Debt-ridden, repeatedly blocked from alternate economic opportunities, and accustomed to various forms of relief for over two centuries, Indians became so evidently demoralized in the 20th century, but the groundwork for this was laid in the more distant past. (Ray, 1984: 17)

The geographic expression of dependency on the fur trader and its consequences for Indian economies is illustrated in an 1820 map constructed by Heidenreich and Galois (Harris, 1987: Plate 69). They classify the Indian economies into seven types, depending on their involvement in the fur trade. The disruption to local Indian economies was magnified as the level of involvement in the fur trade increased. The more disrupted Indian economies were so entangled in the fur economy that the pressure on wildlife, but especially the beaver, often resulted in an ecological collapse. The pressure to overhunt and trap came from the demands of the fur trader for country food and from the need for more trade goods.

The fur trade brought new technology to Indian communities but it also drew them into a different economic system and cultural world. Concepts of private and public property were foreign concepts. In 1870, the transfer of Hudson's Bay Company lands to Canada sent shock waves through the Indian and Métis communities. While the Hudson's Bay Company supported the fur economy and discouraged agricultural settlements, Ottawa was determined to settle the West. Therefore, the land transfer facilitated the agricultural settlement of the Canadian Prairies; it sparked two Métis rebellions, and it resulted in the relocation of Prairie Indians to reserves where they became prisoners in their own land. Fortunately for the Woodland Indians, the forested lands of the Subarctic were not suitable for agriculture and therefore the Crown lands remained available for hunting and trapping. While landownership had changed with the transfer of Rupert's Land to Canada, the daily lives of the Native peoples remained firmly tied to the fur trade.

Trapping Comes to the Arctic

Until the beginning of the twentieth century, fur trading was confined to the Subarctic. When European fur buyers decided that the Arctic white fox pelt had commercial value, the Hudson's Bay Company quickly spread its operations into the Arctic and soon had a series of Arctic trading posts, including Wolstenholme (1909) on the Ungava coast, Chesterfield (1912) on the Hudson Bay coast, Aklavik (1912) near the mouth of the Mackenzie River, and Padlei (1926) in the Barren Lands. As with the Indian tribes, the fur economy changed the traditional Inuit ways. In the Repulse Bay area, Inuit camps became sites of winter trapping, while sealing at the ice edge began to replace breathing-hole sealing as the main winter activity (Damas, 1968: 159).

Exploration and the Fur Trade

The fur trade had always been tied to exploration, as the traders continued to search for new trapping areas. Fur traders were eager to explore new lands and to make contact with distant Indians who might supply them with furs. As always, the push into new lands was driven by the need to reach the Indian hunters before a rival fur trader.

Fur traders occasionally undertook exploration for other reasons. For example, Samuel Hearne's remarkable overland journey from Fort Prince of Wales at the mouth of the Churchill River to the Arctic Ocean in 1771–2 was motivated by the desire to substantiate reports of a 'rich' copper deposit along the Arctic coast. In 1768, northern Indians had brought several pieces of copper to the Hudson's Bay trading post of Fort Churchill (Morton, 1973: 291). The governor of the post, Moses Norton, sent Samuel Hearne in search of the deposit. In his first two attempts, Hearne failed. Crossing the Barrens was no easy feat, even with Indian guides and company servants. Only with the help of Matonabbee and his Chipewyans was Hearne able to reach the mouth of the Coppermine River in 1771 and examine the copper deposit (Hearne, 1959; Rich, 1967: 298). The success of this amazing journey was due to Chipewyan knowledge of the land and animals. Hearne not only reached the shores of the Arctic Ocean but he also travelled west to Slave River. Near Great Slave Lake, Matonabbee traded European goods for furs trapped by Dogribs, which he would later exchange for more trade goods at Fort Churchill (Morton, 1973: 298).

Hearne made a number of important observations about the Chipewyans. For the first time, Europeans had some inkling of the enormous extent of travel by Indians living in the Subarctic. Matonabbee and his Chipewyans ranged a vast hunting territory, extending from Hudson Bay to the Arctic Ocean to Great Slave Lake. These forested and tundra lands, interconnected by rivers and lakes, were not the exclusive hunting grounds of the Chipewyans, nor were they marked by fixed boundaries. For example, during the summer, some of these Indians moved into the Barrens, which also served as the hunting territory of the Inuit. But in these sparsely populated lands, the chance of contact was slim and direct contact could easily be avoided. Yet, at this particular time in history, the Chipewyans were the dominant group on the Barrens, partly because of their leader and partly because they were armed with muskets and other European weapons.

As middlemen in the fur trade, they were able to terrorize the Inuit and exploit neighbouring Indian tribes such as the Dogribs and still profit from trade at Fort Churchill.

Whaling and the Inuit

English, Scottish, and American ships were drawn to the Arctic waters in search of another form of wealth—whales. In the eastern Arctic, Baffin Bay and Hudson Bay were popular whale-hunting areas; in the western Arctic, whaling ships followed the Alaskan coast to the mouth of the Mackenzie River. These whalers and British naval expeditions of the first half of the nineteenth century helped find the elusive Northwest Passage. The tragic loss of the Franklin expedition (Vignette 3.6) indicates the perilous nature of these voyages.

Vignette 3.6 The Search for Franklin

In 1845, a British naval expedition headed by Sir John Franklin set out to find the Northwest Passage. Franklin needed to find a sea link from Barrow Strait to the Arctic coast near the mouth of the Mackenzie River and from there to the Pacific Ocean. By 1848, Franklin's expedition was assumed lost and efforts to find him, his crew, and ships sparked the greatest search in Arctic history. In 1853, a Hudson's Bay Company search party headed by John Rae first learned of the fate of the Franklin expedition from local Inuit. Six years later, an expedition headed by McClintock and Hobson, and sponsored by Lady Franklin, was successful in finding the remains of part of the Franklin party near King William Island, as well as the only written account of the Franklin expedition.

SOURCE: Cooke and Holland (1978: 212–16).

Whaling began in Davis Strait in the seventeenth century. Later, whaling ships ventured further north and even into Lancaster Sound. Dutch, German, English, and Scottish whaling ships plied these Arctic waters in summer voyages. Between 1820 and 1840, whaling reached its greatest intensity with over a hundred ships involved. By 1860, American ships appeared in Hudson Bay, and several decades later the Americans were whaling in the Beaufort Sea. Wintering over by whaling ships was most common in the more inaccessible areas, such as Hudson Bay and the Beaufort Sea. By the time a sailing ship reached Hudson Bay or the Beaufort Sea, sea ice had begun to form, making whaling impossible. These ships, spending the winter months frozen in a sheltered harbour, would get an early start in the spring, leaving time to sail south before the beginning of the second winter.

The impact of the whalers on the Inuit was greatest in places where wintering over was common. While the population of whalers was not great (perhaps 500 men annually wintered in the Beaufort Sea and 200 in Hudson Bay), this contact drew the Inuit into a new economic system. Engaged in the whaling industry as pilots, crewmen, seamstresses, and hunters, Inuit hunters, now armed with rifles, greatly increased their take of caribou in order to supply the whalers with game. In exchange for these services, the Inuit obtained trade goods. Contact with the whalers had its downside,

TABLE 3.2 Mackenzie Eskimo Population, 1826–1930

Year	Population Estimate	Source
1826	2,000	Franklin (1828: 68-228)
1850	2,500	Usher (1971a: 169-71)
1865	2,000	Petitot (1876a: x)
1905	250	RCMP (1906: 129)
1910	130	RCMP (1911: 151)
1930	10	Jenness (1964: 14)

SOURCE: Smith (1984: 349).

however, counterbalancing economic gains. Excessive drinking sometimes led to violence, but by far the most negative impact of contact with Europeans and Americans was exposure to new diseases. Epidemics of smallpox and other contagious diseases swept through contact Inuit communities, reducing their populations. Table 3.2 shows the estimated population decline of one group of Inuit over the course of a century. Even so, the sudden disappearance of the whalers upon whom many Inuit had come to depend was a blow. The whaling industry saw its products lose favour with southern consumers as new products came into the marketplace. First, petroleum replaced whale oil in the late nineteenth century as a fuel for lighting. Then, a few decades later, the market for baleen collapsed when steel products were substituted. By World War I, commercial whaling in the Arctic had ceased.

THE THIRD PHASE: RESOURCE DEVELOPMENT

The Canadian North came into being in 1870 when Rupert's Land and other holdings of the Hudson's Bay Company were transferred from Britain to Ottawa. At one stroke of the pen, the fur monopoly of the Honourable Company was broken, its southern, more temperate lands were opened for settlement, and its inhabitants were now under Ottawa's tutelage. A decade later, the British government transferred to Canada the rest of its Arctic possessions, the Arctic Archipelago (even though all the islands had not yet been discovered). By 1880, the geographic extent of Canada had been realized, though Newfoundland was to join Confederation much later.

Ottawa did little to integrate the North and its Aboriginal peoples into Canada's economy. The main reason was that Ottawa had its hands full with nation-building in southern Canada. The national priority was the settlement of western Canada. The other reason is that Ottawa had no plan for the North except to wait for the private sector to undertake resource development and to allow the Indians, Métis, and Inuit to remain in the fur economy (Vignette 3.7). Then, too, Ottawa chose to keep its administrative costs to a minimum, meaning that education and health services for Aboriginal peoples and investments in transportation received little attention.[6] This laissez-faire policy of the federal government continued until the 1950s (Rea, 1968).

Vignette 3.7 Aboriginal People: Who Are They?

'Aboriginal people' refers to Indians, Métis, and Inuit. The term 'Aboriginal' obscures their heterogeneous nature. Geographically, Aboriginal people are spread across Canada in relatively small groups; culturally, they have evolved in somewhat different historical contexts; and linguistically, they form more than 50 distinct language groups. While most now speak English (and/or French in Quebec), major Aboriginal languages still widely spoken are Cree, Ojibwa, and Inuktitut. Métis may speak Michif, a mixture of Cree and French. A growing number have left their Aboriginal communities and now live in major cities and towns in southern Canada.

The Constitution Act, 1982, section 35(2), recognizes three Aboriginal groups —Indians, Inuit, and Métis. But this simple definition masks their diversity and the administrative classification of Canadians of Indian ancestry as status Indians, non-status Indians, and Métis. These legal differences are not based on biological criteria but can be explained through an understanding of the history of the Indian Act (1876). At that time, the British North America Act assigned the federal government responsibility for 'Indians, and Land reserved for Indians'. With the Indian Act, Indians were placed in a different legal position from other Canadians. The Inuit have never been subject to the Indian Act. In 1939, however, a court decision ruled that they were a federal responsibility. In 1982, the Métis gained official recognition as one of the three Aboriginal peoples of Canada. Non-status Indians, for one reason or another, have lost or surrendered their status.

Still, Canada began to wonder what riches it had inherited. In 1888, a Senate Committee on the Resources of the Great Mackenzie Basin investigated this question. Later, the Senate published a 'highly enthusiastic report on the potential for agriculture, fisheries, forestry, mining, and petroleum, setting the precedent for the optimistic and promotional tone that has continued to this day [1970s] to pervade government pronouncements on northern resources' (Rowley, 1978: 79). While the Senate report sparked considerable interest, the national priority was to settle the Prairies. Little commercial activity took place in the Subarctic and northern life continued to revolve around the fur trade and the Hudson's Bay Company.

The Klondike Gold Rush

In 1896, the discovery of gold on the Klondike River in Yukon confirmed the optimistic position of the Senate Committee on the Resources of the Great Mackenzie Basin. As thousands flocked to the newly discovered gold fields, the population of Yukon soon reached 30,000. Yukon was quickly transformed from a fur-trapping economy to a resource economy.[7] Traces of gold had been discovered in Yukon as early as 1866, but the famous Klondike find of 1896 triggered a gold rush. Two Tagish brothers, Skookum Jim and Dawson Charlie, and George Carmack, a prospector married to their sister Kate, made the world's most famous gold strike at Bonanza Creek. As news spread to the outside world, thousands rushed to Yukon. According to Crowe (1974: 121), the coming of so many white men shattered the world of the Tagish, Tutchone, and other

Indian tribes in Yukon. These Indians lost control of their traditionally occupied lands and became involved in the gold economy. Their participation varied from prospecting to packing supplies from the coast over the Chilkoot Pass (ibid., 122). Some found a place as wage-earners as deckhands on the riverboats, or even as carpenters in Dawson. Hunters sold game to the miners.

The dark side of the gold rush saw the outsiders occupying Indian lands, killing wildlife for food, and exposing local people to 'new' diseases. Perhaps even more significant to the Indians was the sudden imposition of another economic lifestyle, forcing major adjustments in their way of life. Some integrated as best they could while others attempted to continue their old ways.

In 1896, with the sudden arrival of so many newcomers in Yukon, the issue of Canadian sovereignty arose. Prior to the gold rush, Indians and a handful of white traders and prospectors had inhabited Yukon. With so few white people, Ottawa had no need to send its officials there. With the sudden influx of prospectors, Ottawa quickly dispatched detachments of the North-West Mounted Police to Yukon to 'show the flag' and to enforce Canadian laws and regulations. The Mounties issued licences, collected taxes, and kept law and order. In this way, Canadian sovereignty was demonstrated. This was important because most miners were American citizens and fears of annexation were widespread in Ottawa (Vignette 3.8).

The police also began to enforce Canadian conservation laws. For the most part, Indians and Inuit could avoid such interference with their ways by keeping away from settlements. However, concerns about wildlife mounted in Ottawa and during 1916–17 Parliament passed legislation—the Northwest Game Act and the Migratory Birds Convention Act—that greatly affected Aboriginal hunting activities. The police were obliged to apply these game laws to Aboriginal hunters, thereby adding another irritant to Aboriginal relations with federal officials.

Vignette 3.8 Changing Aboriginal Society in Yukon

As Ken Coates (1988: 73) has written, 'the Yukon Indians have faced the industrial frontier for over a century. Their situation provides a useful longitudinal study of Native reaction to the forces of cyclical mining development, seasonal industrial activity, and white encroachment on traditional hunting territories.' Change began with fur trading but the discovery of gold quickened its pace. Indians took advantage of wage employment, but for the most part they remained on the land as hunters and trappers. This mixed economy took hold with traditional hunting and trapping activities at its core but supplemented by seasonal wage employment.

The Klondike Gold Rush created the first industrial frontier in the three territories. Keith Crowe (1974: 122) gives this account of its beginnings:

Restless prospectors were exploring the world for more gold, and by about 1870, a few had entered Yukon by different routes. One man, George Holt, was able to cross the Chilkoot Pass, so jealously guarded by the Chilkoot Indians. An Alaskan Indian gave him two gold nuggets, and the stories he told after returning south brought more gold-seekers to the Yukon. Twenty prospectors, protected by a US gunboat, met the Chilkoot chief Hole-in-the-Face, and by firing a few blank rounds from a machine gun forced the Chilkoots to open their mountain pass to all comers. From then on a steady trickle of prospectors toiled up the thousand-foot-high pass and into the Yukon River basin. The Chilkoot, Chilkat, and related Indians, having lost their control of the inland trade, now began to make money as packers, carrying loads over the pass as they had always done. By 1898, when the gold-seekers were desperate to cross the pass, the Indian packers could make $100 a day and more, carrying loads of up to 200 pounds across the mountains.

SOURCES: Coates (1988); Crowe (1974).

Geopolitics Enters the North

During World War II, the North was transformed from a backwater on the international stage to a vital strategic region for the Allied Forces. The North became a military bridge between two theatres of war. Its geopolitical role in world affairs involved providing a safe, inland supply route to the European and Japanese theatres of war. Vast sums were spent to create a military infrastructure. While there was a lull in military activities after 1945, the North soon regained a geopolitical role as a buffer zone between the two superpowers—the United States and the Soviet Union. Now, it served an 'early warning radar' role for the United States, which feared a surprise Soviet air attack.

The first military expenditures in the Canadian North took place during World War II, not to defend the northern territory but to develop supply lines to major theatres of war in the Pacific and Europe, thereby marking the beginning of a modern transportation system. The US government funded most of the projects because it was the most effective way of supplying its troops in Alaska and England. The four main projects were:

- *Alaska Highway and the Northwest Staging Route.* With the threat of a Japanese invasion of Alaska, a secure supply route to Alaska was considered essential by the American military—hence the construction of the Alaska Highway and the upgrading of the Northwest Staging Route, a series of airfields with paved runways that provided an air route for ferrying aircraft from the United States to its military bases in Alaska.
- *Norman Wells Oil Expansion and Canol Pipeline Project.* The United States wanted a secure supply of oil for its troops in Alaska. Since the ocean shipping route from California to Alaska was considered too vulnerable to Japanese submarines, the Americans elected to increase oil production at Norman Wells in Canada's Northwest Territories and ship that oil to Fairbanks, Alaska, by means of a pipeline. The Canol Pipeline connected Norman Wells with Whitehorse, Yukon, where the oil was refined. It was then shipped by pipeline to Fairbanks.
- *Project Crimson.* An air supply route to Britain was essential. At that time, the range of aircraft was insufficient to across the Atlantic Ocean from New York or Halifax to London. The solution called for the construction of a series of landing fields in

Canada's eastern Arctic that would allow Canadian and American military planes to fly to Baffin Island and then on to Greenland, Iceland, and finally to US military bases in the United Kingdom. Using a polar air route, short-range tactical aircraft could easily make the long journey by refuelling at landing strips in the Canadian North, Greenland, and Iceland. Airports and fuel depots were built along two eastern routes leading to Frobisher Bay (now Iqaluit). The Quebec route included the refuelling depot at Fort Chimo (now Kuujjuaq), while the Manitoba route involved The Pas and Churchill.

- *Goose Bay.* The military complex built at Goose Bay served as a major American air base during World War II. In 1941, Ottawa leased the western end of Hamilton Inlet from Newfoundland (at that time still a colony of Britain) for 99 years. This site was not troubled by fog and cloud and therefore had more than twice as many flying days as the air base at Gander, Newfoundland. Both air bases were strategic links in the North American chain of defence and in supplying warplanes to the United Kingdom.

Initial military investment in a northern transportation infrastructure was designed to support the European and Pacific war theatres. Landing strips were built in remote centres and the Alaska Highway provided the first road link from southern Canada to north of the 60th parallel. While this improved transportation system was designed to meet military needs, it also made northern resources more accessible to world markets. Gradually, more and more of the Subarctic became integrated into the market economy, supplying raw materials and energy to the populated areas of Canada and the United States. Like the impact of the permanent fur-trading posts of the Hudson's Bay Company in the late seventeenth century, towns based on primary industries and government services had an impact on the human geography of the North by extending a hierarchical network of trade centres across the North and thereby more closely integrating northern peoples and their activities into the Canadian economy and society.

A second effect of the military was the involvement of Aboriginal people in the wage economy and their subsequent movement into settlements. The Aboriginal workers found employment with the military an appropriate way to obtain Western products, such as steel knives, rifles, and building materials, and southern foods, medical services, and entertainment. As the Aboriginal families became more and more attached to the construction camps, they became known as settlement Eskimos to differentiate them from those who continued to live on the land.

During the Cold War, the United States saw the Canadian North as a buffer zone between it and its superpower rival, the Union of Soviet Socialist Republics. As the military capabilities of the USSR increased, Canada and the United States constructed three early-warning radar systems across Canada in the 1950s. The Pinetree Line (completed in 1954) extended across southern Canada, the Mid-Canada Line (completed in 1957) was situated along the 55th parallel, and the Distant Early Warning Line (completed in 1957) was along the 70th parallel. The Pinetree Line was jointly financed; the Mid-Canada Line was undertaken by Canada; and the Distant Early Warning Line was paid for by the United States. With the end of the Cold War, the strategic importance of northern Canada greatly diminished and the expensive military plans for northern Canada were set aside.

Post-World War II Resource Boom

After World War II, American demand for resources outstripped their domestic supply. American industry sought resources beyond the United States and Canada's North offered many opportunities. Megaprojects were the order of the day. During the late 1940s, the grandest expression of a megaproject took place in northern Quebec and Labrador—the development of iron ore mines and the building of a railway from Schefferville to Sept-Îles. The purpose of this privately funded project was to supply much-needed iron ore, especially to United States steel plants. The principal shipping routes were (1) up the St Lawrence Seaway to Cleveland, Ohio, by lake carriers; (2) along the Atlantic seaboard by ocean carriers; and (3) across the Atlantic Ocean to Rotterdam (Gern, 1990: Appendix A). Watson (1964: 467–8) describes the transformation of a northern region from 'undeveloped to developed' and the link of such development to the American steel industry:

> A railway was built from the little fishing village of Sept-Îles—now a thriving port— up over the high, formidable, scarp-like edge of the faulted Shield, across extremely rugged terrain, deeply eaten into the rejuvenated sharply entrenched rivers, a distance of 360 miles to the Knob Lake iron field. Here the town of Schefferville soon grew up, a major outpost in the wilderness. The making of the port, the building of the railway, and the installation of nearby hydroelectric dams and works, were all major operations, but with American backing they were soon completed, and in 1954 the production of ore started, and over 2 million tons of ore were shipped out to the iron-hungry cities of the St Lawrence and Great Lakes lowland.

Watson fails to mention the social impacts of this project on the local Aboriginal people—the Naskapi and Montagnais (Innu)—or the environmental consequences of open-pit mining in an area underlain by permafrost. Unlike the James Bay Project, no one raised the question of Aboriginal title to these yet unceded lands.[8] As Aboriginal leaders began to comprehend the effect on their people of the massive developments taking place in the North, their voices were raised, challenging two major development projects proposed in the 1970s—the James Bay Hydroelectric Project and the Mackenzie Valley Gas Pipeline Project.

Megaprojects signalled a new phase in northern resource exploitation. Ottawa supported such economic initiatives with new policies and programs designed to promote resource development. In 1957, John Diefenbaker presented a northern development concept, the 'Northern Vision', calling for the opening of the northland by building transportation routes and communication lines, thereby linking northern resources to southern markets. In 1958, a series of programs was put into place, including 'Roads to Resources'. The 'Roads to Resources' program provided funds for new roads leading to potentially valuable natural resources in the northern reaches of the provinces. The federal share of these monies was determined by formula sharing costs with the provincial governments. The territorial counterpart to this program was the Development Road Program, with the federal government paying for all the construction costs.

During the next decade, northern development continued to hold Canadians' attention. In 1969, Richard Rohmer presented a more complex version of public involvement in northern development. His Mid-Canada Development Corridor proposal called for the building of a northern railway across the mid-north, a transportation corridor meant to stimulate settlement and development similar in effect to the building of the CPR across the Canadian West in the 1880s. In many ways, this grand scheme was an elaboration of Diefenbaker's Northern Vision. According to Rohmer, investment and planning would come from the federal government, ensuring Canadian control and ownership. Rohmer envisioned this massive federal undertaking as a means to strengthen both Canada's economy and its national purpose. He saw the Mid-Canada Corridor concept as a counterweight to the American ownership of Canadian natural resources.

Canadians, particularly non-Aboriginal northerners, responded warmly to Rohmer's concept of a developed North. Federal officials, on the other hand, were cool to his idea of building a railway across the Subarctic, partly because of the potential drain to the treasury but mostly because Ottawa considered it 'unsound'. In the West, a handful of provincial officials reacted suspiciously, fearing that this transportation system would serve the interests of central Canada rather than those of the western provinces. The mixed response to this project indicated that while Canadians wished to see the North developed, there were differences of opinion as to how the goal was to be accomplished.

By the late 1960s, environmental and Aboriginal spokespersons surfaced to challenge development schemes. What were the anticipated impacts on the fragile polar environment? How would such industrial projects affect Aboriginal land use? These issues stirred thoughts about social justice, laying the groundwork for social change in the last three decades of the twentieth century.

Social Change

Along with economic growth, a remarkable social change occurred among Aboriginal peoples. Land-based Indians and Inuit relocated into tiny communities and began participating in settlement life. The hunting and trapping economy was weakened by low fur prices, by withdrawal of the Hudson's Bay Company support for trappers, and by the opportunity for wage employment. In the face of stiff competition and the growing presence of the Canadian government in the North, the HBC no longer felt an obligation to buffer Aboriginals from economic swings in the marketplace for fur. A second sign was the involvement of Dene, Inuit, and Métis in military construction work during both World War II and the Cold War. Many of these Aboriginal employees lived at or near the construction sites. A few found jobs and lived on the edge of these military bases in self-built shacks.

In the early 1950s, cases of starvation among hunting families shocked Ottawa and the Canadian public (Vignette 3.9). The fear was that starvation would be repeated because the caribou herds were declining. Moving Aboriginal peoples to settlements was believed to be the solution; in fact, it was an ill-advised response to an apparent wildlife crisis. Ottawa saw relocation as a first step in integrating Aboriginal peoples into Canadian society. The new urban dwellers would live in public housing and their children would attend school. In time, Ottawa assumed that integration into the wage economy would occur. Unfortunately, this strategy had several flaws. First, settlements had no economic base and therefore few employment opportunities existed. Hunting of wildlife around the communities soon resulted in the exhaustion of this resource. The outcome was a new form of dependence, this time on social welfare. At Port Harrison (now Inukjuak) on Quebec's Ungava Peninsula, local officials decided to relocate these Quebec Inuit to the faraway places of Grise Fiord and Resolute Bay in the Canadian Archipelago where game was more abundant. This move turned into a social disaster (Marcus, 1991). Second, the cultural leap from the Aboriginal lifestyle practised on the land to settlement living was simply too great. The result was the so-called 'lost generation'. Those adults who were the leaders of the land-based economy found themselves misfits within the community. Ottawa also saw relocation as a response to the fear that the land-based economy could no longer support the Aboriginal peoples.

Vignette 3.9 Inuit Caribou Hunters Starve

Before the late 1950s, the Caribou Inuit (Ahiamiut) lived inland and hunted caribou. When their chief source of food, the barren ground caribou, became scarce, they fell into difficult times. Their remote location and nomadic lifestyle made communications with the outside world irregular, and therefore little help was available. In the 1950s, their main contact was through the Department of Transport weather station at Ennadai Lake. When word began to reach the outside world that the Ahiamiut were starving and that many had died, the federal government attempted to rescue the survivors by resettling them in coastal villages such as Eskimo Point. Williamson (1974: 90) reported that starvation had reduced the population of the Caribou Inuit from about 120 in 1950 to about 60 in 1959.

SOURCE: Williamson (1974: 90).

Yet, the lure of relocation was strong—the basic amenities of settlement life, including the general store and the nursing station, were well known and much appreciated. In addition, Ottawa promised housing, Family Allowance payments, health services, and schooling for Aboriginal children. These promises drew Aboriginal people into settlements, which were the sites of fur-trading posts. In some cases, there was a deliberate attempt to use programs to 'ensure' such integration. Family Allowance payments, for instance, required that parents send their children to the community school. Since mothers and children tended to remain in settlements, the extended family hunting unit soon disappeared. Now Aboriginal men formed the hunting unit and spent much less time on the land than before.[9]

Aboriginal People's Place in Development

The spread of the resource economy into the North has resulted in conflicts over land. But this conflict is over more than land—it is a struggle between conflicting goals, preferences, and values. Northern development is one goal. Driven by the market economy, its objective is to integrate the North and its people into the Canadian industrial society. The process of integration through economic development goes beyond strictly economic matters and involves the establishment of Canadian institutions and governments in the North. Since the rise of a more liberal trade policy in 1989 with the signing of the Canada–US Free Trade Agreement, the desire to access to northern resources to meet US needs has accelerated this process within the context of an American continental energy policy. For the most part, northern development reflects a set of values, preferences, and values common to most Canadians. By 2000, Aboriginal organizations, formed from land claim agreements, were demanding a place in resource development, not just as workers but as owners.[10]

Two visions—homeland and hinterland—continue to govern Canadian thought and writings about development in the North (Vignette 1.1). Underlying these visions is the reality of different peoples holding differing values, languages, and hopes for the future. Indigenous peoples, for instance, subscribe to a holistic cosmos and therefore do not accept the Western notion that a direct relationship exists between the economy and the land. Often these differences reveal themselves as tensions between Aboriginal and non-Aboriginal peoples. Such tensions lurk beneath the surface of everyday life but break through when the economic or political stakes are particularly high. These tensions, whether small or large, underlie the ongoing struggle for economic and political power in the North. Often this struggle becomes extremely stressful when a large resource project is planned for an area inhabited primarily by Aboriginal peoples. Such conflicts reached a critical phase in the 1970s when Aboriginal organizations opposed two major construction projects: the proposal to build a natural gas pipeline across northern Yukon and along the Mackenzie River (the Mackenzie Valley Pipeline Project) and the construction of hydroelectric dams in northern Quebec (the James Bay Hydroelectric Project). Some 30 years later, Aboriginal organizations are entering the resource economy. By 2002, Quebec Cree and Quebec Inuit had signed resource development agreements with Quebec; and, with the exception of the Deh Cho First Nation, Aboriginal organizations in the Mackenzie Basin had proposed an Aboriginal natural gas pipeline. The nature of these conflicts and their apparent resolution have implications for Canadian society. The original conflict was first articulated by Justice Thomas Berger (1977) and then expanded upon by Dacks (1981), Feit (1981), Usher (1982), Asch (1984), Peters (1999), Nuttall (2000), and Scott (2001). Anderson (1999), Newhouse (2001), and Bone (2002) explored the relatively recent involvement of Aboriginal organizations in the marketplace. Many Aboriginal business organizations operating in the market economy are an outcome of comprehensive land claim agreements: the court-mandated legality of Aboriginal title resulted in the recognition by corporate Canada that Aboriginal participation in resource development is another element in resource development; and governments have insisted that resource projects have 'northern' benefits (Bajda, 1978; Duffy, 1981). These watershed events are discussed in the next two sections as the legal and media turning points.

The Legal Turning Point

Since the 1970s, the legality of Aboriginal land claims has gained strength. Until 1973, Aboriginal title to their historic homelands was not recognized. As long as the North remained beyond the orbit of the market economy, Aboriginal peoples continued to live on Crown land without interference from outsiders. However, when the land became commercially valued, problems arose. Federal and provincial governments believed that Aboriginal peoples could hunt and trap on Crown land at the 'pleasure' of the Crown and therefore had no further claim to the land. Northern development ignored the original inhabitants. For example, in 1949, the Iron Ore Company of Canada undertook a huge resource development project in northern Quebec and the adjacent area of Labrador without a thought about Aboriginal title.

This position was challenged in the courts. In 1973, the Supreme Court of Canada ruled in the *Calder* case that Aboriginal title did exist in law and that where it was not extinguished Aboriginal title to Crown land must still exist (Vignette 3.10). Just what Aboriginal title meant was to be defined by negotiations. At the same time, the Cree and Inuit of northern Quebec were contesting in the courts of Quebec the right of Hydro-Québec to pursue the James Bay Project on their traditional hunting lands. In 1975, an out-of-court settlement resulted in the first modern treaty.[11] By this time, the federal government acknowledged the need for a negotiating process for determining those claims to land where no treaty existed. This process is known as comprehensive land claim negotiations. Much of the North fell into this category. Aboriginal peoples who reached modern land claim agreements—with the federal government in the territories and with the federal and provincial governments in the provinces—took control of their lands and established their own corporations. By 2002, the Cree, Inuit, and Naskapi of Quebec, the Inuvialuit, Gwich'in, and Sahtu of the Northwest Territories, the Inuit of Nunavut, the Yukon First Nations of Yukon, and the Nisga'a of British Columbia had concluded modern treaties, while the Labrador Inuit and Innu had reached an agreement-in-principle (see Chapter 8 for a more detailed account).

Vignette 3.10 The Calder Decision and Aboriginal Title

The 1973 *Calder* decision opened up the debate on Aboriginal title by giving it legal credibility. The *Calder* case was a long legal battle. In 1967, the Nisga'a Tribal Council, the president of which was Frank Calder, launched legal proceedings against the government of British Columbia to obtain recognition of their Aboriginal claim to lands in the Nash Valley. The Nisga'a argument was based on two points: (1) they had not surrendered their lands to the province; (2) they therefore maintained title to these lands. The lower provincial courts ruled against the Nisga'a based on the notion that these rights had been extinguished by historical events, i.e., the creation of the British colony and/or by provincial laws that affected their Aboriginal title but that did not specifically extinguish them. The Nisga'a took their case to the Supreme Court of Canada. In 1973, the Supreme Court ruled as follows: six of the seven judges sitting on the case declared that the Nisga'a had held title originally. Three stated that they retained title. Although the Nisga'a did not win their case, the decision did give Aboriginal title legal credibility, causing Ottawa to rethink its position on Aboriginal title.

The Media Turning Point

From 1974 to 1976, Canadian society became more aware of the hidden costs of northern development through the extensive newspaper, radio, and television coverage of the Mackenzie Valley Pipeline Inquiry. This inquiry, conducted by Thomas Berger, considered the potential social, environmental, and economic impacts of constructing a gas pipeline across the north coast of Yukon and then southward through the Mackenzie Valley. The purpose of this pipeline was to ship Alaskan gas from Prudhoe Bay to the United States. The proponents of this megaproject argued that it would stimulate the economy of the Northwest Territories, add to the national economic well-being, and create a modern transportation corridor in the Mackenzie Valley.[12] In public meetings held in northern communities, Aboriginal residents presented a much less favourable interpretation of this proposed construction project. Local Dene and Métis spokespersons expressed strong concerns about impacts on their environment and their social well-being. Three concerns were the focus of their opposition. One was the potential negative impact of this pipeline construction project on the environment. Second, Dene and Métis leaders saw few economic benefits in this proposed project for their people and they worried about possible social costs that might cause great harm to individuals and to Aboriginal culture. Their third and primary concern, however, involved the settling of their land claim. The initial position of the Dene Nation and the Métis Association of the Northwest Territories was that a land claims agreement must precede the construction of the Mackenzie Valley Pipeline Project.

In southern Canada, the extensive media coverage of the Mackenzie Valley Pipeline Inquiry had a profound impact on public opinion. Night after night, television coverage brought the message into the living rooms of southern Canadians that this proposed industrial project would have a negative impact on Aboriginal communities and permanently damage the fragile northern environment. And for what purpose, other than to supply natural gas to American consumers? Such determined and unyielding opposition from northerners not only challenged the pipeline proposals but cast a shadow over all future industrial developments. By exposing these hidden environmental and social costs, the Berger Inquiry meant that future northern resource projects could be appraised in a more realistic framework.

In the next chapter, demography provides the focus. With the resource boom of the 1950s and 1960s, Canadians moved into northern resource towns and government centres. This migration greatly increased the northern population and created a number of resource towns. At the same time, Aboriginal peoples moved into small settlements, most of which were former trading posts.

NOTES

1. Who the first North Americans were remains a puzzling question for archaeologists. A growing number of archaeologists suspect that early humans arrived in North America well before 13,000 years ago. Their suspicions are partly based on the Bluefish Caves site, where stone tools and bones from several prehistoric animals, including mammoth, antelope, bison, and large cat and dated as 25,000 to 40,000 years old, were found. Unfortunately, the site does not provide geological support that the stone tools can be associated with the smashed bones, i.e., there is a possibility that the stone tools found their way to this site at a more recent time. Other support for the earlier peopling of the Americas comes from the tools dated as 12,500 years old found at Monte Verde in Chile. The Chile find gives support to the earlier arrival of humans some 25,000 to 30,000 years ago. Ancient stone tools found near Grimshaw, Alberta, may have

been left at this site some 20,000 years ago—before the site was covered by the Cordillera Ice Sheet (Chlachula and Leslie, 1998). The distinguished archaeologist J.V. Wright supports the notion of humans arriving before the last ice advance. Wright (1999: 18) wrote that:

> Archaeological, physical anthropological . . . , linguistic . . . , and genetic evidence . . . has been used to argue for three major migrations from Asia into the Western Hemisphere. While controversy exists regarding the specific timing of these events, one sequence has been suggested as follows: the first migration between 30,000 and 15,000 years ago involved the Palaeo-Indians whose descendants would constitute the vast majority of native peoples of the Western Hemisphere; a second migration between 15,000 and 10,000 gave rise to the members of the Eyak-Athabascan linguistic family and probably some of the current linguistic isolates such as Haida and Tlingit; and a third migration between 9,000 and 6,000 years ago resulted in the historic members of the Eskimo-Aleut . . . .

2. From the time of contact to the late nineteenth century, population estimates were based on accounts of explorers, fur traders, and government officials. The Royal Commission on Aboriginal Peoples suggests a pre-contact population of 500,000. Heidenreich and Galois (Harris, 1987: Plate 69) argue that, in the early seventeenth century, there were about 250,000 Aboriginal people living in what is now known as Canada, suggesting a drop of 50 per cent. By the early 1820s, the Aboriginal population in Canada was estimated at 175,000, indicating a substantial decline from both the pre-contact and the early seventeenth-century figures. The Aboriginal population continued to fall well into the nineteenth century. With the formation of Canada, regular census-taking began. In 1871, the first census recorded just over 102,000 Aboriginal people, which may mark the low point in their population size.

    Some tribes, such as the Beothuks, the Mackenzie Delta Inuit, the Sadlermiut, and the Yellowknives, disappeared and their lands were occupied by Europeans or by other tribes. The popular view is that the Beothuks were victims of intentional genocide who were forced to move from the coast by the English and French settlers. Along the coast, food was more plentiful than in the interior where food sources were more restrictive, caribou being the main food source. According to Pastore, the Beothuks did not want to live near English and French settlers, so they decided to remain in the interior of Newfoundland. Prior to the arrival of Europeans, these hunters and gatherers had complex travel and settlement patterns that mixed inland and coastal locations into a successful nomadic lifestyle. Their life depended on being in the right place at the right time to obtain food from the sea and land. This geographic arrangement was interrupted by the arrival of Europeans who occupied coastal sites. A full account is found in Pastore's *Shanawdithit's People: The Archaeology of the Beothuks*.

3. Transportation is indispensable for resource exports, whether fur pelts or gold ingots. In the days of the fur trade, rivers provided natural highways. Later, resource development depended on expensively constructed roads and railways. Provinces were able to incorporate their northern hinterlands into their economies by building roads and railways. The British Columbia government provides one example. In the early post-World War II period, the British Columbia government extended the provincial highway system to the Peace River district to provide the rest of the province with a link to that region and to the Alaska Highway and to give Peace River settlers their long-awaited direct outlet to the Pacific coast. The John Hart Highway, built from Prince George through the Pine Pass to a junction with the Peace River district's road system after 1945, pioneered the route to be followed by the Pacific Great Eastern Railway.

4. The Hudson's Bay Company's royal charter gave the Company 'sole rights to trade and commerce' in Canada. Two trade goods, guns and blankets, were of special importance. Indians preferred blankets of exceptionally pure, bright colours. Each blanket was graded with a point system corresponding to weight and size. The number of points represented the number of beaver skins required for obtaining a blanket.

5. The HBC agreed to surrender Rupert's Land to the British Crown, which transferred it to Canada. Canada paid £300,000 in compensation to the HBC and allowed the Company to keep its 120 trading posts. Canada also agreed that the Company could claim one-twentieth of the land in the Canadian Prairies.

6. In the decades immediately following Confederation, little attention was paid to 'developing' the North; rather, it was a matter of holding on to this vast territory with a minimum of effort and cost. Canada's first Prime Minister, Sir John A. Macdonald, was concerned that American homesteaders might migrate northward into the 'unoccupied' Canadian Prairies, thereby leading to their annexation to the United States. For this reason, his primary concern was to exert political control over the Prairies by building a railway from Ontario to the Pacific Ocean and then to settle these newly acquired fertile lands. The railway was completed in 1885, and the settling of the Prairies continued into the early part of the twentieth century. During all this time, most of Rupert's Land and all of the North-Western Territory and the Arctic Archipelago were left to the fur economy.

7. Resource development also took place in the late nineteenth century along the southern fringe of the North in Ontario and Quebec—forest products and minerals being the main attractions. The building of the two national railways provided access to these northern forests and minerals. In the case of forest resources, the American timber supplies in New England were no longer adequate to meet growing US demands. Soon, Americans looked to their northern neighbour and its vast forests in Ontario and Quebec. In a classic core/periphery relationship, the Subarctic's forests attracted capital from the giant newspaper firms in major American cities; in turn, the Canadian forests supplied these firms with pulp that was processed into paper at plants near American metropolitan centres.

8. Canadian Indians, such as the Quebec Cree, fall under the Indian Act (1876). By 1930, most Indian tribes had signed treaties. The main exceptions resided in British Columbia, Quebec, Yukon, and Newfoundland. Until 1939, Ottawa did not acknowledge a responsibility towards the Inuit, but in that year a Supreme Court decision determined that the Inuit of northern Quebec were a federal rather than provincial responsibility.

9. The emergence of the Chipewyan community of Black Lake in northern Saskatchewan demonstrates the swiftness of change (Bone, Shannon, and Raby, 1973: 22). Prior to 1950, these Chipewyans hunted caribou and trapped fur-bearing animals. Once or twice a year they would visit the Hudson's Bay trading post at Stony Rapids; the rest of the year they spent on the land, moving from one hunting area to another. In their economy, hunting took precedence over trapping. During the early 1950s, a Roman Catholic Church was built on the shores of Black Lake and a few Chipewyan families built log cabins near the church. By 1956, over half of the Chipewyan families had established houses at Black Lake and their children were attending the newly constructed school. Family hunting parties were becoming less common because mothers and school-aged children remained in Black Lake. The decision to become permanent residents of Black Lake was influenced by several factors—proximity to their church and the local Hudson's Bay store, as well as the availability of federal health services and programs such as Family Allowances.

10. Aboriginal homelands form another goal. Aboriginal peoples have made some progress in this direction. The creation of the Territory of Nunavut is one example. While less well defined, most Aboriginal leaders see this goal best achieved by the combination of land claim agree-

ments and the establishment of a series of political homelands for Aboriginal peoples. This approach requires the settling of many outstanding land claims and negotiation of a series of unique political arrangements with Ottawa or the provinces. Efforts by the Quebec Inuit have met with some success while the Dene have seen their political dream of Denendeh evaporate. The Lubicon Lake band of Cree in northern Alberta, on the other hand, have not yet achieved a land claim settlement. The Lubicon band claims 10,000 km^2 where oil production is occurring and where the Daishowa pulp mill has a timber lease. These developments have also led to the extension of highways that facilitate further petroleum and logging activities, but such roads have had a detrimental effect on the wildlife. Without title to land, the Lubicon cannot prevent these changes to the natural environment, nor do they receive any of the resource revenues. The band has claimed around $170 million in compensation for oil and gas taken in the past (Anonymous, 1989: D14). Progress towards a land claim settlement has been slow. In reaction, the Lubicon Cree have tried to block further developments. For example, the band negotiated an agreement with Daishowa in March 1988 that no logging would take place on lands claimed by the band until a settlement was reached. Two years later, however, a logging firm that had a contract with Daishowa wanted to begin logging on lands claimed by the Lubicon (MacDonald, 1990: A7). While this kind of conflict slows down economic development, forces local firms to lay off employees, and may result in legal action, the costs are due to the unfinished business of land claims; another cost, of course, is the diversion of Aboriginal energies away from focusing on their own economic development projects. Clearly, unsettled land claims remain a fundamental problem facing Canadian society.

11. Modern treaties began in 1975 with the signing of the James Bay and Northern Quebec Agreement. In exchange for land, cash, and a form of regional government, the Quebec Cree and Inuit allowed the James Bay hydroelectric construction project to proceed. Recognizing the need for land claim agreements in other areas where no treaty existed, the federal government established a more orderly process for settling land claims known as comprehensive land claim negotiations. In 1984, the first comprehensive land claim agreement, the Inuvialuit Final Agreement, came into force.

12. Thomas Berger (1977) headed the inquiry into the proposed gas pipeline from Prudhoe Bay along the Arctic coast and then southward along the Mackenzie Valley to markets in the United States. Berger saw the project in a much broader context than did the proponents. He believed that the pipeline would lead to other oil and gas developments that would transform the Mackenzie Valley into an energy corridor. The cumulative impact of such development would bring immense and irreversible changes to the region, the environment, and its people. Some 25 years later, Aboriginal organizations joined forces with oil companies to propose to build a natural gas pipeline from the Mackenzie Delta gas fields to markets in the United States. This enthusiasm for industrial projects was not limited to the Mackenzie Valley. By 2002, both the Quebec Cree and Quebec Inuit had signed agreements for further industrial projects on their traditional lands.

REFERENCES AND SELECTED READINGS

Anderson, Robert Brent. 1999. *Economic Development among the Aboriginal Peoples in Canada: The Hope for the Future.* North York, Ont.: Captus Press.

Anonymous. 1989. 'Lubicon Band Patrols Oilfields on Disputed Land', *Saskatoon Star-Phoenix*, 2 Dec. 1989, D14.

Asch, Michael. 1984. *Home and Native Land: Aboriginal Rights and the Canadian Constitution.* Toronto: Methuen.

Bajda, Edward. 1978. *The Cluff Lake Board of Inquiry Final Report.* Regina: Cluff Lake Board of Inquiry.

Berger, Thomas R. 1977. *Northern Frontier, Northern Homeland: The Report of the Mackenzie Valley Pipeline Inquiry.* Ottawa: Minister of Supply and Services.

Bone, Robert M. 2002. 'Colonialism to Post-Colonialism in Canada's Western Interior: The Case of the Lac La Ronge Indian Band', *Historical Geography* 30: 59–73.

———, Earl Shannon, and Stuart Raby. 1973. *The Chipewyan of the Stony Rapids Region.* Mawdsley Memoir 1. Saskatoon: Institute for Northern Studies, University of Saskatchewan.

Bonnichsen, Robson, and Karen Turnmire. 1999. 'An Introduction to the Peopling of the Americas', in Bonnichsen and Turnmire, eds, *Ice Age People of North America: Environments, Origins, and Adaptations.* Corvallis: Oregon State University Press, 1–27.

Canada, Royal Commission on Aboriginal Peoples. 1996. *Report of the Royal Commission on Aboriginal Peoples: Looking Forward, Looking Back,* vol. 1. Ottawa: Minister of Supply and Services Canada.

Census of Canada. 1881.

Chlachala, Jiri, and Louise Leslie. 1998. 'Preglacial Archaelogical Evidence at Grimshaw, the Peace River Area, Alberta', *Canadian Journal of Earth Sciences* 35, 8: 871–84.

Cinq-Mars, Jacques, and Richard E. Morlan. 1999. ' Bluefish Caves and Old Crow Basin: A New Rapport', in Bonnichsen and Turnmire, eds, *Ice Age People of North America,* 200–12.

Coates, Kenneth. 1985. *Canada's Colonies: A History of the Yukon and Northwest Territories.* Toronto: Lorimer.

———. 1988. 'On the Outside in Their Homeland: Native People and the Evolution of the Yukon Economy', *The Northern Review* 1: 73–89.

Cooke, Alan, and Clive Holland. 1978. *The Exploration of Northern Canada, 500 to 1920: A Chronology.* Toronto: Arctic History Press.

Crowe, Keith J. 1974. *A History of Original Peoples of Northern Canada.* Montreal and Kingston: McGill-Queen's University Press.

Dacks, Gurston. 1981. *A Choice of Futures: Politics in the Canadian North.* Toronto: Methuen.

Damas, David. 1968. 'The Eskimo', in C.S. Beals, ed., *Science, History and Hudson Bay,* vol. 1. Ottawa: Queen's Printer.

Denevan, William M., ed. 1976. *The Native Population of the Americas in 1492.* Madison: University of Wisconsin Press.

———. 1992. 'The Pristine Myth: The Landscape of the Americas in 1492', *Annals of the Association of American Geographers* 82, 3: 369–85.

Dickason, Olive Patricia. 2002. *Canada's First Nations: A History of Founding Peoples from Earliest Times,* 3rd edn. Toronto: Oxford University Press.

Driver, Harold E. 1961. *Indians of North America.* Chicago: University of Chicago Press.

Donaldson, Yarmey. 1989. 'Alberta's First Fort', *Western People,* 8 June, 10.

Duffy, Patrick. 1981. *Norman Wells Oilfield Development and Pipeline Project: Report of the Environmental Assessment Panel.* Ottawa: Federal Environmental Assessment Review Office.

Feit, Harvey A. 1981. 'Negotiating Recognition of Aboriginal Rights: History, Strategies and Reactions to the James Bay and Northern Quebec Agreement', *Canadian Journal of Anthropology* 2: 159–72.

Gern, Richard. 1990. *Cain's Legacy: The Building of Iron Ore Company of Canada.* Sept-Îles: Iron Ore Company of Canada.

Harris, R. Cole. 1987. *Historical Atlas of Canada, vol. 1, From the Beginning to 1800.* Toronto: University of Toronto Press.

———. 1997. *The Resettlement of British Columbia: Essays on Colonialism and Geographical Change.* Vancouver: University of British Columbia Press.

Hearne, Samuel. 1958. *A Journey from Prince of Wale's Fort in Hudson's Bay to the Northern Ocean: 1769–1772.* Toronto: Macmillan.

Kroeber, Alfred L. 1939. *Cultural and Natural Areas of Native North America.* Berkeley: University of California Press.

Lux, Maureen K. 2001. *Medicine That Walks: Disease, Medicine and Canadian Plains Aboriginal People, 1880-1940.* Toronto: University of Toronto Press.

MacDonald, Jack. 1990. 'Daishowa Firm Seeks Police Protection', *Edmonton Journal*, 28 Sept., A7.

McGhee, Robert. 1996. *Ancient People of the Arctic.* Vancouver: University of Columbia Press.

McMillan, Alan D. 1995. *Aboriginal Peoples and Cultures of Canada: An Anthropological Overview.* Vancouver: Douglas & McIntyre.

Marcus, Alan R. 1991. 'Out in the cold: Canada's experimental Inuit relocation to Grise Fiord and Resolute Bay', *Polar Record* 27, 163: 285–96.

Miller, J.R. 1989. *Skyscrapers Hide the Heavens: A History of Indian-White Relations in Canada.* Toronto: University of Toronto Press.

Mooney, James. 1928. *The Aboriginal Population of America North of Mexico.* Washington: Smithsonian Institution.

Morton, Arthur S. 1973. *A History of the Canadian West to 1870–71.* Toronto: University of Toronto Press.

Newhouse, David R. 2001. 'Modern Aboriginal Economies: Capitalism with a Red Face', *Journal of Aboriginal Economic Development* 1, 2: 55–61.

Nuttall, Mark. 2000. 'Indigenous Peoples, Self-determination and the Arctic Environment', in Nuttall and Terry V. Callaghan, eds, *The Arctic: Environment, People, Policy.* Singapore: Harwood Academic Publishers.

Page, Robert. 1986. *Northern Development: The Canadian Dilemma.* Toronto: McClelland & Stewart.

Pastore, Ralph T. 1992. *Shanawdithit's People: The Archaeology of the Beothuks.* St John's: Breakwater Books.

Peters, Evelyn J. 1999. 'Native People and the Environmental Regime in the James Bay and Northern Quebec Agreement', *Arctic* 52, 4: 395–410.

Ray, Arthur J. 1974. *Indians in the Fur Trade: Their Role as Trappers, Hunters, and Middlemen in the Lands Southwest of Hudson Bay, 1660-1870.* Toronto: University of Toronto Press.

———. 1976. 'Diffusion of Diseases in the Western Interior of Canada', *Geographical Review* 66: 139–57.

———. 1984. 'Periodic Shortages, Aboriginal Welfare, and the Hudson's Bay Company, 1670–1930', in Shepard Krech III, ed., *The Subarctic Fur Trade: Aboriginal Social and Economic Adaptations.* Vancouver: University of British Columbia Press, 1–20.

———. 1990. *The Canadian Fur Trade in the Industrial Age.* Toronto: University of Toronto Press.

Rea, K.J. 1968. *The Political Economy of the Canadian North: An Interpretation of the Course of Development in the Northern Territories of Canada to the Early 1960s.* Toronto: University of Toronto Press.

Rich, E.E. 1967. *History of the Hudson's Bay Company, 1670–1870,* vol. 2. London: Hudson's Bay Record Society.

Rowley, Graham. 1978. 'Canada: the Slow Retreat of "the North"', in Terence Armstrong, George Rogers, and Rowley, eds, *The Circumpolar North.* London: Methuen, 71–123.

Saku, James C., and Robert M. Bone. 2000. 'Looking for Solutions in the Canadian North: Modern Treaties as a New Strategy', *The Canadian Geographer* 44, 3: 259–70.

Scott, Colin H., ed. 2001. *Aboriginal Autonomy and Development in Northern Quebec and Labrador.* Vancouver: University of British Columbia Press.

Thomas, David Hurst. 1999. *Exploring Ancient Native America: An Archaeological Guide.* New York: Routledge.

Trudel, Marcel. 1988. 'Jacques Cartier', in *The Canadian Encylopedia,* vol. 1. Edmonton: Hurtig.

Usher, Peter J. 1982. 'The North: Metropolitan Frontier, Native Homeland?', in L.D. McCann, ed., *Heartland and Hinterland: A Geography of Canada.* Scarborough, Ont.: Prentice-Hall.

Watson, J.W. 1964. *North America: Its Countries and Regions.* London: Longmans.

Williamson, Robert G. 1974. *Eskimo Underground: Socio-cultural Change in the Canadian Central Arctic.* Uppsala: Institutionen for Allman.

Wolfe, Eric R. 1982. *Europe and the People Without History.* Berkeley: University of California Press.

Wright, J.V. 1995. *A History of the Native People of Canada, vol. 1, 10,000–1,000 B.C.* Mercury Series, Archaeological Survey of Canada. Paper 152. Ottawa: Museum of Civilization.

———. 1999. *A History of the Native People of Canada, vol. 2, 1000 B.C–A.D. 500.* Mercury Series, Archaeological Survey of Canada. Paper 152. Ottawa: Museum of Civilization.

Zaslow, Morris. 1984. *The Northwest Territories, 1905–1980.* Canadian Historical Association Historical Booklet No. 38. Ottawa: Canadian Historical Society.

———. 1988. *The Northward Expansion of Canada, 1914–1967.* Toronto: McClelland & Stewart.

CHAPTER 4

Population Geography

Beyond Canada's ecumene lies the thinly populated land of the Canadian North. Fewer than 5 per cent of Canada's population—less than 1.5 million people—inhabit Canada's North, making it the most sparsely populated region in Canada. Within the North the distribution of people is uneven, resulting in widely varying regional population densities. Of the two northern biomes, for instance, the Arctic contains fewer than 100,000 people, making its population density of 0.01 persons per km^2 one of the lowest in the world. In comparison, the population density of the Subarctic is around 0.10 persons per km^2.

Why does the North with its vast territory contain such a small population? The answer lies in its physical geography, which has a very low carrying capacity, i.e., the ability of the land to support a population. For many, geographic size is equivalent to carrying capacity, but this is not correct. Carrying capacity in the North is related to the region's resources, whether soil, wildlife, or mineral resources. Thus, while the geographic size of the North is enormous, its carrying capacity and therefore its economic potential are extremely limited. Within the North, the resource base of the Arctic has a lower carrying capacity than that of the Subarctic, and this difference is reflected in the population density figures for the two biomes.

From a geographic perspective, four key factors affect economic development and therefore population size:

- The cold climate eliminates the possibility of commercial agriculture and restricts the forest industry to the Subarctic.
- The cold environment makes the cost of living and the operation of businesses much higher in the North, but especially in the Arctic, than in other more temperate areas of Canada.
- The long cold winters limit water transportation to the short summer period and alternate air transportation is extremely expensive. The limitation of the seasonal nature of water transportation is magnified by the weakly developed highway system, forcing many communities to depend on air transportation, especially in the Arctic.
- The great distance to markets means that its export-oriented resource industry has very high transport costs.

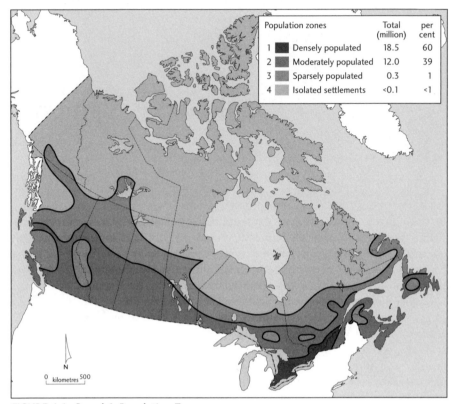

Population zones		Total (million)	per cent
1	Densely populated	18.5	60
2	Moderately populated	12.0	39
3	Sparsely populated	0.3	1
4	Isolated settlements	<0.1	<1

FIGURE 4.1 Canada's Population Zones

In sum, the population geography of the North is distinct from that found in the rest of Canada (Figure 4.1). The demography is characterized by small numbers, concentration of population in settlements, low population density, and a high proportion of Aboriginal peoples. Since the two visions of the North divide along ethnic lines, ethnicity is crucial to understanding the region's population geography. While non-Aboriginal northerners comprise approximately 80 per cent of the North's population, they reside in a relatively small number of cities and resource towns. Outside of these urban centres, non-Aboriginals are a minority. In addition, Aboriginal peoples continue to use the seemingly unoccupied lands for hunting and trapping. This population dichotomy has an economic and cultural spatial pattern. For example, most economic opportunities are found in the cities, regional centres, and resource towns, while Aboriginal culture and language are most easily expressed in First Nation reserves, Métis settlements, and Inuit communities.

POPULATION CHANGE SINCE 1871

Over the past 130 years, the northern population has increased from 60,000 to just under 1.5 million. However, the rate of population growth in the North has varied

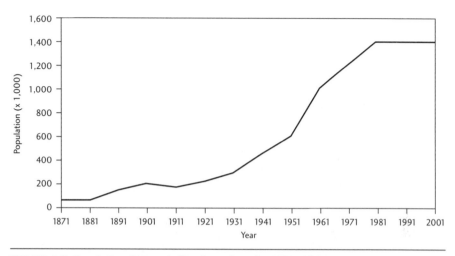

FIGURE 4.2 Population Change in Northern Canada, 1871–2001
Population change from 1871 to 2001 illustrates the irregularity of population from decade to decade. This irregularity is best understood as three distinct demographic phases, with the last phase demonstrating a halt to population growth.
SOURCE: Appendix 2.

over this time period and, for the last 20 years, its growth has stalled (Figure 4.2 and Table 4.1). Change in the size and character of the northern population has been brought about by the interplay of three demographic variables: fertility, mortality, and migration. While a precise comparison from past censuses is difficult because of changes to census boundaries that approximate the North's southern limit, Figure 4.2 provides a general picture of population change over time.[1] These demographic

TABLE 4.1 Population of the Canadian North, 1981–2001

Geographic Area	Population 1981	Per cent 1981	Population 2001	Per cent 2001	Difference 1981–2001	% Change 1981–2001
Territories	68,894	3.3	92,779	6.4	23,885	34.7
Western Canada	414,164	28.1	448,380	31.0	34,216	7.7
Eastern Canada	988,825	67.2	904,006	62.6	(84,819)	(8.6)
Totals	1,471,883	100.0	1,445,165	100.00	(26.718)	(1.8)

SOURCES: Statistics Canada, *Population: Census Divisions and Subdivisions*. Catalogue no. 92–101 (Ottawa: Minister of Supply and Services, 1987); Statistics Canada, 'Population and Dwelling Counts, for Canada, Provinces and Territories, and Census Divisions, 2001 and 1996 Censuses', available at: <http://www12.statcan.ca/english/census01/products/standard/popdwell/Table-PR.cfm>; Statistics Canada, 'Population by Aboriginal Group, 1996 Census', available at: <http://www.statcan.ca/english/ Pgdb/People/ Population/demo39a.htm>.

changes take the shape of an S-curve, suggesting a connection to the biological concept of carrying capacity. The three phases of population change are:

- slow but steady increase from 1871 to 1941;
- rapid increase from 1941 to 1981;
- relative stability from 1981 to 2001.

Phase 1. In 1871, the population of the North was approximately 60,000 (Figure 4.2 and Appendix 2). Over the next 20 years, the settlement of the southern fringe of the Subarctic by non-Aboriginal Canadians plus the slow but steady increase in the Aboriginal population accounted for this population growth. By 1901 the North's population had reached 100,000, and by 1931 it had more than doubled to 250,000.

Phase 2. During the 1941–81 period the population in Canada's North jumped from 350,000 to nearly 1.5 million (Figure 4.2 and Appendix 2). The four main factors accounting for the enormous increase were: (1) a resource boom that began in the late 1940s and triggered a massive in-migration of southern Canadians and the creation of new resource towns; (2) a high rate of natural increase among the Aboriginal population that saw its population more triple; (3) a policy change in Ottawa that began in 1957 with Prime Minister John Diefenbaker's 'Northern Vision'[2] promoting development in the North; and (4) increased public spending by both the provinces and Ottawa that led to a northern bureaucracy and facilitated the relocation of these government officials to the North through a series of northern benefits.

Phase 3. From about 1981 to the present the North's population has remained relatively stable at just under 1.5 million (Figure 4.2 and Appendix 2). Since the 1980s, out-migration has sometimes equalled or exceeded in-migration. In 1981 the North had a population of 1.47 million (Bone, 1992: 244). Twenty years later the figure was slightly lower, at 1.45 million (Table 4.1). The reasons for this demographic reversal from fast growth prior to the 1980s are complex, but are related to the slowing of the in-migration and an increase in out-migration. By 1996, the population of the North had reached 1.49 million (Appendix 3). From 1996 to 2001, however, the population declined slightly to 1.45 million. During that time, few parts of the North experienced population increases. (Appendix 3 shows that the populations of most northern census subdivisions declined between 1996 and 2001.) How long this demographic situation will continue is unknown, but if the Aboriginal rate of natural increase continues to lessen and if there is a net out-migration, the next decade could see the North's population fall below 1.4 million.

STALLED POPULATION GROWTH

Why has population growth in northern Canada stalled? The chief reason has been a sharp downturn in world demand for natural resources in the 1980s, which in turn reduced the demand for workers. The cyclical nature of the world economy is amplified in the northern economy. When the global economy is humming, the northern economy is expanding. However, when the world economy slows, the repercussion for the North is most severe—mines and mills close or reduce the size of their labour force, causing workers and their families to relocate to southern Canada.[3] The second reason has been the increased productivity in the resource industry. High wages in the resource sector drove companies to take advantage of technological innovations. Companies therefore were attracted to substitute capital for labour. However, in times of economic slump, the very survival of the company depends on lower production costs. The quickest approach in this regard is to reduce the company's payroll by purchasing machinery to replace workers. The third reason for stagnant growth in the northern population has been the use of airplanes to bring workers to remote work sites instead of building resource towns. This not only keeps workers and their families in southern Canada, but it diverts northern 'economic benefits' in the form of wages and purchasing power to southern Canada. Yet a fourth reason has been the cutback in hiring of public employees. By the 1990s, Ottawa was concentrating on reducing the federal debt, making increases in federal transfers to Yukon and Northwest Territories governments more difficult. Since these transfers are partly linked to population numbers, both Yukon and the Northwest Territories were only able to argue that they needed more money to deliver services to their residents because of the rising cost of reaching remote places and because of the special needs of their Aboriginal citizens. With the creation of Nunavut, the Northwest Territories was also faced with a transfer of some civil service positions from Yellowknife to Iqaluit.

The private-sector service industry suffered, too. As the resource industry's workforce diminished in size, the ripple effect on the service industry was hurtful, leading to business failures and the loss of service jobs, especially in resource towns. Two positive factors have partially offset these losses. One is the injection of cash into the northern economy from land claims agreements; the other is the entry of Aboriginal groups into the business world. Many communities declined in size and a few resource towns closed. Exceptions to the economic slump in the North have occurred. In the 1990s, Fort McMurray's service industry was bursting with activity associated with the massive expansion of the oil sands industry; in Yellowknife, the tertiary service sector benefited from the discovery of diamonds; and Iqaluit, gaining from its new role as a capital city, saw its population jump by 24.1 per cent from 1996 to 2001.

From a regional perspective, population change has not been uniform. Over the last 20 years, regional population losses have outstripped those areas witnessing a population increase (Table 4.1 and Appendix 3). The greatest losses are associated with regional centres and resource towns in northern areas of Ontario, Quebec, and Newfoundland and Labrador, and in the territories of Yukon and the Northwest Territories (Tables 4.2 and 4.5). On the other hand, the Territory of Nunavut and the northern areas of the western provinces have experienced population increases (Vignette 4.1 and Appendix 3). The explanation for these regional increases is twofold:

• A more robust resource economy in western provinces resulted in a net in-migration.
• An extremely high fertility rate and a net in-migration in Nunavut kept its population growing.

Vignette 4.1 Population Explosion in Nunavut

While the rate of population increase has diminished in most areas of the North, Nunavut's high fertility rates continue to fuel its rapidly expanding population. From 1996 to 2001, Nunavut's population increased from 24,730 to 26,745, an increase of just over 8 per cent, while the other two territories suffered a population decline (Table 4.2). Much of the reason for this difference lies in the fertility rates found in the three territories. In 2001–2, for example, Nunavut's fertility rate was more than twice that of Yukon and over 50 per cent higher than that of the Northwest Territories (Table 4.3).

POPULATION DISTRIBUTION

The North's population is spread unevenly across its vast territory. Such a distribution can be examined from three geographic perspectives, but all reveal a north/south division with most people living in the southern half of the North.

The first perspective views northern population in terms of the two biomes. The Arctic, with a population of approximately 80,000, contains only a small fraction of the North's total population. The Subarctic, on the other hand, is home to nearly 1.4 million people or 94.5 per cent of the northern population. The chief explanation for this difference lies in their respective resource bases.

The second perspective looks at population distribution in terms of the two political norths. Here, too, comparison of the Territorial North and the Provincial North reveals an extreme population dichotomy (Table 4.1). In 2001, 92,779 people or 6.4 per cent of the North's population lived in the three territories, while 1,352,386 or 93.6 per cent inhabited the northern areas of provinces. Within the Provincial North, Table 4.1 illustrates two demographic factors: (1) that the northern areas of eastern Canada account for the bulk of the population, and (2) that the same areas suffered a substantial population decline of 8.6 per cent from 1981 to 2001.

The third perspective allocates the northern population into the four nordicity zones of the Near North, the Middle North, the Far North, and the Extreme North (Figure 1.3). The Near North is the most southerly area of the Canadian North where approximately one million people are located. Most live in cities and towns. Sprinkled among them are northern gateway cities that function as the core within a micro core/periphery model serving sparsely populated hinterlands. Thunder Bay is an important gateway city for northern Ontario. Within the large, sprawling Thunder Bay Census Division that extends from Lake Superior to well beyond the Canadian National Railway, some 150,860 inhabitants live. This microcosm of the North is divided into the Near North (Thunder Bay and vicinity), where approximately 98 per cent of these people live, and the Middle North (north of the Canadian National Railway tracks) that contains over half of the land base of this census division but has fewer than 2 per cent of the total population. The explanation lies in its physical geography. Dominated by the Canadian Shield, this rough, rocky landscape is ill-suited to agriculture but is suitable for logging, hunting, trapping, and fishing. These economic activities mark a fundamental characteristic of northern land use: most land is not occupied but is used, particularly by resource companies and

Aboriginal hunters and trappers. In sharp contrast, the city of Thunder Bay serves as a transportation and processing centre as well as a northern gateway. Its geographic location on Lake Superior and its position on the main east-west rail and water transportation route have played a key role in its development.

Canada's Middle North has a population of approximately 400,000. Most of its towns are closely involved in resource industries, especially energy, forestry, and mining. Prince George in British Columbia is the centre of the interior forest industry. Alberta's heavy oil centre, Fort McMurray, with a population of nearly 41,000, is the fastest growing city in the Middle North. Other resource towns in the Middle North include Thompson, Manitoba, Gagnon, Quebec, and Labrador City.

The Far North lies in the Arctic biome. It contains approximately 80,000 inhabitants. Most are Inuit. Iqaluit, the capital of Nunavut, is located on Baffin Island. Iqaluit is by far the largest centre in the Far North with a population of 5,236 (2001).

The Extreme North is limited to the northernmost islands of the Arctic Archipelago. Less than 300 people live in the Extreme North. Resolute is the largest centre with a population of 215 (2001).

THE NUMBER AND DISTRIBUTION OF ABORIGINAL PEOPLES

The number of Aboriginal peoples in the Canadian North and their percentage of the total northern population are increasing, but the rates are slowing. In 2001, approximately 300,000 Aboriginal Canadians lived in northern Canada[4] and Aboriginal peoples constituted 21 per cent of the northern population, up from 16 per cent in 1986. Most significantly, all three territories witnessed an increase in the proportion of their Aboriginal populations from 1996 to 2001. Over this five-year period, the total Aboriginal population reached nearly 48,000, or 51.7 per cent of the total population (Table 4.2). The explanation for this increase lies in the out-migration of non-Aboriginals and the high rate of natural increase among Aboriginal populations, especially among the Inuit.

The Aboriginal population is unevenly distributed across the Canadian North. While the vast majority (nearly 90 per cent) reside in the Subarctic, the Indian and Métis populations form only 14 per cent of the total population in the Subarctic. In sharp contrast, the Inuit represent the majority inhabiting the Arctic, accounting for 85 per cent in 2001. The distribution in 1996 of Aboriginal Canadians in the territories, the eastern provinces, and the western provinces is shown in Table 4.3. At the more detailed level of census divisions for 1996, the highest percentages of Aboriginal peoples are found in Nunavut (83.9 per cent), Saskatchewan's Census Division 18 (80.1 per cent), Manitoba's Census Division 22 (66.7 per cent), Quebec's Nord-du-Québec (48.9 per cent), and the Northwest Territories (48.2 per cent). In contrast, Yukon's Aboriginal population is only 20.2 per cent of its total population.

POPULATION DENSITY

Population density figures provide a rough indicator of the capacity of a country or region to support a given population at a particular standard of living. The population density of northern Canada is among the lowest in the world and is far below the

TABLE 4.2 Population Size, Density, and Aboriginal Population in the Three Territories

Territory	1996 Population	2001 Population	% change	Aboriginal Population 2001	Aboriginal Population as % of Total Population, 2001	Population Density (per km²)
Yukon	30,766	28,674	(6.8)	6,540	22.8	0.06
NWT	39,672	37,360	(5.8)	18,725	50.1	0.03
Nunavut	24,730	26,745	8.1	22,720	85.0	0.01
Territorial North	95,168	92,779	(2.5)	47,985	51.7	0.02

SOURCES: Statistics Canada, 'Population and Dwelling Counts, for Canada, Provinces and Territories, and Census Divisions, 2001 and 1996 Censuses', 2002: <http://www12.statcan.ca/english/census01/products/standard/popdwell/Table-PR.cfm>; Statistics Canada, 'Population by Aboriginal Group, 1996 Census', 1996: <http://www.statcan.ca/english/Pgdb/People/Population/demo39a.htm>; Statistics Canada, Aboriginal Peoples of Canada: A Demographic Profile, 2003: <http://www12.statcan.ca/english/census01/>; Statistics Canada, 'Land and Freshwater Area', 2002: <http://www.statcan.ca/english/Pgdb/>.

TABLE 4.3 Aboriginal Population, Selected Administrative Units, 1996*

Administrative Unit	Total Population	Aboriginal Population	Percentage of Aboriginal Population
Northern Saskatchewan CD 18	31,085	25,145	80.1
Manitoba CD 22	35,840	23,865	66.6
Nunavut	25,085	21,095	83.9
Ontario Kenora District	62,925	20,030	31.8
Quebec Nord-du-Québec	38,350	18,740	48.9
Northwest Territories	39,335	18,600	48.2
Alberta CD 17	54,445	17,860	32.8
Yukon	30,650	6,175	20.2

*The figures in Table 4.3 are rounded while those in Table 4.2 are actual census figures.

SOURCE: Statistics Canada. Aboriginal Statistics—1996 Census. Catalogue no. 95F0181XDB-4: <http://library.usask.ca/data/social/census96/profile/aboriginal.html>.

Canadian average. Expressed as the number of people per unit of land area, Canada's 2001 population density figure was three persons km^2 while the figure for the North was 0.14 km^2. The population density of Canada is roughly 20 times more than that of the North. The low population density figure for northern Canada does not imply that the Canadian North is underpopulated, but rather that its carrying capacity is limited. A different measure of carrying capacity is known as physiological density (Vignette 4.2). In comparing world countries, the United Nations devised a modified version called physiological density that measures not the total land area but only the amount of arable land per person. Applying this measure to the Canadian North would result in a much higher physiological density than a population density.

Within the North, population densities vary widely between the Arctic and Subarctic—the Arctic has an extremely low population density of approximately 0.01 persons per km^2 compared to 0.10 persons per km^2 for the Subarctic. For most of the Subarctic the figure is closer to 0.05 persons per km^2, but in the southern fringe of the Subarctic the density is much higher, reaching nearly two inhabitants per km^2.

Vignette 4.2 Physiological Density

Variations in population density do not necessarily imply that there are too many people in one country or region compared to another one. The capacity of countries and regions to support a given population depends on many factors, including the local resource base. The Food and Agriculture Organization of the United Nations recognized this problem when comparing population densities of various countries. It attempted to devise a more meaningful measure by expressing population density by the amount of arable land per person. This measure is called physiological density. For northern Canada, a physiological measure would have to be adjusted to recognize its non-agricultural land use. Such a measure might well indicate that, given its natural land base and resource economy, the North is overpopulated!

SOURCE: Newman and Matzke (1984:34–5).

MIGRATION

The migration of southern Canadians into the North is no longer a dominating demographic factor. However, during the rapid expansion of the resource industry from 1950 to 1980, in-migration was large enough and persistent enough to accelerate the North's population growth, alter its demographic structure, and affect its ethnic composition. These three impacts did not occur uniformly across the North but were concentrated in Yukon, the Northwest Territories, and the northern areas of western provinces, where economic opportunities and relocation benefits attracted many newcomers. Relocation benefits took the form of cost-of-living allowances and subsidized housing. As well, prospects for rapid advancement (often a result of workers replacing those who have opted to return south) were another attraction. These 'extra' benefits have helped southern workers to overcome their concerns about the cold climate and lack of amenities in the North.

Northern migration, especially to the territories and resource towns, was often temporary. Many young people came to 'make money' for five years or so and then return home with 'money in their pockets' for a new start. Some southerner transplants, however, do become enamoured with the North and make it their home (Vignette 4.3). In resource towns and regional centres along the southern fringe or in the three territorial capital cities, more and more newcomers are taking root and making the North their home. The recent closure of Faro in Yukon and Leaf Rapids in Manitoba caused many long-term residents to lament the loss of their community and to complain about uprooting their families to relocate elsewhere. Regional loyalties are readily acknowledged as a key geographic theme. However, for southern migrants, such loyalties are more easily formed in the Subarctic for three reasons. First, the climate found in the Subarctic is more readily acceptable to southern Canadians than is the Arctic climate. Second, the Subarctic contains a number of urban centres, especially resource towns, where community design and structure are similar to that found in southern Canada and where the pace and pattern of life are also similar to that found in southern centres. Third, the Arctic, with 85 per cent of the population Inuit, represents a different cultural setting from that familiar to southern Canadians.

Nevertheless, many southern Canadians are 'economic' migrants who are attracted by high-paying jobs. For these transplanted Canadians, the North is a frontier where they have come for economic opportunity but not to make a permanent home. A common goal is to make a 'nest egg' and then return to the south. As newcomers, they remain highly mobile and, if their employment ends or an attractive job opens up elsewhere, they are likely to move. Few stay longer than five years. In Yukon, a recent report indicated that the median length of residency for newcomers was two years (Yukon Bureau of Statistics, 2002: 7). This tendency to move back home so quickly is reinforced by a desire to be closer to family and friends, to enjoy a wider range of urban amenities, and to return to a more temperate climate. Over the longer period, two other factors often motivate people to return to the south:

- A high degree of job uncertainty common to all resource industries, whether mining, forestry, or oil exploration. During times of expansion there is an in-migration of workers, but during economic contraction the same workers may seek employment outside the North.
- A tendency for young couples to leave the North when their children reach school age. The general feeling is that schools in the North do not provide the same level of education as schools in the south.

Vignette 4.3 Southerners Moving North: Economic Migrants or New Northerners?

I've often asked myself why, four years ago, I jumped at the chance to work in the Arctic. In all honesty, I needed a job and the money was good. Heck, the money was excellent. And I think that's why most southerners come here. Our curiosity about the North is dwarfed by our thoughts of compound interest. But for the people who stay, it changes. Perhaps it's because we get used to food prices that are double and triple those in the South and money becomes less valuable. Perhaps our fascination with money is replaced by a fascination with the land and the people who were here long before we ever heard of the place. Perhaps one day, people will be willing to come to live in the North to seek that fascination. Perhaps one day, there will be no need to entice people north with high salaries, big benefits and two free trips a year. But let's not rush things.

SOURCE: Petrovich (1990: 41).

NATURAL INCREASE

Natural increase of a population consists of differences between births and deaths for a given time period. The North has the highest rate of natural increase in Canada. In 2001, the natural rate of increase for Canada was 0.3 per cent while it was 1.3 per cent for the Territorial North and just under 1 per cent for the entire North. For the three territories, the natural rates were 0.7 per cent (Yukon), 1.3 per cent (NWT), and 2.0 per cent (Nunavut) (Table 4.4). This high rate is due to the Aboriginal fertility rate, which is over two times the national figure. We can help to explain this difference by placing these high rates in cultural and historical context. Fears of a Malthusian trap are far-fetched but a population dependence trap may have already occurred (Vignette 4.4).

Vignette 4.4 A Modern Version of the Malthusian Population Trap

In 1971, Milton Freeman expressed concern about the imbalance between Inuit population size and their resource base. Freeman was particularly concerned that 'a rapid rate of population growth generally prevents any successful attempt to remedy the prevailing unfortunate economic situation.' In 1988, Colin Irwin repeated this concern. Since then, the population has continued to increase at a greater rate than the economy, and a fear has arisen of an Arctic version of the Malthusian population trap. In classical Malthusian terms, this trap eventually results in severe food shortage and starvation until a balance between population size and food supply returns. In Nunavut, a modern version of the Malthusian trap leads not to starvation and a reduction in numbers, but to a greater dependency on government.

SOURCES: Freeman (1971); Irwin (1988).

In the broad scheme of demographic change, the demographic transition theory provides a historical explanation linked to socio-economic changes in industrial societies (Vignette 4.5). This theory provides a historical interpretation of long-term vital (birth/death) shifts by linking them with socio-economic changes in industrial societies. Is this theory useful for explaining the lag between low national birth rate and the much higher northern Aboriginal one? Since a reduction in family size (and therefore the birth rate) depends on the attitudes, needs, and values of a particular population, has the relocation of Aboriginal northerners to settlements been long enough to have had an impact on their birth rate and therefore on family size? Historic evidence indicates that family size rose sharply at first, perhaps encouraged by Family Allowance payments, access to modern health care, and public housing. In the last decade, however, a downward trend is noticeable, though the birth rate remains well above the national figure. One likely factor in this downward trend is that Aboriginal women are remaining in the education system for a longer period of time and then entering the workforce, thus delaying family formation. Another factor may be overcrowding in public housing for Aboriginal families and a general shortage of housing for newly formed families. Housing therefore may cause young families to limit the number of children to avoid crowded housing conditions. A third factor may be that family planning is now more accepted within the Aboriginal community.

Vignette 4.5 Demographic Transition Theory

The demographic transition theory provides a basis for interpreting major changes in population growth at a global level. It is based on demographic, social, and economic events that took place in Europe over several centuries. These events are linked to the process of industrialization, which originated in Western Europe. Its essential argument is that factors associated with a rise in the economic well-being of a society lead to a reduction of mortality and, after a short time lag, a drop in fertility. During these demographic changes, there is a large increase in population but the final phase culminates in little or no natural increase, i.e., zero population growth.

In northern Canada, there is no doubt that improved access to medical services accounts for the drop in the mortality rate in the post-World War II decades. Similar declines in mortality have taken place in most Third World countries. Yet the second vital decline, that of birth rates, has not occurred at the same rate in most Third World countries or in northern Canada. In both cases population rates of increase remain very high. Since the demographic transition theory calls for such a drop in birth rates to occur when incomes rise substantially, the existing low incomes for Aboriginal families may have the opposite effect. It stands to reason that, if the theory is correct, Aboriginal birth rates are unlikely to decline to levels approximating Aboriginal death rates until well after their income levels rise sharply.

SOURCES: Weinstein (1976); Newman and Matzke (1984).

The rate of natural increase varies across the North. The highest rates are found in areas where the indigenous peoples form most of the population, as in Nunavut (Table 4.4). Over the last decade, high rates of natural increase also existed in the Northwest Territories and the Provincial Norths of Manitoba and Saskatchewan. Low rates were found in the Provincial Norths of Alberta, British Columbia, Ontario, and Quebec because of the predominance of the non-Aboriginal population.

Fertility in the North is declining, however. For example, Nunavut's birth rate dropped from over 30 births per 1,000 persons in the 1990s to 25.4 in 2000–1. In the previous year, Nunavut's birth rate was higher, at 28.5 births per 1,000 persons (Statistics Canada, CANSIM Matrix 5772). The fertility rate for the Aboriginal population is declining as a result of the changing nature of the social fabric of Aboriginal peoples. Demography stresses three points: (1) as the education level of women increases, fertility declines; (2) as the participation rate in the wage economy for women increases,

TABLE 4.4 Components of Population Growth for the Territories, 1980 and 2000-1

Demographic Event	Canada 1980	Canada 2000-1	Yukon 1980	Yukon 2000-1	NWT* 1980	NWT 2000-1	Nunavut 2000-1
Births/1,000 persons	15.1	11.0	19.4	12.0	28.2	16.6	25.4
Deaths/1,000 persons	7.0	7.6	5.2	4.8	5.2	3.8	5.3
Natural Rate of Increase (%)	8.1	3.4	1.4	0.7	2.3	1.3	2.0
Net Interprovincial Migrants			400	(846)	(900)	(606)	220

*Includes Nunavut.
SOURCE: Bélanger (1999: 16); Statistics Canada, CANSIM II, Table 051-0004.

fertility declines; and (3) as family income increases, fertility levels decline. All demographic theories acknowledge that couples in industrial societies decide whether or not to have an additional child on the basis of their personal situation (a kind of cost-benefit analysis within the context of the family's economic, religious, and social situation) and the conventions and customs affecting women in their society/religion. Martel and Bélanger (1999: 164-5) support this proposition based on family planning concepts:

> And indeed, reproduction has become a matter of choice, because of a major revolution in the history of human populations: the control of fertility through contraception. With the development of effective birth control methods, couples were able to choose relatively accurately the maximum number of children that they wanted and the timing of the births, giving them, to a large degree, control over their fertility.

DEMOGRAPHIC STRUCTURE

The demographic structure of a population—its age and sex composition—is measured in age cohorts, usually based on five-year intervals. Since the population processes of fertility, mortality, and migration shape a population over time, the demographic structure or population pyramid provides a profile of the particular shape of the age and sex of that population for a particular instant in time, as well as significant clues regarding its population future and probable implications for its economy and society.

A high proportion of the population in Canada's North is under the age of 15. In 2001, over 25 per cent of the northern population was under the age of 15 compared to the national figure of 20 per cent. While an older population exists in most areas of northern Ontario and Quebec, the rest of the North has a much younger population. Several northern areas have figures almost double the national average. In 2001, for example, 37 per cent of the Nunavut population was under 15 years of age (Statistics Canada, 2002b).

Demographers describe this phenomenon as a child dependency ratio, where those aged under 15 form a large group compared to those aged 15–64. Demographers also consider those between the ages of 15 and 64 to be the 'productive' population. The implications of a young population are considerable. First, a young population requires more investment in social infrastructure and social programs ranging from daycare facilities to additional classroom space for kindergarten and primary students. Second, as this young population bulge moves through its natural demographic cycle, public investment must be directed to new high schools and post-secondary facilities and then to job training and job creation programs.

Canada's male/female ratio indicates a slight predominance of females. The reverse is true in the North. A preponderance of males is characteristic of resource frontiers. The demographic gender structure found in Yukon exhibits this 'frontier' characteristic. In 1986, Yukon's sex ratio indicated a majority of males, i.e., 110.4 males for every 100 females. By 2001, Yukon's sex ratio had dropped to 105.2, which may reflect the predominantly male out-migration associated with the closure of the Faro lead/zinc mine.

The age of Canada's population is increasing. This demographic fact is reversed in the North. A unique variation to the North's age pyramid is due to the in-migration of more young males than females. For example, Yukon has a population 'bulge' in its age structure between the ages of 20 and 45. This bulge is more prominent among the male population than female one. Other areas of the North, such as Nunavut, have been less affected by economic development and therefore by in-migration. Consequently, their age structures do not exhibit such a bulge. In other northern areas, but especially northern Ontario, Quebec, and Newfoundland and Labrador, economic retrenchment has seen an outflow of surplus populations to cities in southern Canada. Since the migrants tend to fall in the 20–45 age range, these areas have lost a segment of their labour force, causing a retraction in age structure.

URBAN POPULATION

The North's urban population has five primary characteristics. First, virtually all northerners live in urban centres. Second, large towns and cities are located in the Subarctic of northern provinces. Third, the vast majority of urban centres have populations under 5,000. In the Arctic, for example, only one centre, Iqaluit, has a population over 5,000. Fourth, northern centres have functions that allow their communities to be classified into three groups: Native settlements, resource towns, and regional service centres. Fifth, most Aboriginal people live in small communities that originally served as fur-trading posts and have insufficient economic activities to support their workforces.[5]

Most people live in urban settings because the North's cold climate presents few opportunities for rural activities such as farming. Most agricultural settlement in the Canadian North took place in the late nineteenth and early twentieth centuries in the pioneer fringe of the clay belts of Quebec and Ontario. These marginal farmlands soon lost their appeal. A combination of land abandonment and consolidation reduced the rural agricultural population. Since the 1950s, many farmers abandoned or sold their farms and moved to towns and cities. A second reason for the lack of rural presence on the land is that Aboriginal people left their nomadic hunting/trapping lifestyle and relocated into settlements, at the urging of federal officials, where they could more easily access health and social services and where they could receive Family Allowance payments by keeping their children in school. As a consequence, almost all northern Canadians live in urban areas where jobs, services, and business opportunities are concentrated.

The three largest cities in the North are Chicoutimi-Jonquière (160,454 in 2001), Thunder Bay (126,643), and Prince George (85,035). These cities are located on the southern edge of the Subarctic. Chicoutimi-Jonquière, Thunder Bay, and Prince George owe their population size more to their economic role within their provincial economies rather than to their northern connections. Chicoutimi-Jonquière forms the centre of Alcan's industrial complex, with the Saguenay River providing easy and inexpensive access for importing bauxite and exporting the processed aluminum products. Thunder Bay is located on Canada's east/west transportation system. As a major port on the Great Lakes, Thunder Bay is an important transshipment point, especially for western grain and forest products. As a major forestry and transportation centre, Prince George is the regional hub for the northern interior of British Columbia. Like Chicoutimi-Jonquière and Thunder Bay, Prince George houses a major university with a mandate to develop northern themes in its course offerings and to conduct research on northern issues and problems. In this way, these cities have added another dimension to their regional role. The next cities and towns of some size are much smaller. Timmins and Fort McMurray have populations of 43,686 and 41,466, respectively, followed by towns like Rouyn-Noranda (28,269), Val-d'Or (22,748), and Labrador City (20,103). With the exception of Fort McMurray, these cities and towns saw their populations decline from 1996 to 2001 (Table 4.5).

The vast majority of Arctic centres are small, with all but one centre having fewer than 5,000 inhabitants (Table 4.5). Arctic communities, unlike most Subarctic ones, have increased in size from 1996 to 2001. In the territories, 95 per cent of the communities fall into this category. Only three centres, Whitehorse, Yellowknife, and Iqaluit, have populations over 5,000 (Table 4.6). Many communities have populations under 500. In 2001, the Yukon Bureau of Statistics reported that 12 of its 16 urban settlements had populations under 500 persons (Yukon Bureau of Statistics, 2002).

As noted above, northern urban environments are classified into three types of communities: regional centres, resource towns, and Native settlements. *Regional centres* range from small service centres like The Pas in northern Manitoba to capital cities like Yellowknife in the Northwest Territories. In all instances, the capital cities are the major service centres in the territories. These regional centres are the source of certain goods and services for those living within their catchment areas. The central place theory seeks to explain the relative size and geographic spacing of urban centres as a function of shopping behaviour. Its central argument is that basic or lower-order goods and services are found in all urban centres while specialized or higher-order ones are found only in larger urban centres. Successively larger centres offer a greater variety of goods and services and so command a broader market territory. For example, Yellowknife provides a wider range of goods and services than do smaller centres like the nearby village of Rae-Edzo. Residents of Rae-Edzo have to travel to Yellowknife to obtain a higher order of good or service not available in their home community. For a firm to offer a set of goods at a particular place, it must sell enough to meet operating costs and,

TABLE 4.5 Population Changes in Arctic and Subarctic Communities, 1996–2001

Community	1996 Population	2001 Population	% Change
Greenstone, Ont.	6,530	5,662	(13.3)
Mackenzie, BC	5,997	5,206	(13.2)
Kirkland Lake, Ont.	9,905	8,616	(13.0)
Elliot Lake, Ont.	13,588	11,956	(12.0)
Baie-Comeau, Que.	25,554	23,079	(9.7)
Port Cartier, Que.	7,070	6,412	(9.3)
Flin Flon, Man.	6,572	6,000	(8.7)
Iroquois Falls, Ont.	5,714	5,217	(8.7)
Rouyn-Noranda, Que.	30,936	28,269	(8.6)
Chibougamau, Que.	8,664	7,922	(8.6)
Labrador City	8,455	7,744	(8.4)
Timmins, Ont.	47,499	43,686	(8.0)
Kapuskasing, Ont.	10,030	9,238	(8.0)
Happy Valley-Goose Bay, Labrador	8,655	7,969	(7.9)
Thompson, Man.	14,385	13,256	(7.8)
Val-d'Or, Que.	24,479	22,748	(7.1)
Roberval, Que.	11,640	10,906	(6.3)
Sault Ste Marie, Ont.	83,619	78.908	(5.6)
Yellowknife, NWT	17,275	16,541	(4.2)
Thunder Bay, Ont.	126,643	121,986	(3.7)
Smithers, BC	5,624	5,414	(3.7)
Chicoutimi-Jonquière, Que.	160,454	154,938	(3.4)
Kenora, Ont.	16,365	15,838	(3.2)
Prince George, BC	87,731	85,035	(3.1)
Whitehorse, Yukon	21,808	21,405	(1.8)
Alma, Que.	30,377	30,126	(0.8)
Slave Lake, Alberta	6,553	6,600	0.7
Fort St John, BC	15,021	16,034	6.7
Fort McMurray, Alberta	35,213	41,466	17.8
Iqaluit, Nunavut	4,220	5,236	24.1

SOURCE: Statistics Canada, 'Community Profiles', 2002. Available at: <http://www12.statcan.ca>.

TABLE 4.6 Top Ten Territorial Urban Centres by Population Size, 2001

Urban Centre	2001 Population
Whitehorse	19,058
Yellowknife	16,541
Iqaluit	5,236
Hay River	3,510
Inuvik	2,894
Fort Smith	2,185
Rankin Inlet	2,177
Arviat	1,899
Rae-Edzo	1,552
Cambridge Bay	1,309
Total	56,361
Percentage of Territorial Population	59.2%

SOURCE: Statistics Canada, *Statistical Profile of Canadian Communities*, 2002.

presumably, to turn a profit. The concept that a minimum level of demand is necessary to allow a firm to stay in business is called the threshold. The same argument can be made for public services, i.e., a hospital and high school are located in regional centres while nursing stations and primary schools are found in smaller centres. Fort Simpson and Wrigley provide a simple example of the urban hierarchy. Fort Simpson, with a population in 2001 of 1,163, is the regional centre in the Deh Cho region of the Northwest Territories. Fort Simpson has both a hospital and a high school. Wrigley, with only 165 residents in 2001, has neither a hospital nor a high school. Students from Wrigley who wish to attend high school must travel or move to Fort Simpson. Similarly, residents of Wrigley requiring medical care have to go to the Fort Simpson hospital.

Resource towns or single-industry towns are products of the resource economy. Many were created in the resource boom from 1950 to 1980. Resource towns are vulnerable to the vicissitudes of global demand for their natural resources. Resource towns are also susceptible to plant closures, especially those based on non-renewable resources. While forest industry towns are founded on a renewable resource, mining towns are not so fortunate. Many mines cease operations after about 30 years. During that time, these towns have gone through rapid population growth, population stability, and population collapse. Pine Point in the Northwest Territories, Uranium City in northern Saskatchewan, Leaf Rapids in northern Manitoba, and Schefferville in northern Quebec provide examples of mining towns that have gone through such a 30-year cycle of population expansion and decline. All lost their primary mining function, causing the miners and their families to move. By 1993, Pine Point was abandoned while Schefferville

---

Vignette 4.6 Dominance of Capital Cities in the Territories

Whitehorse is the capital of Yukon. Whitehorse is also the transportation, business, and service centre for the territory. In 2001, its population was 19,058, making it the largest city in the three territories. Whitehorse makes up 55 per cent of the territory's population. This modern city is located in the Yukon River Valley and along the surrounding terraces. In the past, the Yukon River represented a major transportation link between Whitehorse and Dawson. Since 1947, the Alaska Highway not only connected the major urban centres of Watson Lake (population 912 in 2001), Whitehorse (19,058), and Dawson (1,251) but also has provided a link with both Alaska and the provinces of British Columbia and Alberta.

Yellowknife is the capital of the Northwest Territories. Located on the north shore of Great Slave Lake, Yellowknife was originally a gold-mining town. In 1967, Yellowknife was selected as the capital of the Northwest Territories. Its population in 2001 was 16,541, making it the second largest city in the three territories. With the recent development of a diamond mine, Yellowknife has become a centre for diamond processing. The next largest communities are Hay River (3,510), Inuvik (2,894), and Fort Smith (2,185). The remaining 28 communities have populations ranging from Trout Lake (70) to Rae-Edzo (1,552).

Iqaluit is the capital of the newly created Territory of Nunavut and the third largest city in the territories. Located on Baffin Island, Iqaluit has a population of 5,236. The next largest communities in Nunavut are Rankin Inlet with 2,177 residents and Cambridge Bay with 1,309. Most remaining communities are much smaller, having less than 1,000 inhabitants.

---

and Uranium City had shrunk to less than 200 inhabitants each, most of whom were either Métis or Indians who lived in the area prior to the mining developments.

These three communities went through a classic boom/bust cycle (Bone, 1998: Table 2). As resource towns go through this cycle they undergo five phases of expansion and contraction, each marked by dramatic changes in population. The first phase precedes a company announcement about developing a local resource. At that time, the site is uninhabited (though it may form part of a traditional hunting territory). The second phase occurs as workers and their families arrive to occupy the newly constructed town. As production reaches its peak during phase three, the demand for additional workers ceases and the town's population stabilizes and then begins to decline as the ore body becomes more difficult to mine and technological advances reduce the number of workers. The fourth phase is linked to the company's announcement that the mine will soon close. At this point, there is a sharp decrease in the town's population. With the closure of the mine, the town is abandoned and its population drops precipitously. The mining town of Pine Point illustrates the full cycle of a boom/bust scenario (ibid., 252–3). In the late 1950s, Cominco decided to develop a lead/zinc mine just south of Great Slave Lake. The problem of access to outside markets was solved by the construction of the Great Slave Lake Railway by the Canadian National Railway. With considerable help from Ottawa, construction of the new town of Pine Point and its lead/zinc mine began in 1962. Three years later, the mine was in full production. From 1962 to 1976, this resource town witnessed extremely rapid growth, reaching nearly 2,000 inhabitants by 1976. By that time, the company had extracted most of the more accessible and higher-quality ore and the cost of mining began to increase. In 1983, the mine ceased production and most work was focused on milling the ore for shipment to a smelter at Trail, British Columbia. From 1976 to 1986, the size of the community began to decrease, dropping to 1,500 by 1986. With the final export of processed ore in 1988, the mill was closed and preparations were underway to abandon the former resource town. By 1991, the town of Pine Point had been erased from the landscape.

Some resource towns, such as Fort McMurray, are still growing. Situated in the heavy oil sands of northern Alberta, Fort McMurray is undergoing a spectacular expansion. Its population has increased from 35,213 in 1996 to 41,466 in 2001, an increase of 17.8 per cent. With several huge oil sands construction projects underway plus the expansion of existing heavy oil plants, the demand for workers exceeds the supply, driving wages higher and higher. High wages and steady employment attract many from across Canada and beyond, especially from economically depressed areas troubled by high rates of unemployment.[6] Not surprisingly, Newfoundland has supplied so many workers that Newfoundlanders make up around one-third of Fort McMurray's population (Mahoney, 2002: A6).

Native settlements are a relatively new form of urban unit in Canada and are the most numerous type of settlement in the Canadian North. Most have populations under 1,000 inhabitants. As former trading posts, they were strategically located with respect to access to hunting and trapping. Many, but particularly the smaller Native settlements, have continued to have close ties to hunting, trapping, and fishing. Two governments, Quebec and Nunavut, have recognized the importance of hunting and trapping to Aboriginal peoples by providing financial assistance. Native settlements are a sign of cultural dysfunction. While such sites are well suited for accessing game, such activity counts for little in the cash economy. Consequently, almost all Native settlements are located on the margins of the northern economy and therefore can offer their residents few economic opportunities now and in the future.

The fur-trading companies discouraged Aboriginal peoples from remaining at their fur posts and, by means of a 'grub stake', kept them on the land where they could trap furs. In sharp contrast, the Canadian government encouraged Aboriginal northerners to move to or remain in settlements located at trading posts. In a sense, the federal government 'paid' them to stay in settlements, directly through cash payments such as Family Allowances, old age pensions, and welfare payments, and indirectly in the form of housing, schools, and nursing stations. Ottawa's rationale was twofold: (1) food supplies and medical care would be readily available in settlements, thus preventing starvation and other hardships taking place on the land; and (2) relocation was the first step in the process of modernization leading to integration into Canadian society and its economy. In addition, new settlements established in the Extreme North during the 1950s helped to maintain Canadian claims to sovereignty over the Arctic Archipelago.

Unfortunately, the state plan had an Achilles heel, namely that these former fur-trading posts were poorly located for modernization, let alone integration into Canada's

economy. With no solid economic base, local employment opportunities were insufficient to meet demand, and, as a consequence, unemployment rates were extremely
high. Few Native settlements have escaped from a new form of economic dependency,
which has led to a heavy reliance on welfare payments and other forms of public assistance. Temporary solutions to unemployment come from public work projects but no
long-term solution is in sight. Thus, Native settlements are troubled by a host of social
ills. Even the new Innu community of Natuashish, created at a cost of $152 million,
offers no escape from these social ills. The observations of Hicks and White (2000: 48)
regarding the Inuit apply equally well to other northern Aboriginal peoples:

> It would be hard to underestimate the extent and the speed of social and cultural
> change experienced by the Inuit in recent decades. Most Inuit over the age of 40 were
> born on the land in snow houses or tents to nomadic families whose lives depended
> almost entirely on hunting, fishing and trapping, and who had almost no exposure to
> mainstream North American society. They now watch cable television in their living
> rooms while their children play video games or surf the Internet. Life in permanent
> communities built upon the wage economy, the welfare state and modern technology
> changed Inuit society fundamentally. Profound changes in economic activity were
> linked to other changes: traditional patterns of authority (for example, the respect
> accorded elders) were challenged by new forces, single-parent families (rare in tradi-
> tional Inuit society) became common, and a range of traditional values and practices
> were weakened. The impaired capacity of Inuit to hunt was critical since hunting was
> not only the economic mainstay but also the cultural focus of traditional Inuit society.

The operating cost of Native settlements is high because of their remote location
(high cost of delivering public services) and small size (lack of economies of scale). With
a negligible local tax base, local councils depend on transfer payments from territorial
and provincial governments. Given rising costs of delivering existing services and the
costs of building additional facilities, a major question facing governments is whether
they can properly support these communities. As the 1999 draft report on Clyde River
indicated, there is no easy answer to this question (Vignette 4.7). In 2002, the government
of Saskatchewan, faced with the costly task of providing sewerage and water services to
a small community in northern Saskatchewan with less than 100 residents, advised its
residents to relocate to the nearest community with adequate facilities.

Vignette 4.7 Are 'Have-Not' Native Settlements Doomed?

A draft consultant's report on Clyde River in the Territory of Nunavut suggested that
the very existence of this community might have to be 'reviewed'. According to this
report, the problem in Clyde River is not unique and is found in many other Arctic
communities. Such communities have no economic activities other than hunting
and public construction projects. Local tax revenues fall far short of the funds
needed to provide local services. With high unemployment rates, a critical shortage
of housing, and an insufficient tax base to pay for public services, increasing transfer payments from other levels of government are necessary to maintain a minimum

quality of life in these communities. Unfortunately, the territorial government is hard-pressed to keep such funding at its current level and has little room to increase funding to communities. Capital projects, such as sewer and water systems, provide temporary relief, but the cost of maintaining these systems becomes an additional burden on the community. A local Clyde River official, Mr Palluq, bitterly said of the consultant's report: 'The guy writing this was getting $200 a day. And he says we should cut back employee benefits. Lots of these people have been working for the municipality for $12 an hour for 15 years on half-days.' But cuts are coming and retiring hamlet employees may no longer receive a payment for unused sick leave. Clyde River's mayor, James Qillaq, unhappily said, 'it seems like it's a slope and we're still sliding down.'

SOURCE: McKibbon (1999).

NOTES

1. Within territories and provinces, the statistical units employed by Statistics Canada may change over time. Territories and provinces have the right to ask for boundary changes to meet their particular statistical needs. Within territories and provinces, the next geographic level of a statistical unit is the census subdivision.

2. A huge immigration was associated with the resource boom of the 1950s and 1960s. Ottawa played a role in that boom. In 1957, Prime Minister John Diefenbaker announced his 'Northern Vision'. Abandoning its earlier laissez-faire policy, Ottawa began to aggressively promote northern development: highways were built to resource sites, and new administrative and resource towns were created. In these southern-style communities, Ottawa and resource companies hoped that southern Canadians would feel more at home and thus consider relocating to the North and possibly establishing roots in these modern frontier communities. In addition, companies and governments sought to attract skilled workers and professional employees to the North with high pay and incentives.

3. The out-migration of northerners varies across the North by ethnicity and by internal regions. Southerners who settled in the North often relocated to southern Canada within five years. This high turnover is partly due to the uncertainty within mining towns. Downsizing or even mine closing usually translates into most miners and their families leaving the North. Aboriginal residents have shown little interest in relocating to southern cities and towns, although some (usually the more educated ones) are gravitating to regional centres or capital cities (but not to resource towns).

4. The census enumeration asked Canadians to state their ethnicity. This approach means that ethnicity is based on the respondent's perception of his or her ancestral background. The number of Aboriginal peoples by ethnicity in 1986 was 711,725, with some 210,000 living in the North. According to the 1996 census, the Aboriginal population in Canada has reached over a million persons, with about 275,000 residing in northern Canada.

5. In the 1950s, Aboriginal Canadians relocated to small settlements where they traditionally traded their furs. These tiny villages are classified as Native settlements. Few relocated to regional centres and virtually none settled in resource towns. Within a decade, some moved to regional centres for a variety of reasons, including specialized health services and employment opportunities. Most migrants were drawn from the growing number of young, more educated Aboriginal Canadians. Some have settled in regional centres, where many are now employed by Aboriginal organizations and government agencies.

6. In terms of its potential labour force, the North has very few professional and skilled workers, especially among the Aboriginal members of the potential labour force. For that reason, most skilled workers are hired in southern Canada and brought to the northern work site. Since these workers face much higher costs of living and a lack of urban amenities found in southern centres, they will not move to the North unless the employer (companies and governments) pays high wages and offers incentives. Often these incentives include subsidized housing and an allowance to travel to southern Canada. The federal government provides several additional incentives, including a northern isolation allowance for its employees and a northern personal tax deduction for all northern employees and business people. Since northern communities vary widely in terms of their isolation, how could government determine who should get these incentives? As well, the degree of isolation could change with a highway reaching a community. Northern isolation allowance payments provide cash compensation. Revenue Canada (now the Canada Customs and Revenue Agency) has used Hamelin's concept of nordicity to create two northern zones. Places in Zone A are more isolated than locations in Zone B and therefore individuals in Zone A filing personal income tax receive more tax relief than those in Zone B. All places in Yukon, the Northwest Territories, and Nunavut fall into Zone A. Zone B corresponds to places in the Provincial Norths, including resource towns. Examples include Chibougamau in Quebec, Red Lake in Ontario, The Pas in Manitoba, La Ronge in Saskatchewan, Fort McMurray in Alberta, and Tumbler Ridge in British Columbia.

REFERENCES AND SELECTED READINGS

Bélanger, Alain. 1999. *Report on the Demographic Situation in Canada 1998–1999*. Statistics Canada Catalogue no. 91–209. Ottawa: Minister of Industry.

———, Yves Carrière, and Stéphane Gilbert. 2001. *Report on the Demographic Situation in Canada 2000: Current Demographic Analysis*. Statistics Canada Catalogue no. 91–209 XPE. Ottawa: Minister of Industry.

Bone, Robert M. 1992. *The Geography of the Canadian North: Issues and Challenges*. Toronto: Oxford University Press.

———. 1998. 'Resource Towns in the Mackenzie Basin', *Cahiers de Géographie du Québec* 42, 116: 249–56.

Choinière, Robert, and Norbert Robitaille. 1987. 'The Fertility of the Inuit of Northern Quebec: A Half-Century of Fluctuations', *Acta Borealia* 1/2: 53–64.

Freeman, Milton M.R. 1971. 'The Significance of Demographic Changes Occurring in the Canadian East Arctic', *Anthropologica* 13, 1–2: 215–37.

Hicks, Jack, and Graham White. 2000. 'Nunavut: Inuit self-determination through a land claim and public government?', in Jens Dahl, Jack Hicks, and Peter Jull, eds, *Nunavut: Inuit Regain Control of Their Lands and Their Lives*. IWGIA Document No. 102. Copenhagen: Centraltrykkeriet Skive A/S, 30–115.

Irwin, Colin. 1988. *Lords of the Arctic: Wards of the State*. Special Edition of *Inungnut*. Rankin Inlet: Keewatin Inuit Association.

Légaré, Andre. 2000. 'La Nunavut Tunngavik Inc.: Un examen de ses activités et de sa structure administrative', *Etude/Inuit/Studies* 24, 1: 97–124.

Mahoney, Jill. 2002. 'Where the jobs are', *Globe and Mail*, 12 Mar., A6.

Martel, L., and Alain Bélanger. 1999. 'An Analysis of the Change in Dependency-Free Life Expectancy in Canada between 1986 and 1996', in Bélanger, *Report on the Demographic Situation in Canada 1998–1999*. Statistics Canada Catalogue no. 91–209. Ottawa: Minister of Industry, 164–86.

Maslove, Allan M., and David C. Hawkes. 1990. *Canada's North, A Profile*. Statistics Canada Catalogue no. 98–122. Ottawa: Minister of Supply and Services.

McKibbon, Sean. 1999. 'Report: Clyde River's Very Existence Is Questionable', *Nunatsiaq News*: <http//:www.nunatsiaq.com/nunavut/nvt91029_01html>.

McNiven, Chuck, and Henry Puderer. 2000. *Delineation of Canada's North: An Examination of the North-South Relationship in Canada*. Geography Working Paper Series No. 2000–3. Ottawa: Statistics Canada.

Newman, James L., and Gordon E. Matzke. 1984. *Population: Patterns, Dynamics, and Prospects*. Englewood Cliffs, NJ: Prentice-Hall.

Northwest Territories Bureau of Statistics. 1998. *Community Population Estimates, Nunavut*. <http://www.stats.gov.nu.ca/Statinfo/Demographics/population/Nunaest/popest_nunavut.p df>. Accessed 4 Mar. 2002.

———. 2001. *Population Estimate and Projections*. <http://www.stats.gov.nt.ca/CPWeb/mergedEstPro/WRIEstPro.html>. Accessed 4 Mar. 2002.

Petrovich, Curt. 1990. 'The Best Reason to Come North . . . Or is it?', *Arctic Circle* 1, 1: 36–41.

Robitaille, Norbert, and Robert Choinière. 1987. 'The Inuit Population of Canada: Present Situation, Future Trends', *Acta Borealia* 1/2: 25–36.

Statistics Canada. 1997. Aboriginal Statistics—1996 Census. Catalogue no. 95F0181XDB–4. <http://library.usask.ca/data/social/census96/profile/aboriginal.html>. Accessed 7 Mar. 2002.

———. 2002a. *Statistical Profile of Canadian Communities*. <http://ceps.statcan.ca/english/profil/PlaceSearchForm1.cfm>. Accessed 28 Feb. 2002.

———. 2002b. *Population by Age Group*. <http://www.statcan.ca/english/Pgdb/People/Population/demo31c.htm>. Accessed 3 Mar. 2002.

———2003. *Aboriginal Peoples of Canada: A Demographic Profile*. <http://www12.statcan/english/census01/>. Accessed 21 Jan 2003.

Weinstein, Jay A. 1976. *Demographic Transition and Social Change*. Morristown, NJ: General Learning Press.

Wonders, William C. 1984. 'The Canadian North: its nature and prospects', *Journal of Geography* 85, 5: 226–33.

———. 1987. 'The Changing Role and Significance of Aboriginal Peoples in Canada's Northwest Territories', *Polar Record* 23, 147: 661–71.

Yukon Bureau of Statistics. 1999. *Annual Statistic Review: 1999 Annual Report*, Table 1.3. <http://www.yukonweb.com/government/ybs/annual.html>. Accessed 4 Mar. 2002.

———. 2002. *Yukon Population Estimates, 2001*. <http://www.yukonweb.com/government/ybs/annual/pop0601.pdf>. Accessed 4 Mar. 2002.

CHAPTER 5

Resource Development

The Canadian North is part of the global economy. Resource development is critical to its economic growth but is controlled by international companies and Crown corporations located outside of the North. The pattern of resource development in hinterlands follows the classical lines of the core/periphery model: capital flows to the North from large companies and Crown corporations to construct megaprojects that serve the interests of the provinces, the nation, and the international community. Economic spinoffs flow from resource projects to the North in the form of employment, business opportunities, transportation infrastructures, and royalties, and these spinoffs have the potential to diversify the North's economy. But, unfortunately, most Aboriginal peoples in the North have gained little from resource development and, marginalized from their land-based economy, suffer from the resulting economic and social consequences. During the construction phase of large-scale industrial projects, economic gains are enormous, but they are also short-lived and do not necessarily build towards the stability and diversification of the northern economy. In fact, such a sharp burst of intense economic activity, by focusing on a small geographic area, overheats the local economy, places heavy demands on the public infrastructure, and draws the local Aboriginal workforce into temporary jobs and contracts. On the positive side, long-term economic benefits that flow from the operational phase of a resource project may lead to economic diversification within the local area and even the region.

Historically, resource development has played a key role in opening Canadian frontiers to economic development. In various regions of Canada, resource development initiated a process of economic growth by exploiting a key resource that, in some cases, led to further economic activities and eventually to the diversification of the region's economy. The first stage of diversification of the North's economy, though difficult, would see an expansion of resource processing and growth in the resource service sector. In 1930, Harold Innis first conceived of regional diversification flowing out of resource development as the staple thesis, thus presenting a new interpretation of Canadian regional economic history. Mel Watkins (1963) transformed Innis's thesis into a more conventional theory of regional development. Regional development is not an automatic process of the market economy. In fact, the most positive outcome of staple projects is a broadening and maturing of the resource economy, but in the worst-case scenario the resource economy flounders and eventually slides into a staple trap where, instead of development, underdevelopment takes hold (Watkins, 1977). Hayter and Barnes (2001: 37) put it more gently: 'But as Innisians emphasized, there is nothing automatic about such diversification.' The question posed in this chapter is: 'Can resource development in the North lead to economic stability and diversification?' In Chapter 8 (Aboriginal Economy and Society), the limited role of First Nations people in past resource projects and hopes for more involvement in future projects are discussed more fully.

RESOURCE HINTERLANDS

The Canadian North is but one of many resource hinterlands interlocked into the global economy. In this way, prices for primary products remain low due to overproduction and stiff competition among the world hinterlands to sell their products in the world market. Within the continental economy of North America, trade barriers pose another danger for Canadian producers. In spite of the North American Free Trade Agreement, the United States government has made the export of Canadian forest products into the United States difficult. Energy and mineral resources have not felt the sting of US trade restrictions because these products are in short supply in the United States.

As small cogs in the world economic system, the Canadian North and other resource hinterlands have a number of common characteristics:

- World demand for primary resources and energy dictates the course of hinterland development.
- Hinterland economies have a narrow economic base, making them extremely vulnerable to sharp economic fluctuations.
- Multinational corporations, with their capital, management skills, and technical knowledge, are the leading force in the development of hinterland resources.
- The global demand for raw materials and energy is cyclical, following the global business cycle. These cycles are more pronounced in resource hinterlands, leading to a 'boom-and-bust' pattern of economic development.
- Resource hinterlands in different countries often compete against each other, driving the price of primary products down.
- Primary resource exploitation in resource frontiers is associated with severe economic leakage: most of the economic benefits generated by resource projects find their way to other, more developed regions.
- Most resource projects characteristically require a small but well-trained labour force.
- While large construction projects employ enormous numbers of workers for short periods of time, relatively few employees are required for the operation of these resource projects. This pattern is especially noticeable in hydroelectric and pipeline projects.

VALUE OF RESOURCE DEVELOPMENT

Canada's geography and world circumstances have shaped the course of its economic development. With a small domestic market and vast natural resources, Canada had no choice but to sell its surplus production in foreign markets. Energy, forest, and mineral resources are developed in response to external demand. In recent years, the value of these export-oriented natural resources amounted to $35 billion. By far the bulk of this production comes from the northern areas of the seven provinces. The Provincial Norths of British Columbia, Manitoba, Quebec, and Newfoundland/Labrador export electricity to energy-deficient areas of the United States. The provincial Norths of British Columbia and Alberta ship petroleum to the west coast and Midwestern areas of the United States by pipelines. All seven provinces sell minerals and forest products to American customers. In total, the northern provinces provide 96 per cent of the value of the North's production of natural resources. Of the three territories, the Northwest Territories accounted for just over $1.3 billion of mineral and petroleum production or roughly 70 per cent of the territorial output in 2001. Converting these economic activities into the geographic areas of the Arctic and Subarctic, the Subarctic accounts for over 95 per cent of the value of natural resource production.

THE AMERICAN MARKET

North America forms a natural marketplace. With the signing of the Canada–US Free Trade Agreement in 1989, Canada's north/south trade began to increase. Today, Canada sends over 85 per cent of its exports to the United States and many resource exports come from the Canadian North. While Canadian exports have always found their way into the huge American market, Canada's reliance on this single marketplace has grown since World War II.[1] By then, America had grown into the largest economy in the world. At that time, American supplies of energy and raw materials could no longer satisfy the ever-increasing demands of its industries. The impact on Canada was profound. American industrialists looked to Canada and other foreign countries for these primary products. Canada was an attractive source for three reasons. It contained the desired resources; it was close to factories in the United States; and Canada was perceived as a politically stable country that offered a safe place for American investments. America soon espoused a continental foreign policy, thereby drawing Canada and its resource-rich North more closely into the American economic orbit. Two large-scale resource projects illustrate the powerful pull of the American market.

The first project marked the beginning of American megaprojects in Canada's North. In 1947, American iron and steel interests announced plans for the first large-scale, privately funded resource project in northern Canada.[2] This plan called for the exploitation of the vast iron deposits in northern Quebec and Labrador and the building of a rail-sea transportation system capable of supplying iron ore to American steel plants. Until the James Bay Project, this iron mining project represented the largest capital investment in the Canadian North. By the early 1950s, this massive iron mining and transportation system was completed. In spite of a decline in the demand for iron ore and the closing of the first iron mining town of Schefferville, the Quebec and Labrador mines still supply the North American market.

The second project is, in fact, a series of massive construction efforts now underway in Alberta's oil sands. American oil companies are pouring billions of dollars into Alberta's vast oil sand deposits for two reasons. First, these deposits represent the world's largest source of bitumen (a thick, sticky form of crude oil) and therefore they represent a long-term supply of oil for the American market. Second, these deposits are deemed 'secure' to American interests and thus have the potential to reduce significantly America's dependency on oil from the Middle East. By 2002, oil companies had already committed $86 billion in proposed energy projects (Collum, 2002: EJ1), making the oil sands the largest northern capital investment, surpassing both the Quebec/Labrador iron mining project and the James Bay hydroelectric project.

Access to the American market is a keystone of Canada's foreign policy. Since 11 September 2001, when terrorists attacked the World Trade Center in New York and the Pentagon in Washington, Ottawa has been concerned about both access to and border delays in reaching American markets. To overcome this potential problem, the United States has advocated a North American perimeter that, by harmonizing immigration, trade, and defence policies, would allow the easy flow of goods and people across the US–Canada border. If Canada agreed to such a concept, the North's resource economy would be even more closely linked to markets in the United States.

RESOURCE BOOM-AND-BUST CYCLES

With its narrow economic base the northern economy is vulnerable to wide fluctuations in its economy. It is especially troubled by non-renewable resource 'boom-and-bust' cycles characterized by a rapid increase in economic activity followed by an inevitable collapse. Three types of boom-and-bust cycles exist. One is the non-renewable resource cycle that follows the opening and eventual closing of a single mine, oil field, or similar non-renewable resource enterprise. The second type involves the construction period associated with the building of a megaproject. The third type is associated with a cyclical slowdown in the global economy that has repercussions for all resource companies.

Non-Renewable Resource Cycle

Many areas of the North have experienced the opening and closing of a mine (Vignette 5.1). While the opening of a new mine is exhilarating, closure has a devastating impact on the workers and their families. In 1981, Uranium City, Saskatchewan, had a population of nearly 2,500. When the Eldorado uranium mine was closed in 1982, the town lost its economic base and, within five years, its population plummeted to less than 200 inhabitants. The closures of the Faro lead/zinc mine in Yukon provide another example and illustrate the vulnerability of mining operations to declining world prices. Yukon, like other northern areas, is heavily dependent on the non-renewable resource industry, leaving the region vulnerable to external forces. For example, the first of three closures of the mine at Faro took place in 1983; the second in 1993; and the third in 1998. Each closure had a negative ripple effect through the community and the territory. The loss of the Faro mine depressed the Yukon economy, reduced government revenues, and triggered an out-migration (Vignette 5.2).

The closure of a mine ends the life cycle of a resource town (Table 5.1). Resource companies, for instance, have no influence on the price of their products and relatively little control over the cost of production. The international marketplace, through such institutions as the London Metal Exchange, determines the price of mineral commodities based on perceptions of world supply and demand. For the northern mining company, a sudden drop in the world price of its product will threaten its operation and perhaps force the company to cease production.

Vignette 5.1 The Boom-Bust Life Cycle of Pine Point

Single-industry towns in remote locations are often characterized as 'boom-and-bust' communities. The appearance of a new town on the northern landscape represents the 'boom' and its later abandonment marks the 'bust'. Since they are based on a finite resource, resource towns have a limited economic life. The classic life cycle falls into five phases (Table 5.1). While some resource towns are able to diversify their economy, remote mining towns usually follow the classic life cycle culminating in mine and community closure. Pine Point illustrates this cycle.

Pine Point was a mining town located on the south shore of Great Slave Lake in the Northwest Territories. In 1961, the federal government agreed to supply 70 per cent of the cost to build a town at the site of the lead/zinc ore body and to construct a railway. The total cost was $125.1 million, including $79 million for the railway (Kendall, 1992: 132). The population of this new town grew rapidly, reaching a peak of nearly 2,000 in 1976. From this point, the population declined slightly due to improved productivity. In 1985, the company decided to restrict its operations to the highest-grade ore. At that time, zinc prices had fallen to 45 cents per pound, well below the cost of production. In 1986, the Pine Point population was 1,558. Mining operations ended in 1987 while milling continued until 1988. The ore concentrate was stockpiled and shipping continued until 1990. By 1991, the residents of Pine Point had left and the town was but a memory. Families had lived in Pine Point for up to 20 years, sufficiently long to raise children and to call Point Point 'home'. Leaving was psychologically hard. One resident put it this way:

Don't think people realise how hard it is to leave a town where all three children were born . . . . Seems unreal to see your home town slowly disappear. It's too bad that some other industry couldn't have been brought in to keep the town alive. . . . It's a shame to see buildings (arenas, school, etc.) abandoned when so many other settlements have nothing of the sort and could use the facilities. (Ibid., 134)

SOURCES: Kendall (1992); Bone (1998).

Vignette 5.2 Metal Prices Rule

In 1969, the Cyprus Anvil Mine opened an open-pit lead/zinc mine and built the company town of Faro, Yukon. During the 1970s, the Faro mine was Canada's largest producer of lead and by far the most important company in Yukon. When metal prices dropped sharply, the Faro mine closed in 1982. In 1986, the mine was sold to Curragh Resources and reopened with an $8.4 million federal government incentive grant. Public support took other forms—Ottawa and Whitehorse guaranteed loans obtained by Curragh Resources. As well, the federal government paid for the upgrading of the highway to the port of Skagway, Alaska. The improved highway allowed Curragh Resources to achieve substantial transportation savings by using large ore-carrying trucks to haul the concentrates to ore freighters, which would deliver the concentrates to overseas buyers. One negative outcome of this decision was the closure of the White Pass and Yukon Railway in 1983. Even with this more efficient transportation system, when world prices for lead and zinc dipped again in the early 1990s the Faro mine was no longer viable. Curragh Resources continued production until 1993, when it, too, went bankrupt. Another firm, Anvil Range Mining Corporation, took possession of the Faro mine in 1994. Commercial production began the next year when the price for zinc soared to over 54 cents a pound. In 1997, the price for zinc slumped to 48 cents a pound, well below the cost of production (*Whitehorse Star*, 1998). Within a year, Anvil closed the mine and went into receivership.

TABLE 5.1 Classic Population Life-Cycle Model for Resource Towns

Phase	Population Characteristics	Associated Events
1	Uninhabited site	Company announces plans to build a resource town.
2	Sharp increase in population size	With the completion of the construction of a company town, workers and their families arrive.
3	Population size stable	Resource production reaches its peak and the demand for additional workers ceases.
4	Sharp decrease in population size	Company decides to close its operations. Workers and their families depart
5	Population size returns to zero	Company closes its mine and the town is abandoned.

Source: Bone (1998: 250).

Regional centres close to a mine or construction site find their economies stimulated by the boom and depressed by the bust, but these towns continue to function. Yellowknife, for example, saw its economy suffer with the closure of the Giant gold mine, but it quickly recovered with the commencement of diamond production.

At a broader geographic level, the economy of the Arctic, with its heavy dependency on mining, is much more vulnerable to mine closures and their ripple effect through the region's economy than is the more diversified economy of the Subarctic. For example, the imminent closure of the Nanisivik mine and the possible closure of Nunavut's other two mines (Polaris and Lupin) within five years would devastate that territory's economy—unless new mines were established.

Construction Cycle

Megaprojects take place at remote resource sites that require an intense construction effort over a short period of time. Such construction has a profound impact on the local community. In the case of the Norman Wells Oil Expansion and Pipeline Project (1982–5), the residents of the small community of Norman Wells (about 650 inhabitants) enjoyed the economic boom, suffered from the construction noise and traffic, and saw their public services stretched to the limit. By the end of the construction, local businesses that had expanded during the boom had to face the harsh reality of a much smaller local market.

Global Induced Cycle

From the end of World War II to the late 1970s, the Canadian North enjoyed a resource boom. Rapidly rising oil prices fuelled this expansion. By the 1980s, however, the global economy began to slow and the repercussions for its resource hinterlands were hurtful. Mine closures and layoffs caused many workers and their families to return to southern Canada. In the 1990s, the economic situation improved, but resource firms continued to restructure their operations by substituting new technology and equipment for high-priced labour. Resource towns were particularly vulnerable, partly because their geographic location resulted in very high transportation costs, thus making these mines and mills marginal producers. A slight shift in price would hurt these primary producers first, causing the layoff of workers or the closing of the plant. Companies sought different means of reducing their costs, but often that translated into reducing the size of the labour force. By the start of the twenty-first century, the resource industry, while continuing to account for most of the value of production in the North, employed far fewer workers than in the 1960s. The gradual reduction in the labour force at these resource towns partly explains the decline of the North's population over the past 20 years.

ACCESSIBILITY

Accessibility to resources is a critical factor in the Canadian North. The existing northern transportation system is very limited, especially in the Territorial North. The reason is simple: because so few people live in the Territorial North, highway construction is difficult to justify. Take the new Territory of Nunavut as an example. Few people—less than 30,000—occupy the largest territorial area in Canada. Not surprisingly, however, no part of Nunavut is connected to the rest of Canada by a highway, nor does a highway link any two communities in Nunavut. The transportation systems in each of the seven Provincial Norths are more developed than those in the territories for three reasons. First, provincial governments have larger tax bases from which to pay for northern highways and railways. Second, the distance to the national transportation system is much shorter in the Provincial Norths than in the Territorial North. Third, provinces see the benefits of developing their Provincial Norths and hence can justify such expenditures as 'opening up' their northern hinterland. In the Territorial North, no such core-periphery dynamic exists.

The cost of highway construction is so high in the North as a result of four main factors. These are:

- Physical terrain, particularly the Canadian Shield and the presence of muskeg and permafrost, increases costs of construction.
- A short summer construction season often extends the construction work for another summer, thus increasing assembly cost.
- A high cost is related to assembling workers and equipment in remote areas.
- The costs of bringing southern supplies to the construction site are also high.

Resource development is often stalled by the absence of a modern transportation system. The mineral-rich Slave Geologic Province of the Canadian Shield found in the Northwest Territories and Nunavut presents such an example. With a modern highway from Yellowknife to the Lupin gold mine in Nunavut, geologists estimated that at least six known mineral deposits, including the Izok Lake lead/zinc deposit, would be viable. An all-season highway would reduce capital investment in storage facilities for ore, reduce capital costs in the trucking fleet, lower operating and maintenance costs of the mine, and employ a part of the workforce year-round rather than on a seasonal basis. In the early 1990s, the German firm, Metall Mining Company, was prepared to develop the Izok Lake deposit, but the firm wanted the federal government to provide the necessary transportation infrastructure. The federal government declined to provide financial support for such an enterprise and the cost, estimated at around $400 million, is well beyond the capacity of the two territorial governments. Besides the high cost of the transportation system, the proposed mining operation only had a 20-year supply of ore. Ottawa simply could not make such an investment for such a relatively short mining period, nor was Ottawa prepared to gamble that other deposits might become viable as a result of the highway system.

Transportation costs dictate that the more valuable resources, e.g., gold and silver, are exploited first because of their relatively low transportation costs. When refined, these highly valuable minerals can be shipped to market by small aircraft. In such cases, there is no need for an expensive all-season highway or railway. On the other hand, base metals like lead and zinc remain bulky products even after milling the ore. Bulky, low-value products require rail, road, or sea transportation. The degree to which various mineral deposits are deemed exploitable is largely a function of the value of that commodity's per unit of weight, that is, the higher the per-unit value of the mineral, the greater distance it can be shipped. In the case of iron ore and lead/zinc ore, milling reduces the ore into a more concentrated form. Still, both the Pine Point lead/zinc mine in the Northwest Territories and the iron ore mine at Schefferville, Quebec, required rail transportation to ship their products to southern markets.

Provincial governments have tried to overcome this distance barrier to resource development within their jurisdictions by building modern transportation routes into their hinterlands.[3] In the 1920s, the British Columbia government tried to stimulate resource development in its northern territory by building the Pacific Great Eastern Railway (PGE). Until 1952, the popular name for this railway was 'the railway that begins nowhere and ends nowhere'. In that year, some 30 years after construction began, the rail link from the northern interior of British Columbia to a seaport was finally completed, thereby transforming this vast wilderness area into a resource hinterland. The PGE, by connecting Prince George with North Vancouver, opened the vast forests of British Columbia's interior to global markets for forest products. In time, the PGE reached further north to Fort St John and further east to Dawson Creek and the Peace River country. At Dawson Creek, the PGE established a link with the Northern Alberta Railway. During the 1960s, resource development of northern British Columbia began in earnest and the PGE both assisted and benefited from the resource boom in forestry and energy. This railway was renamed British Columbia Railroad in 1972 and BC Rail in 1984.

In general, each provincial government has provided some form of access to its northern resources. Similar strides to overcome the problem of inaccessibility have occurred in the Territorial North but not in such a determined manner. The transportation situations in the three territories vary somewhat—parts of Yukon and the Northwest Territories are connected to the national highway system, but Nunavut has neither road nor rail connection with the rest of Canada. For resource companies, this remoteness means that known resources in relatively inaccessible areas of the Territorial North are less likely to be brought into commercial production than similar resources that are more accessible.

Accessibility to resources is affected by prices. In the late 1990s, rising natural gas prices called for the development of natural gas reserves north of 57° in Alberta and British Columbia and the construction of the Alliance Pipeline to transport this gas to the energy-deficient Chicago market. Early in the twenty-first century, many believe that natural gas prices will continue to rise so that the huge natural gas reserves in the Mackenzie Delta at 69°N will be developed and connected by pipeline to the Chicago market. The offshore Beaufort Sea natural gas fields are more costly to develop. For that reason, their exploitation will come later.

RESOURCE DIFFERENCES IN THE ARCTIC AND SUBARCTIC

The resource geographies of the Arctic and Subarctic differ sharply. The Subarctic has a number of advantages in each area: its resource base is much broader and includes major energy, mineral, timber, and water resources; its geographic location makes it more accessible to the American market; and its natural environment presents less of a barrier to industrial projects because of a milder climate, a longer navigation season, and a land less affected by permafrost. All of these advantages translate into lower costs of resource development in the Subarctic than in the Arctic. In addition, sustainable development prospects are more promising in the Subarctic than the Arctic because of the greater array of renewable resources in the Subarctic.

Resource development began much earlier in the Subarctic. While resource development began in earnest in the post-World War II period, commercial forestry and mining had its start along the southern edge of the Canadian Shield in northern Ontario and Quebec in the late nineteenth century. Rivers flowing southward from the Canadian Shield were used to bring northern logs to sawmills and pulp mills in southern Quebec, such as at Trois-Rivières at the mouth of the St Maurice River, and in northern Ontario, such as at Kenora on the English River. In 1885, the completion of the Canadian Pacific Railway provided access to the forest and mineral resources of northern Ontario. By the 1930s, access to resource development across the southern edge of the Subarctic had greatly improved and mines were established at Goldfields, Saskatchewan, Keno City, Yukon, Kirkland Lake, Ontario, Sherridon, Manitoba, and Yellowknife, Northwest Territories. Small-scale, often locally owned, resource firms were found across the southern edge of the Subarctic and even into Yukon and the Northwest Territories.

In the 1950s, America's demand for energy and raw materials created a resource boom in the Subarctic. Often the boom took the form of megaprojects—large-scale resource developments that cost billions of dollars and take years to complete, but have the advantage of economies of scale. All were built in the Subarctic. Megaprojects often involved public financial support, with public funds spent on transportation and settlement infrastructure. Initially, the driving force behind these enormous industrial undertakings was American industry. No longer able to supply themselves with raw materials and minerals from within the United States, American corporate giants turned to the rich primary resources of northern Canada. This prompted nationalists like Richard Rohmer to refer to the Subarctic as Canada's last major resource frontier, which, in his opinion, required a railway to connect northern centres like Whitehorse, Inuvik, and Yellowknife and to bring northern resources to Canada's industrial core. While Rohmer's dream of a transcontinental railway across Canada's 'Green North' faded quickly, transportation routes continued to follow a north/south orientation within each Provincial North. Pushed by massive investments in exploration for oil and natural gas in the sedimentary rock formations in the Interior Plain and hardrock minerals in the Canadian Shield, promising discoveries soon turned into resource towns with north/south road connections to the national highway system. By the end of the resource boom, the Subarctic was no longer on the edge of the global economy but an integral part of its resource hinterland.

The resource boom drew Ottawa into the Subarctic. While the resource companies pushed the resource economy further and further into this hinterland, the federal government expanded the transportation network to reach the newly formed resource towns. Under Prime Minister Diefenbaker's Roads to Resources program, roads were built to resource towns in the Subarctic and beyond. The construction of the Dempster Highway represented the most ambitious and costly of these undertakings. Begun in 1959, the Dempster Highway stretches from Dawson, Yukon, to Inuvik, Northwest Territories, and was the first road to reach the Arctic. In 1979, the Dempster Highway was opened to the public.

From the 1980s on, north/south energy transportation lines were constructed between sites in the Subarctic and markets in southern Canada and the United States. Three north/south regional electrical transmissions lines were built, linking hydroelectric facilities in the Subarctic with American and Canadian markets: northern British Columbia with its Lower Mainland and the American west coast; northern Manitoba with Winnipeg and Minneapolis; and northern Quebec with Montreal and New England. Similarly, the petroleum basins discovered in the sedimentary rocks of Alberta, British Columbia, the Northwest Territories, and Yukon required natural gas pipelines to reach markets in southern Canada and the United States. In 1985, the Norman Wells oil pipeline was completed and oil was flowing to southern markets. The network of natural gas pipelines is not only more extensive but the initial pipeline from the Fort St John area to Vancouver and on to American markets along the Pacific coast took place in the late 1950s. Most natural gas pipeline construction took place after 1980. In the late 1990s, the longest pipeline in North America, Alliance Pipeline, was completed, allowing natural gas from northern British Columbia to reach markets in the Chicago area of the American Midwest.

During the same time, little resource development occurred in the Arctic. By the late 1950s, the only mine in the Arctic was the North Rankin nickel mine, a 'marginal and very small-scale operation' that operated from 1957 to 1962 (Rea, 1968: 148). Since then, seven other mines have opened (Asbestos Hill, Cullaton Lake, Hope Bay, Lupin, Nanisivik, Polaris, and Raglan), but three (Asbestos Hill, Cullaton Lake, and Hope Bay) have already ceased production. Asbestos Hill mine, located along the shores of Arctic Quebec, opened in 1972 and closed in 1983. Keewatin's Cullaton Lake gold mine (1981–5) and Hope Bay silver mine located 150 km southwest of Cambridge Bay (1973–5) had much shorter existences. The Lupin gold mine (1982 to present) is on the shores of Contwoyto Lake, the Nanisivik lead/zinc mine (1976 to present) is on the northern tip of Baffin Island, and Polaris (1981 to present) is located on Little Cornwallis Island in the Arctic Archipelago. All three may exhaust their reserves within five years. Raglan nickel mine, situated in Nunavik, began production in 1998. Nickel concentrate is trucked 100 km to Deception Bay and then shipped to Quebec City. From there, the nickel concentrate is sent by rail to Falconbridge's smelter in Sudbury. A winter road from Yellowknife to the Lupin mine provided an essential transportation link for importing heavy equipment, diesel fuel, and construction supplies. Sea access was one factor that made the Nanisivik and Polaris mines commercially viable (Figure 5.1).

The Arctic does contain vast petroleum reserves. Frontier exploration took place as a result of the funds made available by the Trudeau Liberal government.[4] However, these resources are too far from market and remain undeveloped. Large oil and gas deposits exist in the Beaufort Sea and in the Sverdrup Basin, which is centred on Melville Island. Token shipments of crude oil were sent from the Bent Horn field in the Sverdrup Basin to Montreal in 1985 and 1986, and from the Amauligak field in the Beaufort Sea to Japan in 1986. The more accessible Beaufort Sea petroleum and gas deposits are first in line for commercial exploitation while the Sverdrup Basin deposits will be much later because of the high costs of building pipelines and the difficulty of reaching the mainland— unless global warming permits oil tankers routinely to sail in the Arctic Ocean.

The Arctic has yet to be fully drawn into the global economic system. The problem, obviously, is high transportation costs. Except for the Lupin gold mine, the key factor permitting the other mines to function profitably has been their access to ocean transportation. The Lupin gold mine has a high-value product, which can be flown to market,

FIGURE 5.1 Major Mines, 2002

and a winter road from Yellowknife allows incoming supplies to arrive with acceptable transportation costs. The two lead/zinc mines, Polaris and Nanisivik, have a different solution to their transportation problem. They are able to ship their low-value product (lead and zinc) by sea to European markets. They store their production for about 10 months and then ship it to European markets during the short navigation season. The Lancaster Sound sea route to the Polaris mine site on Little Cornwallis Island may be filled with floating ice at any time during the short navigation period. Both companies ship their freight and concentrated ore in the MV *Arctic*, which has a double steel-reinforced hull, advanced radar, sonar, and satellite navigation systems. All workers commute by air to these three mines, though a road connects the Inuit community of Arctic Bay to the Nanisivik mine. Most employees live in southern Canada (and in a few cases, in other countries). When these mines close, the three mine sites will be abandoned.

Voisey's Bay, at latitude 56° N, lies along the Arctic coast of Labrador. At this remote location one of the world's richest nickel deposits was discovered. The size of this deposit is staggering, with 150 million tons of proven nickel ore plus smaller deposits of cobalt and copper. The ore is located in three sites: the Ovid, the Eastern Deeps, and the Western Extension. Inco purchased this deposit for $4 billion. Over the 30-year life of this mine, a total investment of $2.9 billion is anticipated (Vignette 5.3). Difficult and time-consuming negotiations took place with the government of Newfoundland and Labrador, and with the affected Aboriginal groups (the Labrador Inuit, Innu Nation, and Labrador Métis), and Inco now plans to begin construction of a mine and a mill/concentrator in 2003. This construction project, costing $710 million, should be completed by 2006. During this four-year construction phase, some 1,700 person years of employment will be generated. Once operational, the mill/concentrator will employ some 400 workers and the mining operation (at first open pit and later underground) will involve some 800 miners. Though Inco has reached impact and benefit agreements with the Labrador Inuit Association and Innu Nation, the company has not said how many workers might be selected from the ranks of the Labrador Inuit, Innu, and Métis (Vignette 5.4). While St John's had expected that the smelter would be located within the province, Inco plans to ship the first concentrates to its smelter in Sudbury.

Vignette 5.3 Voisey's Bay Timeline

Year	Activity
June 2002	Inco signed a $2.9 billion development agreement with the Newfoundland/Labrador government.
2002–3	Preparation work clearing land and building construction facilities at Voisey's Bay and Argentia begins.
2003	Construction commences on the open-pit mine at Voisey's Bay, the Inco Innovation Centre in St John's, and the hydro-metallurgical demonstration plant in Argentia.
2004	Inco's Innovation Centre completed.
2006	Voisey's Bay begins production and Argentia pilot plant receives first concentrates.
2007	Testing of hydromet process at Argentia demonstration plant starts.
2008	Inco decides whether to build a commercial hydromet processing facility or to build a matte processing facility that will produce finished nickel from concentrate smelted elsewhere.
2018	Inco decides whether to expand the open-pit mine at Voisey's Bay into an underground mine.
2036	With ore exhausted, Inco closes its Voisey's Bay mining operation.

SOURCE: Adapted from Hasselback (2002: FP7).

STRUCTURE OF THE NORTHERN ECONOMY

Each economy has a basic structure containing four industrial sectors. These four sectors involve primary, secondary, tertiary, and quaternary economic activities. Primary activities include agriculture, mining, quarrying, logging, fishing, hunting, and trapping. Secondary activities involve the processing or manufacturing of primary products. Tertiary activities are services provided by public agencies and private business.

TABLE 5.2 Economic Sectors

Economic Sector	Common Economic Activities
Primary	Agriculture, fishing, hunting, trapping, forestry, mining
Secondary	Manufacturing, processing, construction
Tertiary	Public and private services, accommodation, administration, commerce, education, food & beverage, health, government, real estate, retail trade, social services, transportation, wholesale trade
Quaternary	Corporate and state decision-making and related research

Quaternary activities are best described as policy decision-making activities taken by senior government officials and by the management sector of corporations. Table 5.2 indicates the principal economic activities associated with each sector.

By dividing the economy into four sectors, the structure of the northern economy can be appraised. Unfortunately, statistical information is not readily available either for the quaternary sector or for the North as a whole because its southern boundary does not correspond with those created by Statistics Canada. However, the structure of the northern economy can be appreciated by examining the three main economic sectors (primary, secondary, and tertiary). The very small quaternary sector, which comprises less than 1 per cent the labour force, becomes part of the tertiary sector. By using the economic data for the three territories, we can derive an approximation for the economic structure of the entire North.

On first glance, given the dominating role of the resource industry in terms of value of production, it would seem logical that primary activities would dominate. This is not the case. In Yukon, for example, tertiary or service industries accounted for 86 per cent of the employees in 1999, while the primary sector comprised only 6 per cent of the labour force (Table 5.3). The Northwest Territories and Nunavut show a similar pattern, though their primary sectors are larger, at 21 per cent and 18 per cent respectively.

Most are employed in the tertiary sector. Civil servants and public employees in education, health, and social services comprise 29.1 per cent, 38.1 per cent, and 39.4 per cent of the total workforce of the Northwest Territories, Yukon, and Nunavut. Territorial governments employ most public servants, though a significant number work for the federal government and still others are employed by settlement governments, band councils, and other Aboriginal organizations. In Native settlements, tertiary occupations often comprise over three-quarters of the workforce.

The prominence of the tertiary sector is characteristic of hinterlands in industrial countries. Table 5.4 shows the extent and categories of this sector for the three territories. Note, especially, the large percentage of the total workforce in each territory who work for government in one capacity or another. Such a structural pattern is due to the efforts of the industrial state to provide a similar level of public services in each region of the country. This public policy is a cornerstone of Canada's social contract. In the Canadian North, geography and jurisdictional complexity exacerbate the

TABLE 5.3 Sectoral Percentages of Employment in the Territories, 1999

Economic Sector	Yukon	Northwest Territories	Nunavut
Primary	6	21	18
Secondary	8	10	10
Tertiary	86	69	72
Quaternary	>1	>1	> 1
	100	100	100

SOURCE: Adapted from Government of Northwest Territories (2000).

need for a large public sector. Geography, with its combination of a vast space and few people, makes the delivery of public services expensive. In Nunavut, most residents live in very small communities where administration, education, and health services operate without the benefit of economies of scale found in larger centres. The principle of access to public services regardless of the size of the community is a necessary but expensive procedure. For this reason, the ratio of government employees per resident is much higher than in the rest of Canada. Another reason is that administrative bodies representing different levels of government and Aboriginal organizations often exist in the same community. While each has its own mandate, this jurisdictional arrangement provides a series of hierarchical layers of

TABLE 5.4 Tertiary Sector in the Territories, 1999 (% of total employment)

Type of Service	Northwest Territories	Nunavut	Yukon
Transportation	7.5	3.0	6.2
Communications	7.0	0.6	4.3
Wholesale Trade	1.7	0.8	4.0
Retail Trade	4.7	5.8	6.7
Finance	1.9	1.3	2.6
Real Estate	9.3	16.4	11.3
Business Services	3.2	1.7	2.7
Government	16.4	19.7	24.9
Education	8.2	10.9	6.9
Health/Social Services	4.5	8.8	6.3
Accommodation/Food & Beverage	2.4	2.0	7.2
Other Services	2.6	1.4	3.0
Totals	69.4	72.4	86.1

SOURCE: Adapted from Government of Northwest Territories (2000).

government for relatively few people living in urban centres. In Nunavut, for example, Nunavut Tunngavik Inc. (NTI) is the Inuit organization responsible for the implementation of the Nunavut Land Claims Agreement and that responsibility involves regular consultation with government officials according to the Clyde River Protocol that formally outlines the relationship between NTI and the government of Nunavut (Légaré, 2000). NTI's goal is to ensure that Inuit interests are expressed in such legislation. The Tungavik Federation of Nunavut (later renamed as Nunavut Tunngavik Inc.) took the lead in a harvester support program (Wenzel, 2000).

RESOURCE BASE

Resources provide the raison d'être for northern development. After all, the resource economy opens the North to settlement, encourages transportation development, provides employment and business opportunities, and generates revenue for government. The process of resource development requires an agreement with the owner of the land, i.e., the federal or provincial government. Such an agreement or lease allows a company to conduct its business on this Crown land. But Crown land is often subject to land claims by Aboriginal peoples (see the discussion of the *Calder* decision 1973 in Chapter 3). From an Aboriginal perspective, these companies have 'invaded' Aboriginal lands, creating a conflict between the two cultures. Aboriginal peoples and their organizations have responded to resource development on their traditional lands in different ways, but more and more, land claim agreements result in Aboriginal organizations participating in resource development (Slocombe, 2000). Impact and benefit agreements are now commonly arranged between the company wishing to develop a resource and the local Aboriginal group (Vignette 5.4) The impact of resource development on Aboriginal peoples and their cultures is discussed in Chapter 8.

Vignette 5.4 Inco's Agreements with Labrador Inuit Association and Innu Nation

On 11 June 2002, Inco and the province of Newfoundland and Labrador entered into a statement of principles on the development of the Voisey's Bay nickel-copper-cobalt deposits in Labrador. Inco has also finalized separate impact and benefit agreements (IBAs) with the Labrador Inuit Association and Innu Nation. The two IBAs are currently undergoing a ratification process within the memberships of these two Native groups. Both agreements provide employment and business opportunities for the Inuit and Innu as well as a share in the profits of the Voisey's Bay project. For example, the Inuit central government is expected to receive 3 per cent of provincial revenues from the Voisey's Bay project.

Since Canada's market is too small to absorb this production, the exploitation of the North's natural wealth depends on demand from the United States and other foreign industrial countries. This primary sector of the economy focuses on forestry, minerals, oil and gas, and hydroelectric power. A conservative estimate of the total value of all northern resource production in 2002 would exceed $35 billion, with 75 per cent of the production being exported to the US.

The resource base can be divided into two sectors—non-renewable and renewable resources. Non-renewable resources are mineral and petroleum deposits. While the exploitation of these resources does stimulate the economy, their long-term impact is limited because of their finite nature. Renewable resources include forestry, water, and wildlife. Except for trapping, wildlife is not a commercial resource, but it does supply Aboriginal families with meat and fish (see Chapters 8 and 9 for a discussion of the hunting economy and country food). Properly managed, the harvesting of renewable resources can lead to sustainable development and economic diversification. The harvesting of renewable resources does not, however, automatically lead to sustainable development. Long-term management of these resources is necessary to preserve them for future use. Unfortunately, overexploitation has occurred in the past and, in some instances, continues. R.A. Clapp (1999) blames the workings of the market economy, where the desire for short-term gains leads to a destructive cycle of resource exploitation that can also put species at risk. As Dianne Draper (2002: 423) writes, 'It is clear that without adequate and healthy habitat, wildlife (terrestrial and aquatic plants, animals, and microorganisms) cannot survive.' Resource development inevitably represents a trade-off between a healthy environment and economic growth. This trade-off presents a classic dilemma in the industrial world—how much resource development can take place before the environment is harmed or altered too much?

THE FOREST RESOURCE

The northern coniferous forest represents an enormous resource in the Provincial Norths. The boreal forest forms a continuous 'green' belt from Newfoundland to Yukon. Commercial logging takes place in the northern areas of British Columbia, Alberta, Saskatchewan, Manitoba, Ontario, and Quebec. In the territories, Yukon has a small logging industry. With few exceptions, access to forest lands requires a company to obtain a timber lease from a provincial or territorial government. With technological advances in logging, most employment is derived from processing the logs in mills. In recent years, First Nations have obtained timber leases on lands where they claim Aboriginal title and, by forming joint ventures with established forestry firms, have become involved in logging and lumber.

Canada's forest industry relies heavily on the American market. Since the Free Trade Agreement in 1989, Canada's forests have supported an annual harvest of about 200 million cubic metres. Approximately 70 per cent of this harvest is in softwood lumber while the remainder is used in the pulp and paper industry. The annual value of forest production and manufacturing was over $20 billion and most of this output was destined for the US. While Canada and the US have signed a Free Trade Agreement, the United States has restricted Canadian lumber imports several times in order to protect its domestic lumber industry. In 2002, the American government announced a 27 per cent tariff on Canadian lumber entering the United States. The consequences for northern forest companies have been devastating. Small firms, including joint ventures with First Nations and Métis, have had to curtail or ceases their operations because their profit margin is so narrow. One example is provided by a small-scale forestry operation and partnership established in 1999 by Zelensky Brothers Sawmill Company and the Lac La Ronge band. A joint venture company was formed to build a new sawmill near La Ronge with the goal of employing band members in its various operations—in the mill, in logging, and in trucking the logs to the mill (Ellis and Cousins, 1999). The lumber would be shipped to the Minneapolis market in the United States. Access to timber was a key to this partnership. The Saskatchewan government solved the problem by allocating wood from a timber lease earlier granted to the forest giant Weyerhaeuser. The wood is located in an area where band members have traditionally hunted and trapped. These plans were squashed in the spring of 2002 when the US announced the 27 per cent tariff on Canadian lumber.

Because timber is a renewable resource, the forest industry has the potential to sustain its economic activities, thereby providing stability to its mill towns and the regional economy. In granting timber leases to private companies, governments insist that these companies undertake reforestation activities. Sawmills and pulp plants are located along the southern edge of the Subarctic forest where access to highway and railway transportation allows their products to be shipped to American and other foreign markets. Trucks bring the timber from logging areas located much further north. Mills in many small towns along the edge of the boreal forest process the logs into lumber, plywood, and pulp. Meadow Lake in northwest Saskatchewan is such a town (Vignette 5.5).

Vignette 5.5 Meadow Lake, Forest Centre for Saskatchewan's Northwest

Like many small towns along the southern edge of the northern coniferous forest, Meadow Lake is involved in the forest industry. With excellent road and rail connections, Meadow Lake is well placed for the forest industry. Meadow Lake has two major forest plants and a strand board mill. The forest industry in Meadow Lake began with a sawmill. In 1988, NorSask Forest Products Inc. purchased this failing mill and obtained a timber lease from the provincial government. At that time, this sawmill, owned and operated by the Meadow Lake Tribal Council, used the softwood timber found in its 3.3-million-hectare Forest Management Licence Area. The mill employed more than 100 people in the production of lumber used in the construction industry.

In 1992, the Edmonton-based firm of Millar Western Forest Products wanted to expand its pulp operations. However, the province of Alberta had already committed its timber leases to other pulp firms. Millar Western approached NorSask Forest Products to see if its aspen trees were available. As it turned out, the sawmill used the white and black spruce trees for producing lumber and ignored the aspen trees, which were deemed unsuitable for lumber. Since aspen is ideal pulpwood, NorSask Forest Products was pleased to sell its aspen timber to Millar Western. The pulp mill that was established as a result of this new venture now employs 200 people and produces a high-quality, chlorine-free pulp known as bleached chemi-thermo-mechanical pulp (BCTMP). Meadow Lake Tribal Council and its two new partners, Techfor (an employee-owned company) and Millar Western Pulp (Meadow Lake) Ltd, now own NorSask Forest Ltd. Mistik Management is the logging company that produces the pulpwood for the Millar Western plant. Jointly owned by NorSask Forest Products and Millar Western Pulp (Meadow Lake) Inc., Mistik Management has established co-management boards in each Aboriginal community. These boards review logging plans, establish the size and location of the 'cut blocks', decide on methods of harvest, and design reforestation plans.

Resource innovations have affected the forest industry. For example, technological innovations have transformed forestry from a labour-intensive activity to a machine-driven one. Logging, for example, now sees complex machines operated by one worker cut and pile logs. Innovative research has broadened the species of trees suitable for commercial production. For instance, the pulp and paper industry took advantage of a scientific discovery in the early 1980s that the aspen is suitable for producing high-quality paper products. For years, commercial forest companies considered aspen a 'useless weed'. Suddenly, pulp and paper companies aggressively sought timber leases for the 'worthless' aspen stands in northern Alberta, Saskatchewan, and Manitoba (Vignette 5.5). Within 10 years, the three provincial governments had granted timber leases to virtually all of their aspen timber stands. Alberta was particularly anxious to develop its aspen stands. In the 1980s, the Alberta government, seeking to diversify its economy, leased vast northern hardwood forest land to five pulp and paper companies, including two Japanese firms, Daishowa Canada Company Ltd and Alberta-Pacific Forest Industries Inc. The Daishowa plant is located at Peace River and the Alberta-Pacific Forest plant at Athabasca. Daishowa's timber lease extends over lands claimed by the Lubicon Cree band, who have yet to achieve a land claim agreement with Ottawa.

MINING

Canada is the world's leading mineral exporter. Over the past five years, the annual value of mineral exports has been close to $25 billion and over half of this production comes from northern mines. The type of mining ranges from highly precious minerals, such as gold, silver, and platinum, to bulky, lower-valued minerals, such as uranium, lead, zinc, copper, and nickel.

Mineral production is divided into four sectors: metallics, non-metallics, mineral fuels (oil and gas), and structural materials. Metallic minerals and mineral fuels account for the bulk of the mining activity in the North. Very few structural materials (sand, gravel, clay, and lime) and non-metallic minerals (clay, potash, salt, sulphur, and gypsum) are produced in the North. These minerals are extremely bulky, low-valued products, which are very sensitive to transportation costs and therefore must be located near major markets. The former lead/zinc mine at Faro, Yukon, was troubled by the high cost of shipping its concentrates by rail and later by truck to its closest seaport, Snag, Yukon.

Mining operations are frequently the leading edge of northern development. High-value minerals, such as gold, often can sustain a remote location. Overall, mines are found in all areas of the Canadian North and, as a ubiquitous northern phenomenon, they provide a basic transportation infrastructure that can trigger other resource development. Gold is produced at the Lupin mine in Nunavut and at the Con mine near

Yellowknife, iron ore at the Labrador City and Wabush mines in Labrador, lead/zinc at the Nanisivik and Polaris mines in Nunavut, nickel at Thompson, Manitoba, and uranium at fly-in mines in northern Saskatchewan.

The mining industry is based on a non-renewable resource. This fact, plus the volatile nature of metal prices, makes long-term economic stability based on mining very problematic. Mines that last for more than 50 years, such as the Giant gold mine at Yellowknife, provide such stability, but most have a much shorter life span. Many mines remain operative for less than 10 years. But what is the alternative? The some-what ephemeral place of mining in northern development raises a round of interde-pendent issues. Public financial support for mining projects is a key issue for private companies. Without government assistance, mining firms will walk away from risky mining developments. On the other hand, why should the public support such enter-prises? This debate came into focus with the Izok Lake lead/zinc proposal. In the early 1990s, a German firm, Metall Mining Corp., wanted to develop the Izok Lake deposit in the Lac de Gras area of the Northwest Territories. Unlike the nearby Ekati diamond mine or the Lupin gold mine, the products of a lead/zinc mine require a highway to reach the Arctic Ocean before ships can take it to market. The two existing lead/zinc mines in Nunavut are located by the sea and therefore avoid the high cost of land transportation for their bulky, low-value ore. Metall Mining Corp. requested that the governments of the Northwest Territories and Canada build a highway from the pro-posed Izok mine to the Arctic Ocean near Coppermine. As discussed earlier, Ottawa turned down the request and Metall abandoned its efforts.

Clearly, transportation is a key factor in determining the commercial viability of remote mines. Low-grade ore that contains a small percentage of valuable minerals (usually less than 5 per cent) is far too costly to ship. For that reason, milling of the ore into a more concentrated product takes place at the mine site. The concentrate is then shipped south for further refining or, in the case of gold and silver, directly to the pur-chaser. In all cases, the economic purpose is to reduce transportation costs by shipping a concentrate of the mineral. In the case of uranium ore, it is mixed with large quan-tities of water, crushed, and ground into fine particles. The resulting slurry is placed in a settling tank, producing two products—a low radioactive waste product and a highly radioactive product known as yellowcake. The waste is mixed with lime and placed in a tailing pond while the commercial product is dried and bagged for export. Further refining of the uranium concentrate takes place at Canada's only uranium refinery at Blind River, Ontario, or at plants in the United States. For nickel, copper, gold, and silver, the local processing is more involved. Nickel ore, for example, is sent to a concentrator where it is crushed and the sulphide minerals concentrated by flota-tion. The concentrate is smelted to produce nickel matte, which is sent to a refinery where cathodes, anodes, pellets, and other products are made.

In the 1990s, the most exciting mining story unfolded in the Northwest Territories —the discovery of diamonds (Vignette 5.6). Until recently, geologists did not believe that the Canadian Shield contained diamonds. In 1991, two prospectors, Charles Fipke and Stewart Blusson, discovered diamonds near Lac de Gras in the Northwest Territories. Other diamond deposits were found and two of them (Diavik and Snap Lake) have commercial promise. Each deposit has an estimated 120-year supply of

Vignette 5.6 Diamonds in the Northwest Territories

The Northwest Territories is the diamond centre for North America. By 2005, the three major mines, Ekati, Diavik, and Snap Lake, will account for 12 per cent of the world's diamond production. Already, a small proportion of Ekati diamonds are sorted and cut in Yellowknife. Diamonds have been mined in the Northwest Territories only recently. The following timeline outlines the development of diamond mining in the Northwest Territories.

Date	Event
1991	Charles Fipke and Stewart Blusson discover diamonds near Lac de Gras, Northwest Territories, sparking the largest staking rush in Canadian history.
1993	BHP opens an exploration camp just north of Lac de Gras, Northwest Territories. BHP eventually proves the commercial viability of the Ekati mine.
1996	Diavik Diamond Mines continues its exploration work; the Snap Lake diamond deposit is discovered.
1998	BHP Ekati diamond mine opens (Panda open-pit mine); BHP and the NWT government sign an agreement whereby diamond sorting and valuation of some Ekati diamonds will take place in Yellowknife.
1999	Sirius Diamonds Ltd opens a cutting and polishing facility in Yellowknife.
2000	Ottawa approves the Diavik proposal and construction of the Diavik mine begins; De Beers gains control of the Snap Lake deposit; Deton'Cho Diamonds Inc. and Arsianian Cutting Works NWT Ltd open cutting and polishing facilities in Yellowknife.
2001	BHP opens a second open-pit mine called Misery.
2003	Diavik mine plans to start production.
2005	Snap Lake mine is expected to begin production.

SOURCE: NWT Diamonds Timeline, available at: <http://www.gov.nt.ca/RWED/diamond/timeline.htm>.

diamonds. As a result, diamond mining has quickly become the backbone of the economy of the Northwest Territories. By value of production, number of employees, and spinoff effects, BHP Billiton Diamonds, a subsidiary of Broken Hill Proprietary Company Inc., is the leading mining company in the North. Its rich Ekati diamond mine is located abut 300 km northeast of Yellowknife. Ekati mine is linked to Yellowknife by a winter road that services both Ekati and the nearby Lupin gold mine. In 1998, the Ekati diamond mine accounted for $500 million worth of diamonds. By 2001, its production was valued at $847 million. A second mine, Diavik, located near the Ekati mine, is scheduled to begin production in 2003. Work on a third diamond deposit, at Snap Lake, is underway, and if all goes well this will become a commercial venture in 2005. In addition to the mining operation, Yellowknife has gained a new industry—diamond cutting and polishing. While most raw diamonds are exported to the Netherlands for sorting and cutting, a small portion is allocated to the new diamond sorting and cutting industry in Yellowknife.

TABLE 5.5 Mineral Production by Value, 2001 (millions of dollars)

Territory	Gold	Lead	Silver	Zinc	Diamonds	Sand/ Gravel	Total
Yukon	40	0	–	0	0	3	43
NWT	54	0	–	0	847	5	906
Nunavut	59	24	3	233	0	–	319
Totals	153	24	3	233	847	8	1,268

SOURCE: Natural Resources Canada, *Preliminary Estimates of the Mineral Production of Canada, by Provinces, 2001* (Ottawa, 2002), Table 1.

Yellowknife now has an important 'value-added' industry and rightly describes itself as the 'Diamond Capital of North America'.

The mineral industry is particularly important in the Territorial North. In 2001, the value of the territories' mineral production was nearly $1.3 billion, with the Northwest Territories, because of its diamond mining, producing over 71 per cent of this total (Table 5.5). Traditionally, mining has been the largest private-sector employer in the territories. Over the years, mining employment has remained relatively stable at about 11 per cent of the labour force (about five times the Canadian average) while accounting for up to 25 per cent of wages and salaries. In addition, mining creates a significant number of indirect jobs in transportation, electricity, construction, government, and other service sectors. In the Arctic, mineral exploration, mining, and associated service activities are the only practical alternative to employment in the public sector. This heavy dependence on the mining industry means that Nunavut's economy is vulnerable to mine closures. The hope, of course, is that new mining ventures will replace those that have closed. The Northwest Territories recently had this experience in the late 1990s when the Giant gold mine closed and the Ekati diamond mine opened. Yukon did not. When the Faro lead/zinc mine closed in 1998 there were no new mining ventures to take up the slack. Such vulnerability reveals a serious flaw in an economy based on non-renewable resources.

OIL AND GAS

The North contains most of Canada's petroleum reserves. These reserves are found in some 40 sedimentary basins that underlie about half of the land area of Canada and its continental shelves. Discoveries of oil and natural gas have been concentrated to a few basins, particularly the Western Canadian Sedimentary Basin. This basin, extending from the Beaufort Sea to the 49th parallel, is the most important petroleum-producing sedimentary basin in Canada. Oil and natural gas deposits have been found further north, but commercial production is limited to the Provincial Norths of British Columbia and Alberta and the adjacent areas of Yukon and the Northwest Territories. Canada's greatest potential for future sources of oil and gas, however, is found in the Arctic Ocean, particularly in the Beaufort Sea and the Sverdrup Basin.[5] These deposits,

TABLE 5.6 Energy Production by Value, 2001 (millions of dollars)

Territory	Natural Gas	Oil	Totals
Yukon	55	0	55
NWT	58	380	438
Nunavut	0	0	0
Totals	113	380	493

SOURCE: Natural Resources Canada, *Preliminary Estimates of the Mineral Production of Canada, by Provinces, 2001* (Ottawa, 2002), Table 1.

including the heavy oil sands of Alberta, make up over one-half of Canada's hydrocarbon reserves but form less than 20 per cent of Canada's production.

Most production takes places in northern Alberta and British Columbia. The Norman Wells oil field represents the only oil-producing site north of the 60th parallel. While production began at Norman Wells in 1920, exports to southern Canada and the United States did not begin until the Norman Wells Project was completed. In 1979, Esso Resources and Interprovincial Pipeline applied to the government of Canada for approval to expand the Norman Wells oil field and to construct a small-diameter pipeline to transmit oil to Alberta and beyond. This proposal was approved in 1980 and construction work began in 1982. In 2001, the value of its production was nearly $400 million (Table 5.6).

Recent discoveries of 'elephant-size' deposits of natural gas in the Provincial Norths of British Columbia and Alberta and the adjacent Fort Liard area of the Northwest Territories have demonstrated the vastness of these reserves. Size of deposits, coupled with their relative closeness to the national pipeline system, has allowed these natural gas reserves to penetrate the American market at a competitive price. Since the late 1990s, the price of natural gas in the United States has increased significantly, triggering more exploration and production in frontier areas. By 1999, the construction of the Alliance Pipeline from northern Alberta to the energy-starved Chicago market was completed, allowing the newly discovered gas reserves to reach the North American marketplace. Since then, more natural gas has been found. The most recent natural gas discovery, the Ladyfern field, is in the Fort Nelson area of British Columbia. As the largest natural gas discovery in the region, the Ladyfern deposit is similar to the enormous Sable Island gas deposit off the coast of Nova Scotia. Both contain around a trillion cubic feet of natural gas, but unlike Sable Island, the Ladyfern deposit is relatively inexpensive to develop. In July 2002, another major natural gas field (Monkman field) was discovered in the foothills of northeastern British Columbia.

By the beginning of the twenty-first century, the natural gas pipeline system had reached the southernmost areas of Yukon and the Northwest Territories. The next step, expected by the end of the first decade of the twenty-first century, will be a natural gas pipeline from the Mackenzie Delta area to US markets and possibly from Prudhoe Bay, Alaska. Much later, the development of natural gas deposits in the Beaufort Sea and

Sverdrup Basin should take place.[6] Such developments are predicated on higher natural gas prices. Recently, prices have reached a level that would sustain the high cost of building a pipeline from the known natural gas reserves in the Mackenzie Delta to markets in the United States. Still, the risk is high because of the cost of building such a pipeline, the possibility of delays due to unresolved land claims, and the possibility of a drop in natural gas prices. Natural gas prices have proven to be volatile. For example, gas prices did not continue to rise after the 1970s and in fact declined in the 1980s. The Mackenzie Valley Gas Pipeline Project, if approved in the mid-1970s, might have proven too expensive a project because its success was predicated on rising gas prices.

By the end of the twentieth century, natural gas prices again rose, encouraging petroleum companies to reconsider building natural gas pipelines from the Arctic to southern markets. One plan calls for a pipeline from the huge natural gas deposits at Prudhoe Bay to markets in the US (Vignette 5.7). This pipeline, with an estimated cost of $20 billion, would follow the Alaska Highway. The second plan focuses on the Mackenzie Delta gas reserves. In this case, the pipeline would follow the Mackenzie River Valley to US markets. Its construction cost is estimated at $4 billion. Oil companies—Imperial Oil Ltd, Gulf Canada Resources Ltd, Shell Canada Ltd, and Exxon Mobil Corp.—hold large natural gas reserves in the Mackenzie Delta. By 2001, these companies had prepared plans for developing the oil gas fields in the Mackenzie Delta and then shipping this gas by pipeline to southern markets. The next step is for the companies to submit a proposal to Ottawa for review and approval.

In the 1970s, a similar proposal ran into strong opposition from the Dene living in the Mackenzie Valley, in part because the Dene insisted that their land claims be settled before the construction of the Mackenzie Valley Pipeline Project could begin. Also, the Dene had concerns about the impact of this construction project on their lands and people. More specifically, they feared that wildlife would become less plentiful, causing their hunting/trapping lifestyle to collapse. Other concerns were identified, such as the Dene fear that their communities would not gain a fair share of the resulting jobs and business opportunities, and that the expected increase in non-Aboriginal population would generate negative social impacts on Dene culture and the social well-being of Dene people. Now these concerns are no longer seen as a major obstacle by most Dene. One reason is that several land claim agreements have been concluded and another is that the Dene workforce and business community are more comfortable and better prepared to take advantage of such a mega-construction project. In fact, some Dene groups, plus the Inuvialuit, have joined together to form the Aboriginal Pipeline Group. Their goal is to share in the ownership of the proposed pipeline. In November 2002, the Aboriginal Pipeline Group requested a $70 million loan guarantee from the federal government, but the initial reaction from Ottawa has not been favourable. Nellie Cournoyea, chairwoman and chief executive officer of the Inuvialuit Regional Corporation, urged the Prime Minister to support their proposal, arguing that:

> Our aboriginal pipeline group is working with the producer groups, with all the aboriginal people up and around the Mackenzie Valley and trying to put a proposal together that takes in employment opportunity, business opportunities, training and an equity share [for Aboriginal people] in the pipeline. (Cattaneo, 2000: C5).

Still, this pipeline proposal could stumble over the issue of the Deh Cho's unsettled land claim. Since the proposed pipeline would have to cross lands claimed by the Deh Cho, this Dene band may use the pipeline issue in their land claim negotiations (Anderson, 2002). Unlike the other land claim agreements, the Deh Cho have rejected the land selection process employed in the comprehensive land claim agreements. Instead, they are asking for legal, constitutional, and political control over an entire region that would form a Deh Cho homeland. Until the Deh Cho reach an agreement with Ottawa they are unlikely to support the pipeline project. Under this scenario, the federal government would push the pipeline forward by declaring its construction in the national interest. However, such a decision would infuriate the Deh Cho and possibly lead to other forms of protest against the construction of the pipeline (for more on the 'mega' nature of these proposed Arctic pipelines, see the next chapter).

Vignette 5.7 The Rival Arctic Pipeline Proposal

The growing demand for natural gas has triggered a strong interest in Arctic gas. By 2015, demand for natural gas is projected to soar to 31.3 trillion cubic feet a year in North America from current production of 24 trillion cubic feet, possibly pushing prices well over current rates. Over the next 10 years, existing production will diminish as natural gas reserves are exhausted. By then, one of the two proposed Arctic pipelines should be completed. Estimates of North American prices for natural gas favour the construction of Arctic pipelines. Even so, experts have declared that, prior to 2015, North American demand can only absorb gas from one of the major Arctic gas deposits. Otherwise, the gas market would be saturated and the price would drop, thus threatening to make the pipelines uneconomical.

The race to build the first Arctic pipeline to North American markets pits the North Slope of Alaska (which includes Prudhoe Bay) against the Mackenzie Delta. However, unless the US government subsidizes the construction of the much more expensive Alaskan pipeline (estimated at some $20 billion compared to $4 billion for the all-Canadian pipeline), the Mackenzie Delta gas will reach American markets first. The stakes are high, causing much lobbying in Washington. Alaska has two strong points: (1) Alaska's reserves are much larger than those in the Mackenzie Delta—(Alaska holds known reserves of 35 trillion cubic feet and an estimate of an additional 100 trillion cubic feet compared to about nine trillion cubic feet of known reserves at Mackenzie Delta, plus estimated reserves similar in size to those in Alaska; and (2) American security concerns call for the development of American petroleum deposits. Still, the Mackenzie Delta has two main advantages: (1) a much lower construction cost because of a shorter distance to market and because the diameter of its pipe is much smaller (and therefore less costly) than that proposed for the Alaskan pipeline; and (2) a much shorter construction time (six years) compared to the proposed Alaskan pipeline (10–12 years).

SOURCES: Toulin (2001: A1); Howes (2002: FP9).

WATER POWER

The rivers and lakes of the Canadian North contain enormous potential for hydroelectric power development. Crown corporations have undertaken massive hydroelectric projects in three provinces (Quebec, Manitoba, and British Columbia). In all cases, the power is shipped south to Canadian consumers with the surplus sold to American utilities. At first, these huge projects were seen as a solution to both energy shortages and air pollution problems. As it turned out, hydroelectric development had a more serious impact on the environment and the traditional economy of Aboriginal peoples living in the areas than originally contemplated (see Chapters 7 and 8 for a fuller discussion of environmental/social costs).

Development of remote hydro resources depends on transportation in the form of high-voltage power lines. Without access to large markets, large-scale hydroelectric projects would not be viable. For many years, this potential power was unused due to the high cost of transporting electrical energy to major industrial areas. Increased demand and technological advances in electric power transmission have made remote hydroelectric projects commercially attractive. Over the last hundred years, the cost of transmitting electrical energy over long distances has decreased and the technology to build transmission lines has advanced. In 1903, for example, the transmission of electrical power some 140 km from Shawinigan Falls to Montreal was considered an engineering feat. Some 80 years later, Hydro-Québec's James Bay high-voltage transmission lines to southern Quebec are almost 10 times longer.

Coupled with the ability to transmit energy long distances, the demand and price of electrical energy in southern Canada and the United States increased sharply. After 1972, the Organization of Petroleum Exporting Countries (OPEC) began to limit production of crude oil. As the world's chief producers, OPEC controlled world prices. As prices increased, utilities in energy-deficient New England were seeking alternative energy sources, especially non-polluting energy. One alternative was electricity from Quebec's James Bay hydroelectric project.

Most hydroelectric power is generated in two geomorphic areas, the Cordillera and the Canadian Shield, which have ideal conditions for generating electricity: a large volume of water and steep drops in elevation. Potential hydroelectric sites still exist in northern British Columbia, Quebec, Manitoba, Newfoundland and Labrador, and Saskatchewan. Ontario, which has the greatest need for more energy, lacks similar sites in its Canadian Shield because of relatively low elevations.

Major hydroelectric projects require large water reservoirs. To smooth out fluctuations in river flows, storage dams and water diversions supplement the water supply to the reservoirs. Ensuring a reliable flow of water throughout the year maximizes the installed generating capacity of the hydroelectric power plant. Even with a complex system of reservoirs, storage dams, and diversions, a long period of below-average precipitation can reduce river flow and hence electrical power generation. In the 1980s, the Subarctic experienced below-average precipitation and hydroelectric power production at installations in northern Manitoba and Quebec was adversely affected. The following decade saw a return to average precipitation and the restoration of water levels.

The James Bay Project is the largest hydroelectric project in the world. Announced in 1971 by Quebec Premier Robert Bourassa, the James Bay Project is a key component in Quebec's economic development strategy of providing low-cost power to Quebec industry. The James Bay Project calls for the harnessing of the rivers in Quebec flowing into James Bay. These rivers originate in the uplands of the Canadian Shield in the interior of northern Quebec. The James Bay Project consists of three phases. The first phase, known as La Grande Project, began in 1972 and was completed 10 years later at a cost $15 billion. It involved massive diversions of water from three rivers (the Eastmain, Opinaca, and Caniapiscau rivers) to five reservoirs on La Grande Rivière. Eight dams, three powerhouses, and nearly 200 dikes were constructed while La Grande-2 powerhouse (LG-2), the world's largest underground power facility, was completed in 1982. Two years later, La Grande-3 powerhouse (LG-3) and La Grande-4 powerhouse (LG-4) were finished and began to produce power.

The first phase, La Grande, overshadowed other hydro developments in the North for two reasons. First of all, the sheer scale of the project is staggering. The amount of power produced is more than 10,000 megawatts annually, making it the largest hydroelectric project in North America. Second, the project resulted in the first modern land settlement (the James Bay and Northern Quebec Agreement) with the Quebec Cree and Quebec Inuit. This agreement recognized that the Cree and Inuit had Aboriginal title to these lands and therefore warranted compensation for potential damage to their traditional hunting and fishing territory.

In 1985, the Quebec government announced the second phase of the James Bay Project, the Great Whale River Project. Located just north of La Grande Project, this second phase would again involve a massive rearrangement of the natural environment with river diversions, storage dams, powerhouses, and numerous dikes. Its construction would be financed from advanced sale of its power to New England utility companies. The Grand Council of the Cree and environmental organizations, including the Sierra Club, vigorously opposed the Great Whale River Project. By mounting an impressive publicity campaign to attract American support, they hoped to convince American utilities not to purchase electricity from the proposed second phase of the James Bay Project. Perhaps the most spectacular media event occurred in the summer of 1990 when the Cree paddled canoes down the Hudson River to New York City. Economic factors also affected the project. At that time, a surplus of natural gas in North America existed, making natural gas prices lower than most other forms of energy. The extension of a gas pipeline from Canada to the New England area resulted in more secure natural gas supplies at a lower price and, in turn, triggered the construction of more gas-burning thermal-electrical plants in New England. New England electrical utilities, concerned about pollution, shifted from coal-burning thermal-generating plants to natural gas ones. The cost of operating the new gas-driven plants was well below the cost of the old coal-burning plants. As energy prices in New England declined, American utilities sought to negotiate a lower long-term price for electricity from Quebec. In 1994, the government of Quebec announced that the Great Whale River Project would not proceed until the demand (and price) for electricity in New England improved. By the end of the 1990s, natural gas prices had increased substantially, making hydro-electricity from James Bay more attractive to New England customers.

The James Bay Project took on a new life in 2001 when the Quebec government announced a 50-year agreement with the Cree of northern Quebec (Gouvernement du Québec, 2001), and in the following year a similar agreement was reached with the Quebec Inuit (George, 2002). The essence of the agreement with the Cree is that they would support resource development in James Bay, including the construction of the Nottaway Hydroelectric Project. In exchange, the Cree would receive $3.4 billion over 50 years, beginning with $23 million in 2002–3, $46 million in 2003–4, and $70 million in 2004–5. In the years to come, the annual payment is indexed to a formula that reflects the value of production in the fields of forestry, mines, and hydroelectric power. The Cree were also promised jobs in future developments in forestry, mining, and construction. In the original James Bay plan, the Nottaway Basin was designed as the third phase of the James Bay Project. This agreement with the Cree was ratified on 7 February 2002 following a plebiscite among the Cree in which 70 per cent supported the agreement. Given the past acrimony between the two parties, this agreement marks the beginning of a new era in relations between the government of Quebec and the Grand Council of the Cree and signals new opportunities for more hydroelectric developments in northern Quebec.

RESOURCE DEVELOPMENT IN THE TWENTY-FIRST CENTURY

While resource development persists as the backbone of the northern economy, economic leakage siphons most spinoff benefits to firms in southern Canada and even to foreign countries. Economic leakage slows regional economic growth and, in extreme cases, blocks economic diversification. Three issues that affect and interact to drive northern resource development are crucial to the future course of the northern economy:

- Is sustainable development possible?
- Can megaprojects avoid extensive damage to the environment?
- Do Aboriginal groups have a place in resource development?

Governments, of course, play a role in influencing and hopefully steering these issues towards prescribed goals and positive resolution. The issues are discussed in the following three chapters, beginning with megaprojects. Large-scale resource projects in the North are controversial. Some have heralded such massive development as the triggering device for a strong northern economy, while others see it as the exploitation of northern resources by outside interests. Megaprojects are expensive and require large capital investments and secure markets. Since only large international companies (and governments) have the necessary resources to undertake such projects, these firms are major players in the northern economy. Given the scope of their projects, these corporations are often able to obtain special concessions from the federal or provincial governments, such as improved transportation links to the resource, tax concessions, or loan guarantees. In this way, large companies are able to reduce the risk and enhance the profitability of large-scale projects. Should the public fund such enterprises? For Canada, the national interest is served so the answer is yes; but for the North, where the costs of such development are borne, a positive answer is more problematic. And yet, what is the alternative? The complex subject of large-scale projects is discussed in the next chapter, while the role of governments, the search for sustainable development, and the issue of economic diversification are left for the concluding chapters.

NOTES

1. After World War II, America's seemingly insatiable demand for energy and raw materials extended its reach to the Canadian North, especially the Subarctic. The first megaproject, the development of the iron deposits in northern Quebec and Labrador, began in 1947. Public financial support for large-scale energy and mineral projects accelerated the pace of development. The objectives of both federal and provincial governments were to expand and diversify national, provincial, and territorial economies. The North soon became a critical resource hinterland serving Canada, the United States, and other industrialized nations. The new economic landscape consists of mines, oil wells, pulp mills, and hydroelectric power stations, all connected to southern markets by a modern transportation network. The construction of these industrial projects and the building of a complementary infrastructure consisting of towns, roads, and a wide range of public facilities generated a demand for goods and equipment produced in southern factories, created job opportunities in both northern and southern Canada, and increased the volume of Canadian exports, thereby improving Canada's balance of trade. Both federal and provincial levels of government (but to a much lesser degree territorial governments) have benefited from increased tax revenues generated by the resource industries and the associated service industries, as well as from their employees' personal income taxes. At that time, the booming resource economy drew many southern workers and their families into the North.
2. Iron ore deposits in northern Quebec and Labrador were developed in response to a growing demand from the United States. The rich Mesabi Iron Range in Minnesota was near exhaustion, and United States iron and steel plants began to look abroad for alternative sources. The previously worthless ore bodies of the Labrador Trough, known for over a half-century, suddenly became a valued resource. By 1947, plans were laid for large-scale open-pit mining around Knob Lake in northern Quebec. Several mining towns were built, including Gagnon, Schefferville, Labrador City, and Wabush. In 1954, Schefferville was connected by a 571-kilometre railway to the port of Sept-Îles on the north shore of the St Lawrence River. Iron concentrate was shipped by rail to Sept-Îles and then by iron ore ships from Sept-Îles to the iron and steel plants in the US Midwest. Six large American iron and steel companies supplied the capital for this enormous project. These same companies now had a reliable supply of iron ore for their steel plants in Ohio and Pennsylvania. With a downturn in the demand for iron ore in the US, coupled with foreign steel displacing American steel, US production levels of the 1970s fell by half by 1983 and several mines were closed. With the demise of US steel and the new landscape known as the 'Rust Belt', the days of rapid growth were over, resulting in an equally depressing northern mining landscape with its abandoned operations.
3. Under the terms of Confederation, the federal government had no responsibility for highway construction in the provinces. Ottawa did become involved in railway-building in order to unite the country. After World War I, political pressure from western farmers caused Ottawa to build the Hudson Bay Railway to Churchill, Manitoba. Completed in 1929, it was designed to provide an alternative route to European markets for western grain. Prairie farmers believed that the shorter Hudson Bay rail route to their major European customers would reduce their total shipping costs. Unfortunately, the new railway never became an important export route for grain because of the high cost of marine insurance in the ice-ridden waters

of Hudson Strait and Hudson Bay. Instead, the Hudson Bay Railway was instrumental in unlocking the mineral, forest, hydro, and fishing resources of northern Manitoba. Unlike the original dream of the Prairie farmers, however, the Hudson Bay Railway did not serve to export grain through the port of Churchill but rather to bring resource products south into the markets of southern Canada and the United States.

By the late 1950s, Ottawa began to play a role in northern transportation, thus abandoning its laissez-faire policy. The reason was straightforward: the federal government saw northern development as a way to strengthen the nation and to ensure Canadian sovereignty. As well, Ottawa hoped resource development would provide jobs to Aboriginal northerners who were by then living in settlements. In 1958, the newly elected Conservative government sought to increase the rate of resource development in the North by using public funds to extend the southern transportation system into the North. In its Roads to Resources program, the federal government agreed to fund half the cost for building roads in northern areas of the provinces, leaving the provinces responsible for the remainder. A similar program was available in the territories, but in this case the federal government covered all the costs. Under these two programs, roads were built to help private companies reach world markets. One example was the road built to connect the asbestos mine at Cassiar (now closed) in northern British Columbia with the port of Stewart. Other highways were constructed to provide major northern centres with a land connection to southern Canada. For example, the Mackenzie Highway from Edmonton to Hay River was extended to Yellowknife. In all, from 1959 to 1970, over 6,000 kilometres of new roads were built under this program at a cost of $145 million (Gilchrist, 1988: 1877).

4. In the early 1970s, the Trudeau government intervened in the market economy by creating the Foreign Investment Review Act (1974) and established the Crown corporation, Petro-Canada. These political actions were designed to break the dominance of the multinational oil and gas companies in Canada. Petro-Canada, like the foreign-owned multinational companies, has the financial strength, technology, and long-term perspective to undertake large, expensive projects like oil sands development and Arctic exploration. In 1980, the government announced the National Energy Program, which increased the federal taxation of petroleum revenues and took away the tax write-offs that had encouraged exploratory drilling in the 1970s. In place of these tax write-offs, the government created the Petroleum Incentive Program (PIP), which paid grants to Canadian-owned firms undertaking oil exploration. These grants were based on the level of Canadian ownership and the location of the wells. The largest grants were awarded to companies with at least 75 per cent Canadian ownership, drilling for petroleum in frontier areas like the Beaufort Sea and the Sverdrup Basin.

5. In 1972, TransCanada PipeLines, Panarctic Oils Ltd, Ontario Energy Corporation, Petro-Canada, Pacific Lighting Gas Development Company, and Tenneco Oil of Canada formed the company Polar Gas. Their first proposal, in 1977, called for the construction of a pipeline along the Hudson Bay coast. Their 1984 proposal called for the construction of a natural gas pipeline from the Drake Point field located in the northern part of Melville Island to service the Ontario, Quebec, and neighbouring US markets. This 3,763-kilometre pipeline would interconnect with the TransCanada PipeLines system just east of Lake Nipigon in northern Ontario. The proposal allowed for a spur line to connect to the Beaufort Sea natural gas fields. The main pipeline route would begin on Melville Island, cross to Victoria Island, and reach the mainland near Coppermine (now Kugluktuk). It would then travel in a southeasterly direction into northern Saskatchewan east of Lake Athabasca and cross the Subarctic of Manitoba and Ontario. The construction of this large-diameter pipe would present two major engineering challenges. The first would be to construct a gas pipeline in the zone of continuous permafrost. Because the heat generated by the flowing gas would destabilize the

permafrost and therefore threaten the integrity of the pipe, there are two possible solutions. One would be to build an elevated pipeline, and the other would be to chill the natural gas below the freezing point. The second challenge would be to lay pipe on the bottom of the Arctic Ocean. The longest underwater stretch would be the crossing from Melville Island to Victoria Island. The length of this crossing beneath the ice-covered waters of Viscount Melville Sound would be about 150 kilometres. The successful completion of this pipeline would be a major engineering feat. In 1981, the Arctic Pilot Project proposed an alternative way of transporting natural gas from the Arctic islands to southern markets. Sponsored by Petro-Canada, Dome, Nova, and Melville Shipping, the Arctic Pilot Project advocated the use of ice-breaking liquefied natural gas tankers (LNG). This plan called for two LNG tankers to collect gas from Melville Island and deliver it to a re-gasification plant either near Quebec City or at Melford Point on the Strait of Canso in Nova Scotia. This gas would supply the Quebec and Atlantic Canada markets. The reinforced LNG tankers would follow the Parry Sound route by entering through Lancaster Sound, crossing Barrow Strait and Viscount Melville Sound to Melville Island. While this sea route may be ice-free during the short summer period, it would be covered by thick ice during the long winter period and the tankers might well encounter pack ice in Parry Sound and icebergs in Baffin Bay.

6. More than 200 wells have already been drilled in the Mackenzie Delta-Beaufort Sea region. Approximately one-third of these wells were drilled from ships or floating platforms. By the early 1980s, there were nearly 200 billion cubic metres of recoverable natural gas and around 120 million cubic metres of recoverable crude oil (Nassichuk, 1987: 279). The potential reserves are thought to exceed the proven reserves by perhaps as much as 20 times (Procter, Taylor, and Wade, 1984). In 1984, the discovery of the Amauligak 'elephant' field gave some indication of the potential size of the Beaufort Sea hydrocarbon deposit. This single discovery doubled the proven oil reserves of the Beaufort Sea deposit. Two years after the discovery of the Amauligak field, a token shipment was sent by tanker to Japan. The significance of this shipment was twofold: that oil could be produced commercially from the Beaufort Sea deposit, and that an Arctic tanker route could be used to ship its oil to world markets.

REFERENCES AND SELECTED READINGS

Anderson, Mark. 2002. 'Brinkmanship and Betrayal', *National Post Business* (Jan.): 40–52.

Bone, Robert M. 1998. 'Resource Towns', *Cahiers de Géographie du Québec* 42, 116: 249–59.

Cattaneo, Claudia. 2000. 'Inuvialuit press PM for pipeline support', *National Post,* 24 Nov., C5.

Christensen, Bev. 1995. *Too Good To Be True: Alcan's Kemano Completion Project.* Vancouver: Talonbooks.

Clapp, R.A. 1999. 'The Resource Cycle in Forest and Fishing', *The Canadian Geographer* 42, 2: 129–44.

Collum, Peter. 2002. 'Canada's Energy Eldorado', *Edmonton Journal* (Special Fort McMurray Economic Report), 10 May, EJ1.

Draper, Dianne. 2002. *Our Environment: A Canadian Perspective,* 2nd edn. Scarborough, Ont.: Nelson.

Duerden, Frank. 1992. 'A Critical Look at Sustainable Development in the Canadian North', *Arctic* 45, 3: 219–25.

Ellis, Bob, and Brian Cousins. 1999. 'New Forestry Partnership in La Ronge', news release from Economic and Cooperative Development, 10 May 1999. Available at: <http://www.gov.sk.ca/newsrel/1999/05/10-413.html>.

Gilchrist, C.W. 1988. 'Roads and Highways', *The Canadian Encyclopedia,* 2nd edn. Edmonton: Hurtig, 1876–7.

Gouvernement du Québec. 2001. 'Le Premier Ministre Landry et Le Grand Chef Moses Signent une Entente Historique', Communiqué de presse, 23 Oct.

Froschauer, Karl. 1999. *White Gold: Hydroelectric Power in Canada.* Vancouver: University of British Columbia Press.

George, Jane. 2002. 'Quebec, Inuit Reach $900M Hydro Deal', *National Post,* 5 Apr., A4.

Government of Northwest Territories. 2000. *Gross Domestic Product, Northwest Territories, 1999,* Table 5. Available at: <http://www.stats.gov.nt.ca/Statinfo/Economic/GDP/1999_NWTGDP.html>. Accessed 7 Aug. 2001.

———. 2001. *Statistical Quarterly* 23, 4: 44.

Hamilton, Frank. 1996. *The NorthSask Forest Story.* Edmonton: University of Alberta Press.

Hasselback, Drew. 2002. 'Voisey's Bay deal is done, next comes big writedown', *National Post,* 12 June, FP7.

Hayter, Roger, and Trevor J. Barnes. 2001. 'Canada's Resource Economy', *The Canadian Geographer* 45, 1: 36–41.

Howes, Carol. 2002. 'Pumping up Pipelines', *National Post,* 24 Jan., FP9.

Innis, Harold A. 1930. *The Fur Trade in Canada.* Toronto: University of Toronto Press.

Johnston, Margaret, ed. 1994. *Geographic Perspectives on the Provincial Norths.* Toronto: Lakehead University and Copp Clark Longman.

Légaré, André. 2000. 'La Nunavut Tunngavik Inc.: Un examen de ses activités et de sa structure administrative', *Études/Inuit/Studies* 24, 1: 197–224.

Nassichuk, W.W. 1987. 'Forty Years of Northern Non-Renewable Natural Resource Development', *Arctic* 40, 4: 274–84.

Neil, Cecily, Markku Tykklaine, and John Bradbury. 1992. *Coping with Closure: An International Comparison of Mine Town Experiences.* London: Routledge.

Nuttall, Mark, and Terry V. Callaghan, eds. 2000. *The Arctic: Environment, People, Policy.* Singapore: Harwood Academic Publishers.

Procter, R.M., G.C. Taylor, and J.A. Wade. 1984. *Oil and Natural Gas Resources of Canada, 1983.* Geological Survey of Canada Papers 83–31. Ottawa: Minister of Supply and Services.

Rae, K.J. 1968. *The Political Economy of the Canadian North: An Interpretation of the Course of Development in the Northern Territories of Canada to the Early 1960s.* Toronto: University of Toronto Press.

Rohmer, Richard. 1970. *The Green North.* Toronto: Maclean-Hunter.

Scott, Colin H., ed. 2001. *Aboriginal Autonomy and Development in Northern Quebec and Labrador.* Vancouver: University of British Columbia Press.

Slocombe, D. Scott. 2000. 'Resources, People and Places: Resource and Environmental Geography in Canada', *The Canadian Geographer* 44, 1: 56–66.

Toulin, Allan. 2001. '$20-Billion Pipeline to be Biggest Private Project ever in N. America', *National Post,* 27 July, A1

Watkins, Melville H. 1963. 'A Staple Theory of Economic Growth', *Canadian Journal of Economics and Political Science* 29: 160-9.

———. 1977. 'The Staple Theory Revisited', *Journal of Canadian Studies* 12, 5: 83–95.

Wenzel, George. 2000. 'Inuit Subsistence and Hunter Support in Nunavut', in Jens Dahl, Jack Hicks, and Peter Jull, eds, *Nunavut: Inuit Regain Control of Their Lands and Their Lives.* Copenhagen: Centraltrykkeriet Skive A/S, 180–95.

Whitehorse Star. 1998. 'Hundreds Laid Off'. Available at: <http://www.whitehorsestart.com/Archives/>. Accessed 14 Apr. 1999.

CHAPTER 6

Megaprojects in Northern Development

Megaprojects hold the key for resource development in the Canadian North.[1] But what exactly are megaprojects and why are they so important? Megaprojects are huge industrial undertakings that transform a hinterland area into an industrial node and add greatly to world production of primary products. These large-scale projects can unlock the vast wealth of the North by overcoming the North's adverse geography, especially its costly construction and operating expenses due to the cold climate, great distances to markets, and extra costs of construction in permafrost areas. Given the size and cost of such projects, only large corporations but especially multinational corporations have the capacity to design, construct, and operate megaprojects. Multinational corporations also have excellent political connections that often lead to various forms of government support, including price supports, tax concessions, and outright grants.

Megaprojects have two phases: construction and operation. Of the two, the construction phase places the greatest pressure on the impacted community and surrounding area. The construction phrase creates an intense work atmosphere where thousands of workers live in trailers, work long hours, and take home big paycheques. The impacted community is under immense pressure from the constant noise from the equipment and trucks, from the construction dust and air pollution, from the number of new families and their demand for community services, and from the shortage of housing. During construction, the common characteristics of megaprojects are:

- Construction costs alone exceed $1 billion and can reach $20 billion.
- The construction period exceeds two years and can extend to 10 years.
- Short-term but substantial employment and business opportunities are generated.
- Outside labour and businesses play a key role because local workers and firms are unable to satisfy demands from the megaproject.
- The sheer size of construction workforce overwhelms existing community services and infrastructure.
- Construction work damages the local environment.
- The local transportation system is hard-pressed to meet the needs of the megaproject.

Multinational corporations are the dominant economic force in our global economy. Centred in the world industrial core, multinational corporations reach into world hinterlands for a variety of primary products. Within world hinterlands, such as the Canadian

North, multinational corporations often direct the course of regional economic development. Circumstances within the global community, however, are forcing these firms to acknowledge their political and social responsibilities when operating in world hinterlands. The Mackenzie Valley Pipeline Inquiry that brought Aboriginal political and social conditions into the decision-making process in the mid-1970s provides such an example. Yet, the very nature of the global economy emphasizes corporate profits, not social responsibilities. Given their dominant role in resource development, what responsibility, if any, do these firms have for social development and the environment? (Vignette 6.1).

Vignette 6.1 Corporate Responsibility

In 1939, Peter Drucker wondered how the vast power held by multinational corporations could be justified within the tradition of Western political philosophy. As a leading social philosopher, Drucker recognized that the corporation was not inherently conservative, such as the state, church, and army. On the contrary, the corporation, but especially the multinational corporation, must constantly transform itself to meet new circumstances. Drucker believed that the corporation was the ideal candidate for the leadership of a rapidly changing modern industrial society. Indeed, if corporations refuse to take responsibilities for solving social and environmental problems besetting the global community, who else will have the power to do so?

SOURCE: Drucker (1939).

MEGAPROJECTS: POSITIVE AND NEGATIVE IMPACTS

Megaprojects are the engine of northern development. These enormous undertakings greatly add to Canada's industrial capacity, stimulate regional development, and expand local and regional transportation systems. At the same time, they generate new demands for goods and services, thus expanding and diversifying the regional economy. During the heyday of the resource boom, megaprojects were touted as the new engine of economic growth for the North. In 1981, a federal task force, headed by Robert Blair of Nova Corporation and Shirley Carr of the Canadian Labour Congress, estimated that the construction of a series of northern megaprojects would inject nearly $400 billion into the northern economies during the last 20 years of the twentieth century, thus transforming the North from a hinterland to an industrial region (Blair and Carr, 1981).

But megaprojects have a dark side. Along with the arrival of large numbers of construction workers, social problems arise. Fort McMurray is currently experiencing 'the price of prosperity'. Tom Barrett of the *Edmonton Journal* (2002: EJ15) wrote:

> Big salaries, boredom leads to trouble [in Fort McMurray]. The latest economic boom to sweep through Fort McMurray has brought with it a predictable increase in crime. Crime, crack, and cocaine are problems for a community that plays as hard as its works. Take a lot of disposable income, add a huge population of single men without roots in the community and you can expect some problems, says RCMP Staff Sgt. Scott Stauffer. Money buys cocaine, ecstasy and a host of softer drugs, plus plenty of liquor. Heavy drinking often leads to fights and traffic accidents.

During the construction phrase, the local community is overwhelmed and the newcomers, by their sheer numbers, place enormous pressure on the community's housing stock, infrastructure, and recreational facilities, thereby forcing radical changes to the community's character and lifestyle. Business opportunities abound but the small northern business sector cannot satisfy the needs of the construction firms, and economic spinoffs generated by the construction are lost to southern Canada. In 2001, drilling rigs designed for the Mackenzie Delta were not manufactured in the North but in southern Canada.[2] The explanation is simple: the North does not have a manufacturing capacity. Similarly, the small and relatively unskilled northern labour force results in labour leakage as firms employ air commuting systems to obtain their workers from labour pools in southern Canada and these workers spend their wages in their home communities. The net result is that virtually all of the multiplier effects accrue to other regions of Canada (Vignette 6.2). In short, the disadvantages are:

- Profits flow out of the North.
- Manufacturing of special facilities or equipment takes place in southern Canada.
- Managerial experience and technical knowledge gained from the development are retained by the company.
- Public funds are often used to encourage such developments, thereby reducing their risk and enhancing their prospects of profitability but doing little for the North.
- The influx of workers without ties to the community can cause social problems as neither the community nor the workers are able to cope successfully with this sudden demographic change.

Vignette 6.2 Regional Multiplier

In neo-classical economic theory, the most common form of economic impact analysis is based on the Keynesian concept of the multiplier effect. The multiplier effect is a measure of the economic impact of a new development, such as a factory or mine, on the local or regional economy. A high regional multiplier translates into a region heading towards economic diversification.

There are three types of impacts: the direct impact of the wages, salaries, and profits of the new development; the indirect impact from payments to regional industries supplying goods and services to the new firm; and the induced impact, which is the increase in payments to retail stores and their regional suppliers brought about by the spending of the new income.

The regional multiplier is expressed mathematically as $1/(1-s)$ where s is the marginal propensity to consume goods and services within the region. Goods and services purchased outside the region represent economic leakage. For example, let us assume that the induced impact is determined by a regional multiplier of 1.5. This multiplier indicates that $0.33 of every dollar spent on supplies and wages by the owners of the new enterprise occurs within the region. It is calculated from the expression $(1/1-s)$ where $1/(1-0.33) = 1.5$. Arriving at the total annual income impact involves applying the multiplier to the total expenditures from direct and indirect impacts within the region. If this annual amount was $4 million, then by applying the multiplier of 1.5, the indirect impact is $2 million and the total impact is $6 million ($4 million direct impacts and $2 million indirect impacts).

In the case of the Alberta-Pacific pulp project, the multiplier was used to calculate the number of anticipated indirect jobs (jobs not directly associated with the project). In this example, the multiplier was assumed to be low—1.2—and the number of jobs in the northern region was calculated as follows: 600 direct jobs x 1.2 = 720 total jobs (120 indirect jobs).

THE ERA OF MEGAPROJECTS

The era of megaprojects began after World War II when the North's resources became more attractive as supplies elsewhere were either exhausted or insufficient to meet the demand. American firms initiated this pattern of resource development in Canada's northern hinterland. Their first huge investment took place in northern Quebec and adjacent areas of Labrador where iron mines, mining towns, a railway, and port facilities at Sept-Îles were built to supply ore to US steel plants (Table 6.1).

In the following decades, a resource boom took place in northern Canada fuelled not only by demands from the United States but also from other foreign countries such as France, Germany, and Japan. Multinational corporations based in these and other foreign countries invested in Canada's natural resources. These firms were seeking a reliable source of raw materials and energy. French and German firms are involved in uranium mining, partly to supply their nuclear-powered electrical thermal stations. Japanese companies have obtained long-term leases for virtually all the remaining commercial timber in northern Alberta.

In 1991, the discovery of diamonds opened a new chapter in resource development. Diamond mining in the Northwest Territories has made Canada a major diamond producer. Now that the geology of diamond deposits in the Canadian Shield is better understood, other discoveries have occurred in the Northwest Territories, Quebec, Ontario, and Saskatchewan. The discovery of diamonds in the Northwest Territories sparked one of the largest staking operations in Canada and several multinational corporations joined the action, including Australia's large mining firm, Broken Hill Proprietary Company, and South Africa's legendary diamond firm, De Beers. By 1998, production began at Broken Hill's Ekati diamond mine in the Northwest Territories. The value of its production overshadows other energy and mineral developments in the Northwest Territories. Two more diamond mines, Diavik and Snap Lake, are coming on stream within the next few years. De Beers has a major interest in both mines, and each mine has an estimated 120-year supply of diamonds.

Megaprojects are concentrated in the Subarctic. Leading examples are the Alberta oil sands, the James Bay Project, and the Norman Wells Oil Expansion and Pipeline. Diamond mines, both operating and planned, lie in the transition zone between the Arctic and Subarctic. The potential for Arctic development is enormous but their time has not yet come. The first Arctic megaproject will likely be the development of the

TABLE 6.1 Megaprojects

Project	Resource	Production Date	Major Market	Ownership	Transportation
Quebec/Labrador Iron Ore Project	Iron ore	1954	United States		Rail and lake carriers
Great Canadian Oil Sands Plant	Heavy oil	1967	United States	Sun Oil Company	Pipeline
Syncrude Canada Plant	Heavy oil	1978	United States	Syncrude Canada Ltd.	Pipeline
Peace River Hydroelectric Project	Electricity	1980	United States	BC Hydro	Transmission lines
Northwest Coal Project	Coal	1984	Japan	Denison Mines	Rail & ocean ship
Norman Wells Oil Project	Oil	1985	United States	Esso Resources Canada	Pipeline
James Bay Hydroelectric Project	Electricity	1986	United States	Hydro-Québec	Transmission lines
Peace River Pulp Plant	Pulp	1990	Japan	Daishowa	Rail/ship
Alberta-Pacific Forest Plant	Pulp	1993	Japan	Mitsubishi & Oji Paper Company	Rail/ship
BHP Diamond Project	Diamonds	1998	United States	BHP	Aircraft
McArthur River Project	Uranium	2000	United States	Cameco Corporation	Truck
Alliance Gas Pipeline	Natural Gas	2000	United States	Alliance Pipeline Inc.	Pipeline
Suncor Millennium Project	Heavy Oil	2001	United States	Exxon Mobil Corp.; Royal Dutch/Shell Group; and Petro-Canada	Pipeline

Mackenzie Delta natural gas field. Since 1995, when natural gas prices tumbled to a low wellhead price of US$1.15/thousand cubic feet, prices have strengthened. By 2000, natural gas prices had jumped to US$3.69/thousand cubic feet (Table 6.4). At this price level, Mackenzie Delta natural gas can be sold in American markets.

CROWN CORPORATIONS AND HYDROELECTRIC POWER

Water power falls under the control of provinces. Each provincial government has created a Crown corporation designed to develop and market hydro and thermal electrical sites. In this way, provincial Crown corporations play a key role in the development of water resources in northern areas of provinces. As such, they are an expression of provincial strategies for economic development. Provincial hydroelectric Crown corporations in British Columbia, Manitoba, and Quebec have built huge hydroelectric projects to produce low-cost energy for their consumers and to sell surplus energy to the United States.

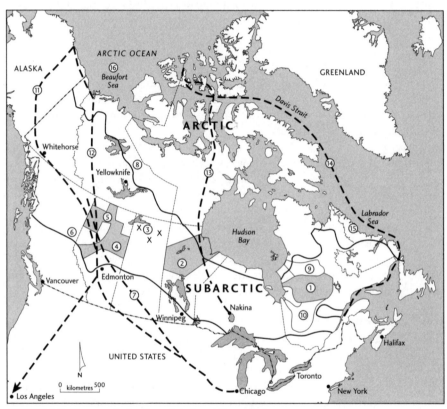

FIGURE 6.1 Megaprojects: Completed and Proposed

Completed	Proposed
1 La Grande hydroelectric project	9 Great Whale River hydroelectric project
2 Churchill/Nelson hydroelectric project	10 Nottaway-Broadback-Rupert hydro project
3 Uranium mines in Saskatchewan	11 Alaska Gas Pipeline
4 Alberta oil sands open-pit mines	12 Mackenzie Valley Gas Pipeline
5 Timber leases for pulp plants in Alberta	13 Polar Gas Pipeline
6 Northeast BC coal mines	14 Arctic Pilot Project
7 Alliance Gas Pipeline	15 Voisey's Bay nickel mine
8 Ekati and Diavik diamond mines	16 Beaufort Sea oil development

ENERGY

Energy is not only a resource but also a vital component in industrial activities. For energy-deficient Americans, Canadian energy is essential to their domestic economy. Supplies are not only close at hand but politically secure. Energy is central to American continental resource policy and to a rationalized North American market. Hydro-electricity, because of its limited transmission range, lends itself to a regional distribution pattern within the North American marketplace. Geography dictates that power generated in northern British Columbia supplies the densely populated Pacific coast markets from BC's Lower Mainland to the population clusters in Washington, Oregon, and California while natural gas and oil production from Alberta, Saskatchewan, the Northwest Territories, and Yukon are delivered to energy-deficient areas of Canada and the US, with the American Midwest forming the major market.

Northern oil, however, holds a special significance in American strategic planning. Dependence on Middle East oil sits uneasily in Washington. Canada could reduce this dependency if oil production from the Alberta oil sands could be quickly brought on stream. For this reason, exports of competitively priced Canadian oil are quickly absorbed into American markets.

Energy production in the North far exceeds the needs of the Canadian market and most is sold in foreign markets. In many cases, energy proposals require firm commitments from foreign buyers before construction begins. For example, Japan wants western Canadian coal for its steel mills, and France, Japan, Korea, and Germany import Canadian uranium under long-term contracts. Energy, then, is sought not only by the US but also by industrial countries around the world. The significance of Canadian energy to industrial countries is revealed by the willingness of foreign companies to sign long-term energy purchase agreements or, through their Canadian subsidiaries, to provide the investment capital. This pattern of development in Canada's North is clear from the following discussion of several energy megaprojects.

The Northeast Coal Project

The vast coal reserves along the western slopes of the Rocky Mountains were well known but the great distance from global markets prevented their exploitation until the 1970s. At that time, with world prices for high-quality coal soaring, Japanese steel mills were concerned about future prices and secure supplies. Under those circumstances, the Northeast Coal Project was launched. The government of British Columbia saw this megaproject as the key to creating an industrial node in the northeast area of the province and the transshipment of coal at Prince Rupert stimulating the local economy of this underutilized Pacific port. Japanese steel mills provided the long-term contracts that guaranteed for this very expensive project. The project not only consisted of developing open-pit coal mines and creating a new resource town, Tumbler Ridge, but also involved building the transportation infrastructure by upgrading and extending the CNR rail line from the coal fields to the port of Prince Rupert. The Northeast Coal Project was predicated on coal prices reaching $100 per tonne before the end of the century. Unfortunately, coal production began as the global economy slid into a recession, thereby reducing the world demand for steel. In turn, the

need for coal declined, causing coal prices to drop. By the early 1980s the world economy was sputtering; spot coal prices were declining; and the future of the Northeast
Coal Project was in jeopardy.

The Northeast Coal Project consisted of three coal-mining operations. Denison
Mines owned the Quintette and Gregg River mines while Teck Corporation ran the
Bullmoose mine. The total investment was about $4.5 billion, with the federal and
British Columbia governments providing a total of $1.5 billion to build two railways
and port facilities from which to ship coal to Japan. In addition, some 50 banks loaned
a total of $1 billion to Quintette Coal Ltd, a subsidiary of Denison Mines, to develop
the Quintette mine and the town of Tumbler Ridge. The Japanese steel mills were
willing to purchase the entire production of Quintette's operations (nearly 5 million
tonnes annually) at prices above the world market in order to obtain a secure supply
of coal. Both Quintette and a consortium of Japanese steel producers were confident
that time was on their side. A 14-year contract set the price at $75 a tonne in 1980 but
with annual escalations possible to a ceiling price of $104 a tonne. The contract also
called for three price reviews, one in 1987, another in 1991, and the last in 1995. In
1984, when the Quintette mine opened, the contract price was $90 a tonne, which was
about 10 per cent above world spot prices for coal.

In 1987, the contract price for Quintette coal was to be reviewed. At that time, the
contract price was nearly $100 a tonne while the world spot price had dropped to just
under $60 a tonne. The Japanese consortium wanted the price decreased to world spot
price levels while Quintette demanded the fully escalated contract price of $104. The
dispute was taken to arbitration and the arbitrated prices were set at about $96 for the
period from 1987 to 1990 and at $82.40 for next three years. At that contract price,
the mining companies began to lose money. Part of Denison Mines' financial problem
was due to servicing its $700 million debt. In the early 1990s, Denison Mines had to
file for bankruptcy. Teck Corporation gained control of the Quintette coal mine.
Prices for coal remained low and Teck was forced to shut down the Quintette mine
in 2000, leaving the town of Tumbler Ridge without an economic function. Some
600 miners and their families left the community. According to Statistics Canada,
Tumbler Ridge's population dropped from 3,775 in 1996 to 1,851 in 2001, a decrease
of 51 per cent. While the future of Tumbler Ridge is in doubt, efforts to turn the
community into a recreation/retirement centre are underway.[3] Its primary asset is
its community infrastructure and housing stock.

The James Bay Project

The James Bay Project ranks among the world's largest hydroelectric undertakings.
The first of three construction phases has been completed and the next two may be
completed in the twenty-first century. The strategy of Hydro-Québec was to sell the
surplus electricity to utilities in New England. In fact, without long-term agreements
with American utilities, the first phase of the James Bay Project would not have been
a viable project. In 1971, Premier Bourassa announced the first phase, known as Le
Grande Project. This massive construction project was completed in 1985. It supplies
low-cost electrical power to industries along the St Lawrence Valley. Surplus energy
is sold to the utilities in New England. The Great Whale River Project forms the

second phase. The natural market for this electricity is New England. Announced in 1985, the strategy of Hydro-Québec was to seek long-term contracts for its electricity and to use the initial payments to pay for the construction costs. Maine, New York, and Vermont all negotiated contracts with Hydro-Québec Although hydroelectric power is touted as environmentally friendly energy, environmental organizations, including the Sierra Club and the New York Energy Efficiency Coalition, and the Quebec Cree under the leadership of Mathew Coon Come strongly opposed the development of the Great Whale River Project, claiming that it would cause great harm to the land and people of northern Quebec. In 1992, the state of New York cancelled two contracts with Hydro-Québec totalling $17.6 billion. These contracts were critical for the project. While the relatively low price of natural gas was the principal factor affecting the decision of New York Governor Mario Cuomo, environmental concerns related to the flooding of 5,000 km^2 of land in northern Quebec also played an important role. Ironically, much of the natural gas purchased by thermal electricity plants in New England came from western Canada via the extension of the TransCanada Pipeline network in Ontario to the Duke Pipeline network in New York. In 1994, the Quebec government announced that the Great Whale River Project would not proceed until the demand and price for its electricity improved. In 2002, the Quebec government entered into agreements with the Quebec Cree and Inuit. These agreements call for the development of the natural resources of northern Quebec and the sharing of the profits from these developments. The agreement with the Cree clears the way for the development of the third phase of the James Bay Project, the Nottaway-Broadback-Rupert Project.

The Norman Wells Project

Since the 1930s, oil from the Norman Wells field supplied the local communities and mines along the Mackenzie River and the two major lakes, Great Bear and Great Slave. With oil prices soaring in the 1970s, Esso Resources Canada saw an opportunity to expand production at its Norman Wells oil field, construct a pipeline to reach the continental pipeline system in northern Alberta, and supply much of the new production to American markets. As the first megaproject to take place in the Northwest Territories, this project was caught up in the political undertow caused by the Mackenzie Valley Pipeline Inquiry and its report (the Berger Report). While much smaller than the Mackenzie Valley pipeline proposal, the Norman Wells proposal raised many similar concerns to those expressed by opponents to the Mackenzie Valley Project. Ottawa saw this proposal as a viable alternative to the failed Mackenzie Valley Gas Pipeline proposal, as a way to circumvent the Dene resistance to such developments prior to a land claim agreement, and, most importantly, as a means to encourage economic and social development in the Mackenzie Valley. With Ottawa's help, construction began only five years after the publication of the Berger Report.

The Norman Wells Project called for drilling additional wells to increase output from the shallow oil field[4] lying beneath the Mackenzie River and for the construction of a pipeline from Norman Wells to Zama, Alberta, in order to ship the additional oil to southern markets. In 1978, Esso submitted its plans to Ottawa for an environmental review that would lead to the approval of its oil expansion and pipeline proposal.

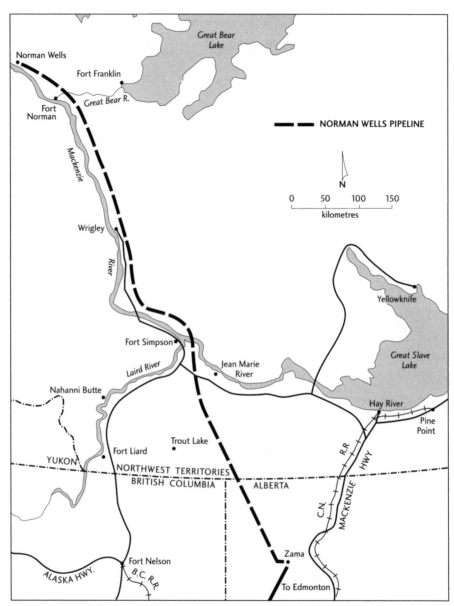

FIGURE 6.2 Norman Wells Pipeline Route
SOURCE: Bone (1984: 63).

In 1980, the federal Environment and Assessment Review Office recommended that the project proceed, but that construction be delayed until 1982 to permit further land claim negotiations. Even though an agreement was not reached, construction began in 1982. By 1985, the project was completed at a cost of just under a billion dollars.

TABLE 6.2 Production and Value of Norman Wells Petroleum, 1981–2002

Year	Oil Production (000 m^3)	$ Value (millions)
1981	172	13
1982	173	15
1983	169	19
1984	175	20
1985	1,148	195
1986	1,478	103
1987	1,570	145
1988	1,833	124
1989	1,885	178
1990	1,864	248
1991	1,872	202
1992	1,834	188
1993	1,819	165
1994	1,655	174
1995	1,590	206
1996	1,747	254
1997	1,690	241
1998	1,650	172
1999	1,640	231
2000	1,536	382
2001	1,528	380
2002	1,530*	380*

*Estimate.
SOURCE: Bureau of Statistics, Government of the Northwest Territories, *Statistics Quarterly.*

Production from the new wells increased the total output by over eight times, from 180,000 cubic metres/year to nearly 1,500,000 cubic metres/year (Table 6.2). In addition, a water injection technique increased oil recovery from 17 per cent to 42 per cent, making a more efficient use of the oil field. Facilities required for increasing production would include 200 new oil and water injection wells, six artificial islands to serve as drilling platforms, an oil-gathering system, and a central processing plant to condition oil for pipeline transmission. The relatively small-diameter (324 mm) pipeline, buried

TABLE 6.3 World Oil Prices, 1973–2002 (based on US domestic prices)

Year	$US/barrel	Year	$US/barrel
1973	3.89	1988	12.58
1974	6.87	1989	15.86
1975	7.67	1990	20.03
1976	8.19	1991	16.54
1977	8.57	1992	15.99
1978	9.00	1993	14.25
1979	12.64	1994	13.19
1980	21.59	1995	14.62
1981	31.77	1996	18.46
1982	28.52	1997	17.23
1983	26.19	1998	10.87
1984	25.88	1999	15.56
1985	24.09	2000	26.72
1986	12.51	2001	21.84
1987	15.40	2002	23.30*

*Estimate.
SOURCES: World Oil Prices: <http://www.eia.doe.gov/emeu/mer/txt/mer9-1>.

along its entire length, would have a capacity of around 5,000 cubic metres/day. It would transport oil at near ground temperature, thereby reducing the potential for frost heave. Three pumping stations were to be located near Norman Wells, Wrigley, and Fort Simpson. Esso assigned Interprovincial Pipe Lines Ltd (IPL) the task of constructing a buried pipeline. The pipe was laid during the winter to minimize damage to the environment. Both Esso and IPL subcontracted the work to other firms, including local companies. Surveying and line cutting took place in the winter months of 1982–3 while the pipe was assembled, welded, and buried in a trench over the course of two winter seasons (1983–4 and 1984–5).

Industry and government saw this project as a model for future energy developments. From an industry perspective, Norman Wells was built without serious environmental or social impacts. As well, it was built some 30 per cent under the original cost estimate of $1.4 billion and was completed slightly ahead of schedule. While Esso Resources Canada has profited from this oil field, world prices unexpectedly sagged in the late 1980s and they did not recover until 2000 (Tables 6.2 and 6.3). Again, this unexpected decline in oil prices indicates the high risk of large-scale industrial projects (see the subsection 'Price Considerations' in this chapter).

Alliance Gas Pipeline

As the longest natural gas pipeline in North America, the Alliance Gas Pipeline extends over 3,700 km from Fort St John in northern British Columbia to Chicago, Illinois. The Alliance Pipeline was built in response to two factors: rising gas prices and a growing demand in the United States. Construction began in 1999 and work was completed in 2000 at a cost of US$3 billion (Alliance Pipeline news release, 1 June 1999). The Alliance Gas Pipeline represents an important element in the continental energy system. It is designed to carry 1,325 billion cubic feet per day of natural gas from the sedimentary basins found in northwestern Alberta and northeastern British Columbia to the American Midwest. While its major market is the Chicago area, natural gas products are distributed throughout North America. While most natural gas heats residential and institutional buildings, some is converted into ethane, propane, and butane at an extraction and fractionation plant in Channabon, Illinois (just west of Chicago).

The deregulation of the natural gas industry played a role in the building of the Alliance Gas Pipeline. Until 1986, the National Energy Board closely regulated the natural gas industry. Under this system, the existing pipeline owners (primarily Nova Corporation and TransCanada Pipelines Ltd) had a virtual monopoly. With a limited pipeline capacity, Alberta has a surplus of natural gas and low prices. The problem was too much gas and not enough pipes. At about this time, American demand for natural gas began to increase, as natural gas replaced coal for both heating purposes and for generating thermal electricity in many jurisdictions. Gas-producing firms complained about low gas prices because of this quasi-monopoly. They wanted more competition between pipeline companies and more access to the lucrative American market. In 1986, Ottawa deregulated the industry. With both demand and prices rising in the United States, the time for a pipeline from Alberta to the American Midwest had arrived. In 1997, Alliance Pipeline submitted its proposal to the National Energy Board. Two years later, its application, including its environmental impact assessment statement, was approved for the construction of a natural gas pipeline from Fort St John, BC, to the US border near Estevan, Saskatchewan. Fears that the Alliance Pipeline had too much export capacity and would depress US prices proved false. In 2000 and 2001, the average price in the United States was US$3.69 and $4.12/thousand cubic feet respectively. The US government estimate for 2002 was US$4.92 (Table 6.4).

Oil Sands Expansion

The Alberta oil sands contain vast quantities of oil that rival the size of reserves found in the Middle East. Yet, the cost of removing the oil from the sand makes the oil sands much more expensive and this separation process requires large quantities of energy. Still, as conventional crude oil gets harder to find, oil companies have shifted their focus to this huge source. Following the 11 September 2001 terrorist air attacks on New York and Washington, the place of the Alberta oil sands in America's continental energy policy was greatly enhanced, causing American and Canadian multinational firms to invest billions in the tar sands. As Sheik Zaki Yamani, head of the Centre for Global Energy Studies, stated: 'Output from Canadian oilsands and heavy oil projects, projected to equal as much as 80 per cent of current US imports from the Middle East by 2007, may pose a serious threat to the Organization of Petroleum Exporting Countries' (Laverty, 2002: FP1). Yamani also noted that 'OPEC needs to be cautious because the projections imply that the cost of alternative non-OPEC sources of oil like tar sands and heavy oil is not particularly high' (ibid.). US President George W. Bush has earmarked Alberta oil sands as a major source of increased North American oil supplies, adding a political urgency to oil sands development (Cattaneo, 2001: C2). Bush's logic is based on the increasing gap between American oil production and consumption. In 2000, for instance, US oil production slipped to 7.7 million barrels per day, while consumption rose to 18.7 million barrels per day. With American demand for oil continuing to outstrip its capacity to satisfy that need, sales of additional Canadian oil to the United States (unlike Canadian lumber exports) are most welcome by the US government.

Alberta oil sands are found in four major deposits. While some deposits are close to the surface, most lie beneath some 50 metres of overburden. The best-known deposit is the Athabasca oil sands near Fort McMurray. The other three deposits are Peace River, Wabasca, and Cold Lake. Together, they contain more than 1.7 trillion barrels of bitumen or 1 trillion barrels of synthetic crude oil, which exceeds the known reserves of Saudi Arabia. Unlocking this black gold is expensive and already substantial investments have been made. In 2001, an additional $86 billion was committed to 63 different projects that will be built over the next decade. As a result, Fort McMurray and the Athabasca oil sands region are undergoing an unprecedented economic boom. Skilled labour is in such short supply that some projects have been delayed and others have had serious cost overruns.

The two major oil sands companies are Suncor Energy Inc. and Syncrude Canada Ltd. Both have already invested billions and are engaged in major expansion projects. Both companies operate open-pit mines and send their liquid-like bitumen by pipeline to their refineries near Fort Saskatchewan, Alberta. Over time, these two companies have successfully cut costs of mining and refining bitumen to drive their cost per barrel from near $20 to $12. In January 2003, a third open-pit operation (the Athabasca Oil Sands Project) came on stream. The Athabasca Oil Sands Project (also known as the Albian Project) was completed in December 2002 and production began in January 2003. Diluted bitumen is shipped by its Corridor Pipeline to the Scotford upgrader refinery near Fort Saskatchewan, Alberta. The Athabasca Oil Sands Project is owned by Shell Canada Ltd (60 per cent), Chevron Canada Ltd (20 per cent), and Western Oil Sands Inc (20 per cent). In December 2002 several other projects, including the Fort Hills Project, the Meadow Creek Project, and the Horizons Project, were about to move from the design stage to the construction stage, but construction may be delayed until the costs of the Kyoto Protocol are clarified (see below for a fuller discussion of the impact of the Kyoto Protocol on new oil sands projects).

The history of Suncor began in 1967, when the Great Canadian Oil Sands Company (later it became Suncor) opened the first commercially successful oil sands plant. Some 34 years later, Suncor completed its Project Millennium, a $3.4 billion expansion of its existing facilities that doubled the size of its mining, extraction, upgrading, and supporting infrastructure and increased its capacity to 210,000 barrels of oil per day, more than double its 1999 production. The next expansion by Suncor focuses on a new mining operation called Firebag located some 40 km northeast of its existing plant. By 2005, the extra production from Firebag will boost total production to 260,000 barrels of oil per day and to 400,000 barrels of oil per day by 2010. The Syncrude plant began production in 1978 and it soon became the leading producer. In 1996, Syncrude announced an $8 billion oil expansion project called Syncrude 21. By 2002, the first two stages were completed and the $4 billion third stage was given approval that will increase production by 100,000 barrels per day to 360,000 barrels per day. At the completion of the Syncrude 21 expansion project in 2010, 465,000 barrels will be produced each day. Four other projects, valued at $20 billion, should be completed within four or five years.

The extraction of oil from the tar sands results in high levels of greenhouse gases escaping into the atmosphere. For that reason, the Kyoto Protocol might chase investment out of the oil sands and into countries that either have not signed this international agreement (the United States) or countries that are not industrialized but contain vast oil reserves (Venezuela) and therefore are exempt from reducing greenhouse gas emissions (Vignette 2.9). For example, in August 2002, Petro-Canada announced a $6 billion project with construction beginning in 2003, but following Ottawa's announcement in early September 2002 that it is signing on to the Kyoto agreement, Petro-Canada got cold feet. Chris Dawson of Petro-Canada stated that 'These aren't threats. These are business realities. We are in an extremely competitive business and if our dollars are best invested elsewhere then that's what we're prepared to do' (Seskus, 2002: FP1). On 14 January 2003, TrueNorth Energy Inc., a subsidiary of the US-based energy giant Koch Industries Inc., decided not to proceed with its $3.3 billion Fort Hills construction project because of the unknown costs associated with the Kyoto agreement. At the same time, Petro-Canada and Canadian Natural Resources Ltd announced that negotiations were continuing with Ottawa regarding the Kyoto costs after 2012. In December 2002, Ottawa limited the exposure to Kyoto costs to 2012 by setting the emissions targets for the oil and gas sector at a level not more than 15 per cent of discharge levels in 2010, and Ottawa capped its Kyoto costs at $15 a tonne of greenhouse gases to 2012. Petro-Canada's $5.2 billion Meadow Creek Project and Canadian Natural Resources' $8 billion Horizon Project may be delayed or both firms may locate their upgraders in the United States, which has refused to sign on to the Kyoto agreement.

The Mackenzie Delta Natural Gas Field

With prices for natural gas increasing in the late 1990s, the huge natural gas reserves contained in the Mackenzie Delta are close to becoming commercially viable. The question is price stability at current levels. If the price of natural gas remains at or exceeds US$3.00 per thousand cubic feet over the next 20 years, then the Mackenzie Delta gas deposits will be a profitable venture. With a pipeline in place the offshore gas in the Beaufort Sea would only require a slightly higher price, perhaps US$3.50 per thousand cubic feet, to be commercially viable for exploitation.

Price increases in the late 1990s to US$2.00 per thousand cubic feet made the natural gas field in northern British Columbia commercially viable for the US market. At these prices, the construction of pipelines from southern Yukon and southern

Northwest Territories made business sense. In the territories, three active gas fields at Fort Liard (Northwest Territories), Pointed Mountain (Northwest Territories), and Kotaneelee (Yukon Territory) supply part of the gas flowing to American markets. The Fort Liard deposit alone has 1.5 trillion cubic feet of proven reserves and another six trillion cubic feet of probable reserves. In comparison, the Mackenzie Delta/Beaufort Sea has an estimated nine trillion cubic feet of proven reserves with probable reserves estimated at about 64 trillion cubic feet.

By 2000, plans were being formulated to bring Mackenzie Delta gas to US markets. Such a pipeline would be almost twice a long as the Alliance Gas Pipeline and would cost at least twice as much. Once before, the same companies tried to develop these resources but failed. In the 1970s, social and environmental issues derailed this massive project to bring Prudhoe Bay natural gas to US markets via the Mackenzie Valley. We need to revisit what happened in the 1970s to see the nature of these barriers to development and to determine if these barriers still exist.

The Background

In the 1970s, demand for energy was growing in the United States. At the same time, oil prices were increasing due to the efforts of OPEC to curtail their production of oil. The net result was to push all energy prices higher. Americans felt vulnerable because more and more of their energy came from the volatile Middle East. The huge oil and gas reserves located along the Arctic coast of Alaska at Prudhoe Bay offered the United States an alternative source of oil (though at a higher price than imported oil), thereby fulfilling two national objectives—to supply much-needed energy to continental America and to reduce American dependency on foreign oil. In 1974, the construction of an oil pipeline across Alaska was begun. Since the Prudhoe Bay oil deposit also contains natural gas (an estimated 20 trillion cubic feet), the question on the minds of executives of gas companies was, 'Can we sell this gas too?'

Canadian Arctic Gas Pipeline Limited, composed of 27 Canadian and American companies, including Exxon, Gulf, Shell, and TransCanada Pipelines, had an answer. They proposed to build a pipeline from Prudhoe, Alaska, across the Arctic coastal plain of Yukon to the Mackenzie Delta and then, after extending the pipeline to the Mackenzie Delta gas fields, ship both Alaskan and Canadian natural gas along the Mackenzie Valley to Alberta and on to Chicago and other centres in the energy-deficient Midwest.[5]

The Berger Inquiry

The Arctic Gas pipeline would have been the longest in the world, stretching nearly 4,000 km, and the greatest construction enterprise ever undertaken.[6] The engineering problems of building a pipeline across permanently frozen ground were monumental and the potential impacts on the northern environment and Native peoples were significant. A federal inquiry, led by Judge Thomas Berger, was appointed in 1974 to consider the proposal and the possible social and environmental impacts on the North. The Inquiry held community hearings across the western Arctic and Subarctic, beginning in 1975 and ending in 1976, to learn of the concerns of Aboriginal people and environmentalists. The Berger Report, issued in 1977, concluded that a pipeline from the Mackenzie Delta up the Mackenzie Valley to Alberta was feasible. But Justice Berger determined that such a pipeline should proceed only after the major obstacles had been overcome, specifically, after further study of how a buried and chilled gas pipeline would avoid frost heave in areas of discontinuous permafrost, and after Native land claims were settled. Berger ruled against building a pipeline across the Yukon coastal plain because of its fragile nature and because of its importance as a calving ground for the Porcupine caribou herd.[7] He felt that the building of a gas pipeline through this calving ground on the Yukon coastal plain would threaten the survival of the caribou herd and the hunting economy of the local people. Now, more than 25 years later, to what extent has the economic, environmental, and social climate changed?

Price Considerations

Megaprojects are vulnerable to long-term price declines. In fact, companies often begin construction based on the assumption that prices will rise. Therefore, determining (or trying to determine) future prices is particularly crucial. First, investment decisions based on such projections are made some five to ten years before the project is completed. Second, non-market factors such as concern for the environment can affect the type of energy used. For example, concern over air pollution caused by coal-burning thermal electrical plants in New England resulted in a shift from coal to natural gas thermal plants in the 1990s. Third, growing non-OPEC oil production could result in overproduction, thus causing prices to decline. In sum, the complexity of market forces and the effect of non-market forces make the estimate of future prices difficult, creating a sense of uncertainty.

For example, if a megaproject comes on stream during a long economic slowdown, low prices can lead to the failure of the project and the bankruptcy of the firm. The Northwest Coal Project, previously discussed, provides a perfect example of such a scenario. This explains why American companies considering building a natural gas pipeline from Prudhoe Bay to Chicago sought financial support from Washington. For that reason, the US Senate passed a bill that would subsidize the price of natural gas from Alaska in order to spur construction of the pipeline from Alaska to the continental United States. The purpose of this subsidy was to reduce US dependency on Middle East oil. Under this bill, the price of Alaska natural gas would have a base price of $3.25/thousand cubic feet. Hal Kvisle, the CEO of TransCanada Pipelines, interpreted this bill in the following manner:

> We absolutely understand the problem that is faced by Alaska producers—how do you underpin the investment of more than $10-billion US dollars to get that gas to market when you have no idea what the gas price is going to be five years out? It's the biggest single challenge that the pipeline industry has in North American today. (Jones, 2002: FP5)

While the Senate bill did not become law, two important questions surfaced. First, would a subsidy for Alaska gas distort the deregulated North American market? Second, would such a distortion put the Mackenzie Delta natural gas project on hold?

Without a doubt, the suggested base price of $3.25/thousand cubic feet eliminates the risk of low prices for the Alaska Highway pipeline. This price is well above the long-term price (the average annual price of natural gas over the last two decades), which was under US$2.00/thousand cubic feet. From 1986 to 1996, consumption increased but prices remained relatively stable at less than US$2.00 per thousand cubic feet. The reason was simple—a surplus of gas had developed in Alberta and Mexico. With supply outstripping demand, natural gas prices sagged well below $2.00 per thousand cubic feet for 10 of the 15 years between 1985 and 2000 (Table 6.4). At such prices, the development of the gas fields in Alaska and the Mackenzie Delta were not viable. In time, however, these surpluses disappeared. By 1996, growing demand for natural gas in the United States saw an increase in natural gas prices to over US$2.00 per thousand cubic feet. As well, advances in drilling and pipeline technology have reduced the cost of exploration, extraction, and transportation of natural gas. By 2000, the price had reached US$3.69 per thousand cubic feet. At those prices, both the Alaskan and Mackenzie Delta gas reserves could be delivered to southern Canada and the United States at a profit (Vignette 6.3).

Vignette 6.3 Pipeline Rivals

The state of Alaska and the Yukon government are lobbying for the construction of a gas pipeline from Prudhoe Bay along the Alaska Highway to markets in the energy-deficient American Midwest. A rival proposal comes from the government of the Northwest Territories, which supports a proposal for a gas pipeline stretching from the Mackenzie Delta to supply energy to the same American market. Under normal market conditions, the Mackenzie Valley pipeline would proceed first because it is much less expensive (US$4 billion compared to US$20 billion); it can be built over a short time because the Mackenzie Valley route is much shorter; and it is further ahead in the regulatory procedure. Yet, the Alaskan pipeline may be built first because of the geopolitical strategic thinking in Washington, which may cause the US government to intervene by providing some form of subsidy to pipeline companies supporting the Alaskan route.

SOURCE: Gillis and Seskus (2002).

Natural gas prices increased in recent years because more and more natural gas is converted into electricity. Traditional energy sources for producing electricity were coal, oil, and water. Since the late 1980s, natural gas has become an important fuel for producing electricity in both the United States and Canada due to three factors. First, the supply of natural gas in the major population areas of Canada and the US became more secure due to the construction of new pipelines. Second, the price of natural gas was very competitive with both coal and hydro-generated electricity. Third, natural gas satisfied the desire for a clean-burning fuel. Construction of thermal electrical plants in the 1990s greatly favoured the use of natural gas and some coal thermal stations were converted to natural gas. Even hydroelectricity fell into disfavour.

Natural gas prices are largely set by demand from the United States. Since the 1990s, US demand for natural gas outstripped both oil and coal. Since 1995, virtually all new capacity has been based on natural gas (US Department of Energy, 2001: Table 2). By the late 1990s, the increased consumption of natural gas for electrical power generation placed pressure on US supplies of natural gas and thus increased its price. The result was short-term price fluctuations because the market adjustment system needed more time to increase its capacity to deliver gas to its customers (Vignette 6.4).

Vignette 6.4 Long-Term and Short-Term Market Adjustment Mechanisms

Market adjustment mechanisms in the natural gas industry are designed to maintain a long-term stable price regime. For example, high prices stimulate well-drilling, construction of new LNG terminals, and pipeline construction. However, these developments often take several years to complete. During this time, the price of natural gas remains high. Such prices can trigger the substitution of other forms of energy, which can dampen demand for natural gas. For example, utility companies install coal- or oil-burning thermal electrical generators.

Short-term price fluctuations occur when the natural gas industry is unable to supply customers with needed gas. Usually these price spikes do not last more than a few days to a month. Sudden increases in spot prices are often related to extreme seasonal variations in temperatures. Season variations in demand for natural gas take place in both winter and summer. In winter, energy required to heat residences, institutions, and factories reaches a peak when a severe cold spell affects the major population clusters in southern Canada and the northern parts of the United States. Similarly, summer demand for electrical energy to operate air-conditioning units takes place when a long heat wave strikes the same geographic area. Weather can indirectly affect the price of natural gas. For example, in prolonged dry spells, low water levels at reservoirs at hydroelectric facilities result in reduced electrical production. This shortfall forces more output from electrical thermal stations, causing a short-term spike in natural gas prices.

The main limiting factor is not natural gas reserves, which have been increasing in Canada, but the capacity of the pipeline system to bring Canadian natural gas to its American customers. The construction of the Maritimes & Northeast Pipeline from Sable Island gas fields to New England (1999) and the Alliance Pipeline from northern British Columbia to the American Midwest (2000) has enhanced Canada's capacity to supply energy-deficient areas of the United States with natural gas and has led to a softening of natural gas prices. Still, prices remain well above US$2.00 per thousand cubic feet, indicating that the demand for natural gas has absorbed this additional supply (Table 6.4).

TABLE 6.4 Average Natural Gas Prices in the United States, 1985–2002
(US dollars per thousand cubic feet)

Year	Wellhead
1985	2.51
1986	1.94
1987	1.67
1988	1.69
1989	1.69
1990	1.70
1991	1.64
1992	1.74
1993	2.04
1994	1.85
1995	1.55
1996	2.17
1997	2.32
1998	1.96
1999	2.19
2000	3.69
2001	4.12
2002	4.92*

*Estimate.
SOURCE: Adapted from US Department of Energy (2001: Figure 1), and US Department of Energy (2002): Table 4): <http://www.eia.doe.gov/oil_gas/natural_gas/data_publications/naturalgas_monthly/ ngm.html>.

PERMAFROST

In the area around the Mackenzie Delta, the ground is permanently frozen. Further south, discontinuous permafrost is encountered, meaning that some ground is not frozen. Chilled gas flowing through a buried pipeline would not pose a problem in the zone of continuous permafrost but frost heave is a possibility in the discontinuous zone. Frost heave might occur because the chilled pipe may cause the water in the ground to freeze and expand, pushing the ground and pipe upward. If large amounts of water freeze, then sufficient pressure in the form of frost heave could break the pipe. This problem remains unresolved, but much has been learned from the Norman Wells pipeline.

The Norman Wells pipeline is the first completely buried oil pipeline in permafrost terrain in Canada. This pipeline extends over a distance of 869 km through both permafrost terrain and non-permafrost terrain. The pipeline begins at Norman Wells and ends at Zama, Alberta, where it joins the national pipeline system.

In 1985, the Norman Wells pipeline began operation. This small-diameter pipeline operates as an ambient temperature line, that is, oil is chilled before entering the pipe and the average temperature of the oil in the line is kept below zero. By chilling the oil, the threat of warming the pockets of ice in frozen ground is removed, but the freezing of ground (and water) in non-frozen terrain has resulted in several cases of frost heave where the pipe has been pushed upward by close to a metre. Thus far, however, the pipe has not broken. Steep slopes are another area of concern. In the summer, the surfaces of south-facing slopes are subject to solar warming that melts both snow and ice embedded in the frozen ground. The melt can then cause stream erosion, which can expose the pipe. One solution is to insulate such slopes with a layer of wood chips to prevent the strong summer sun from warming the upper layer of the frozen slopes, thus reducing the possibility of rapid melt and stream erosion on such slopes.

Special design and construction measures are required for permafrost environments. The Geological Survey of Canada is undertaking such research and is using the Norman Wells pipeline as a case study of research in permafrost terrain. Its goal is to develop new design standards for pipelines to improve methods for predicting the impact of upheaval buckling, ice scour, slumping, and the thawing and freezing soils surrounding pipe. The Geological Survey (2001) hopes that its initial 'results provide a basis for establishing regulations and they help industry make decisions regarding safe and cost-effective pipeline design and maintenance strategies.'

ECONOMIC AND SOCIAL DEVELOPMENT

Back in 1939, Peter Drucker wondered how the vast power held by multinational corporations could be justified within the tradition of Western political philosophy (Vignette 6.1). Part of the answer may lie in joint ventures such as those between Aboriginal organizations and multinational corporations. Within this business structure, economic and social development could then coalesce. The potential for Aboriginal groups is enormous. One example is provided by the quest to develop the Mackenzie Delta natural gas deposits and to construct a pipeline from these deposits to markets in the United States. Such participation may take the form of a joint venture between the Mackenzie Delta Producers Group, which represents Imperial Oil Resources, Conoco Canada, Shell Canada Limited, and ExxonMobil Canada, and the Mackenzie Valley Aboriginal Pipeline Corporation, which represents most Aboriginal groups in the Northwest Territories. The two groups took an important step forward in June 2001 when they signed a Memorandum of Understanding. According to this agreement, the Aboriginal Pipeline Corporation would have a one-third share in the enterprise subject to their obtaining the necessary capital. The next step took place on 7 January 2002 when the two groups announced their intent to begin preparing regulatory applications needed to develop onshore natural gas resources in the Mackenzie Delta, including a Mackenzie Valley pipeline (Imperial Oil, 2002).

During the Berger Inquiry, the Dene made it clear that they wanted to conclude their land claim agreements before allowing large-scale industrial developments to proceed. Dene leaders believed that only then could they truly benefit from megaprojects like the Mackenzie Valley Pipeline. Strong opposition from the Aboriginal peoples posed a major stumbling block for that pipeline proposal (see Chapter 5 for more details). Over the past 30 years, the relationship between pipeline developers and Aboriginal groups has changed because some Aboriginal organizations have entered the marketplace in various ways, including joint ventures with private firms such as that between the Aboriginal Pipeline Group and the Mackenzie Delta Producers Group. While the corporations have accepted their Aboriginal partners, funding remains a barrier. With the pipeline costs estimated at $4 billion, the Aboriginal group's share of investment would amount to $1.3 billion. Such funds are well beyond their capacity. For that reason, Nellie Cournoyea, chairwoman and chief executive officer of the Inuvialuit Regional Corporation, called for federal support to ensure that Aboriginal peoples have an ownership stake in this gas pipeline. As she said, this would signal 'the recognition [that] we are building the capacity to participate in the economy of the twenty-first century' (Weber, 2001). This joint venture faces another obstacle. Some Aboriginal First Nations in the Mackenzie Valley are not members of the Aboriginal Pipeline Group. The leading opposition comes from the Deh Cho First Nation, which has not yet settled its land claim with Ottawa. These difficulties indicate that the path to joint economic ventures between multinational corporations and Aboriginal organizations is not an easy one and may involve political considerations beyond the power of either partner. However, once achieved, joint ventures are one path to the seemingly elusive goal of combining economic growth and social development in Canada's North.

NOTES

1. The Klondike Gold Rush of 1897–8 was the first major mining operation in the North. However, it is the opposite of megaprojects, which are controlled by corporations. The Klondike Gold Rush, on the other hand, drew thousands of individual prospectors into the North seeking the gold nuggets found in the streambeds of the Klondike River. While the Klondike Gold Rush was a major mining operation, it involved many individuals, not a large company. Placer mining involved the recovery of auriferous deposits found in streambeds by simple and inexpensive technology called panning or surface sluicing. This technology enabled seasoned prospectors and greenhorn amateurs to recover the most accessible nuggets and fine sand-like gold particles from tributaries of the Klondike River, particularly Bonanza Creek. Within a few years, placer gold became harder and harder to find. Gold was buried in frozen ground well below the surface but individuals had neither the capital nor the organization necessary to mine this gold. This type of mining was much more capital-intensive, requiring expensive dredging and hydraulic equipment along with separate, highly organized water-supply systems and electric power supplies. Large companies gradually took over the gold-mining industry in Yukon. The Yukon Gold Corporation was the largest of these operations. In order to supply its mining sites on Bonanza and Eldorado creeks with water and electrical power, it built a hydroelectric dam and a hundred-kilometre-long water distribution system (Rae, 1968: 99-100). This more complex mining was limited to the summer months when the frozen ground (permafrost) could be thawed and the gravel sorted. During

the long summer days, the dredges operated around the clock, although the existence of permafrost made hydraulic operations more difficult and time-consuming.

2. Three oil-drilling rigs specially outfitted for the Mackenzie Delta in 2001 cost a total of $50 million, five times more than rigs used in southern Canada. They were manufactured in Edmonton and the nearby town of Nisku. *National Post*, 15 Feb. 2001, C7.

3. In a recent study Lana Sullivan (2002) reveals the struggle between the economic realities of a resource town, Tumbler Ridge, BC, that has lost its economic base and the desire of the residents to keep the town alive. This desire is reflected in a quotation from the Tumbler Ridge local newspaper:

> Despite the media messages, and the abandonment of Tumbler Ridge as a disposable community by Provincial politicians, there is a strong current of confidence about our future running through town. Many residents are survivors from other mining towns ... Pine Point, Faro, Uranium City, Cassiar, and Granisle, to name a few. A significant number of residents call Tumbler Ridge their permanent home and are not willing to move.

Sullivan also reported on the action plan to save the community. This plan involved local, regional, and provincial leaders who joined together to form the Tumbler Ridge Revitalization Task Force. The purpose of this group was to focus on the town and its ability to deliver municipal, educational, community health, and social services to a viable and stable community infrastructure.

4. The Norman Wells oil field, discovered in 1920, has proven oil reserves of around 100 million cubic metres of light grade oil (Esso, 1980). A small refinery was erected at the site and oil was produced to meet the needs of the residents of the Mackenzie Valley. In 1925, operations ceased because the demand for oil was too small. In 1932, production recommenced because the mining operation at Port Radium on Great Bear Lake needed fuel oil. In 1936, the gold mine at Yellowknife also required fuel oil. Given the slow growth of a market for oil in the Mackenzie Basin, production increased very slowly. However, during World War II the Japanese threat to Alaska caused the Americans to seek an alternative supply of oil for their military bases in Alaska. The inland oil field at Norman Wells was expanded and a pipeline built from the oil production site to Whitehorse, where a refinery was built. The US Army undertook this project because Washington wanted an alternative supply of oil, which could not be impeded by an enemy submarine or aircraft attack. This wartime megaproject was the Canol Project (Canol was an acronym for Canadian Oil). Work began in 1942 and was completed in early 1944, by which time the threat of an attack on Alaska by the Japanese had diminished considerably. Without military demand, Canol oil could not compete with lower-priced California oil. The refinery was closed, the new wells at Norman Wells capped, and the pipeline abandoned. By 1947, the pipeline, pumping equipment, and support vehicles were sold as surplus war assets. Imperial Oil purchased the Whitehorse refinery and moved it to Edmonton, where it processed oil from the Leduc field in central Alberta. With the loss of its military market, Norman Wells returned to supplying customers in the Mackenzie Valley. From 1946 on, the local market grew as Indians and Métis moved into settlements where their houses were heated by fuel oil. The demand for fuel oil increased as community infrastructures grew and more mines appeared.

5. A Canadian firm, Foothills Pipe Lines Ltd, proposed to build a pipeline from the Mackenzie Delta gas deposits through the Mackenzie Valley to markets in Canada and the United States.

6. In 1977, Foothills Pipe Lines proposed an alternative route along the Alaska Highway to Fairbanks and then parallel to the Trans-Alaska Pipeline. Five years later, Ottawa approved

this route. However, this pipeline was not built because the estimated cost of construction was so high that the price of this natural gas in the Chicago market would have been well above the existing market price. Market prices had dropped since the late 1970s because the demand for natural gas had been satisfied by Alberta and Mexico, both of which could deliver gas to the Chicago market at a lower price than Alaskan gas.

7. The creation of the Ivvavik National Park, while suggested by Berger, was a direct response to the Inuvialuit Final Agreement. The park falls within the Inuvialuit Settlement Region and the Inuvialuit have hunting and fishing rights within the park. The park stretches along the Yukon coastal plain near the border with Alaska. The Inuvialuit and the federal government co-manage this park

REFERENCES AND SELECTED READINGS

Barrett, Tom. 2002. 'Big salaries, boredom lead to trouble', *Edmonton Journal* (Special Fort McMurray Economic Report), 10 May, EJ15.

Blair, S. Robert, and Shirley G.E Carr. 1981. *Major Canadian Projects: Major Canadian Opportunities. A Report by the Consultative Task Force on Industrial and Regional Benefits from Major Canadian Projects.* Calgary: Nova Corporation.

Bone, Robert M. 1984. *The DIAND Norman Wells Socio-economic Monitoring Program.* Report 9–84. Ottawa: Department of Indian Affairs and Northern Development.

Bureau of Statistics, Government of the Northwest Territories. Various years. *Statistics Quarterly.* Yellowknife: Bureau of Statistics.

Cattaneo, Claudia. 2001. 'Oil sands project takes on new importance', *National Post,* 15 Sept., C2.

Difrancesco, Richard J. 1996. 'The Crown, Territorial Jurisdiction, and Aboriginal Title: Issues Surrounding the Management of Oil and Gas Lands in the Northwest Territories', *Energy Studies Review* 8, 3: 232–48.

———. 1999. 'Developing Canada's Arctic Oil Reserves: An Assessment of the Interregional Economic Impacts', *Environment and Planning* 31, 3: 459–76.

———. 2000. 'A Diamond in the Rough?: An Examination of the Issues Surrounding the Development of the Northwest Territories', *The Canadian Geographer* 44, 2: 114–34.

Drucker, Peter F. 1939. *The End of Economic Man: A Study of the New Totalitarianism.* New York: John Day.

———. 1993. *Post Capitalist Society.* New York: HarperBusiness.

Duffy, Patrick. 1981. *Norman Wells Oilfield Development and Pipeline Project: Report of the Environmental Assessment Panel.* Ottawa: Federal Environmental Assessment Review Office.

Esso. 1980. *Norman Wells Oilfield Expansion: Development Plan.* Calgary: Esso Resources Canada Ltd.

Flaherty, John E. 1999. *Peter Drucker: Shaping the Managerial Mind.* San Francisco: Jossey-Bass.

Geological Survey of Canada. 2001. *Pipeline-Permafrost Interaction: Norman Wells Pipeline Research.* Available at: <http://sts.gsc.nrcan.gc.ca/permafrost/pipeline.htm>. Accessed 1 May 2001.

Gillis, Charlie, and Tony Seskus. 2002. 'Canadian arctic pipeline has edge, Alaska concedes', *National Post,* 7 June, FP3.

Green, Milford B., and David A. Stewart. 1986. *Community Profiles of Socio-Economic Change, 1982-1985.* Report 9–85. Ottawa: Department of Indian Affairs and Northern Development.

Imperial Oil. 2002. 'Mackenzie Delta Producers Group and Mackenzie Valley Aboriginal Pipeline Corporation Advance to Project Definition Phase', news release, 7 Jan. Available at: <http://www.imperialoil.com/news/_release/mn_news_020107.html>.

Jones, Jeffrey. 2002. 'TCPLQ1 profit rises 15% on gas and cost-cutting', *National Post*, 27 Apr., FP5.

Laverty, Gene. 2002. 'Oilsands pose threat to OPEC', *National Post*, 29 Jan., FP1.

Natural Resources Canada. 2002. Preliminary Estimates of the Mineral Production of Canada, by Provinces, 2001, Table 1. Available at: <http://www.nrcan.gc.ca/mms/efab/mmsd/production/production.htm>. Accessed 11 Apr. 2002.

Rae, K.J. 1968. *The Political Economy of the Canadian North: An Interpretation of the Course of Development in the Northwestern Territories of Canada.* Toronto: University of Toronto Press.

Seskus, Tony. 2002. 'Kyoto puts oilsands at risk', *National Post*, 4 Sept., FP1.

Sullivan, Lana. 2002. 'Community Capacity for a Town in Transition: The Case of Tumbler Ridge, British Columbia', paper presented at the annual meeting of the Canadian Association of Geographers, Toronto, 29 May.

Stewart, David A., and Robert M. Bone. 1986. *Norman Wells Socio-Economic Monitoring Program: Summary Report.* Report 1–86. Ottawa: Department of Indian Affairs and Northern Development.

US Department of Energy. 2001. *U.S. Natural Gas Markets: Mid-Term Prospects for Natural Gas Supply.* Washington: Energy Information Administration.

———. 2002. 'Selected National Average Natural Gas Prices, 1996–2002', *Natural Gas Monthly.* Washington: Energy Information Administration: <http://www.eia. doe.gov/oil_gas/natural_gas/data_publications/natural_gas_monthly/ngm.html>. Accessed 16 Jan. 2003.

Weber, Bob. 2001. 'Energy companies sign deal with northern aboriginal partners for gas pipeline', *Canoe News,* 16 Oct. Available at: <http://www.canoe.ca/AllAboutCanoesNews Oct01/16_pipe-cp.html>. Accessed 12 Apr. 2002.

CHAPTER 7

Environmental Impact
of Resource Projects

Canada's North has not escaped from the environmental degradation caused by our industrial economy (Figure 7.1). In fact, industrial development has hit the North especially hard for three reasons. First, the North's environment is more easily damaged by industrial activities and its effluents because of the existence of permafrost. Second, the North's cold biological regime requires a much longer time for the environment to repair itself from various forms of industrial damage. Third, the global atmospheric and oceanic circulation systems bring industrial pollutants to the North.

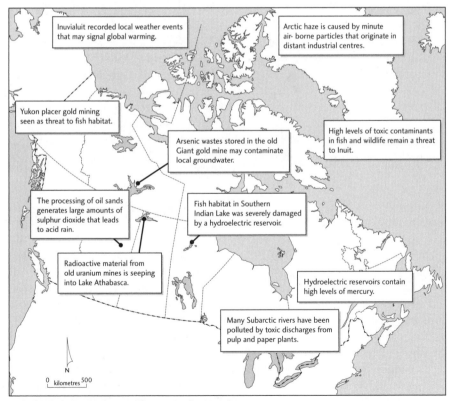

Inuvialuit recorded local weather events that may signal global warming.

Arctic haze is caused by minute air-borne particles that originate in distant industrial centres.

Yukon placer gold mining seen as threat to fish habitat.

Arsenic wastes stored in the old Giant gold mine may contaminate local groundwater.

High levels of toxic contaminants in fish and wildlife remain a threat to Inuit.

The processing of oil sands generates large amounts of sulphur dioxide that leads to acid rain.

Fish habitat in Southern Indian Lake was severely damaged by a hydroelectric reservoir.

Radioactive material from old uranium mines is seeping into Lake Athabasca.

Hydroelectric reservoirs contain high levels of mercury.

Many Subarctic rivers have been polluted by toxic discharges from pulp and paper plants.

N

0 ___ 500
kilometres

FIGURE 7.1 Environment Change in the North

Vignette 7.1 Restoring the Environment

Toxic wastes left behind by mining operations pose a major threat to biological life in the immediate area surrounding a mine site and possibly to a much wider area comprising the mine site's water basin. In the past, companies did not clean up these sites at the end of the mine's economic life. Now they must. Royal Oak Mines Inc. began production well before these new environmental requirements came into effect. When Royal Oak Mines closed its two gold mines, it simply abandoned them. In 1997, when mining ceased at its Colomac mine located some 250 km north of Yellowknife, Royal Oak Mines left behind an environmental time bomb in the form of a poorly constructed tailings pond containing cyanide-polluted water that threatened to overflow and contaminate surface waters. The recently closed Giant Mine near Yellowknife poses a much bigger threat. In this case, the environment is confronted with a toxic mess consisting of 270,000 tonnes of arsenic trioxide, a by-product of gold refining. The cost of eliminating these two dangerous toxic materials amounts to over $1 million in the case of Colomac tailings pond and over $250 million for removing the arsenic stored in an old mine shaft.

Since the late 1990s, more stringent rules govern the restoration of former mine sites. For example, Ottawa required BHP Diamonds Inc. to submit environmental management plans to deal with environmental matters during the construction and production phases of the project. BHP submitted its first annual report in 1998. As well, the company must submit an environmental report every three years. Before the time of mine closure, BHP will be required to submit a reclamation plan to the Department of Indian Affairs and Northern Development (DIAND), the government of the Northwest Territories, and the monitoring agency (Independent Environmental Monitoring Agency) outlining the company's plans for reclamation of the project site. The agreement requires that BHP provide security deposits totalling $11 million for performance of its non-water-related obligations. In addition, BHP has provided a financial guarantee of $20 million to ensure proper site restoration.

SOURCES: McKinnon (1999); Pedersen (2001).

In the past, environmental degradation went unchecked by governments and the resulting damage represented the 'hidden costs' of resource development, including reducing the region's biodiversity. Fortunately, such costs are now recognized and are embedded in environment impact assessments of industrial projects, though the issue of cumulative effects of a series of industrial projects remains contentious. Reclamation agreements represent a new approach and are most commonly arranged between companies undertaking a resource megaproject and the appropriate level(s) of government. A recent example is the environmental agreement between the diamond-mining company Broken Hill Proprietary Company Inc. (BHP) and the federal and Northwest Territories governments (Vignette 7.1).

Environmental degradation of the North has affected local residents, especially Aboriginal residents who still depend on wildlife for much of their food. Arctic ecosystems, for example, are particularly vulnerable to contamination by toxic compounds transported by westerly moving air masses from major industrial cores located in China, Japan, and Russia. Chemical compounds, such as PCBs, accumulate in fatty tissues of mammals at the top of the food chain through the process of bioaccumulation. The consumption of meat from these animals on a regular basis by Inuit may adversely affect their health. The effects of both direct and indirect industrial contaminants on humans are not always clear, but the presence of toxic chemicals in the food chain is, at the very minimum, a danger sign. Health Canada scientists now suspect that subtle behavioural changes through nerve damage may have occurred in young Inuit children who have been exposed on a regular basis to a mix of pollutants, including those found in country food (Spears, 2002: A13). Such subtle damage to the human central nervous system begins in a most insidious manner—in the womb and during breast-feeding[1] (see 'Pending Disasters', below, for a fuller discussion).

The original inhabitants of the North have much knowledge about their environment through their long-standing relationship with the land and wildlife. This local expertise is called traditional ecological knowledge (TEK). TEK is an essential element of the holistic nature of Aboriginal culture; however, it does not fit well within Western scientific approaches to resolving environmental problems. Still, TEK has become part of environmental investigations and offers both an alternative view of how to identify potential threats to the environment associated with a proposed industrial project and help in formulating research hypothesis. One example was provided by Fikret Berkes in a public lecture at the University of Saskatchewan (Berkes, 2003). Berkes revealed that during his work with the Inuvialuit on global warming at Sachs Harbour, Northwest Territories, an Elder mentioned that, as a child, thunderstorms were rare events but now were much more frequent. When Berkes relayed this information to a climatologist, the climatologist recognized its meteorological significance, namely that the Arctic storm track may have shifted further north. Formal scientific investigation can use this information about a northward-shifting storm track as a plausible hypothesis.

TYPES OF ENVIRONMENTAL IMPACTS

By their size alone, megaprojects must have a serious impact on the environment. Examples are found in every type of resource industry. Pulp and paper mills have fouled northern waters by discharging toxic effluent, uranium mills have spilled radioactive waste onto the landscape, and heavy oil upgraders have emitted huge quantities of sulphur dioxide into the atmosphere.

Environmental pollution falls into two categories: that which originates in the area, such as the North, that has been polluted, and that which comes from outside the area or region. While pollution from outside blankets the entire North, local industrial projects affect the environment within a more restricted geographic area, though there is a 'shadow effect', which refers to all the indirect but related activities such as roads and power lines that are associated with an industry. For example, remote mining operations take place in a relatively small geographic area but indirect effects extend into a much larger area. With this understanding, we can consider northern industrial projects as having three types of impact on the environment: linear, areal, and accumulated effects.

Linear effects are associated with highways, seismic lines, and pipelines. While small in total area, these changes to the landscape have a greater effect than their areal extent would suggest. For example, wildlife is affected by such developments, especially migrating animals such as caribou. Also, access by hunters to wildlife is enhanced by new roads. Back in the late 1970s, the Berger Inquiry called for a wilderness zone along the Arctic coastal plain stretching from Alaska to Yukon so that the Porcupine caribou herd would not be disturbed by the presence of the proposed Mackenzie Valley Gas Pipeline.

Areal developments affect huge geographic areas. A hydroelectric project, for example, can have an impact on entire river basins by diverting rivers, creating giant reservoirs that flood extensive areas, and reversing the seasonal peak flows of the rivers, thus transforming the natural landscape into an industrial one. Hydroelectric development in northern Quebec has had a massive impact on the Grande River Basin—some describe the project as bordering on an ecological disaster (Berkes, 1982, 1998; Peters, 1999; Roebuck, 1999; Rosenberg, Bodaly, Hecky, and Newbury, 1987). Similar impacts have occurred in northern British Columbia, Manitoba, and Labrador at large-scale hydroelectric sites.

Cumulative environmental damage is more widespread than generally recognized. Certainly, few environmental impact assessment reviews have paid serious attention to the combined effect of several industrial projects within a single geographic area. The first major examination of cumulative effects focused on the Mackenzie River Basin that extends into Alberta and British Columbia. The environmental assessment review began by focusing on a single industrial proposal, the Alberta-Pacific pulp mill on the shores of the Athabasca River. After considerable political pressure from the government of the Northwest Territories, the environmental review board was drawn into the much broader issue of cumulative effects of toxic wastes discharged from Alberta mills into streams that eventually flow into the Mackenzie River and thereby affect residents of the Northwest Territories. Mitigating changes were made. Not only did Alberta-Pacific replace one chemical agent, chlorine, which is a major source of dioxins and furans, with another one, hydrogen peroxide, which produces much lower levels of dioxins and furans, but Edmonton announced that other pulp mills would be required to lower the level of dioxins and furans discharged as industrial effluent. Even after these changes, however, Yellowknife continued to argue that the proposed mill should be rejected on the grounds that residents of the Northwest Territories who eat the fish and drink the water from the Mackenzie River will be negatively affected and receive none of the benefits.

Pollution from the highly industrialized countries in the northern hemisphere reaches the seemingly pristine lands and waters of northern Canada in the form of minute particles and gases. These tiny substances originate from factories, farms, and urban centres in Russia, China, and other industrial nations. As these pollutants enter the global atmospheric and oceanic circulation systems, some eventually are deposited in Canada's North, where they are absorbed into the vegetation cover and water bodies. Gradually but inevitably, these chemical compounds enter the food chain. Most toxic pollutants originate as residue from the spraying of chemicals on crops, exhaust from automobiles, and effluent produced by industrial factories. A substance is declared toxic when it has an inherent potential to cause adverse effects to living organisms, including humans. Arctic haze, a form of smog caused by aerosols and by carbon particles from coal-based industries in Europe and Asia, is an example of global pollution affecting the North (Vignette 7.2). The danger of global pollution in the North is difficult to determine but is now considered a serious threat to the health of Inuit, who consume large quantities of meat from seal and caribou (see 'Pending Disasters', below, for further discussion).

Vignette 7.2 Arctic Haze and Ice Fog

Visibility in the Canadian North is generally clear. However, certain conditions dramatically limit visibility near the ground. Two features unique to the North are Arctic haze and ice fog. In the 1950s, airplane pilots flying in Alaska first identified a brownish haze on the horizon that later was called Arctic haze (Mitchell, 1956). This haze was an accumulation of gases from aerosols of sulphate and minute carbon particles. Both were carried from the industrial areas in the middle latitudes into the high latitudes of the Arctic by global winds. Some scientists believe that the Arctic may act as an atmospheric 'sink' for such contaminants.

Ice fog is a local phenomenon that occurs in urban areas in the winter. Ice fog forms when a continuous supply of water vapour is released into air with a temperature of -30°C or below and condenses into tiny ice crystals. Such conditions are common in Arctic towns where an inversion causes low temperatures and restricts mixing of air, and where combustion associated with vehicles and heating plants contributes more water to the atmosphere than can be absorbed without condensing. Whitehorse is a notorious example; when temperatures remain below −40°C for a week, visibility at ground level is reduced to less than 10 metres. More serious than the ice crystals themselves is the pollution associated with the fog. Lead and carbon dioxide concentrations exceed those found in any other city. Ice fogs may occur in Whitehorse any time from late November to the end of March. They are a growing problem in smaller Canadian Arctic towns such as Inuvik and Iqaluit.

SOURCES: Mitchell (1956: 195–211); Sugden (1982: 60); Reiesen (2000: 575–6).

Industrial countries have gained economically, pushing their gross national products to new heights. But these economic gains involve hidden costs associated with the pollution of environments not only in the immediate area surrounding the industrial development but also in areas far removed from the industrial site. The Canadian North, while not benefiting from such industrial development, shares the burden of industrial pollution. Such pollution is increasing. In a recent study by the Commission for Environmental Co-operation of North America covering 1995 to 1999, the release of toxic wastes by Canadian firms was reported to have increased by 8 per cent (Mittelstaedt, 2002: A6). The implications for Canada's North are ominous. The Canadian North faces an ever-growing threat from outside its borders, whether from plans to dispose of Toronto's garbage in northern sites, to store nuclear wastes in abandoned mine shafts, or to build new industrial plants in the middle latitudes.

Some pollutants are air-borne particles while others are water-borne. Evidence of environmental damage in the North is not always obvious. Such damage includes acid rain, whereby northern forests and lakes in eastern Canada have been adversely affected by emissions of sulphuric acid from industrial plants in southern Canada and the United States; the thinning of the ozone layer over the Arctic caused by the discharge of aerosols into the atmosphere; and the appearance of toxic chemicals in the Arctic food chain, which may have originated in industrial factories found in other parts of the northern hemisphere. Then there is the greenhouse effect, which suggests that global atmospheric pollution will warm the northern climate by over 5 degrees Celsius over the next 100 years. Such a rise in surface temperatures would have a profound effect on the polar environment by eliminating the ice cover on Hudson Bay and by causing the Arctic ice pack to retreat. Such global warming would destabilize the permafrost equilibrium, causing subsidence that might threaten bridges, pipelines, and buildings. In addition, the boreal forest would extend northward to the Arctic Ocean, thereby eliminating much habitat for Arctic animals, including polar bears.

EMERGENCE OF THE ENVIRONMENTAL MOVEMENT

In 1962, Rachel Carson's epoch-making *Silent Spring* appeared. Carson revealed the extent of industrial pollution, shocking Americans and galvanizing many to support and to join environmental organizations. After the publication of *Silent Spring*, the media reported more and more examples of industry disposing of toxic wastes in a haphazard manner. While these practices save the companies money, such activities can create ecological disasters. In the 1977, the seeping of chemicals from the Love Canal chemical waste site in Niagara Falls, New York, provoked an outrage from residents. Some years earlier, chemical wastes were dumped into the canal and later covered with soil. Then the site was developed into a residential area. Residents complained of ill health and even deaths from these chemicals. The state purchased 250 houses and spent US$250 million on a cleanup operation (McDonald, 2001: 23). In Canada, one of the worst examples is the abandoned gold mine at Deloro on the southern edge of the Canadian Shield in eastern Ontario, where the arsenic in the soil is 24 times the allowable level (Damsell, 1999: FP1). In addition, the Deloro site was used as a dump in the 1940s for uranium waste from the Manhattan Project in the US that produced the first atomic bombs and also received radioactive waste from an Eldorado Nuclear uranium refinery in Port Hope, Ontario. Companies, in many instances, have taken the position that they had not broken any laws and therefore had every right to release toxic materials into the atmosphere, rivers, and land. In doing so, industry destroyed the myth that 'business knows best'.

Why did such pollution take place in the past? Two factors came into play. First, the popular image of the North as a pristine region with few people was widespread. How could a few northern industrial developments harm such a vast wilderness and its inhabitants? Some assumed that nature would heal any damage to the environment. Canada saw this vast resource hinterland as a bottomless source of wealth and sought to exploit its natural riches by encouraging private developers. No one appreciated how such uncontrolled development would damage the environment for generations to come. For instance, many were unaware that industrial effluent injected into the North's rivers and lakes would spread into their watersheds or seep into the groundwaters. By the end of the twentieth century, some 10,000 abandoned mines in Canada contained toxic wastes (ibid.). The reclamation of these contaminated industrial sites will be very expensive—likely over $10 billion. In northern Saskatchewan, a number of tailings from abandoned uranium mines exist adjacent to Lake Athabasca. Like a ticking time bomb, these radioactive tailings, the legacy of a series of small-scale uranium mines in the 1950s, are slowly seeping into the groundwater and the waters of Lake Athabasca. The promised cleanup by the Saskatchewan government has not yet begun, but it will be very expensive, perhaps exceeding $1 billion (Saskatchewan Environment, 2002). How many more radioactive industrial sites exist across Canada is unknown.

Second, prior to environmental legislation in the 1970s, the discharge of industrial wastes into the environment was not regulated and resource companies simply discharged toxic wastes in the most efficient and cheapest manner. One frightful example took place in northern Ontario when a pulp mill at Dryden discharged its mercury-laced effluent into the Wabagoon River. The results were disastrous for the members of the Grassy Narrows and Whitedog Indian reserves, whose diet consisted of large quantities of fish (see 'Past Environmental Disasters', below). Another example is the toxic tailings that abound in Yukon from the days of the Klondike Gold Rush to the more recent mining operations at the lead/zinc mine at Faro. Lastly, construction firms paid little attention to the effect of removing the vegetative cover in permafrost areas; when the permafrost is thus disturbed, a process of erosion and subsidence begins that will last for decades. In sum, the legacy of careless and irresponsible actions by industry has scarred the northern environment and continues to haunt us by leaving the costly cleanup of dangerous materials or damaged landscapes for the Canadian taxpayer.

The environmental movement demanded legal regulations to protect the environment and ultimately the quality of human life. By the late 1960s, the environmental movement gained such political strength that governments could not ignore it. Support for the environmental movement grew, and NGOs (non-governmental organizations) were formed. By the 1970s, the Sierra Club, Greenpeace, and Pollution Probe were well known for their role in trying to protect the environment and wildlife from further damage by industry. In the Canadian North, the Canadian Arctic Resources Committee played an active role, often joining forces with Aboriginal organizations to confront resource development proposals and publishing its findings in *Northern Perspectives*. At the same time, scientists discovered that the damage to the environment was more extensive than earlier believed. Chemicals previously thought to be benign were actually toxic and such human-induced contaminants were found in wildlife consumed by Aboriginal peoples. Among these chemicals was chlorine, which is used extensively by the pulp and paper industry. Pesticides such as DDT were also found in northern food chains. In 1971, Canada banned the use of DDT. In the years to come, Ottawa passed other legislation to regulate the discharge of toxic wastes into the environment and it entered into an agreement with the United States to reduce acid rain. New pulp and paper mills, for example, must meet higher standards for toxic waste discharge. Owners of older mills are under pressure to upgrade their operations and some are claiming that the costs are too high for these mills to remain commercially viable.

More and more, the resource industry has to abide by strict environmental legislation. Recent scientific advances allow instruments to detect minuscule amounts of toxic contaminants undetectable only a decade ago. This allows regulatory agencies to lower the levels of toxic waste permissible in industrial effluent. Dioxins, for example, were declared toxic by Environment Canada in 1990 and new controls were introduced under the Environmental Contaminants Act to regulate chemicals harmful to health and/or the environment. The key contaminants are organochlorine (OC), pesticides (toxaphene, cholordane, and DDT), and industrial chemicals (PCBs).

ENVIRONMENTAL AGENCIES

By the early 1970s, the Canadian public had become aware of the hidden costs of industrial development and expressed their concerns to federal and provincial governments. In turn, governments passed legislation to protect the environment and created regulatory agencies to conduct environmental impact assessments of new industrial projects. A federal agency, the Federal Environment and Review Office (FEARO), was formed in 1973, and provinces organized similar agencies. In both cases, their purpose was to enforce federal and provincial environmental legislation. Provinces are responsible for assessing proposed projects in their respective provinces, while their federal counterpart (now the Canadian Environmental Assessment Agency) has jurisdiction in the three territories and in the provinces when federal interests are involved. In the territories, Aboriginal groups who have completed land claim agreements have gained a modicum of control over local environmental issues through co-management of resources and environmental impact assessments in their settlement areas (see 'Aboriginal Involvement in Environmental Impact Assessment' for more on this subject).

Under the Canadian Environmental Assessment Act 1995, the environmental assessment process consists of three basic stages: screening, comprehensive study, and a review panel.[2] Once a project is submitted, it undergoes an environmental screening. The screening procedure has three possible outcomes: (1) the project can proceed without further environmental review other than compliance with existing policies and standards; (2) if the potential adverse environmental effects are not fully known, then a more detailed assessment (comprehensive study) takes place; and (3) if the potential adverse effects are considered significant, then a review panel is established. Most projects, but especially small projects, are assessed and approved quickly under the screening process. On average, around 5,000 proposals are approved at the screening stage each year. Larger projects that have potential for greater environmental impacts undergo a comprehensive study where the developer submits a detailed report describing the proposed industrial project. If environmental impacts of the submitted project are considered potentially significant, then a review by an independent review panel takes place.

Under this review process, environmental impact assessment agencies are not attempting to halt industrial projects but rather to ensure that damage to the environment is minimized. However, several proposals have been rejected or withdrawn. The most famous case was the proposed Mackenzie Valley Pipeline Project. The Windy Craggy Project, while less well known, was also rejected. In the late 1980s Geddes

Resources of Toronto sought approval for mining an extremely rich deposit of copper and gold in the river valley of the Tatshenshini River in northwest British Columbia, one of the most pristine wild rivers in North America. However, the risks posed to the local water table and streams by the sulphur-rich tailings were considered too high and the company was forced to withdraw its application. But that is not the end of the story. In 1993, the area was designated as the Tatshenshini-Alsek Wilderness Park and, in 1994, this wilderness park was named a World Heritage Site (Vignette 7.3).

Vignette 7.3 From a Mining Proposal to a World Heritage Site

The pristine Tatshenshini River nearly became the site of a copper mine, but instead this river basin was named a World Heritage Site. This marks one of the few times that an industrial project has been rejected for environmental reasons. In the late 1980s, Geddes Resources Limited, a Toronto-based mining company, wanted to develop the huge Windy Craggy copper deposit in the mountainous corner of northwest British Columbia near Alaska, only some 80 kilometres downstream from Glacier Bay National Park and Preserve and 32 kilometres from Kluane National Park. This rich copper/gold deposit was valued at $8.5 billion. Geddes applied to the British Columbia environmental agency for permission to proceed with development. The original submission was unacceptable and the company withdrew it. Major flaws in the initial proposal were the danger of highly acidic water draining from the sulphide-rich tailings and the open-pit mine into groundwater and local streams, including the Tatshenshini River. The revised mine plan, released in January 1991, was estimated to increase development costs by $100 million, making the total cost around $600 million. It proposed to accomplish three goals: (1) reduce the amount of waste rock by 50 per cent; (2) separate sulphide-bearing rock from other waste rock (which would still be dumped on the nearby glacier); and (3) place the sulphide-bearing waste rock in a tailing pond. The revised proposal was not accepted, causing the company to abandon its plans for a mine. Efforts by environmental groups such as the Western Canada Wilderness Committee, World Wildlife Fund, Sierra Club, National Audubon Society, and Tatshenshini Wild played a critical role in shaping the final outcome. In 1993, the Tatshenshini-Alsek Wilderness Park was created. The following year, the park was designated as a World Heritage Site.

SOURCES: Environment Canada (1990); Geddes Resources Ltd (1990); Robinson (1991: B1); Searle (1991); Draper (2002: 357).

RECENT DEVELOPMENTS IN ENVIRONMENTAL IMPACT ASSESSMENT

In the Canadian North, Aboriginal groups have gained a measure of control over resource development and land-use management. Some of that control has come through comprehensive land claim agreements that have transferred to Aboriginal groups a measure of political power to govern land-use activities and assess proposed industrial projects. This newly won power is restricted, for the most part, to their settlement areas (areas determined by each specific comprehensive land claim agreement) and goes far beyond the concept of public involvement (Noble, 2000: 106–8). As Bone (1995: 175) observed:

> The Canadian North is undergoing a political realignment. The key to this devolution of political power lies in the resolution of northern land claims and the creation of co-management agencies to oversee the environment. This process began in 1984 with the transfer of the Environmental Impact Assessment process from Ottawa to Inuvik under the Inuvialuit Final Agreement. Out of this realignment, a new co-management arrangement for environmental impact assessment in the Inuvialuit Settlement Region was achieved. The co-managed agencies (Environmental Impact Screening Committee and the Environmental Impact Review Board) have equal Inuvialuit and non-Inuvialuit representatives. Unlike the Ottawa-based agency, these two co-managed boards have placed much more emphasis on possible negative impacts of proposed industrial projects on the environment and wildlife. This new emphasis reflects the Inuvialuit culture and the continuing importance placed on wildlife harvesting.

Within their settlement areas, these Aboriginal groups now share responsibility for environmental impact assessment of industrial proposals with Ottawa. Within the territories, five Aboriginal groups (Inuvialuit, Gwich'in, Sahtu/Métis, Inuit, and Yukon First Nations) have reached land claim agreements. In 1992, for example, the Gwich'in concluded their land claim agreement for some 22,000 square kilometres along both sides of the Yukon-NWT border, and that agreement spawned the Gwich'in Renewable Resource Board (GRRB). The GRRB is a co-management board that manages the renewable resources in the Gwich'in settlement area and deals with environment impact assessments. The Gwich'in Tribal Council and various government departments nominate an equal number of board members. In this way, power is shared between the Gwich'in and governments. Similar arrangements exist with other Aboriginal groups who have negotiated comprehensive land claim agreements.

Other forms of co-management frequently focus on a single resource. The Beverly-Qamanirjuaq Caribou Management Board, for example, is concerned with resource management of caribou over several jurisdictions in the territories and provinces and among several Aboriginal user groups and it must deal with the contentious issue of caribou harvesting by Dene and Inuit communities. While this board has only an advisory role, the various governments responsible for caribou tend to accept the recommendations of the Board. As Kendrick (2000: 1) stated: 'The Beverly-Qamanirjuaq caribou management board plays a unique role as interjurisdictional forum enabling the discussion of ecological issues not easily handled by distinct and formal political organization.'

The Northern Pipeline Environmental Impact Assessment and Regulatory Chair's Committee represents another example of the evolving nature of environment impact assessment bodies. The various members of this committee are involved in preparing a plan for assessing and regulating energy development in the Northwest Territories and their first tasks will likely deal with the Mackenzie Delta gas field and a pipeline leading from this gas field to southern markets (www.mveirb.nt.ca).

THE MACKENZIE VALLEY PIPELINE INQUIRY AND ITS AFTERMATH

In the 1960s, both provincial and federal governments eagerly sought to entice resource companies to invest in the North. Their vision was simple: resource development would provide benefits for everyone as well as transforming an undeveloped area into a resource hinterland. Often, governments gave resource companies complete freedom to construct projects as they saw fit. Such carte blanche may have reduced construction costs but it had negative implications for the environment. All this changed with the Mackenzie Valley Pipeline Inquiry. Headed by Justice Thomas Berger of the British Columbia Supreme Court, who formerly had served as chief counsel for the Nisga'a in the *Calder* case, this inquiry changed the course of northern development. It challenged the claims of large companies and influenced future environmental inquiries by ensuring that they included a strong social component and a place for public participation. But perhaps most importantly the inquiry was able to reach the Canadian public and change attitudes towards industrial development, the environment, and Aboriginal issues. Berger accomplished this by shifting the focus of the inquiry from technical issues to a much broader examination of the consequences of industrial development on the environment and the culture of Aboriginal peoples; by holding meetings in small Aboriginal communities where local people were encouraged to express their concerns; and by ensuring ample coverage by the media. This allowed Aboriginal leaders such as James Wah Shee, president of the National Indian Brotherhood (forerunner of the Assembly of First Nations), to present their views on land claims and other issues directly to the Canadian public. For these reasons, the Berger Inquiry was more than an investigation into a single project; it was an examination of the purpose of northern development, the place of the environment in Canadian society, and the potential role of northern peoples in that development.

The proposed Mackenzie Valley Pipeline Project called for the building of a pipeline to bring natural gas from the Prudhoe Bay field through the Mackenzie Valley to markets in southern Canada and the United States. Two companies, Canadian Arctic Gas Pipeline Limited (Arctic Gas) and Foothills Pipe Lines Ltd, applied to build this pipeline. Arctic Gas was a consortium of Canadian and American petroleum and pipeline companies while Foothills represented Alberta Gas Trunk Line and West Coast Transmissions. The estimated cost of the Arctic Gas proposal within Canada was $8 billion (Berger, 1977: 16). As discussed in Chapter 6, the Inquiry focused on three environmental and social issues: (1) the problem of burying a gas pipeline in areas with permafrost; (2) the threat to the Arctic ecosystem; and (3) the potential disruption of Aboriginal life and the impact on Aboriginal traditional culture.

The Berger Inquiry set the standard for future inquiries. First of all, industrial proposals are more carefully scrutinized by the federal environmental assessment and review process. Second, the role of public participation has been enlarged and hearings are held in the communities affected by proposed projects. Lastly, environmental issues affecting Aboriginal peoples have become a critical area of assessment because environmental impacts caused by industrial projects have a particularly harsh effect on habitat that supports hunting, trapping, and fishing.

Arctic pipeline proposals did not end with the Berger Report. In 1977, Foothills proposed an alternate route for Alaskan gas, the Alaska Highway Gas Pipeline Project. This project was approved in 1982 but has not yet been built because the cost of delivering natural gas from Prudhoe Bay to the Chicago market is still not commercially attractive (though this project is currently being reviewed and may receive financial assistance from the US government). Next in line was a joint project by Esso Resources Canada Ltd and Interprovincial Pipe Lines (NW) Ltd to construct a pipeline from Norman Wells to Zama, Alberta, which has been discussed at length in Chapter 6. The oil industry saw this project as a test case for northern pipelines and, if successful, as a model for much larger pipeline projects to bring Mackenzie Delta gas and Beaufort Sea oil to North American markets.

Issues about building a pipeline in discontinuous permafrost had not changed from the time of the Berger Report. For instance, the Norman Wells pipeline is designed to allow oil to flow near 0°C, thereby minimizing the possibility of the pipe either thawing or freezing the ground around the pipe. Originally, oil was chilled to –2°C before entering the pipe at Norman Wells to minimize ground disturbance such as subsidence caused by frost heave or the melting of ground ice (MacInnes, Burgess, Harry, and Baker, 1989: I and II; Burgess and Riseborough, 1989). After 1993, the company requested a summer/winter temperature regime with the oil chilled to –4°C in winter and raised to 12°C in summer (Burgess, Nixon, and Lawrence, 1998: 95). Over the past 25 years, the Norman Wells pipeline has maintained its integrity, though the pipe has shifted up to a metre in many places and water erosion has exposed the buried pipe (Vignette 7.4). The company has responded by filling in these depressions and by covering exposed steep slopes with wood chips to reduce surface heating of the ground.

The final story of a Mackenzie Valley pipeline should unfold with the development of the Mackenzie Delta natural gas field (see Chapter 6). While the proponents have yet to submit their proposed development plan to Ottawa, the environmental assessment process is already taking shape. The Northern Pipeline Environmental Impact Assessment and Regulatory Chair's Committee has put into place a series of agreements with various interest groups along the Mackenzie River Valley. For example, a Memorandum of Understanding between the federal Minister of the Environment and the Inuvialuit, represented by the Inuvialuit Game Council, was signed on 7 October 2002. This agreement ensures Inuvialuit participation in the environmental review of a gas pipeline and a natural gas field development in the Inuvialuit Settlement Region. Similar agreements are expected to involve the Dene groups that have settled their land claims with Ottawa and therefore have the infrastructure in place to participate in the anticipated environmental review.

PAST ENVIRONMENTAL DISASTERS

Most of the burden of industrial pollution in the North has been borne by Aboriginal Canadians who rely heavily on the land and water for food. One of the worst examples of industrial pollution affecting Indians occurred 30 years ago along the English-Wabigoon River system near Kenora, Ontario (Shkilnyk, 1985). Between 1962 and 1975 Dryden Chemicals Ltd, a subsidiary of Reid Paper Ltd, produced chlorine and other

Vignette 7.4 Integrity of the Norman Wells Pipeline

Scientists at the Norman Wells pipeline hearings were concerned about thermal conduction, warming of the disturbed surface of the pipeline route, and global warming. The first concern was that the moving oil could be expected to conduct heat or cold through the steel pipe and thereby affect the surrounding ground. Two possible problems were identified. One was that the oil could be cooled while flowing through a permanently frozen section of the pipeline route and then cause freezing of ground in an unfrozen section. If the previously unfrozen section contained large amounts of moisture, then the ground and the pipe could be subject to considerable frost heave. In another scenario, areas of frozen ground surrounding the pipe could be warmed and thawed by the flow of oil. Again, should there be ice-rich ground beneath the pipe, considerable subsidence could occur, possibly leading to the rupture of the pipe.

A second problem might arise through the removal of ground cover. In the course of building the pipeline, the forested vegetation was removed to form a right-of-way and a trench was dug and then refilled. The surface of this exposed right-of-way would absorb more solar energy, causing much greater thawing. Repeated freezing and thawing of the ground around the pipe over a decade or so could lift the pipe out of the ground.

Lastly, the scientists testifying at the hearing argued that the greenhouse effect could result in the warming of the northern hemisphere by as much as 3 C° over the life span of the pipeline.

SOURCE: Duffy (1981: 33–4).

chemicals used as bleach in the pulp and paper mill of Reid Paper. The mill flushed its waste products into the Wabigoon River. The mill effluent contained a relatively high level of mercury, which worked its way into the aquatic food chain of the river system. In 1970, the Ontario government discovered that the level of mercury found in fish in a 500-km stretch downstream from the pulp and paper mill was dangerous to health, and advised the Ojibway communities at Grassy Narrows and Whitedog reserves not to eat fish from these rivers. It also banned commercial fishing on all lakes and tributaries of the English and Wabigoon rivers. The impact on the Ojibway was staggering. First, 90 members from the White Dog and Grassy Narrows reserves exhibited serious neurological symptoms characteristics of methyl mercury poisoning (Roebuck, 1999: 80). Second, the Ojibway lost their economic base with the collapse of commercial fishing and guiding income. Third, they could no longer trust their environment because one of their traditional sources of food, fish, was the source of their illness. This loss of trust in a basic tenet of their culture represented a devastating psychological blow.

At that time, governments had very few regulations regarding industrial waste. For the most part, untreated industrial wastes, like those of the pulp and paper mill at Kenora, were discharged into water bodies. Once society realized that such pollution was affecting the quality of life, pressure was placed on governments and industry to reduce industrial damage to the environment. With the various regulatory agencies and environmental groups now in place, most industrial projects built 40 years ago would not pass current environment standards. Resource industries, too, have accepted the new government regulations and the costs associated with cleaning up industrial sites and properly disposing of toxic wastes. However, companies that fouled the environment in the past have left the Canadian taxpayer to foot the bill. All of these events have made the Canadian public very wary of new resource projects even though companies are much more concerned about their impact on the environment. To some degree, resource companies have accepted their social responsibility to protect the environment from toxic wastes. While environmental protection has been reinforced by government regulations, companies are more willing to pay the extra costs to keep from damaging the environment *providing that their rival companies are compelled to pay for the same costs.* This acceptance is based on the so-called 'level playing field' model found in competitive capitalism.

Each resource project has a distinct environmental footprint. Most are highly localized. Not so with hydroelectric projects. They have a 'regional' impact on river basins. Dams flood vast areas of land, alter stream flows, cause shoreline erosion, and increase the mercury content of the water in reservoirs. In the past, the cost of pre-flood clearing of trees was considered too expensive, and anyone who has visited a reservoir is struck by shoreline slumping and vegetation debris. Unfortunately, nature does not correct such man-made problems quickly. Some 70 years after the construction of the Island Falls Dam on the Churchill River in Saskatchewan, standing snags (dead trees) lie just below the surface of the reservoir (Sokatisewin Lake) while along its shoreline, trees have a tilted or 'drunk' appearance.

Major hydroelectric projects have altered the physical character of river basins in British Columbia, Manitoba, and Quebec. In all cases, hydroelectric development is an important element of the provincial economy. The purpose of energy development is to supply low-cost electrical power to industrial users and to export surplus power to markets in neighbouring provinces and the United States. In Manitoba, initial plans called for the construction of hydroelectric projects on the Churchill and Nelson rivers. In 1961, the Kelsey hydroelectric dam was built and the nickel smelter at Thompson consumed most of its output. Five other dams have been constructed: Grand Rapids, Jenpeg, Kettle Rapids, Long Spruce, and Limestone. In the early 1990s, the Conawapa Dam proposal was presented but the project was shelved because markets in the United States were unable to absorb the power at high enough prices (the Great Whale River Project in northern Quebec faced a similar problem). In November 2002, plans to build the Conawapa Dam gained new strength because of a combination of growing energy needs in Ontario and the pressure to reduce greenhouse gases, which eliminates the possibility of new coal-fired thermal electric plants in Ontario. For the Conawapa Dam to proceed to the construction phase, the high cost of building a hydroelectric power line from Manitoba to southern Ontario would have to be resolved. If this line is conceived of as the start of a national power grid, Ottawa might help with its financing (Benzie, 2002: A4).

In the early 1970s, Manitoba decided to increase the water flowing through the Nelson River by diverting most of the flow of the Churchill River. A control dam was built at the outlet of Southern Indian Lake to prevent water from continuing to flow to the mouth of the Churchill River, and a channel was dug between the southern edge of the lake and the Rat River, which flows into the Nelson River. The water level on Southern Indian Lake rose by three metres and in 1976 water began to flow into the Nelson Basin. While the amount of electric power generated by existing power stations on the Nelson River increased, the diversion of water from the Churchill River to the Nelson River is seen as an ecological disaster (Rosenberg, Bodaly, Hecky, and Newbury, 1987: 81). Submerged vegetation still chokes the lake, causing oxygen depletion during the winter, and mercury levels in fish have risen, making frequent consumption unwise. Changes in the depth of water in the lake have greatly diminished the white-fish population, resulting in the collapse of the commercial whitefish fishery. Commercial fishers, most of whom are of Indian ancestry, have received compensation from Manitoba Hydro through the Northern Flood Agreement or, in the case of those fishers living in the Indian village of South Indian Lake, from special compensation agreements with Manitoba Hydro (ibid., 83).

PENDING DISASTERS?

Global pollution, particularly toxic particles belonging to chlorine-containing organic compounds, has affected the food chain and Aboriginal peoples. Starting with single-celled algae, these toxic substances move up the food chain, becoming more concentrated with each step. This biological process is known as biomagnification. The main sources of these pollutants are the pesticide known as DDT and a chemical waste from industrial processes referred to as PCBs (polychlorinated biphenyls). By the 1970s, federal scientists were well aware of the presence of toxic elements in the Arctic food chain and its potential hazard to human life. Efforts by NGOs, especially the Canadian Arctic Resources Committee, succeeded in alerting the general public to this problem and more recent studies have confirmed the danger to humans (Tesar, 2000; Delormier and Kuhnlein, 2000; Spears, 2002). But this problem was clearly known in 1989 when a federal government official announced that a study of PCBs found relatively high levels in seals and caribou, the principal game consumed by Inuit. Furthermore, the study revealed that virtually all of the PCBs and related organochlorine contaminants found in southern Canada are also present in the Arctic, though usually at much lower levels. Beluga whales in the St Lawrence River, for example, have PCB levels 25 times higher than those in the eastern Arctic.

For the Inuit, whose diet consists partly of country food, the presence of PCBs in wildlife is disturbing and is a potential serious health hazard. Government officials have stressed that they did not believe there was any immediate danger to those eating country food and that these traditional foods have greater nutritional value than many of the prepared foods available in the local stores. In 1990, a study of Arctic beluga whales in the western Arctic revealed extremely high levels of cadmium and mercury. While the federal government has not yet set guidelines for cadmium, the Health Protection Branch in Ottawa recommends that people not eat fish containing more than 0.5 parts mercury per million. Since the whales captured by Aboriginal hunters had levels of mercury well above the federal guideline, the consumption of these mammals by the Inuit may be injurious to their health. But the scientific world expressed conflicting views over the threat of mercury to northern peoples. According to Caulfield (2000: 491–2):

> Preliminary research suggests that mercury levels in some regions of the Arctic are already high enough to put children at risk. People in northern Greenland and Inuit and Cree in the eastern Canadian Arctic have the highest exposures. Fully 29 per cent of Canadian Inuit in the eastern Arctic have daily intakes above limits recommended by the World Health Organization (WHO). Analysis of archaeological samples from the 15th century Arctic shows that current mercury levels are three times higher than 500 years before.

Roebuck recognizes the trade-off between low levels of mercury in fish and the nutritional value of fish to Cree. He worries that without fish in their diet, the Cree's nutritional and psychological well-being will suffer. Roebuck recommends that those who already have high levels of mercury change their diet, i.e., reduce the number of fish eaten, but that others could continue to consume fish. Roebuck (1999: 88–9) describes this dilemma:

> All food supplies contain undesirable chemicals such as mercury. Because mercury is naturally present in the environment, it has undoubtedly been present in (i.e., has contaminated) fish throughout the world for eons. It was present in the fish of the James Bay region when the ancestors of the present-day Cree first migrated to the area. What is different now is a general and widespread elevation in concentration of mercury in fish due to global and regional industrial activity, and localized elevations from the formation of reservoirs.

Northern peoples are confused and even suspicious of this scientific information. In any case, how could they stop eating the traditional foods that Mother Earth provided to them? What would they substitute for country foods? In the Inuit community of Salluit in northern Quebec (Nunavik), Poirier and Brooke (2000) reported that local resistance to scientific information on contaminants in fish and wildlife is strong. Hunters trust in their own ability to detect a sick animal and the notion of 'poisoned' animals or fish, as described by scientists, is difficult for them to comprehend. But more than that, Inuit ontology is based on a trust relationship between the Inuit and the animal world. As an Inuk woman explained, 'We do not inflict injustices on the animals and trust that they in turn are good for us, we who do not wrong them in some way' (ibid., 87).

Yet, Western science has recorded high levels of toxic chemicals in seemingly healthy wildlife and fish. Scientists are concerned that several groups of persistent organic pollutants (POPs), including lindane (HCH), toxaphene, DDT, and their metabolites such as PCBs, are a growing threat to Aboriginal peoples in northern Canada (Reiersen, 2000: 576). In the late 1980s, minute particles of residues of organo-chlorine compounds were discovered in the Arctic food chain (Bidleman et al., 1989). These invisible contaminants had been transported to the remotest areas of the Arctic and are found in concentrated quantities in large mammals. Given enough accumulation in humans, other industrial substances such as DDT and PCBs can become extremely toxic and eventually poisonous. Since both contaminants are found in the Arctic food chain, and since Inuit eat large amounts of seal, caribou, and whale, a health risk already exists.

HYDROELECTRIC PROJECTS, CROWN CORPORATIONS, AND THE ENVIRONMENT

Hydroelectric projects have an enormous impact on the environment. Crown corporations are the leading agency in the design, construction, and operation of northern hydroelectric projects. Provincial power companies have built large-scale hydroelectric projects across the Provincial Norths. Of these projects, La Grande Project in northern Quebec had the greatest geographic impact on the northern landscape, with massive changes to the ecological system in northern Quebec. Environmental impacts caused by damming the Grande River (the first phase of the James Bay Project) are well documented (Gill and Cooke, 1975; Berkes, 1982; Rosenberg, Bodaly, Hecky, and Newbury, 1987; Cloutier, 1987; Gorrie, 1990; Hornig, 1999). In a recent book on the social and environmental impacts of the James Bay Project, Coppinger and Ryan (1999: 69) played down the direct ecological impact of such a massive project and suggested, rather, that newly constructed roads in the James Bay area would have a much greater impact on the natural vegetation and wildlife because they would increase the number of southern visitors and expand the hunting range of local people.

> As we have pointed out, the La Grande complex is not going to be an ecological disaster. But the roads leading to it and the increasing human population could be. People can have a very real impact on productivity, diversity, and species survival. The increasing number of people, be they miners, foresters, developers, electric workers, vacationers, campers, hunters, anglers, or residents, all change the nature of the region. Habitat loss through construction and development reduces the region's bioproductivity. It is the increasing stresses placed on individual species because of their commercial, ritual, or recreational value that further reduce productivity and diversity.

Fikret Berkes (1998: 106) reported that the Chisasibi Cree took advantage of road access to an area near the LG-4 dam where a large number of caribou had congregated: 'Large numbers were taken (the actual kill was unknown), even though the caribou stayed in the area only for a month or so. Chisasibi hunters used the road, bringing back truckloads of caribou. There was so much meat that, according to one hunter, "people overdosed on caribou".' This hunt involved 'shooting wildly, killing more than they could carry, and not disposing of wastes properly'. Like other caribou hunting peoples, the Quebec Cree strongly believe that caribou must be respected, meaning that hunters must only take what they need. This concept of a mutual relationship between the Cree and the caribou is strongly etched into Cree spirituality. Cree hunting leader Robbie Matthew translated this cultural tradition into a simple but foretelling phrase: 'show no respect and the game will retaliate' (ibid.).

The James Bay Energy Corporation (JBEC) was incorporated in 1971 for the specific purpose of developing the hydroelectric potential of the rivers on the Quebec side of James Bay (Vignette 7.5). It is a subsidiary of Hydro-Québec. This corporation describes the James Bay Project as the symbol of Quebec's creative genius and it sees the hydroelectric project as 'development in accord with its environment' (JBEC, 1988: vii). The James Bay Energy Corporation formed an environment department whose task was to minimize the environmental damage caused by the construction of this massive hydroelectric project. The construction of the James Bay Project created four different types of aquatic systems: reservoirs, diversion zones, rivers with reduced flow downstream from diversion sites, and one river in which the flow was increased. The project also impacted on the surrounding environment through the construction of work camps and roads. According to a JBEC report (ibid., 25), 'the remedial work in each of these habitats had the same goal: either to improve their biological stability and productivity or to facilitate access and improve hunting, fishing, and trapping conditions of Aboriginal people.'

The major physical changes caused by the creation of the James Bay Project include the flooding of large areas and radical changes in seasonal stream flows. Other environmental changes are:

- increase in the mercury concentrations in these flooded waters caused by the biological process associated with the decay of drowned vegetation, particularly trees, and the appearance of mercury in the food chain, including fish, after empoundment;
- shoreline flooding and erosion, which eliminates valuable animal and waterfowl habitat;
- changes in the salinity and temperature of riverine estuaries and James Bay itself that could affect ice cover and the habitat for fish and mammals.

Evidence suggests that beluga whales are affected by changes in the salinity and temperature of waters caused by hydroelectric dams. By increasing the salinity and temperature of sea water at the mouths of rivers, hydroelectric projects have reduced the habitat of beluga whales and eliminated preferred calving sites. The St Lawrence beluga whales have already felt this environmental impact and no longer congregate at the mouths of the Bersimis, Manicouagan, and Outardes rivers (all of which are dammed), and the dammed rivers flowing into James Bay could have the same impact on the estuarine habitat of the Hudson Bay beluga whales (Brunett et al., 1989: 24).

FOREST INDUSTRY AND THE ENVIRONMENT

The forest industry is one of the major employers in the Subarctic. Consequently, local residents are often inclined to minimize the potential environmental damage caused by a pulp and paper mill. Provincial governments also support the mills and encourage the development of new ones because they are anxious to expand and diversify regional and provincial economies. On the other hand, many Canadians—particularly those downstream from such mills—are adamant that the effluents should be reduced and toxic substances eliminated. In the late 1980s, the federal government introduced stiffer

Vignette 7.5 The James Bay Project

The scope of the James Bay Hydroelectric Project is staggering. It involves the transformation of the northern landscape in Quebec and a new lifestyle for the Indians and Inuit living in this area of the Subarctic. This project will eventually harness the energy of all the rivers flowing through 350,000 square km of northwestern Quebec, thereby producing up to 28,000 megawatts of electrical power. At least a dozen rivers will have their water diverted, leaving shrunken waterways with pools of water and dried-up riverbeds. The water is to be collected in vast reservoirs and directed towards generating stations where electric energy is or will be produced. This massive project involves some 20 rivers and about one-fifth of the total area of Quebec. The James Bay Project is to develop three river basins.

1. *La Grande River Basin.* The first phase of the James Bay Project was completed in 1985 at a cost of about $16 billion. Three dams, reservoirs, and power stations were built on La Grande River. These installations are named LG-2, LG-3, and LG-4. Five rivers were diverted to provide more water for La Grande River. Additional developments were completed in 1996, including six dams, reservoirs, and power stations at LG-1, Brisay, Eastmain 1 and 2, and Laforge 1 and 2.

2. *Great Whale River Basin.* Located north of La Grande Basin, plans to develop the Great Whale River Basin were cancelled in 1994 when potential American utility customers backed out of tentative agreements to purchase electrical power from this development. Originally, Hydro-Québec planned to create three power stations, which would require the diversion of two rivers.

3. *Nottaway River Basin.* This hydroelectric development involves three large rivers, the Nottaway, Broadback, and Rupert. Water from the Nottaway and Rupert rivers is to be diverted into the Broadback River, where eight power stations are planned.

regulations affecting the discharge of untreated or toxic industrial wastes into the environment. The forest industry must now meet much higher environmental standards. The critical question is, what level of pollution is society willing to accept?

Degradation of the environment by pulp and paper mills in the past was so severe that the industry has been singled out for stiffer regulations. In the late 1980s, for example, it was responsible for half of all the industrial wastes discharged into water bodies and 6 per cent of those sent into the atmosphere (Sinclair, 1990: 39). No industry is more vulnerable to public pressures than the forest industry, for it depends on Crown-owned timber leases for its raw material. The forest industry realized that it must be more environmentally sensitive or else it could be denied timber leases, particularly in the more fragile northern environments. Two critical issues face the forest industry: clear-cut logging practices, and the discharge of toxic chemicals into the environment by pulp and paper companies.

Clear-cutting has been banned or restricted in many parts of the developed world. The argument for clear-cutting is economic efficiency. Forest industry officials maintain that sustainable, balanced development of forests can best be achieved by clear-cutting because natural and artificial regeneration can then take place. Environmentalists disagree and argue that regeneration is best after selective cutting. Other environmental problems associated with clear-cutting occur in mountainous and hilly terrain where serious erosion and flooding problems may result. The sizes of clear-cut areas normally are limited. Yet, many environmental groups strongly oppose any form of clear-cutting. The Canadian forest industry's continued practice of clear-cutting has raised the ire of European 'greens', who have urged the European Parliament to pass legislation boycotting Canadian forest products (forest exports to Europe reached $5 billion in 2001).

The economic attraction of clear-cutting often outweighs the damage to the environment in the eyes of industry and governments. In the 1980s, the Alberta government jumped at the opportunity to lease its northern forests to allow the construction of new pulp and paper plants. The province and the federal government provided public funds. Alberta-Pacific Forest Industries Inc., for example, has received a $300 million loan and public funds estimated at $75 million to pay for the access roads and rail lines to its proposed bleached-kraft pulp mill near the community of Athabasca. The major companies behind these massive investments totalling $4.5 billion into the Alberta forests were two Japanese firms (Daishowa Canada and Alberta-Pacific Forest Industries Inc.) and four North American firms (Procter and Gamble Cellulose Ltd, Weldwood of Canada Ltd, Alberta Newsprint Company Ltd, and Alberta Energy Company Ltd).

While there are undoubtedly benefits of economic diversification and new jobs for northerners in these projects, the northern environment will be negatively affected, primarily by industrial wastes discharged into the air and water. This trade-off has meant that economic benefits far outweighed environmental losses. Over the past 25 years, a slow but steady shift in this relationship has taken place, i.e., the trade-off is now more balanced. This shift began in Alberta when public concern forced the proponents of the Alberta-Pacific plan to change their milling operation to reduce the volume of toxic chemical residues of dioxins and furans to be discharged into the Athabasca River. These changes were made after the environmental review board recommended halting the project until more was known about the potential impact of effluents from the mill on the Athabasca, Slave, and Mackenzie rivers. The federal environmental agency approved the company's proposal to replace chlorine with hydrogen peroxide in its bleaching process, in conjunction with the provincial government announcement that it would force other pulp mills on the Athabasca River to lower the level of waste discharge containing dioxins and furans. These mills include Weldwood at Hinton, Millar Western and Alberta Newsprint near Whitecourt, and Alberta Energy Company at Slave Lake. All of these mills discharge higher levels of toxic chemicals into the Athabasca River than the estimated figures for the proposed Alberta-Pacific mill. Nonetheless, the government of the Northwest Territories continues to oppose the project.

INDUSTRIAL DEVELOPMENT AND THE ENVIRONMENT

Society must make choices between industrial development and the northern environment. Often this trade-off is simplified into a 'jobs versus the environment' argument. In making these choices, decision-makers too often underestimate or, worse yet, ignore the cumulative effects of a series of industrial projects and the long-term costs to society. While Ottawa has passed environmental legislation that limits damage to the land, older military and mining developments paid little heed to the environment. Unfortunately, the cost of repairing a damaged environment often falls to the tax-payers. Two examples illustrate this point.

- The removal of PCBs and contaminated soil from 21 Distant Early Warning radar sites cost Ottawa some $250 million.
- The cost of removing some 270,000 tonnes of arsenic waste from the Giant Mine near Yellowknife is estimated at $250 million. Since the arsenic could seep into the groundwater and affect local sources of drinking water, measures must be taken to remove this toxic waste. When the owners of Giant Mine—Royal Oak Mines— declared bankruptcy, the federal government was stuck with the costly environ-mental cleanup. Another mining company, Miramar Mining Corporation, struck an agreement in 2001 with the federal Department of Indian Affairs and Northern Development (DIAND) to keep the mine operating, but this agreement requires DIAND to pay $300,000 per month towards environmental compliance costs. In addition, it does not resolve the costly problem of disposing of the arsenic waste.

Geopolitics favours industrial development over the environment. For instance, even though Canada was a signatory to the Sustainability Protocol of the UN Conference on Environment and Development (UNCED—'Earth Summit'), held in Rio de Janeiro in 1992, economic and political realities continue to dictate that the environment takes second place to development. Global events can intervene into our national decision-making.[3] The Middle East crisis has implications for a secure sup-ply of oil for America. Washington's reaction is to expand energy supplies from North America. For that reason, President Bush approved oil drilling in the ecologically sensitive Arctic National Wildlife Refuge in Alaska in 2001. However, the President's proposal did not have the support of the US Senate and the Senate rejected his proposal in 2002. Still, President Bush came down on the side of industrial development. He rejected the argument that drilling activity would harm the Porcupine River caribou herd, which travels 400 miles from the Yukon to the Alaskan coastal plain for calving in May and June. Of course, America's dependency on Middle East oil provides the overriding political reason for continued interest in opening the Arctic National Wildlife Refuge to oil exploration and this interest has been magnified by the events following 11 September 2001. In January 2003, the Republican-controlled Congress and Senate began plotting a new strategy to pass legislation permitting oil exploration in the Arctic National Wildlife Refuge (Morton, 2003: FP1).

Some 25 years earlier, Justice Thomas Berger had come to an opposite decision by declaring that the fragile Arctic coastal plain extending beyond Alaska into Yukon and the western edge of the Northwest Territories should forever remain a wilderness refuge. The entire ecological zone serves as the grazing and calving area for the Porcupine River caribou herd. As Berger pointed out in 1977, hunting of the caribou by Gwich'in hunters remains an essential element of their economy and culture.

Without a doubt, economic development does affect the environment. The key question is 'does its impact fall within acceptable limits?' Drilling for oil in the Arctic coastal plain, for example, may not fall within acceptable limits, while the construction of a pipeline along the Mackenzie River Valley may be considered acceptable. Society must choose between development and the environment. Through the environmental impact assessment process, society has exerted its power to control the type of development and to put constraints on the amount of damage to the natural environment. Some 50 years ago, the environment was a virtual dumping ground for industrial wastes. No effective controls were in place, but no one worried because society had yet to recognize the pollution problem. The law was no help because it left private individuals and companies affected by pollution problems caused by others to seek a negotiated settlement with the polluter or to turn to the courts. Governments did not protect Crown land because they were too interested in promoting industrial development to pay attention to industrial pollution. Today, society is more conscious of the hidden costs of industrial projects, and governments have been pressured to pass legislation to protect the environment and to require developers to factor these hidden costs into their project proposals.

Society makes choices by means of long-term land-use planning and the impact assessment process. Since the 1980s only a handful of industrial proposals have been rejected, but, much more important, the vast majority have had to be modified to accommodate environmental concerns. In this way, Canadian society is able to encourage resource development and still maintain a reasonable level of protection for the environment. Environmental impact assessment aims at minimizing industrial impacts. This process is one of checks and balances, evolving over time and now placing more emphasis on ensuring that the industrial site is returned to its natural state. Industry and the need for jobs remain of paramount concern. Land-use planning, whether urban or rural planning, offers society a means of regulating industrial proposals and setting long-term land-use development goals. Company proposals must be submitted to an environmental impact assessment panel for approval, rejection, or modification. Under the comprehensive land claim agreements, environmental impact assessment for land claim settlement areas is shared between the particular Aboriginal group and governments. Co-management of environmental impact assessment has allowed local issues, especially those affecting wildlife, to receive much more attention than under the former system controlled by Ottawa. While the assessment process is not perfect, the current version is a vast improvement over the initial procedures of the 1970s. Still, our society must address four related questions:

- Given that new industrial projects will be announced, is there an acceptable level of industrial pollution?
- Do the recent advances in EIA ensure an acceptable level of cumulated industrial pollution?
- Is there a point when environmental concerns come before jobs, i.e., when industry is not allowed into certain areas?
- How do we halt the toxic chemicals that originate in foreign countries from reaching the North and then enter the food chain, water supplies, and atmosphere where they threaten the health of Canadians but especially northern Aboriginal peoples?

TRADITIONAL ECOLOGICAL KNOWLEDGE

The discussion so far has taken place using a Western 'ecological' paradigm. Aboriginal peoples have a different paradigm, steeped in their long-standing relationship with the land, that evokes a different spiritual context. While Western culture sees humans at the top of a hierarchical arrangement of living creatures, Aboriginal culture views the world from a holistic perspective where all life is seen as a series of relationships among equals. Can this non-Western approach to the land and wildlife help in addressing the questions posed above and in formulating a gentler and more respectful approach to the environment when the prospect of resource development enters the equation? Sheila Watt-Cloutier, the president of Inuit Circumpolar Conference Canada, made these poignant remarks at Kuujjuaq, Nunavik, the site of the Ninth Circumpolar General Assembly (Watt-Cloutier, 2002: 2):

> As Inuit, we think in holistic ways. We know that everything is interrelated—the threads of our lives are woven into a garment that is inherently sustainable. Our culture reflects our values, spirit, economy, and health. Our land and natural resources sustain us, and the health of these resources affects our health. If we use and develop these resources with respect, our environment will remain healthy and so will we. The process of the hunt is invaluable, through it we learn what is required to survive and how to gain wisdom—the key to living and acting sustainably.

Peter Usher (2000) argues that traditional ecological knowledge (TEK) must be an essential element in environmental assessment and management. While Usher's view is specific to the Territory of Nunavut, the concept, if valid in Nunavut, could complement Western scientific approaches to environment assessment and management questions in other jurisdictions as well. How the Western capitalist and TEK paradigms can be meshed remains troublesome because attitudes, customs, and values in the two cultures are so different.

Perhaps a bridge between the two paradigms, based on the principle of respect for the land, does exist. Such respect is found at the core of Cree tradition. But Cree hunters sometimes fail to show such respect. Earlier, an account of the Chisasibi Cree killing more caribou than necessary was presented. Fikret Berkes, in an essay entitled 'Indigenous knowledge and resource management systems in the Canadian subarctic', has described how Chisasibi hunters violated the traditional code in 1983–4. The following winter, 1984–5, no caribou appeared on the road where thousands were seen the previous year. The elders recalled that a similar disaster took place at the turn of the century when hunters with repeating rifles lost all self-control and slaughtered the caribou at a crossing point along the Caniapiscau River, leaving many carcasses rotting in the water. Again the caribou disappeared. Elders, who know that change occurs in cycles, said that the caribou would return but that the hunters must respect them, taking only what they need. The caribou did return and the Chisasibi hunt in 1985–6 was conducted in a controlled and responsible manner, illustrating that the Cree can exercise self-management. The question is, can corporations and Crown corporations show the same respect for the land?

NOTES

1. Spears (2002) reported that the Health Canada documents stated that:
   - People living in the Arctic are exposed to a wide variety of persistent environmental pollutants but most toxicological studies . . . only test single compounds or simple mixtures.
   - It is not clear these single chemical studies accurately represent the toxicity associated with chemical mixtures.
   - Fetuses and young infants are especially sensitive to these pollutants, which have been associated with a wide range of toxic effects including learning and developmental deficiencies.
   - Subtle behavioural changes through nerve damage can happen in young children even where there is no obvious evidence of 'gross toxicological effects'.
2. On 20 March 2001 the Minister of the Environment tabled Bill C-19, An Act to Amend the Canadian Environmental Assessment Act, which was passed into law the following year.
3. Acid rain is an important type of global pollution. In the case of North America, the source of most acid rain is found in the United States while much of it is deposited in Canada. The term 'acid rain' refers to the deposit of acidic pollutants, chiefly oxides of sulphur and nitrogen, on the earth's surface. The principal source of these air-borne pollutants is industrial and urban emission of sulphur dioxide (SO_2). Current annual emissions of SO_2 in Canada and the United States are nearly 30 million tonnes, most of which come from coal-fired thermal electrical power plants in the United States. In Canada, significant sources of SO_2 emissions are copper and nickel smelters and heavy-oil upgrading plants. Once in the atmosphere, sulphur and nitrogen dioxides are easily absorbed in water vapour and converted into sulphuric and nitric acids. When washed out of the air by rain, snow, or fog, this acidic precipitation sets off a chain of chemical and biological reactions. The effects of acid rain are most pronounced on rivers and lakes, where an increase in the acidity of the water can have a devastating effect on aquatic life, particularly fish populations. Thousands of lakes in eastern Canada have already lost their fish populations due to water acidification and many more are threatened.

REFERENCES AND SELECTED READINGS

Benzie, Robert. 2002. 'PM touts Manitoba hydro dam to Eves', *National Post,* 27 Nov., A4.

Berger, Thomas R. 1977. *Northern Frontier, Northern Homeland: The Report of the Mackenzie Valley Pipeline Inquiry.* Ottawa: Department of Supply and Services.

Berkes, Fikret. 1982. 'Preliminary Impacts of the James Bay Hydroelectric Project, Quebec, on Estuarine Fish and Fisheries', *Arctic* 35, 4: 524–30.

———. 1998. 'Indigenous knowledge and resource management systems in the Canadian subarctic', in Berkes and Folke (1998: 98-129).

———. 2003. 'Inuit Observations of Climate Change: Designing a Collaborative Project', public lecture at the University of Saskatchewan, 9 Jan.

——— and Carl Folke, eds. 1998. *Linking Social and Ecological Systems: Management Practices and Social Mechanisms for Building Resilience.* Cambridge: Cambridge University Press

Bidleman, T.F., G.W. Patton, M.D. Walla, B.T. Hargrave, W.P. Vass, P. Erickson, B. Fowler, V. Scott, and D.J. Gregor. 1989. 'Toxaphene and Other Organochlorines in Arctic Ocean Fauna: Evidence for Atmospheric Delivery', *Arctic* 42, 4: 307–13.

Bone, Robert M. 1995. 'Power Shifts in the Canadian North: A Case Study of the Inuvialuit Final Agreement', in Roland Vogelsang, ed., *Proceedings of Canada in Transition Symposium: Results of Environmental and Human Geographical Research*. Kanada-Studien im Auftrag des Instituts für Kanada-Studien, Band 22, Bochum: Universitätsverlag Dr. N. Brokmeyer, 175–90.

Brunett, J.A., C.T. Dauphiné Jr, S.H. McCrindle, and T. Mosquin. 1989. *On the Brink: Endangered Species in Canada*. Saskatoon: Western Producer Prairie Books.

Burgess, Margaret M., and Daniel W. Riseborough. 1989. *Measurement Frequency Requirements for Permafrost Ground Temperature Monitoring: Analysis of Norman Wells Pipeline Data, Northwest Territories and Alberta*. Geological Survey of Canada, Paper 89–1D. Ottawa: Energy, Mines and Resources Canada.

———, J.F. Nixon, and D.E. Lawrence. 1998. 'Seasonal Pipe Movement in Permafrost Terrain, KP2 Study Site, Norman Wells Pipeline', in A.G. Lewkowicz and M. Allard, eds, *Proceedings of the Seventh International Conference on Permafrost*. Ste Foye: Centre d'étude nordiques, Université Laval, 95–100.

Cameron, Marjorie, and I. Michael Weis. 1993. 'Organochlorine Contaminants in the Country Food Diet of the Belcher Island Inuit, Northwest Territories, Canada', *Arctic* 46, 1: 42–8.

Carson, Rachel. 1962. *Silent Spring*. Boston: Houghton Mifflin.

Caulfield, Richard A. 2000. 'The Political Economy of Renewable Resource Management in the Arctic', in Mark Nuttall and Terry V. Callaghan, eds, *The Arctic: Environment, People, Policy*. Amsterdam: Harwood Academic Publishers, ch. 17.

Chenard, M. Paul. 1990. 'Global Atmospheric Change', in Environment Canada, *Proceedings of the 4th Conference on Toxic Substances*. Ottawa: Minister of Supply and Services.

Cloutier, Luce, 1987. 'Quand le mercures élevé trop haut à la Baie James . . .', *Acta Borealia* 4, 1/2: 5–23.

Coppinger, Raymond, and Will Ryan. 1999. 'James Bay: Environmental considerations for building large hydroelectric dams and reservoirs in Quebec', in Hornig (1999: 41–72).

Damsell, Keith. 1999. 'Mining's Toxic Orphans Come of Age', *National Post*, 18 Sept., FP1.

Davies, John A. 1985. 'Carbon Dioxide and Climate: A Review', *The Canadian Geographer* 29, 1: 74–85.

Delormier, Treena, and Harriet V. Kuhnlein. 1999. 'Dietary Characteristics of Eastern James Bay Cree Women', *Arctic* 52, 2: 182–7.

Draper, Dianne. 2002. *Our Environment: A Canadian Perspective*, 2nd edn. Toronto: Nelson.

Duffy, Patrick. 1981. *Norman Wells Oilfield Development and Pipeline Project*. Report of the Environmental Assessment Panel. Ottawa: Minister of Supply and Services.

Environment Canada. 1990. *Detailed Review Comments on the Windy Craggy Stage 1 Environmental and Socioeconomic Impact Assessment*. Ottawa: Environment Canada.

Fast, Helen, and Fikret Berkes. 1994. *Native Land Use, Traditional Knowledge and the Subsistence Economy in the Hudson Bay Bioregion*. Ottawa: Hudson Bay Program.

Geddes Resources Limited. 1990. *Windy Craggy Project: Stage 1: Environmental and Socioeconomic Impact Assessment*. Toronto: Geddes Resources Limited.

Gill, Don, and Alan D. Cooke. 1975. 'Hydroelectric Developments in Northern Canada: A Comparison with the Churchill River Project in Saskatchewan', *The Musk-Ox* 15: 53–6.

Gorrie, Peter. 1990. 'The James Bay Power Project', *Canadian Geographic* 110, 1: 21–31.

Hornig, James F., ed. 1999. *Social and Environmental Impacts of the James Bay Hydroelectric Project*. Montreal and Kingston: McGill-Queen's University Press.

James Bay Energy Corporation. 1988. *La Grande Rivière: A Development in Accord with its Environment*. Montreal: James Bay Energy Corporation.

Keith, Robbie. 1998. 'Arctic Contaminants: An Unfinished Agenda', *Northern Perspectives* 25, 2: 1–3.

Kendrick, Anne. 2000. 'Community Perceptions of the Beverly-Qamanirjuaq Caribou Management Board', *Canadian Journal of Native Studies* 20, 1: 1–33.

Lockhart, W.L., P. Wilkinson, B.N. Billeck, R.V. Hunt, R.Wagemann, and G.J. Brunskill. 1995. 'Current and Historic Inputs of Mercury to High Latitude Lakes in Canada and Hudson Bay', *Air and Soil Pollution* 80, 1/4: 603–10.

McDonald, Adrian. 2001. 'Environment at the Crossroads', in Jacqueline West, ed., *The USA and Canada 2002*, 4th edn. Old Woking, Surrey: Unwin Brothers, 22–8.

MacInnes, K.L., M.M. Burgess, D.G. Harry, and T.H.W. Baker. 1989. *Permafrost and Terrain Research and Monitoring: Norman Wells Pipeline.* Environmental Studies No. 64, vols 1 and 2. Ottawa: Minister of Supply and Services.

McKinnon, Ian. 1999. 'Royal Oak may leave taxpayers on hook', *National Post*, 9 Mar., C1.

Maxwell, B. 1987. 'Atmospheric and Climatic Change in the Canadian Arctic: Causes, Effects, and Impacts', *Northern Perspectives* 18, 5: 243.

Mitchell, M. 1956. 'Early Identification of Arctic Haze—Reference to the Alaskan Arctic', *Journal of Atmospheric Terrestrial Physics,* Special Supplement: 195–211.

Mittelstaedt, Martin. 2002. 'Toxic Output Posts 8% Rise, Study Finds', *Globe and Mail,* 30 May, A6.

Morton, Peter. 2003. 'New push for drilling in refuge', *National Post,* 20 Jan., FP1.

Nadasdy, Paul. 1999. 'The Politics of TEK: Power and the Integration of Knowledge', *Arctic Anthropology* 36, 1–2: 1–18.

Nikiforuk, Andrew, and Ed Struzik. 1989. 'The Great Forest Sell-Off', *Report on Business Magazine* (Nov.).

Noble, Bram F. 2000. 'Strengthening EIA through Adaptive Management: A Systems Perspective', *Environmental Impact Assessment Review* 20: 97–111.

Northern Pipeline Environmental Impact Assessment and Regulatory Chair's Committee. 2002. <http://www.mveirb.nt.ca>. Accessed 27 Nov. 2002.

Pedersen, Red. 2001. *Annual Report 2000-2001 of the Independent Environmental Monitoring Agency for the Ekati Diamond Mine.* Yellowknife: Independent Environmental Monitoring Agency.

Peters, Evelyn J. 1999. 'Native People and the Environmental Regime in the James Bay and Northern Quebec Agreement', *Arctic* 52, 4: 395–410.

Poirier, Sylvie, and Lorraine Brooke. 2000. 'Inuit Perceptions of Contaminants and Environmental Knowedge in Salluit, Nunavik', *Arctic Anthropology* 37, 2: 78–91.

Reiesen, Lars Otto. 2000. 'Local and Transboundary Pollutants', in Mark Nuttall and Terry V. Callaghan, eds, *The Arctic: Environment, People, Policy.* Amsterdam: Harwood Academic Publishers, ch. 20.

Robillard, S., G. Beauchamp, G. Paillard, and D. Bélanger. 2002. 'Levels of Cadmium, Lead, Mercury and Caesium in Caribou (Rangifer tarandus)', *Arctic* 55, 1: 1–9.

Robinson, Allan. 1991. 'Exploring the Risks at Windy Craggy', *Globe and Mail,* 19 Jan., B1.

Roebuck, B.D. 1999. 'Elevated Mercury in Fish as a Result of the James Bay Hydroelectric Development: Perception and Reality', in Hornig (1999: ch. 4).

Rosenberg, D.M., R.A. Bodaly, R.E. Hecky, and R.W. Newbury. 1987. 'The Environmental Assessment of Hydroelectric Impoundments and Diversions in Canada', in M.C. Healey and R.R. Wallace, eds, *Canadian Aquatic Resources.* Ottawa: Department of Fisheries and Oceans, 71–104.

Saskatchewan Environment. 2002. *An Assessment of Abandoned Mines in Northern Saskatchewan.* File R3160. Regina: Clifton Associates Ltd.

Saunders, Alan. 1990. 'Pulp and Paper on the Athabasca: Economic Diversity vs. Environmental Disaster', *Northern Perspectives* 18, 1: 1–12.

Searle, Rick. 1991. 'Journey to the Ice Age: Rafting the Tatshenshini, North America's Wildest and Most Endangered River', *Equinox* 55, 1: 24–35.

Sinclair, William F. 1990. *Controlling Pollution from Canadian Pulp and Paper Manufacturers: A Federal Perspective*. Ottawa: Environment Canada/Minister of Supply and Services.

Shkilnyk, Anastasia M. 1985. *A Poison Stronger Than Love: The Destruction of an Ojibwa Community*. New Haven: Yale University Press.

Spears, Tom. 2002. 'Arctic pollution causing Natives serious health problems: study', *National Post*, 19 Aug., A13.

Sugden, David. 1982. *Arctic and Antarctic: A Modern Geographical Synthesis*. Oxford: Blackwell.

Tener, John S. 1984. *Beaufort Sea Hydrocarbon Production and Transportation Proposal: Final Report of the Environmental Assessment Panel*. Ottawa: Minister of Supply and Services.

Tesar, Clive. 2000. 'POPs: what they are; how they are used; how they are transported', *Northern Perspective* 26, 1: 2-5.

Usher, Peter. 2000. 'Traditional Ecological Knowledge in Environmental Assessment and Management', *Arctic* 53, 2: 183–93.

Watt-Cloutier, Sheila. 2002. 'Speech Delivered by Sheila Watt-Cloutier, President ICC Canada and Vice-President ICC International, at the 9th General Assembly and 25th Anniversary of the Inuit Circumpolar Conference', *Silarjualiriniq: Inuit in Global Issues* 12 and 13: 1–8.

Wenzel, George W. 1999. 'Traditional Ecological Knowledge and Inuit: Reflections on TEK Research and Ethics', *Arctic* 52, 2: 113–24.

Williams, Peter J. 1986. *Pipelines and Permafrost: Science in a Cold Climate*. Ottawa: Carleton University Press.

CHAPTER 8

Aboriginal Economy and Society

Over the last 30 years, Aboriginal peoples have taken giant strides towards securing a new place in Canadian society. In that short time frame, Aboriginal peoples have moved from a restrictive colonial world to a more open post-colonial one where they have gained a measure of control over their lives and where some have become participants in the market economy. But progress is uneven among Aboriginal groups and their place in that post-colonial world, its market economy, and Canadian society has yet to be determined. Among the defining questions that will shape their new world are:

- Can Aboriginal individuals, families, and corporations strengthen their economic position by participating in the market economy?
- Can they retain and perhaps redefine their Aboriginal identity and culture while participating in this economy?
- Can Nunavut, as the highest level of government achieved by an Aboriginal group, serve as both a cultural and economic model for Aboriginal peoples?

In this chapter, our attention is concentrated on the involvement of Native peoples in the northern resource economy. The one exception is the emergence of the Inuit homeland, Nunavut. While the northern resource economy forms only one piece of a much larger puzzle, participation in the resource economy, whether as individuals or as corporations, marks a quantum leap into the capitalistic world by Aboriginal peoples. With the broad parameters for their journey through the twenty-first century already set, the ramifications for their traditional land-based economy and society are both profound and irreversible. The search for Aboriginal self-government, for instance, loses much of its meaning if this political gain is not accompanied by similar economic advances. Our discussion begins with an examination of two key events: (1) the shift from the land to settlements; and (2) the acceptance of a broader interpretation of Aboriginal title.

GEOGRAPHIC SHIFT

The shift from the land to settlements was both a remarkable feat and the beginning of a new way of life. Relocation to settlements took place in the 1950s and 1960s.

Native settlements, however, are not like other urban places, which were founded for economic reasons. The lack of an economic foundation has proven to be the Achilles heel of the relocation 'strategy' (Vignette 4.7). Under normal circumstances, urban places that lose their economic function soon die, whether they are single-industry towns or rural communities. Native settlements do not follow this pattern of urban evolution because they generally have been located within cultural homelands and are close to traditional hunting lands. While some, especially the younger members, have moved to larger centres in search of employment, most of the people are content to remain in these familiar and culturally supportive homelands. In addition, the relatively small out-migration is often more than offset by high birth rates, causing populations in Native settlements to increase.

Regardless of the reasons for the formation of Native settlements, they remain a permanent expression of the larger Canadian society and of Canada's urban network. Adjusting to life in Native settlements has not been easy. Initially, social change that took place in these settlements was particularly difficult for adults, who often spoke only their native tongue. Skills that served hunters and trappers well were of little use in the settlement. Education and job training were the supposed basis of the wage economy. For adults who lacked the schooling and occupational skills necessary for wage employment, if indeed any wage employment was available, trapping provided an occupation that brought both income and prestige. Charlie Thomas, a trapper from the Old Crow band in the Northwest Territories, offers an insight into the trapping life in the 1980s:

> I have been a trapper all my life. I had a family, but I lost my wife. I am just by myself now. I am 69 years old now, I draw the old age pension and I am still trapping. I have never been to school. I just live in the bush. All I know is how to sign my name on a cheque. I cannot read one word, but I make a living anyway. (Schellenberger and MacDougall, 1986: 16)

Some 50 years after settlements in the North became the primary habitat for Aboriginal peoples, how has the 'relocation strategy' worked? At the beginning of the twenty-first century, Native settlements remain troubled by high unemployment rates, which have inevitably led to widespread poverty, poor health, and a host of social problems. Unlike living on the land, the cost of living in settlements is much higher. Store food, for example, is often more than twice as expensive as it is in southern towns and cities. Store food has also been a contributing factor to poor health (Vignette 8.1). But with little chance to find employment, people have become resigned to their lot and are heavily dependent on social welfare. Davis Inlet, a small Innu community along the Labrador coast, represents one of many Aboriginal communities in crisis. In the early 1990s, the Canadian public saw television images of young children from Davis Inlet sniffing glue. While these children were sent to a rehabilitation centre in St John's, the problem has not been resolved. According to Michael MacDonald of the Canadian Press, 'Everyone in Davis has stories to tell about personal battles with alcoholism, solvent abuse and family violence. Studies show the community has one of the highest suicide rates in the world.' Davis Inlet (Itshimassits or 'place of the boss') is located on an island, making it inaccessible to traditional hunting grounds for part of the year. At an estimated cost of $150 million, the modern settlement of Natuashish, which means 'break in the river' in Innuaumin, has been built for the Mushuau Innu by the federal government. While Natuashish will not provide a solution to the social problems besetting the Innu, it will move them from a squalid village that lacks running water to a new town with a sewer and water system, and it will improve their access to caribou herds (MacDonald, 2001). Like other Native settlements, however, Natuashish is confronted by a dismal economic future that will hamper the resolution of serious social problems. The location of Natuashish and many other Native settlements does not lend itself to economic development within the market economy. For that reason alone, a support program for the hunting economy makes sense.

Vignette 8.1 Diet and Health

One of the curses of settlement life for Aboriginal peoples has been the deterioration of their health. Diabetes, for instance, has affected an unusually high proportion of Aboriginal peoples, including those under 30 years of age. Many are overweight. Health officials point to inactivity and diet as two causes for the poor state of their health. Prior to the 1950s, Aboriginal people were extremely active as hunters, fishers, and food gatherers. Their diet was based on fresh meat and fish (country food) that supplied them with most of their caloric and nutritional needs. As well, country food was an important cultural anchor providing both an economic and spiritual link with the land and wildlife. While tea, flour, sugar, and salt were purchased at the local trading store, it was not until the indigenous peoples moved into settlements that a wide range of foods with high levels of sugar and starch were purchased and consumed. As Collings, Wenzel, and Condon (1998: 303) reported, 'This shift from a high-protein, polyunsaturated fat diet to one high in carbohydrates and saturated fats, especially among the generation(s) raised in the settlement, has not been without adverse health effects.'

THE POLITICAL SHIFT

Shortly after World War II a series of world events caught the eye of Aboriginal leaders, political activists, and intellectuals. First, colonial empires were replaced by independent states in Africa and Asia. Second, the American civil rights movement was challenging segregation by taking to the streets. Third, separatist parties in Europe and Canada were seeking political independence and their activities often led to violent acts. The turbulent political atmosphere not only recast world geopolitics but ideas of independence and self-determination spread to the oppressed Aboriginal minorities in North and South America. In the 1970s, the unthinkable happened in Canada. The Parti Québécois formed the opposition party in the Quebec legislature and then it became the Quebec government in 1976. The question for Aboriginal students and political leaders of the day was simple—what about our political future within the Canadian federal system?

In 1969, Ottawa produced a White Paper on Indian affairs in which the government described its aim to end inequalities in Canadian society by abolishing the Indian Act and treating Aboriginal peoples like all other citizens. One result would have been that benefits received by Indians through treaties would cease. Indian opposition to Ottawa's proposal caused a political firestorm (Cardinal, 1969). By the 1970s, the Dene tribes in the Mackenzie Basin were moving towards what then seemed like a dangerous and even threatening political position. In 1975, they made a radical political statement with the Dene Declaration that called for political independence within Canada (Erasmus, 1977: 3–4). In their land claim negotiations with Ottawa, the Dene demanded a separate territory and government for the Dene tribes in the western half of the Northwest Territories. This new state would be called Denendeh. Ottawa was taken aback by such a bold request, which, it seemed, could lead to a series of semi-autonomous Aboriginal states within Canada. However, by 1991, the Dene land claim, which had reached the advanced stage of an agreement-in-principle, had unravelled, thus putting an end to their political dream of Denendeh. For the Inuit of the eastern Arctic, however, their political dream was translated into reality with the formation of Nunavut. Though the Inuit had also proposed an ethnic state and government at the same time, they were able to adjust to the political realities of the day. In their revised version, the Inuit called for a public government rather than an ethnic one, i.e., a government that treats all residents equally. In 1999, the Inuit wish for a separate territory was fulfilled with the creation of the Territory of Nunavut.

NUNAVUT

Nunavut is the most promising and innovative political development to appear on the northern horizon. In 1976, Inuit Tapirisat of Canada proposed creating an Arctic territory called Nunavut ('our land' in Inuktitut) that would represent the political and cultural interests of Canada's Inuit. It took nearly 25 years, but on 1 April 1999 Nunavut was formally carved out of the Northwest Territories. As the largest political unit in Canada, Nunavut extends over 2 million km^2. At the same time, Nunavut has the smallest population (26,745 inhabitants in 2001), but most are Inuit (85 per cent). Its population, however, is growing rapidly, at an annual rate of 1.6 per cent, due to its high birth rate (the highest in Canada). Its people are scattered across the tundra in small, isolated settlements without a series of highways connecting these places. Nunavut, like the other two territories, is heavily dependent on the mining industry. Three mines (Lupin, Nanasivik, and Polaris) account for most of the value of production in Nunavut. Yet, these mines all employ a fly-in and fly-out air-commuting system so that the majority of the miners reside in southern Canada and spend their salaries on southern goods and services. Most Inuit families rely on a combination of local employment, transfer payments, and hunting rather than full-time employment in one of the three mines.

The creators of Nunavut were far-sighted and determined Inuit leaders who saw Nunavut as a homeland for the Inuit and an embodiment of Inuit culture. In fact, the government of Nunavut is trying to ensure that its policies and operations follow the Inuit way of thinking and living (Inuit Qaujimajatuqangit). Government by consensus and its decentralization to a series of regional centres represent powerful and effective measures in moving towards an Inuit style of government by emphasizing the people as a collectivity and by bringing government close to the people. Another significant step is the role established for the Inuit land claim organization, Nunavut Tunngavik Inc. In fact, it forms a shadow government with the mandate to make sure government legislation, policies, and programs represent the interests of Inuit. The cardinal principles of Nunavut Tunngavik Inc. are to promote the Inuktitut language and Inuit culture. Even so, three major barriers prevent a smooth transition from a traditional Canadian style of government to an Inuit one. One is the shortage of qualified Inuit for jobs within government. As a result, many in the civil service, especially at the senior levels, are non-Inuit. Second, the use of Inuktitut as a working language within the civil service has not been successful. In fact, English tends to be the working language in the capital of Iqaluit while Inuktitut is more commonly spoken in the regional centres. Third, political fulfillment of the Nunavut dream is unlikely unless its economy becomes more diversified. At the moment, Nunavut relies most heavily on transfer payments from Ottawa, and such financial dependence may well curtail the full flowering of Nunavut's political development. The fear is that these three barriers will cause Nunavut to slide into a Canadian version of territorial government, and such a version runs counter to Inuit Qaujimajatuqangit.

In spite of this fear, the concept of Aboriginal self-government holding sway over a vast territory has spread from the territories to northern Quebec, where the Quebec Inuit have proposed a similar political structure called Nunavik that, if approved by the Quebec government, could provide a template for self-government within each Provincial North with a majority of Aboriginal peoples (Bone, 2001). From that perspective, Nunavut and perhaps Nunavik represent the first step in the search for a place within Canadian society. Once the political structure is in place, the Inuit leaders can focus their energies on the issues of culture and economic development. While the Inuit model of political development may be a suitable beginning point for other areas of the North where Aboriginal peoples hold a majority, there is an important difference, namely, that the ethnic homogeneity in the eastern Arctic is not found in the Subarctic.

ABORIGINAL TITLE

Aboriginal title is the legal basis for comprehensive land claims and for obtaining benefits from resource development. Aboriginal title refers to traditional lands used for hunting and trapping that were never ceded or surrendered by treaty or purchase. Canada's First Peoples retain certain rights (Aboriginal title) to these lands. A comprehensive agreement is a legal agreement between a First Nation or other Aboriginal group and the federal government that extinguishes their Aboriginal title in exchange for land and capital. Modern treaties refer to the total land area claimed as the settlement area; Ottawa, however, only cedes a portion, perhaps around 10 per cent, of the settlement area to the Aboriginal claimants. For instance, the 14 Indian First Nations in Yukon claimed virtually all the territory of Yukon but received ownership of 41,440 km^2, which represents 8.6 per cent of the land mass of Yukon. The agreement also requires the government to fulfill a number of commitments.

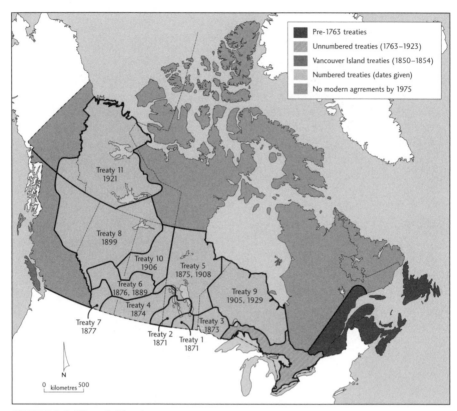

FIGURE 8.1 Historic Treaties

Treaties with northern Aboriginals were slow in coming because Arctic and Subarctic lands held little attraction for settlement and resource development. In 1921, Treaty II was signed because of the discovery of oil at Norman Wells.

The basis of Aboriginal title is found in British justice and was first expressed as a legal document in the Royal Proclamation of 1763.[1] In British North America, treaties and military alliances with Indians were commonplace. This strategy of military alliances ended after the War of 1812 when relations between the United States and Britain became less belligerent. After Canada was formed in 1867, Ottawa continued the tradition of making 'treaty' with the Indian tribes in order to secure access to the land for settlement (Figure 8.1).[2] Except for reserves, the federal government obtained ownership of the remaining land. While Aboriginal peoples could continue to hunt and trap on these Crown lands, they had no other rights to Crown lands. The James Bay Project, announced in 1971 by Premier Robert Bourassa, did not take into account the Cree and Inuit living in northern Quebec. The Aboriginal residents of northern Quebec would simply have to move aside for this important project. It was only after a court battle that the Quebec government undertook negotiations with the Cree and Inuit that resulted in the James Bay and Northern Quebec Agreement of 1975.

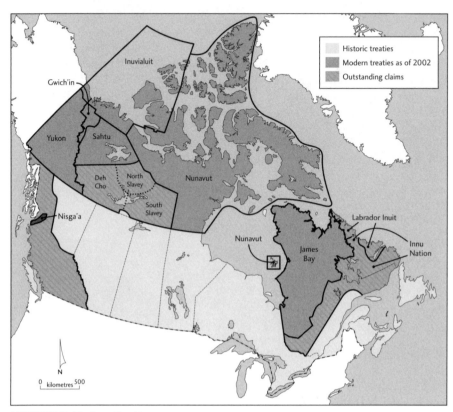

FIGURE 8.2 Modern Treaties
The first modern treaty, the James Bay and Northern Quebec Agreement, was signed in 1975. Since then, modern treaties have fallen into two categories: comprehensive and specific. By 2001, the main areas without treaties were much of British Columbia, Labrador, and lands in Quebec. (The original inhabitants of Newfoundland, the Beothuk, had perished from disease, encroachment, and slaughter by the early nineteenth century.)

As we have seen, the 1973 *Calder* case gave Aboriginal title a new legal interpretation, i.e., Aboriginal title existed if the British or Canadian governments had not extinguished it by a treaty (Vignette 3.10). The 1975 James Bay and Northern Quebec Agreement added additional legal weight to the new concept of Aboriginal title. Shortly thereafter, Ottawa began to negotiate with Aboriginal groups who still had a claim to their traditional lands and therefore Aboriginal title. For Aboriginal peoples living in the Territorial North, the impact of modern treaties has been nothing short of revolutionary. Known as comprehensive land claim agreements, these modern treaties have transformed their economic and political lives because they provide the means and structure to participate in Canada's economy and society and yet retain a presence in their traditional economy and society (Figure 8.2). For Aboriginal peoples in the Provincial Norths, the changes have been less dramatic because, for most of these people, treaties had been signed in the late nineteenth and early twentieth centuries within a colonial context. There are exceptions. The Inuit and Cree of northern Quebec, as well as the Nisga'a of northern British Columbia, negotiated modern land claim agreements. By 2002, nine such agreements have been concluded and the Dogrib First Nation has reached an agreement-in-principle with Ottawa (Table 8.1). These agreements provide three important ingredients for Aboriginal peoples.

- an administrative structure and capital resources necessary to function in the Canadian economy;
- access to natural resources, including subsurface minerals;
- a co-management role in environmental matters, land-use planning, and wildlife management.

From an Aboriginal perspective, this legal agreement represents a blending of the subsistence land-based economy with the commercial economy, thus allowing Aboriginal peoples a foot in two economic systems. The first agreement, known as the Inuvialuit Final Agreement, set the pattern for future negotiations. In the case of the Inuvialuit Final Agreement, the Inuvialuit Regional Corporation represents the business structure while the Inuvialuit Game Council is concerned about the environment and wildlife. Equally important, when resource developments are proposed within the settlement area of an Aboriginal group, the developer must negotiate an 'impacts and benefits agreement' (Vignette 8.2). Such agreements are between the Aboriginal group and the company. As such, they are treated as confidential documents.

TABLE 8.1 Final Comprehensive Land Claim Agreements*

Final Agreement	Date
James Bay and Northern Quebec Agreement	1975
James Bay Naskapi	1978
Inuvialuit Final Agreement	1984
Gwich'in Final Agreement	1992
Tungavik Federation of Nunavut Final Agreement	1992
Sahtu/Métis Final Agreement	1993
Yukon Indians' Umbrella Final Agreement	1993
Nisga'a Final Agreement	1999

*A final agreement is the outcome of successful claim negotiations that have been ratified by the negotiating parties. Canada then passes settlement legislation that gives legal effect to the final agreement. For example, the House of Commons passed the Nisga'a Final Agreement as an Act of Parliament in 2000. The Inuvialuit Final Agreement (1984) marks the first comprehensive agreement. The James Bay and Northern Quebec Agreement (1975) took place before Ottawa had established a process for negotiating comprehensive agreements.

Vignette 8.2 Impacts and Benefits Agreements

Resource companies today must negotiate impacts and benefits agreements with Aboriginal groups who have a claim to the land where development is planned to take place. These agreements are confidential and vary from one group to the next depending on the political strength and negotiating skills of each group. Under most circumstances, the company has an advantage because its negotiators are more experienced and have the legal and other resources of the company at their disposal. The Aboriginal group has one important advantage—Aboriginal title. The company must reach an agreement in order to proceed with their project. However, not all Aboriginal groups are sufficiently aware of the stakes and some have little experience with such negotiations. Two case studies are considered here: Victor Lake diamond deposit in northern Ontario and the Ekati diamond deposit in the Northwest Territories.

De Beers Canada has plans to develop the Victor diamond deposit in northern Ontario. This deposit lies on lands claimed by the Attawapiskat First Nation. De Beers and Attawapiskat signed a memorandum of understanding (MOU) in November 1999. In July 2002, the First Nation declared that it was terminating the MOU but would like to begin negotiation towards an impacts and benefits agreement. For the company, the Attawapiskat First Nation demand that work halt for at least two months was unsettling and costly. This meant that a community consultation process, application for government permits, and work on an environmental assessment had to stop. The reason for the Attawapiskat First Nation demand is simple: the First Nation leaders were unsure of the consequences of the project and needed time to review technical documents and to consult with band members and advisers. They also believed that their interests would be better served by an impacts and benefits agreement, but to achieve such an agreement requires negotiating experience and skills that this First Nation may lack to strike a 'good' deal.

Broken Hill Proprietary Company Inc. (BHP) has negotiated impacts and benefits agreements with each of the four Aboriginal groups whose traditional lands are potentially affected by the Ekati diamond mine. The four groups are North Slave Métis Alliance, Akaitcho Treaty 8, Kitikmeot Inuit Association with the Hamlet of Kugluktuk, and Dogrib Treaty 11. These agreements ensure that the project will not interfere with these Aboriginal groups. In return, the company agrees (1) to ensure that training, employment, and business opportunities are made available to these people, and (2) to minimize any potential adverse environmental and social impacts of the project. Other objectives are to respect local cultures and the land-based economy, to provide a working relationship between the company and the Aboriginal groups, and to determine how the local communities will be involved in employment, training, and business opportunities.

SOURCES: Hasselback (2002: FP3); personal communication with Denise Burlingame, Senior Public Affairs Officer, Ekati Diamond Mine, 2 Aug. 2002.

TABLE 8.2 Recent Supreme Court of Canada Decisions on Aboriginal Title

Case	Date	Outcome
Nowegijick	1983	Treaties must be liberally interpreted.
Guerin	1984	Ottawa must recognize the existence of inherent Aboriginal title and a fiduciary (trust) relationship based on title.
Sioui	1990	Provincial laws cannot overrule rights contained in treaties.
Sparrow	1990	Section 35(1) of the Constitution Act, 1982 containing the term 'existing rights' was defined as anything unextinguished.
Delgamuukw	1997	Oral history of Indian people must receive equal weight to historical evidence in land claim legal cases.
Marshall	1999	Mi'kmaq have the right to catch and sell fish (lobster) to earn a 'moderate living'.

ABORIGINAL ACCESS TO NATURAL RESOURCES

Access to natural resources has emerged as a major economic and political development in the Aboriginal world. Supported by favourable court decisions over the last 30 years, the recognition of the right to natural resources by Aboriginal peoples has greatly improved (Bartlett, 1991). In the latter part of the twentieth century, the Supreme Court of Canada made a number of important rulings that have had great impact on Aboriginal peoples and their access to natural resources (Table 8.2). In 1973, the *Calder* case made history when the Nisga'a argued that they retained Aboriginal title to their traditionally occupied land. While the Supreme Court narrowly ruled against this position, the Court did recognize that the Nisga'a had Aboriginal property rights and therefore Aboriginal title existed until the claim was extinguished. After this ruling, the federal government accepted the principle that Aboriginal peoples might have a claim and Ottawa soon thereafter set in motion a process of negotiations. The Inuvialuit Final Agreement (1984) marked the first modern land claim agreement between Ottawa and an Aboriginal group.

Moving from Aboriginal title to a land claim agreement requires a formal process. The land claim process resolves the matter of the size, geographic area, and access to resources. Land selection is a critical factor in this process and it involves geographic concerns such as location and quality of land. Frank Duerden (1990: 35–6), who, as a geographer, continues to work extensively with Yukon First Nations, has outlined four spatial components of the land claims process:

- mapping areas of use and occupancy in order to develop a case for legitimacy of a claim;
- preparation of maps of land-use potential to identify 'optimum' areas to be retained as an outcome of negotiations;

- evaluation of land selection positions as negotiation proceeds to establish the extent to which they satisfy the goals of the process;
- evaluation of non-ownership agreements regarding land to ascertain the effectiveness of the control they offer and their long-term impact on land-use patterns.

THE EVOLVING ABORIGINAL CULTURE

Since contact, Aboriginal cultures have evolved to adjust to new circumstances. Culture, being a dynamic phenomenon, constantly changes, though it must retain at least some of its core elements. This paradox—changing but holding on to core elements—is particularly noticeable in Aboriginal cultures because of the rapid rate of change caused by the intense contact with Western culture since the move to settlements. Cheryl Swidrovich (2001: 99) maintains that 'Aboriginal peoples have, as part of the strength of their traditions, the ability to continually adapt and change as their circumstances demand without losing their sense of cultural integrity.' Swidrovich concludes that 'the adoption of European principles or beliefs should not, in itself, signal a sudden or wholesale change as to who they are as peoples.' David Newhouse (2000: 408), an Onondaga from the Six Nations of the Grand River and Head of Native Studies at Trent University, sees the development of modern Aboriginal societies as a blending of Aboriginal and Canadian cultures:

> The idea of one citizen, one vote gives to an individual a role and power that may be at odds with the roles of individuals within traditional societies. These modern notions are being combined with Aboriginal notions of collectivism and the fundamental values of respect, kindness, honesty, sharing, and caring. Yet, despite these combinations, we still recognize the governments as Aboriginal and the people as Aboriginal. What has happened is that our notion of 'Aboriginal' has changed and now incorporates features of both the traditional and modern worlds.

EDUCATION: THE KEY TO THE FUTURE

Education provides equality of opportunity based on merit. A high school diploma is a start on this journey. With that diploma, students can enter various post-secondary education programs at trades schools or universities. Unfortunately, Aboriginal students, including those living in northern Canada, lag far behind non-Aboriginal students (Vignette 8.3). According to the 1996 census, Aboriginal people 15 years of age and over have much lower levels of schooling than the non-Aboriginal population, regardless of age group (Statistics Canada, 1998). The situation is particularly troublesome for First Nations. The Auditor General's Report in 2000 noted that 18 per cent of the estimated 117,000 First Nations students dropped out of school before finishing Grade 9, compared with 3 per cent of non-Native students. A third of Native people aged 18–20 finished high school, compared to 63 per cent of non-Natives in the same age group (Kyle, 2002: A4). Over one-half (54 per cent) of the Aboriginal population aged 15 and over had not received a high school diploma, compared with 35 per cent of the non-Aboriginal population. At higher levels of attainment, 4.5 per cent of Aboriginal people were university graduates with degrees or certificates, compared with 16 per cent of the non-Aboriginal population (Statistics Canada, 1998).

Vignette 8.3 The Gap between Aboriginal Education and Employment

Canada faces a shortage of skilled workers. Traditionally, Canada has sought skilled workers from other countries. John Kim Bell, president of the National Aboriginal Achievement Foundation, sees another solution. The demographic explosion among the Aboriginal population has created a large and growing young 'potential' labour force—one that is growing more than twice as fast as the non-Aboriginal workforce. The problem is that most young Aboriginal people are not graduating from high school and therefore cannot enter into trade schools or other post-secondary institutions. In the short run, Bell calls for private industry to draw more Aboriginal workers into their companies by providing on-the-job training. In the long run, the answer lies in eliminating the education gap between Aboriginal and non-Aboriginal students—but how? A geographic disjuncture between where most Aboriginal people live and where most jobs are created represents more than a relocation issue because Aboriginal communities are cultural homelands.

Such a wide variation in workforce participation rates of Aboriginal and non-Aboriginal peoples indicates that a dual labour force along Aboriginal/non-Aboriginal lines exists. In theory, labour segmentation is a long-term, if not permanent, feature where members of the less well-educated and trained labour force are relegated to low-paying, short-term jobs. By the very nature of these jobs, employees have little chance of job advancement. While this theory is often condemned because it is too rigid, the magnitude of variation in education status of the two labour forces provides sobering evidence of the deep-rooted nature of the problem. Not surprisingly, personal incomes of Aboriginal adults are well below those of other Canadians.

SOURCE: Bell (2002: A15).

Figures for the North mirror these national figures. In 1989, for example, a special survey of the labour force in the Northwest Territories revealed that Aboriginal adults had much less formal education than did other NWT residents (at that time, Nunavut was part of the Northwest Territories). A substantial number had less than Grade 9 education, especially those over 50 years of age. As well, this report revealed sharp differences among Aboriginal peoples, with 25 per cent of the Métis adult population with less than Grade 9 education followed by the Inuvialuit at 48 per cent, the Dene at 55 per cent, and the Inuit at 62 per cent (Government of the Northwest Territories, 1990: 26, 28). The reason for the variation between the four Aboriginal groups at that time was largely a result of when schooling became available to each group, i.e., when these people relocated to settlements. In the Arctic, Inuit moved into settlements much later than did other Aboriginal peoples. Once in settlements, public schooling was available to the Inuit but at a later date than for other Aboriginal peoples. Gender differences exist, too. According to Hull (2000: 15–19), more Aboriginal women have completed high school and university than Aboriginal men, and this pattern exists in the North. Hull (ibid., 19) also notes that high school completion rates are low among the youngest age group (15–24 years of age) but increase sharply for those 25–44 years of age. This suggests that older Aboriginal adults recognize the value of a high school degree and enrol in adult education programs.

This education gap forms a barrier to jobs for Aboriginal people. The reasons why young Aboriginal adults have not been more successful in school are complex, but include cultural and psychological factors. Aboriginal students must cross into a different culture at school. Teachers conduct classroom work in English (French in northern Quebec), and they present Western ideas and knowledge. Few role models (parents and other family members) exist. John Bell, president of the National Aboriginal Achievement Foundation, describes the problem:

> At a time when jobs do, and will forever, require more and more education, aboriginal people lag far behind the rest of the Canadian population. A staggering 70 per cent of aboriginal students are not entering into post-secondary studies and the dropout rates starting in Grade 9 are alarming. Unemployment rates for young aboriginal people often stand four and five times above the national average and reflect this educational deficit and reality. (Bell, 2002: A15)

Another factor accounting for this gap is the fact that small Aboriginal communities do not have high schools, thus requiring students to move to a larger centre. Some parents are reluctant to have their children leave their community. A lack of motivation—because everyone living in Aboriginal communities knows that few jobs exist in their community—may also be a factor. Peer pressure and parents' indifference, therefore, may also play a role in such high dropout rates.

THE ABORIGINAL EMPLOYMENT GAP

An Aboriginal employment gap exists in Canada. Such a gap is not surprising because the Aboriginal workforce has recently switched from work on the land as hunters and trappers to wage employment in settlements. Unfortunately, employment requires preparation, and such preparation only began after relocation to settlements when children had an opportunity to attend schools. Preparation had two components. Formal preparation involved attending schools where Native students learned a second language, in most instances English, obtained a basic knowledge of Euro-Canadian society, and became aware of the customs and values of that larger society. Informal preparation involved observing those who were employed, selecting role models in the workplace, and assessing the work opportunities in the community. Paul Okituk, an employment officer with the Nunavik regional government in northern Quebec who is responsible for finding Inuit workers for the Raglan nickel mine in northern Quebec, provides several insights into this situation: 'because of isolation, poor schools and a tradition that does not include education, only a minority of Inuit adults have the skills and education needed to work at a world-class mine' (Stackhouse, 2001).

In 1996, the employment gap was around 20 percentage points—62 per cent of Canadians were employed compared to 43 per cent of registered Indians and 56 per cent of Métis and Inuit (Hull, 2000: iii). Employment rates are determined by dividing the potential labour force (those between the ages of 15 and 64) into the number of employed workers. The biggest gains have occurred in the public sector, where a substantial number of Aboriginal employees hold positions in governments and Aboriginal organizations. Hicks and White (2000: 41) describe the growing public sector in Nunavut:

> Nunavut's economy depends to an extraordinary degree on government. Well over half the territory's jobs are in the public sector and many others, in service and construction for example, are (directly or indirectly) dependent on government activities. Public sector employment involves far more than government bureaucrats [many of whom are non-Inuit middle and senior management levels]; teachers and health care workers are important—and numerous—examples of para-public sector employees.

But again, lack of education has kept Aboriginal employees from obtaining middle and senior management positions and professional jobs. In the territorial governments, Aboriginal employees are underrepresented, especially among senior managers, technical workers, and professional employees, simply because few Aboriginal adults have the necessary educational background to qualify for such jobs.

The conventional explanation for the gap between non-Aboriginal and Aboriginal peoples falls into two categories. First, Aboriginal workers are less well educated and have less job experience than non-Aboriginal workers. Second, many Aboriginal adults reside in communities far from job opportunities. The less conventional explanation lies in cultural resistance to working in an industrial workplace where the strict routine is foreign to many Aboriginal adults and the need to make social adjustments with fellow workers creates a high level of stress. Put differently, the economic gain obtained from employment has to be weighed against two factors: (1) the social discomfort that takes places at the workplace; and (2) the cultural 'comfort' of remaining at home.

The North has an even larger Aboriginal employment gap. Figures from the 1999 NWT Labour Force Survey (Government of the Northwest Territories, 2000: 7) illustrate the magnitude of the gap—just over 36 percentage points. The employment rate for the non-Aboriginal workforce was 84.1 per cent compared to 47.9 per cent for the Aboriginal workforce. Among the Aboriginal population, the Métis had the highest employment rate at 62.3 per cent followed by the Inuvialuit/Inuit at 52 per cent. The Indian workforce had the lowest employment rate at 41.4 per cent. Gender differences exist as well, with Aboriginal females having a much higher employment rate than both Aboriginal males and non-Aboriginal females. However, the gap is narrowing. A decade of recording the employment rate for the Aboriginal labour force in the Northwest Territories reveals a modest increase from 41.8 per cent in 1989 to 47.9 per cent in 1999, while the non-Aboriginal rate remained constant (Government of the Northwest Territories, 2000: Table 5).

Geography also affects the Aboriginal employment rate, with the highest rate (59.2 per cent of Aboriginal people employed) in Yellowknife. In comparison, small communities like Kakisa (32.1 per cent) and Wha Ti (36.8 per cent) and a large Native settlement near Yellowknife, Rae-Edzo (29.5 per cent), had very low employment rates.

Scholars interpret such statistics differently. Modernists and the traditionalists represent two extreme positions. The most popular interpretation is the modern one. Here, the growing involvement in the wage economy is seen as part of the modernization of Aboriginal society (Stabler, 1989: 829). Participation in the wage economy by Aboriginal workers is strongest in the major centres, indicating a spatial variation in Aboriginal employment rates. Not surprisingly, young Aboriginal workers come to these centres to seek employment. Many holding the modernist view foresee the integration of Aboriginal society within the larger Canadian society, a consequence of which will be the narrowing but not the elimination of the cultural differences between the two groups. This narrowing of cultural differences is reflected in the thinking of David Newhouse, cited above. Newhouse (2000: 407) claims that:

> The fundamental change in the last two decades has been the acceptance by both Aboriginal people and mainstream Canadians of the way in which traditional Aboriginal people have viewed themselves and the resultant construction of new identities, not as victims or as noble savages or primitive beings but as, for example, Cree, Ojibway, or Inuit who have dignity and knowledge and are deserving of respect and a place in contemporary society.

Traditionalists have a different explanation, arguing that continued involvement in hunting and trapping represents a desire to hold onto traditional culture. This view was particularly popular in the early decades of Native settlements, when many realized that (1) there was very little to do in these artificial urban places, and (2) without a link to the land, Aboriginal culture would suffer. Those Aboriginal workers who devoted some cash for land-based activities, such as purchasing a snowmobile, did so for cultural reasons (Berger, 1977: 93–100). For them, hunting and trapping are preferred, but the cost of outfitting for a hunter/trapper is beyond the resources of many Native people. The solution is to enter the wage economy to generate capital for their land-based activities. Dacks (1981: 13) supported this line of reasoning by observing that 'many Aboriginal people who are employed—and therefore do not have an economic need to do so—continue to hunt, fish, or trap in their spare time or in interludes between periods of wage employment. An Aboriginal person, for instance, may prefer a mix of summer employment and winter trapping/hunting even though more money could be secured by full-time employment.[3] Trapping in the Territorial North was valued at between $2 and $6 million for most years prior to the 1990s but now is under $1 million annually (Government of Northwest Territories, 1998, 2001). Despite sweeping political, social, and economic changes across the Canadian North, hunting remains an important social activity for many, including some younger adults. The problem is cash—hunting and trapping cannot satisfy the need for cash. Still, Aboriginal peoples place a high value on country food (Bone, 1988; Condon, Collings, and Wenzel, 1995; Myers, 1996, 2002; Collings, Wenzel, and Condon, 1998).

EMPLOYMENT AND AIR COMMUTING

Few employment opportunities, as we have noted, exist in Native settlements. Already, a small number of Aboriginal families and individuals have moved to larger regional centres, but few have moved to resource towns. Resource towns are more mainstream and southern Canadian in their attitudes and lifeways, making it much more difficult to adjust culturally. In fact, in the 1960s government efforts to relocate Aboriginal families to resource towns failed (Stevenson, 1968; Williamson and Foster, 1975). Such social engineering programs have good intentions but fail because they ignore the enormity of the cultural adjustment required. Peter Usher, speaking at a research seminar on the North associated with the Royal Commission on the Economic Union and Development Prospects for Canada, argued that:

> Looking for either mega-project (or even mini-project, such as mining) development as the solution for Aboriginal employment is barking up the wrong tree. There is absolutely no evidence that Aboriginal people are longing to move out of their communities to a few points where economic opportunity is so much greater. (Whittington, 1985: 17)

Air commuting offers a form of cultural mobility where the Aboriginal workers have access to the workplace but their families remain in their home community. Recruitment of Aboriginal workers by construction and mining companies has met with some success using an air-commuting system. During the construction of the Norman Wells Project from 1982 to 1985, over 500 Aboriginal project workers commuted by air to the construction site. Over the past 20 years, approximately 400 Aboriginal employees have worked at fly-in mines each year. In 2002, the largest number, some 350 Indians and Métis, were employed in the uranium mines in northern Saskatchewan; approximately 100 Quebec Inuit worked at the Raglan mine in northern Quebec; and a similar number were employed at the three mines in Nunavut. Ekati, the diamond mine in the Northwest Territories, expects to employ around 250 Aboriginal workers. Salaries are high: the starting wage at these mines is around $65,000 a year. Within their home communities, such wages move Aboriginal families out of poverty and into a position of relative affluence. In some cases, social tensions have arisen between families because of the income differential.

The record of northern and Aboriginal employment varies by region and by company. Northern Saskatchewan has the best employment record, with one company recruiting at least half of its workforce from the North, most of them workers of Aboriginal ancestry. The three mines in Nunavut have not done so well—only 10 per cent of the workers at the Nanisivik, Polaris, and Lupin mines reside in Nunavut. Within this context, it is interesting to note that over half of the Norman Wells Project rotational workers employed by Esso and its subcontractors resided in the Mackenzie Basin of the Northwest Territories.

In all cases, a dual air-commuting system is necessary to meet the company's goals of employing Aboriginal workers and securing workers for their mining operation. The first goal is met by a northern air system that links Native settlements with the mine site. The second goal is satisfied by a southern-based system that connects a major city such as Edmonton or Montreal with the mine site. While air commuting from the south could supply the entire labour force for a mine or other resource project, the additional cost of a northern system of air commuting is a fact of doing business in the northern hinterland and ensuring that there are 'northern benefits'. Companies have not come to this conclusion without help from governments. Back in the late 1970s, the Saskatchewan government insisted that the uranium mines employ residents from its small northern population—otherwise, companies would not receive surface leases.

COMMUNITY DEVELOPMENT

Native settlements lack a solid economic base because of their small populations (meaning small markets) and because they are located on the margins of the Canadian economy. Private investors and firms see few opportunities in such places. Without private investment, Native settlements must depend on the public sector for capital and on community and individual initiatives for business ideas and customer support. Public and community ventures are the heart of community development in Native settlements.[4] The attractions of community development are that economic control is vested with the community, wages and profits remain in the community, and local expertise can be developed (Robinson and Ghostkeeper, 1987, 1988). Co-operative stores are widespread in Nunavik and Nunavut. Originally, co-operatives were designed to bring the business of furs and other renewable resources into the hands of local Inuit. They soon expanded into other areas, including handicrafts and the arts, but most importantly into retail (general) stores. However, such ventures operate in a marginal business environment. Consequently, they rarely make a profit and more often than not lose money. Governments and/or Aboriginal organizations often supply the capital investment and, in the case of an office building, for example, help with the operating expenses by agreeing to long-term rental contracts. Over the years, co-operatives have received annual grants from Ottawa and, more recently, from the governments of Nunavut and Quebec.

In spite of these efforts, Native settlements remain places of chronic unemployment. In Nunavut, the difference in unemployment rates between large and small communities illustrates this problem confronting Native settlements. In 1999 more than 65 per cent of the adult population in the three largest centres in Nunavut (Iqaluit, Rankin Inlet, and Arviat) had jobs compared to less than 35 per cent in the much smaller communities of Clyde River and Gjoa Haven (Hicks and White, 2000: 41).

In such an environment, social problems, such as alcohol and substance abuse, are widespread. A recognition that Native settlements are unable to develop an economic base leads to support for an alternative approach—the land-based economy. One of the most successful land-based programs is the Income Security Program for Cree hunters and trappers that arose out of the James Bay Agreement.[5] The Income Security Program is designed to encourage people living in settlements to spend time on the land rather than remain idle in their communities. The objectives are threefold:

- to provide an alternative to settlement unemployment and exposure to settlement social problems;
- to reinforce Cree culture by spending more time on the land;
- to reduce reliance on social assistance programs such as welfare.

The Quebec program is not inexpensive. The Quebec government spent about $6 million in 1981 (Salisbury, 1986: 94) and nearly $12 million in 1985 (Ames et al., 1989: 275). By 2002, the cost had reached $21 million (Government of Quebec, 2002). Over the same period, the number of participants has more than doubled. In comprehensive land claim negotiations with other Aboriginal groups, the federal government has refused to agree to similar programs, arguing that these are the responsibility of provinces and territories (Légaré, 2000). For the territories, of course, Ottawa's argument seems somewhat hollow because most of the territorial revenues come from Ottawa. Ottawa may be avoiding such support because: (1) the integration of Aboriginal families but especially children into Canadian society will be retarded by such a program, i.e., spending time on the land rather than in school; (2) such a program could perpetuate a marginal economic activity; and (3) by agreeing to such a program, the government would be committed to subsidize this activity for a long time.

The Cree program guarantees full-time hunters a minimum cash income each year plus an allowance for each day spent on the land. It ensures that hunting, fishing, and trapping remain a viable way of life for the Cree and that individual Cree who elect to pursue such a way of life are guaranteed a measure of economic security. In 2002, the Cree population in northern Quebec totalled over 13,000 and the rate of participation in this program varies between 11 per cent and 32 per cent depending on the village (Government of Quebec, 2002). In 1976–7, the first full year of this program, 1,012 families or single individuals registered, thereby indicating their intention to hunt all winter and, in return, to receive a grubstake payment before departing for their hunting or trapping areas (Salisbury, 1986: 76). By 2000–1, the number registered for this program was over 2,500. In 2002–3, a family of four (two adults and two children) who stayed on the land for 200 days would received a payment of $27,882 plus a share of revenue generated from the sale of furs. In May 2002, the Quebec government agreed to increase funding over the next four years. By 2004–5, a family of four staying on the land for 200 days would receive approximately $32,500 (Government of Quebec, 2002).

ABORIGINAL CORPORATIONS

Aboriginal leaders in some instances have taken advantage of commercial opportunities resulting from Aboriginal title and modern land claim agreements by forming Native-owned corporations. Now operating within the market economy, they, like other entrepreneurs, are confronted with many issues, including finding qualified Aboriginal staff, especially senior managers, ensuring that these operations are profitable, which may mean laying off workers in slow times, protecting the environment, and, above all, avoiding overexploitation of renewable resources.

Just as the political movement created political leaders, business leaders represent a new social class within the Aboriginal community. Aboriginal title, however, is an important factor in allowing such businesses to come into being. The Innu of Labrador provide one example. Aboriginal title has favoured the Innu, who have a claim to land around the Gull Island hydroelectric project. Quebec and Newfoundland/Labrador have joined forces to development the Gull Island site, which is 225 kilometres downstream from Churchill Falls on the Churchill River. At full capacity, Gull Island hydroelectric project will generate 2,000 megawatts of power, making it one of the largest hydroelectric generating stations in North America. Both Quebec and Newfoundland/Labrador will reap major economic rewards, but only if the Innu of Labrador consent to the project. Under this proposed joint arrangement, Hydro-Québec would buy the surplus electricity and Newfoundland/Labrador would undertake the construction of the hydro facility. Through negotiations related to their Aboriginal title the Innu should obtain some benefits, but only when the project is approved by both provincial governments. So far, St John's has withheld its approval.

While Aboriginal title provides an opportunity to participate in resource developments, comprehensive land claim agreements supply the beneficiaries with a business structure as well as a large cash settlement.[6] The cash settlements obtained by Aboriginal groups through comprehensive agreements in the Territorial North exceed $1 billion. In northern Quebec, agreements signed in the 1970s with the Cree, Inuit, and Naskapi totalled $234 million. More recently, the Cree and Inuit have reached new agreements with the Quebec government. Over the next 50 years, the total value of the Cree/Quebec agreement is $3.6 billion, with annual payments for the first three years reaching $23 million, $46 million, and $70 million. These funds are committed to economic and community development and release Quebec from its responsibilities under the James Bay and Northern Quebec Agreement in these two fields. In exchange, the Cree have consented to the construction of the third and final stage of the James Bay Project, known as the Nottaway-Broadback-Rupert Project. This project will involve the construction of the Eastmain hydroelectric station and the diversion of the Rupert River (Vignette 8.4). The Quebec Inuit reached a 25-year agreement (the Sanarrutik Agreement) with the Quebec government in April 2002 (George, 2002). Again, the agreement links northern development with community and economic projects in Nunavik. The Quebec government has approval to commence work on developing the rivers flowing into Hudson Bay and Hudson Strait (the Nastapoka, Whale, George, and Caniapiscau rivers). In June 2002, the Makivik Corporation received the first payment of $7 million. At the end of 25 years, Makivik Corporation will receive just over $360 million.

Circumstances have allowed some Aboriginal groups to move boldly into the resource economy. Two Aboriginal corporations, the Inuvialuit Regional Corporation and Kitsaki Management Limited Partnership, exemplify this Native entrepreneurial spirit. The Inuvialuit Regional Corporation (IRC) is located in Inuvik, NWT, while the headquarters of Kitsaki Management Limited Partnership, the business arm of the Lac La Ronge Indian band, is located near La Ronge, Saskatchewan.

In 1984, the IRC was formed as a result of the Inuvialuit Final Agreement. Its purpose was to receive and manage the lands and cash settlement of $55 million (in 1979

Vignette 8.4 Shining Model or Trojan Horse?

In November 2001, Quebec Premier Bernard Landry and Cree Grand Chief Ted Moses agreed to the $3.8 billion Nottaway-Broadback-Rupert hydroelectric project in exchange for annual payments over 50 years totalling $3.6 billion. These funds are for economic and community development and will help to address the shortage of housing in the Cree villages and create construction jobs for local workers. As part of the deal the Cree must drop their $8 billion in lawsuits filed against the province of Quebec.

The agreement puts an end to years of disputes over the impact of the hydroelectric projects on the Cree and their claim of unfulfilled promises from the James Bay and Northern Quebec Agreement. It commits the traditional territory of the Cree to economic development—hydroelectric, forestry, and mining. Some might argue that the Cree have been co-opted. Guy Chevette, Quebec Native Affairs Minister, proclaimed this agreement to be a shining model for the rest of Canada. Chevette (Roslin, 2001: FP7) stated: 'The path of the future for native people is to give them the opportunity to exploit resources and share in that.' Peter Kulchyski, writing in 1994, warned that 'regardless of the level of power provided to Aboriginal governments, every decision that is made following the dominant logic, in accordance with the hierarchical and bureaucratic structures of the established order, will take Aboriginal peoples further away from their own culture.'

SOURCES: Kulchyski (1994: 121); Roslin (2001: FP7).

dollars) flowing out of this agreement. As a company, the IRC sought to invest these funds in profitable enterprises, and, by doing so, to provide both employment and dividends for its members. Its strategy has been to form a number of subsidiaries to undertake specific business activities. For example, the Inuvialuit Development Corporation (IDC) is responsible for investing in a wide range of business ventures. By 2001, IDC was a major shareholder in over 20 enterprises and joint ventures in seven sectors—transportation, petroleum services, construction/manufacturing, environmental services, northern services, real estate, and tourism/hospitality. From an initial investment of $10 million in 1977, IDC's asset base has grown to over $135 million due in large part to its petroleum investments. Since the North has few commercial opportunities, most investments are outside of the North, such as real estate properties on Vancouver Island (Riverside Park Developments Inc.). Major northern investments include Northern Transportation Company Ltd, which operates the barge system on the Mackenzie River, Aklak Air Ltd, which provides regional air service in the western Arctic, and Grimshaw Trucking and Distributing Ltd, which transports foodstuffs and other goods to the communities along the Mackenzie Valley highway system. Ownership of these firms does provide employment opportunities for the Inuvialuit, but relatively few have joined these companies.

The Inuvialuit economic strategy has three weaknesses. One is that, with the exception of Inuvik, Inuvialuit communities have not been the beneficiaries of Inuvialuit investment capital because these isolated communities contain virtually no profitable investment opportunities. Second, while ownership of resource firms opens up employment and training opportunities for Inuvialuit adults, for two reasons few have joined these firms: most Inuvialuit lack sufficient education (high school diploma) to enter into the lowest level of employment with any of these Inuvialuit-owned companies, and those who do may refuse to relocate to other communities, especially those in southern Canada. Third, more government attention needs to be placed on the long-term goal of economic diversification within the North that would support Inuvialuit regional development and therefore support Inuvialuit culture.

Kitsaki Management Limited Partnership, the business arm of the 7,000-plus Lac La Ronge band, operates at a much smaller scale and without the advantage of a modern land claim settlement. Kitsaki came about when the provincial government insisted that northern mining companies provide employment and business opportunities for northern residents. Unlike the IRC, Kitsaki has little capital and has had to move slowly and cautiously into business opportunities in the mining and forestry industries. Often, the provincial government, as a means of ensuring 'northern benefits', has encouraged forestry and mining companies to offer Kitsaki business opportunities. In the early 1980s, the Lac La Ronge band entered into a joint venture with a private trucking firm to supply goods to the uranium mines in northern Saskatchewan. Without experienced truck drivers, few band members were employed at first, but the trucking firm was willing to train and then employ people from Lac La Ronge. The chief at that time, Myles Venn, saw these new opportunities as a means to achieve 'Aboriginal ownership that will enable us to possess the control we need to secure jobs for our people' (Bone, 2002: 70). By 2001, Kitsaki employed over 500 workers and up to 1,000 seasonal employees. Kitsaki's gross revenue for the year ending 31 March 2001 exceeded $67 million from diverse enterprises, including: Northern Resource Trucking, Athabasca Catering, La Ronge Wild Rice Corporation, La Ronge Motor Hotel, Prince Albert Inn, Dakota Winds Kitsaki Mechanical Services Ltd, Wapawekka Lumber, Kitsaki Meats, Keewatin/Procon Joint Venture for contract mining services, Pihkan Askiy/Nih-Soreldhen Joint Venture environmental cleanup services, and CanNorth Environmental Services.

Kitsaki, like the Inuvialuit Regional Corporation, is finding the business world a difficult one to 'make a dent' in its immediate and pressing employment and social problems. Still, both corporations have made a difference, although the direct impact on their respective communities has been limited. The relatively small number of people benefiting may, in the eyes of the majority, have created a form of Aboriginal elitism. Local support for these business initiatives wavers, partly because of the complexity of their operations, high expectations, and the slowness of visible impacts on the two Aboriginal groups.

SUMMARY

For better or worse, the economic and political landscape of the Aboriginal world has changed. The shift towards self-government has reached a high level of government with the creation of the Territory of Nunavut. But the economic landscape has seen the most profound changes—changes driven by the need to participate in the market economy or else remain on the margins. While not abandoning their land-based activities, more and more Aboriginal groups have ventured into the always risky market economy through a variety of business organizations. Some involve the commercial use of their natural resources; some are assisted by northern affirmative action; and some represent individuals starting a business. Joint ventures have proven to be a successful way for Aboriginal business people to become involved in the economy of the North. For centuries Aboriginal people lived on the land, practising a distinct way of life in northern Canada. With the move to settlements, their land-based economy was no longer able to meet all their needs and wants. Aboriginal northerners now required a much larger cash income to satisfy needs and wants common to all those living in an urban environment. Two such adaptations are participation in the wage economy and involvement in the business community. Tom Mason (2001: 45) has described the range of new Aboriginal business developments across Canada:

> Impressive as they may be, the strides that Millbrook [Nova Scotia] residents [having built a multipurpose retail and industrial park near Truro, Nova Scotia] are making are far from unique. In fact, they're part of a new wave of native-run businesses sweeping Canada, bringing once-poor First Nations a newfound prosperity. The Lac La Ronge Indian Band in northern Saskatchewan has developed Kitsaki Management Ltd to manage a portfolio of businesses that includes mining, insurance, trucking, and hospitality. BC's Osoyoos Indian Band Development Corp. is now operating eight businesses, including a vineyard and a sawmill. And Peace Hills Trust, an Alberta First Nations-based financial institution with about $800 million in assets, may soon be a Power Centre tenant.

While Mason's article is upbeat and focused on a few commercial successes, most First Nations are struggling to find their way in this commercial world that is so foreign to their traditional culture. No one is sure how to balance ventures into the market economy with Aboriginal culture, and, not surprisingly, not all members are supportive of these commercial initiatives. Yet, Aboriginal corporations are seeking commercial solutions to tackle the problem of poverty and related social and health problems. Those Aboriginal groups that have negotiated comprehensive land claim agreements have several advantages, including a substantial cash settlement and a dual administrative structure that together can allow participation both in the new world of commerce and in the old world of hunting and trapping. Aboriginal commerce also has the attraction of reducing dependency, but it carries with it the possibility of failure. The key questions posed at the beginning of this chapter will be answered by the success or failure of 'Red capitalism' (Newhouse, 2001). It is still too soon, however, to know whether or not Aboriginal communities can retain and redefine their identity while participating in the market economy, or whether such participation will strengthen communities as opposed to some individuals within those communities. Nunavut, as we have seen, may serve as a model for Aboriginal economic involvement and political success. The years to come should be interesting indeed, and will, it is hoped, provide some answers to these questions.

NOTES

1. The Seven Years' War between the British and French took place between 1756 and 1763. In the struggle for supremacy in North America, each European nation allied itself with Indians living on lands that it controlled or claimed. The British allied themselves with the Iroquois. At the end of this war, George III issued the Royal Proclamation declaring that lands west of the Appalachians were to remain Indian lands. The British needed the support of the Iroquois to control these lands, which formerly fell under French control. The problem facing Britain was that British subjects in the American colonies wanted to settle on these lands, but under the Proclamation they were not to cross a 'line' following the Appalachian Divide from Maine to Georgia and then to the St Marys River in Florida. Efforts to prevent settlers from moving west proved futile, however, and just before the American Revolution as many as 100,000 colonists may have been living west of this imaginary line (Hilliard, 1987: 149). After the American Revolution, the newly formed United States of America declared the lands extending from the Appalachians to the Mississippi River open for settlement. Thousands of Americans poured over the divide. Within several decades, virtually all of the land east of the Mississippi had passed into American ownership and the original inhabitants were exterminated, assimilated, or living on reservations (ibid., 163).

2. Treaties involved the surrender to the Crown of the property rights to lands traditionally used by Indians for hunting and trapping. In exchange for their surrender of land, the Indians received reserves, lump-sum cash payments, an annual payment to each member of the band, and promises of hunting and fishing rights on unoccupied Crown lands. While the exact terms varied somewhat, the basic elements of treaties were protection of the Aboriginals by the Crown from the settlers and prospectors, and the establishment of their own land base. The land was granted to the tribe or band and ownership was communal, so it could not be sold. In the case of the Métis, however, they received scrip, which entitled them to either cash or land. For the most part, the scrip was sold.

3. In Western economic terminology, people may choose a less attractive economic option because it results in greater personal satisfaction. Thus, a suboptimal rather than an optimal economic decision may occur. The 'cost' of that decision is the difference between the higher economic gain that could have been derived and the actual monetary gain resulting from the suboptimal decision. This difference is called 'psychic income'.

4. Coffey and Polese (1984) described local development as a particular form of regional development where an injection of public capital is necessary and where it operates at a micro-spatial level in which local factors play a central position. Coffey and Polese proposed a four-stage model of local development: (1) the emergence of local entrepreneurship; (2) the 'take-off' of local enterprises; (3) the expansion of these enterprises beyond the local region; and (4) the achievement of a regional economic structure based on local initiatives and locally created comparative advantages. In theory, community development has much appeal, but in reality such development is troubled by a small market and high cost of operation, resulting in high prices for goods and services. Local consumers' loyalty to buying locally is often severely tested, causing some to purchase goods and services outside of their community. Given this situation, most forms of community development require annual operating grants to offset losses.

5. Salisbury (1986: 76–84) describes changes in hunting among the Cree of northern Quebec. Under the subsidized Income Security Program for hunters and trappers, the increased availability of cash meant that they could make more use of modern technology and transportation. Prior to 1975, hunters took little equipment into the bush and often travelled only short distances. By 1981, the Cree hunters could use chartered aircraft to fly their

families into remote bush camps, which now were as comfortable as village housing. As well, hunting has become more mechanized and less physically exhausting because these Cree hunters can now afford to fly a snowmobile to their winter camps. The snowmobile is the workhorse of the hunter. It allows a quick inspection of his trapline and the easy hauling of big game and firewood from the bush to camp. Mechanization, made possible by the Income Security Program, has made hunting less strenuous and more productive. From 1974 to 1979, Salisbury reports that there was a 20 per cent increase in the overall amount of game killed by these Cree hunters and their families (whose number increased by more than 50 per cent over the same time period).

6. Land is a fundamental element in the well-being of Aboriginal peoples. Canada has made treaty with many southern Indian tribes. In exchange for surrendering their rights to their traditional hunting lands, treaty Indians received reserve lands, a right to hunt and fish, and other benefits. In some cases, treaty Indians did not receive their correct allotment of land. In such cases, they can file a specific land claim. Some status Indians have not taken treaty. They and other Aboriginal peoples have not surrendered their Aboriginal right to traditional lands. Both can make a comprehensive land claim. Métis residing in the Northwest Territories are eligible to make a claim but, as of 2001, Métis living in provinces could not.

Many treaty Indians claimed that they did not receive their full allotment of land at the time of signing the treaty or that they lost land. To answer these claims, the federal government established the Office of Native Claims in 1974. Since the 1980s, this role has been assigned to the Department of Indian Affairs and Northern Development. After documenting their case, a band is eligible to make a specific land claim. Specific land claims are often based on a grievance about the federal government's administration of Indian land. Land shortages have occurred in three ways. (1) The original land grant was correct but government officials took some land from them without proper authorization. (2) Lands that should have been granted never were granted. (3) Reserve populations have increased. Most claims are based on 'lost' lands. In Saskatchewan, for example, almost a third of the land placed in reserve under treaty was surrendered to the government and then sold to settlers (Brizinski, 1993: 231). In many cases, since Crown land is either not available or is not suitable, land must be purchased from private landowners. Given the price of agricultural and urban land, the cost of settling specific claims may run into billions of dollars. The Saskatchewan settlement reached $500 million divided among 27 First Nations.

Comprehensive land claims are considered modern treaties. Like earlier treaties, they are based on the concept of Aboriginal title to land. Comprehensive land claim settlements are designed to extinguished Native claim to their traditional land occupancy in exchange for ownership of a block of land, hunting and trapping rights (but not subsurface rights) on selected lands, and monetary compensation. So far, modern land claim agreements have been ratified in Quebec (the James Bay and Northern Quebec Agreement is a modern treaty but not a comprehensive one), Yukon, the Northwest Territories, and British Columbia. Others are pending in the NWT, Newfoundland/Labrador, and BC. See Table 8.1 for a list of these agreements and Figure 8.1 for their geographic location.

REFERENCES AND SELECTED READINGS

Abel, Kerry, and Jean Friesen, eds. 1991. *Aboriginal Resource Use in Canada: Historical and Legal Aspects*. Winnipeg: University of Manitoba Press.

Ames, Randy, Don Axford, Peter Usher, Ed Weick, and George Wenzel. 1989. *Keeping On the Land: A Study of the Feasibility of a Comprehensive Wildlife Harvest Support Program in the Northwest Territories*. Ottawa: Canadian Arctic Resources Committee.

Anderson, Robert B. 1999. *Economic Development Among the Aboriginal Peoples in Canada: The Hope for the Future.* North York, Ont.: Captus Press.

———. 2002. 'The Mackenzie Valley Pipeline Inquiry', in *Aboriginal Entrepreneurship and Business Development.* Toronto: Captus Press, 22–5.

Bartlett, Richard. 1991. *Resource Development and Aboriginal Land Rights.* Calgary: University of Calgary, Canadian Institute of Resources Law.

Bell, John Kim. 2002. 'Build native future working with private sector', *Saskatoon Star-Phoenix*, 21 June, A15.

Berger, Thomas R. 1977. *Northern Frontier, Northern Homeland: The Report of the Mackenzie Valley Pipeline Inquiry.* Ottawa: Department of Supply and Services.

Bone, Robert M. 1988. 'Cultural Persistence and Country Food: The Case of the Norman Wells Project', *Western Canadian Anthropologist* 5: 61–79.

———. 2001. *Nunavik Political Model: Is it an appropriate model for other provinces—the case of Northern Saskatchewan.*. Report prepared for the Department of Indian and Northern Affairs. Saskatoon: Signe Research Associates.

———. 2002. 'Colonialism to Post-Colonialism in Canada's Western Interior: The Case of the Lac La Ronge Indian Band', *Historical Geography* 30: 59–73.

——— and Milford B. Green. 1984. 'The Northern Aboriginal Labor Force: A Disadvantaged Work Force', *Operational Geographer* 3: 12–14.

Cardinal, Harold. 1969. *The Unjust Society.* Edmonton: Hurtig.

Collings, Peter, George Wenzel, and Richard G. Condon. 1998. 'Modern Food Sharing Networks and Community Integration in the Central Canadian Arctic', *Arctic* 51, 4: 301–14.

Condon, Richard G., Peter Collings, and George Wenzel. 1995. 'The Best Part of Life: Subsistence Hunting, Ethnicity, and Economic Adaptation among Young Adult Inuit Males', *Arctic* 48, 1: 31–46.

Dacks, Gurston. 1981. *A Choice of Futures: Politics in the Canadian North.* Toronto: Methuen.

Duerden, Frank. 1990. 'The Geographer and Land Claims: A Critical Appraisal', *Operational Geographer* 8, 2: 35–7.

———. 1996. 'An Evaluation of the Effectiveness of First Nations Participation in the Development of Land-Use Plans in the Yukon', *Canadian Journal of Native Studies* 16: 105–24.

——— and R.G. Kuhn. 1998. 'Scale, Content, and Application of Traditional Knowledge of the Canadian North', *Polar Record* 34, 188: 31–8.

Erasmus, George. 1977. 'We The Dene', in Mel Watkins, ed., *Dene Nation—The Colony Within.* Toronto: University of Toronto Press, 3–4.

George, Jane. 2002. 'Nunavik Leaders Celebrate First Quebec Payout', *Nunatsiaq News.* Available at: <http://www.nunatsiaq.com/news/nunavik/20621_1.html>.

Government of Quebec. 2002. 'Complementary Agreement to the James Bay and Northern Québec Agreement—the Quebec Government allocates an additional $4.4 million to the income security program for Cree hunters', news release, 22 May 2002. Available at: <http://communiques.gouv.qc.ca/gouvqc/communiques/GPQE/Mai2002/23/c8749.html>.

Government of the Northwest Territories. 1990. *Statistics Quarterly.* Yellowknife: Bureau of Statistics.

———. 1998. *Statistics Quarterly.* Yellowknife: Bureau of Statistics.

———. 2000. *1999 NWT Labour Force Survey: Overall Results & Community Detail.* Yellowknife: Bureau of Statistics.

———. 2001. *Statistics Quarterly* 23. Yellowknife: Bureau of Statistics.

Hasselback, Drew. 2002. 'Natives Halt De Beers Diamond Project', *National Post,* 1 Aug., FP3.

Hicks, Jack, and Graham White. 2000. 'Nunavut: Inuit Self-Determination through a Land Claim and Public Government?', in Jens Dahl, Hicks, and Peter Jull, eds, *Inuit Regain Control of*

Their Lands and Their Lives. Skive, Denmark: Centraltrykkeriet Skive A/S, 30–117.

Hilliard, Sam B. 1987. 'A Robust New Nation, 1783–1820', in Robert D. Mitchell and Paul A. Groves, eds, *North America: The Historical Geography of a Changing Continent.* Totowa, NJ: Rowman & Littlefield, 149–171.

Hull, Jeremy. 2000. *Aboriginal Post-Secondary Education and Labour Market Outcomes, Canada, 1996.* Ottawa: Indian and Northern Affairs Canada, Research and Analysis Directorate.

Jull, Peter. 2001. 'Nunavut: The Still Small Voice of Indigenous Governance', *Indigenous Affairs* 3, 1: 42–51.

Kulchyski, Peter. 1994. *Unjust Relations: Aboriginal Rights in Canadian Courts.* Toronto: Oxford University Press.

Kyle, Anne. 2002. 'Nault Calls on Aboriginal Educators to Solve Woes of Native Schooling', *Saskatoon Star-Phoenix,* 18 June, A4.

Légaré, André. 2000. 'La Nunavut Tunngavik Inc.: Un examen de ses activités et de sa structure administrative', *Études/Inuit/Studies* 24, 1: 97–124.

———. 2001. 'The Spatial and Symbolic Construction of Nunavut: Towards the Emergence of a Regional Collective Identity', *Études/Inuit/Studies* 25, 1–2: 143–68.

MacDonald, Michael. 2001. 'Innu of Davis Inlet Prepare for Year of Big Changes', Canadian Press, 21 Dec. Available at: <http://www.canoe.ca/CNEWS2001Review/1223_innu-cp.html>.

Mason, Tom. 2001. 'Tribal Counsel', *Canadian Business* 74, 21: 41–5.

Myers, Heather. 1996. 'Neither Boom Nor Bust', *Alternatives Journal* 22, 4: 18–23.

———. 2002. 'Options for Appropriate Development in Nunavut Communities', *Études/Inuit/Studies* 24, 1: 25–40.

——— and Scott Forrest. 2000. 'Making Change: Economic Development in Pond Inlet, 1987 to 1997', *Arctic* 53, 2: 134–45.

Newhouse, David. 2000. 'From the Tribal to the Modern: The Development of Modern Aboriginal Societies', in Ron F. Laliberte, Priscilla Settee, James B. Waldram, Rob Innes, Brenda Macdougall, Lesley McBain, and F. Laurie Barron, eds, *Expressions in Canadian Native Studies.* Saskatoon: University of Saskatchewan Extension Press, 395-409.

———. 2001. 'Modern Aboriginal Economies: Capitalism with a Red Face', *Journal of Aboriginal Economic Development* 1, 2: 55–61.

Notzke, Claudia. 1994. *Aboriginal Peoples and Natural Resources in Canada.* North York, Ont.: Captus Press.

Peters, Evelyn J. 1989. 'Federal and Provincial Responsibilities for the Cree, Naskapi and Inuit Under the James Bay and Northern Quebec, and Northeastern Quebec Agreements', in D.C. Hawkes, ed., *Aboriginal Peoples and Government Responsibility: Exploring Federal and Provincial Roles.* Ottawa: Carleton University Press, ch. 6.

———. 1999. 'Environmental Impact Assessment and the James Bay and Northern Quebec Agreement', *Arctic* 52: 395–410.

———. 2000. 'Aboriginal People and Canadian Geography: A Review of the Recent Literature', *Canadian Geographer* 44, 1: 44–55.

Robinson, Michael, and Elmer Ghostkeeper. 1987. 'Native and Local Economies: A Consideration of Economic Evolution and the Next Economy', *Arctic* 40, 2: 138–44.

——— and ———. 1988. 'Implementing the Next Economy in a Unified Context: A Case Study of the Paddle Prairie Mall Corporation', *Arctic* 41, 3: 173–82.

———, Michael Pretes, and Wanda Wuttunee. 1989. 'Investment Strategies for Northern Cash Windfalls: Learning from the Alaskan Experience', *Arctic* 42, 3: 265–76.

Roslin, Alex. 2001. 'Cree Deal a Model or Betrayal?', *National Post,* 10 Nov., FP7.

Salisbury, Richard F. 1986. *A Homeland for the Cree: Regional Development in James Bay, 1971–1981.* Montreal and Kingston: McGill-Queen's University Press.

Schellenberger, Stan, and John A. MacDougall. 1986. *The Fur Issue: Cultural Continuity, Economic Opportunity.* Report of the House of Commons Standing Committee on Aboriginal Affairs and Northern Development. Ottawa: Queen's Printer.

Slocombe, D. Scott. 2000. 'Resources, People and Places: Resource and Environmental Geography in Canada', *Canadian Geographer* 44, 1: 56–66.

Stabler, Jack C. 1989. 'Dualism and Development in the Northwest Territories', *Economic Development and Cultural Change* 37, 4: 805–40.

———. 1989. 'Jobs, Leisure and Traditional Pursuits: Activities of Aboriginal Males in the Northwest Territories', *Polar Record* 25, 155: 295–302.

Stackhouse, John. 2001. 'Increasing Raglan's Inuit workforce', *Globe and Mail,* 14 Dec. Available at: <http://www.globeandmail.com/series/apartheid/stories/20011214-5.htm>.

Stevenson, D. 1968. *Problems of Eskimo Relocation for Industrial Employment.* Ottawa: Department of Northern Affairs and National Resources, Northern Co-ordination and Research Centre.

Statistics Canada. 1998. '1996 Census: Education, mobility and migration', *The Daily,* 14 Apr. Available at: <http://www.statcan.ca/Daily/English/980414/d980414.htm>.

Swidrovich, Cheryl. 2001. 'Stanley Mission: Becoming Anglican But Remaining Cree', *Native Studies Review* 14, 2:71–108.

Usher, Peter J. 1982. 'Unfinished Business on the Frontier', *Canadian Geographer* 26, 3: 187–90.

——— and George Wenzel. 1987. 'Aboriginal Harvest Surveys and Statistics: A Critique of Their Construction and Use', *Arctic* 40, 2: 145–60.

——— and ———. 1989. 'Socio-Economic Aspects of Harvesting', Chapter 1 in Randy Ames, Don Axford, Usher, Ed Weick, and Wenzel, eds, *Keeping On the Land: A Study of the Feasibility of a Comprehensive Wildlife Harvest Support Program in the Northwest Territories.* Ottawa: Canadian Arctic Resources Committee.

Wenzel, George W. 1986. 'Canadian Inuit in a Mixed Economy: Thoughts on Seals, Snowmobiles, and Animal Rights', *Aboriginal Studies Review* 2, 1: 69–82.

———. 1995. '*Ningiqtuq:* Resource sharing and generalized reciprocity in Clyde River, Nunavut', *Arctic Anthropology* 24, 2: 56–81.

White, Graham. 2002. 'Politics and Government in the Territorial North: Familiar and Exotic', in *The Canadian North: Embracing Change.* The CRIC Papers No. 6. Montreal: Centre for Research and Information on Canada.

Whittington, Michael S., ed. 1985. *The North.* Toronto: University of Toronto Press.

Williamson, Robert G., and T.W. Foster. 1975. *Eskimo Relocation in Canada.* Saskatoon: University of Saskatchewan, Institute for Northern Studies.

CHAPTER 9

Looking to the Future

While the Canadian North remains a region of conflicting goals, preferences, and aspirations, the search for a consensus continues. The image of the North as either a resource frontier or an Aboriginal homeland lies at the root of this struggle. Like myths, these two visions express important yet idealized truths. They organize the past into two different but coherent images of the North, which simplify the complex ebb and flow of past events but resonate in the present and, more importantly, point to the future. Somehow, some way, these two visions must merge, and that is the challenge for the twenty-first century.

At the centre of this struggle for hegemony lie the resource economy and its impact on the environment and Aboriginal peoples. The pattern of northern economic development depends on the extraction of its natural wealth for North American and global markets. While past impacts have rendered great damage to the environment and injured the social fabric of Aboriginal peoples, some positive developments over the past three decades have begun to forge a new northern reality. The two principal forces moulding this new reality are: (1) a shift of power that has greatly improved the position of Aboriginal groups in the resource economy and in the environmental impact assessment of industrial projects; and (2) an emergence of a much stronger environmental regulatory regime plus a willingness of corporations to comply to this regime. Already signs of a consensus are building. Nunavut, an Inuit homeland, represents one sign, while Aboriginal groups seeking part-ownership of the proposed Mackenzie Delta natural gas pipeline are another sign. On the environmental side, proposed industrial projects must undergo much more extensive public consultation, more demanding comprehensive environmental reviews, and meaningful negotiations with Aboriginal groups that would be affected by these projects. The Kyoto agreement signed by Ottawa in December 2002 may encourage movement in this direction.

In the past century, the road to this new northern reality was not an easy one. Yukon lost its principal mine; the dream of Denendeh vanished; and the Voisey's Bay nickel project stalled. Beyond promoting resource development, Ottawa and its provincial counterparts have failed to formulate a long-term northern development strategy that could lead to the eventual diversification of the northern economy. Furthermore, governments have misjudged the aspirations and needs of their Aboriginal populations. As DiFrancesco (2000) concluded:

> The cumulative impact of several decades of federal interventions in the economic and social systems of the NWT has been titanic. This fact notwithstanding, the expenditure of many billions of dollars and the implementation of myriad economic development initiatives has failed to stimulate the development of a viable wage economy. As it exists currently, the wage economy of the NWT is extremely unbalanced, inaccessible to the majority of its population, dependent upon government expenditure, and extremely vulnerable to fluctuations in international commodity markets.

Still, several positive events, including comprehensive land claim agreements, the discovery of diamonds, and the creation of Nunavut, have propelled the North into the twenty-first century on a more hopeful note. We now need to re-examine the three questions posed at the beginning of this book and then explore crucial challenges for the twenty-first century.

QUESTION 1: Can the resource economy support the northern labour force?

While the resource industry remains the driving force behind the northern economy in terms of value of production, its highly efficient operations employ only a small portion of the northern labour force. Future megaprojects will see substantial employment opportunities during the construction phase, but, unless these projects have enormous reserves like the Alberta oil sands, they offer only a short-term and partial solution to the North's unemployment problem. In the Territorial North, the heavy reliance on non-renewable resources exposes the economy to potentially wild fluctuations in demand for labour. As well, there is a serious mismatch between the skilled labour required by resource companies and the qualifications of Aboriginal workers, who often lack the necessary schooling, job experience, and technical skills. Until this gap is overcome, companies will continue to recruit many workers from southern Canada.[1]

Can the resource economy do better? Taking the newly formed Territory of Nunavut as an example, unemployment rates among the Inuit workforce are extremely high. Even with new mines, the Inuit labour force is still some distance from taking full advantage of these economic opportunities unless companies adopt innovative measures. Access to jobs is a critical problem; job qualifications are another serious barrier to employment. Air commuting can overcome the inaccessibility issue and also offer a cultural bridge by providing Inuit workers with employment at the remote mines and still allowing their families to remain in their home communities. But air commuters today number in the hundreds while thousands more want jobs. Perhaps the mining company strategy of adding an Inuit to this crew and another to that crew is at fault. Would an employment breakthrough occur if the companies created an Inuit work environment for one complete crew? Certainly this is not a simple task, and possibly it would be a very expensive one. Yet the stakes are high. Given the cultural hardships faced by Inuit workers in a Canadian mine and the urgency to increase quickly the number of Inuit workers, perhaps many more would join an Inuit crew whose working language is Inuktitut.

QUESTION 2: How can government ensure that the resource industry limits its impact on the environment?

Over the last 30 years, three developments have helped to reduce the threat of environmental damage caused by megaprojects and, at the same time, ensured that the land will be restored to its former natural state. One major step was the passing of legislation that makes environmental regulations more demanding and that ensures the reclamation of the work site after the project has wound down. Another step forward was the creation of co-managed environmental impact assessment agencies in comprehensive land claim settlement areas. The third step involves a shift in corporate attitude about the environment. While the resource industry continues to put its industrial stamp on the northern landscape, its executives have accepted their social responsibilities—care for the environment that is reinforced by legally binding environmental agreements with federal, provincial, and territorial governments.

This was not always the case. During the last 30 years, for example, many resource companies have failed to clean up lands and waters that they fouled. The Giant gold mine near Yellowknife is a classic example. Mining at the Giant mine began long before current environmental regulations came into effect. In those days, mining companies simply walked away from their mine sites, leaving their mess behind. Today's regulations commit companies to decommission mine sites. Such regulations will avoid the past practice of leaving a fouled landscape—unless, of course, the company declares bankruptcy, which, given the nature of resource development and the fluctuations in market prices, is a fairly large caveat.

QUESTION 3: Is there a place for Aboriginal peoples in the resource economy?

Aboriginal groups are now aggressively seeking a place in the resource economy, but one that balances Aboriginal cultural values with the profit motive. The injection of economic and political power into the Aboriginal world by means of modern land claim agreements and Aboriginal title offers them the opportunity to participate in the marketplace, to become involved in resource development on traditional lands, and, at the same time, to ensure a place for harvesting country food from the lands and waters of the North (Table 9.1).

One goal is a share in the ownership of industrial projects. In the Northwest Territories, for example, Aboriginal groups want to participate as a partner in the construction of a pipeline that would pipe gas from the Mackenzie Delta to Chicago. Another goal is to increase Aboriginal employment in the resource industry. This goal is more complicated. High unemployment rates are common among the Aboriginal workforce. In Nunavut, for example, the Inuit have achieved their political goal, but the much more formidable task of economic development remains. The territory faces many economic challenges. Lying mostly within the Canadian Shield,

TABLE 9.1 Modern Land Claim Agreements

Claim	Date	Number of Beneficiaries[1]	Compensation[2] (per capita)	Land (km²)[3] (per capita)
James Bay Cree	11 Nov. 1977	6,650	$135 million ($29,300)	75,539 (11.4)
James Bay Inuit	11 Nov. 1977	4,390	$90 million ($20,501)	89,747 (20.4)
James Bay Naskapi	12 Jan. 1978	390	$9 million ($23,136)	4,943 (12.7)
Inuvialuit	5 June 1984	2,500	$55 million ($22,000)	91,000* (36.4)
Gwich'in	22 Apr. 1992	2,200	$75 million ($34,091)	17,818** (8.1)
NWT Inuit	25 May 1993	19,000	$580 million ($34,118)	351,000** (18.5)
Sahtu	6 Sept. 1993	2,400	$75 million ($31,250)	41,437** (17.3)
Yukon Indians	29 May 1993	7,500	$243 million ($32,400)	41,595** (5.6)
Nisga'a	11 May 2000	6,000	$190 million ($31,667)	2,000*** (0.8)

*Includes subsurface mineral rights.

**Includes subsurface mineral rights and royalties from future resource projects.

***Includes subsurface mineral rights, royalties, and a share of natural resource harvests.

[1]Population figures refer to the date of the agreement.

[2]The purchase value of the dollars shown in the compensation column declines with time because of inflation, i.e., constant dollars for a particular year have not been used so the highest value occurs in the James Bay Agreements and the lowest in the Nisga'a Agreement.

[3]Negotiations for the type of land have evolved over time. In the James Bay Agreement, land is classified into three categories: surface rights; hunting rights; and shared hunting rights. For example, approximately 93 per cent of the land provided them with hunting rights, leaving the James Bay Native groups with only 7 per cent as surface ownership of land. Such land (category 1) surrounds Cree, Inuit, and Naskapi villages while the hunting lands (category 2) form large blocks. Category 3, which is not included in the table above, is by far the largest amount of land and is controlled by the Quebec government. In the case of the James Bay Agreement, the Quebec Cree, Inuit, and Naskapi sought control over land for hunting, fishing, and trapping, while in later negotiations, Aboriginal claimants sought fee simple lands, mineral rights, a share of royalties from resource developments within their settlement areas, and, by 2000, a share of natural resources.

SOURCE: Department of Indian and Northern Affairs Canada, Agreements. Available at: <www.ainc-inac.gc.ca/pr/agr>. Accessed 23 Jan. 2003.

its rocky terrain contains only mineral wealth, and most deposits are not yet commercially viable. Coupled with rapid population growth, the pressure on the Nunavut government to find work for its growing labour force is acute. The public sector has provided jobs in each of the 26 communities as a result of the decentralization policy of the Nunavut government. Still, Nunavut's economic growth depends on new initiatives in the mining sector.

Aboriginal culture must play a role in this new economy. The harvesting of country food, while important in itself, is an essential element of Aboriginal culture and its mixed economy.[2] Here lies the rub—the resource economy must, by its very nature, diminish habitat for wildlife, and, as Scott and Webber (2001: 150–1) have indicated in regard to the Cree, other aspects of Canadian society come into conflict with Cree values—sport hunters take their toll not in the killing of animals but, according to Cree beliefs, in their disrespect for the animals. From a Western materialist perspective, such a matter seems inconsequential. However, cultural clashes may prove to be a major stumbling block for Aboriginal groups in finding a place in the resource economy and may even affect the operations of resource companies.

LOOKING FORWARD

As the twenty-first century unfolds, the integration of Canada's northern hinterland into the North American and global economies continues unabated. The reason for a shift from a national economy to a North American one is simple: the United States is short of energy, lumber, and minerals, while Canada's North has a surplus. As prices rise, more and more resources will be developed and then transported to American markets. In the twentieth century, these resources, with only a few exceptions, came from the Provincial Norths. With energy, for example, the recently constructed Alliance Pipeline takes natural gas from northern British Columbia and Alberta to the Chicago market. With higher prices, Arctic natural gas will flow from the Mackenzie Delta to southern markets, possibly within a decade.

Because the North is a high-cost region, megaprojects are best able to harness the riches in this part of Canada. Increasingly, they require partnerships between the developers and the purchasers. These partnerships represent another form of resource integration within the North American marketplace. Given the high cost of transportation, these partnerships take on a regional nature with Hydro-Québec selling its electricity to utilities in New England, BC Hydro sending its electricity into the Pacific Northwest and California markets, and Manitoba supplying energy to North Dakota and Minnesota. In August 2002, for example, Manitoba Hydro and Xcel Energy, the largest utility company in Minnesota, concluded a $1.7 billion agreement, thus assuring Manitoba Hydro of electrical sales to its largest American customer to 2015 (Perreaux, 2002: FP6).

In the first decade of the twenty-first century, the North faces many issues. I have chosen to explore three issues:

- the diversification of the northern economy;
- the need to strengthen Native settlements;
- the creation of a new political map.

Diversification

Canada has seen its regions diversify over time. Geography dictates the type of diversity possible. Each region has its unique set of natural assets. Ontario has its automobile industry, Alberta has its petrochemical industry, and British Columbia has its lumber industry. Some regions, such as Atlantic Canada, have had more difficulty diversifying their economies. But what about the North? In the twenty-first century, is it heading towards a more broadly based economy or will it fall into a staple trap?[3]

Economic diversification is far from an automatic process for a resource hinterland, but it is a desirable goal for at least two reasons. First, it allows business to expand to new and sometimes serendipitous opportunities. Second, it offers the region's labour force more variety of jobs and, in some cases, upward mobility associated with higher-paying jobs. The processing of diamonds in Yellowknife represents one step towards economic diversification and the promise of highly skilled employment. However, without the intervention of the government of the Northwest Territories, the acceptance of the government's argument about retaining some of the high-value processing in the North by the mining company (BHP Billiton Diamonds Inc.), and the recruitment of experienced diamond cutters from other lands, diamond sorting, cutting, and polishing businesses would not have located in Yellowknife. With two more diamond mines coming on stream, a similar arrangement is anticipated, thereby greatly expanding the business of diamond sorting, cutting, and polishing in Yellowknife.

Natural resources are crucial for economic diversification, but only if more economic benefits can remain in the North. Yet, distance from market rules out all but the most necessary processing. The copper smelter at Flin Flon, Manitoba, removes perhaps 95 per cent of the waste ore, thus greatly reducing the shipping costs of the remaining high-grade copper ore. New ore deposits such as that at Voisey's Bay are a positive development, but the plan to ship this nickel ore to the smelter at Sudbury represents a market solution that underscores the difficulty of establishing processing plants in the northern hinterland. Similarly, the proposal to ship Mackenzie Delta natural gas to refineries in southern Canada and the United States represents an economic decision, i.e., it is more economical to ship the raw product to market where it is processed into a final product. Even with such a decision, other available options would provide economic benefits to communities along the pipeline route. One option would be to supply these communities with low-cost gas, thus lowering their costs of living and perhaps attracting business to locate in these communities. Another option is to build a series of greenhouses near pumping stations to utilize heat generated by these stations. Greenhouses could supply local communities with fresh garden products and employ local workers.

The construction phase of megaprojects offers many employment and business opportunities. The Alberta oil sands represent a striking example, and additional hydroelectric power development in northern Quebec provides another. The construction of these huge projects generates significant spinoff effects and can stimulate local businesses. Since the North is faced with a series of megaprojects, the cumulative effect could make a difference. As noted in the case of the Norman Wells Project (1982–5), the North's commercial infrastructure at that time was limited and therefore most spinoff effects did not stay in the North but went to large firms in southern Canada. Even some employment opportunities leaked to southern Canada as companies flew southern workers to northern construction and mining sites. Successes did occur when the company went to the communities to ensure that local businesses became involved in the project, whether it was a contract to fill sandbags for the pipeline or security services for the construction site. Alberta-Pacific Forest Industries provides another example of proactive recruiting by companies to ensure northern benefits. Alberta-Pacific uses this community approach in its pulp operations in northern Alberta. Its timber lease extends over 25 per cent of northern Alberta's land area and includes 22 Native settlements with a total Aboriginal population of 23,000. Without such an approach, Doug Willy (2002), the director of Aboriginal Business Planning at Alberta-Pacific, believes that Aboriginal business involvement in the work of the company would have been minuscule.

Diversification, then, takes on two elements: a broadening of commercial activities and a diffusion of those activities to small communities. Diversification depends on capturing more of the spinoff effects from the construction of future megaprojects. In this way, three economic benefits can emerge: an expanded northern business community; greater involvement of Aboriginal businesses; and increased business experience for entrepreneurs in small communities. In sum, diversification of the northern economy, including the spread of spinoff effects to small communities, will not come quickly or easily, but it must remain the principal goal for the twenty-first century.

Native Settlements

In the 1950s, the shift from the land to settlements began. This relocation marked the beginning of a new way of life. Native settlements, however, were not formed for economic reasons, but represent cultural homelands that are adjacent to traditional hunting grounds. The absence of an economic raison d'être has led to many social problems, such as family violence, substance abuse, and high suicide rates, and has placed many Aboriginal residents in a state of psychological depression where hope for a better life has vanished and has been replaced by high levels of frustration, grief, and psychic pain. High suicide rates are one measure of the degree of individual and group dysfunction. For example, Nunavut's suicide rate is six times higher than the national average and it is even higher among Inuit males between the ages of 15–29 years (Hicks and White, 2000: 89–90). James Eetoolook, first vice-president of Nunavut Tunngavik Inc. summed up the problem:

> As in other societies, problems of domestic violence are a symptom of deeper economic and social problems in Inuit society that are aggravated by such things as: unemployment, underemployment, inadequate and poorly designed government social policies and programs, and the rapid rate of technological change. (Ibid., 84)

As the Achilles heel of Ottawa's modernization 'strategy', the lack of an adequate economic base for Native settlements results in high unemployment rates, encourages social violence, and creates a dependency on social welfare. Even with an air-commuting system linking these settlements with the mine sites, those Aboriginal adults living in small, remote communities stand little chance of participating because of limited education and few skills suitable for the mining industry. Jull (2000: 119) has described this problem:

Health care saved many lives and sparked a baby boom, while schooling made people want jobs, which did not exist in the Arctic. There is no doubt that under- and un-employment are and will be the fundamental challenge of Nunavut for some time. Big resource projects, if and when they come, do not hire large numbers of unskilled local labour but rely on national and international pools of skilled personnel who move around the world following jobs.

This problem is not new. Air commuting has had positive but limited results in overcoming the distance barrier. Mining companies using an air-commuting system to link northern settlements with mine sites have obtained a stable and loyal workforce. For the most part, Aboriginal workers have received company and/or government training programs to upgrade their work skills, which compensates for limited job experience and schooling. By working for several weeks at the mine site and then returning home, this non-Aboriginal work environment is more culturally acceptable than relocating to a resource town for both the Aboriginal employee and his/her family. For the company, a northern air-commuting system represents an extra cost to operations, but it is an acceptable cost because it results in 'northern benefits'.

Air commuting to mine sites alleviates, but does not solve, the problem of large pools of unemployed and underemployed workers in Native settlements. Coupled with the fact that these settlements have shown little sign of local development, high unemployment rates are destined to plague these Aboriginal communities in the future. For that reason alone, Ottawa should revisit the idea of subsidizing the hunting economy. This idea is not new. Over 25 years ago, Thomas Berger (1977: xxvi) stated: 'The development of the whole renewable resource sector—including the strengthening of the native economy—would enable native people to enter the industrial system without becoming completely dependent on it.'

While there are different ways to subsidize the hunting economy, including the Nunavut Hunter Support Program (Wenzel, 2000: 188–91), the Quebec Cree program extends over a larger number of families, provides much greater financial support, and is more financially secure than the Nunavut program.[4] The Income Security Program for the Cree in northern Quebec is based on the premise that it is better to be productively engaged in land-based activities than to draw social assistance in a Native settlement. The Quebec government recognized that Native settlements could not provide sufficient jobs. Its hunting subsidy program guarantees an income for full-time hunters based on the time spent on the land. At the same time, it reduces the competition for jobs in the settlements. Its only drawbacks are the cost of a hunting subsidy and the possibility that children of hunting families may not opt for an education fitting them for the wage economy. Given the economic and social malaise found in most Native settlements, these drawbacks appear inconsequential. While the Income Security Program for the Cree has been extremely popular, how well it has eased social problems in their communities requires closer examination.

A New Map of the North

An emerging new map of the Canadian North reflects the newly acquired political power of the Aboriginal community. The first step in this reconstituted geography began in 1999 when Nunavut was formally carved out of the Northwest Territories

(Vignette 9.1). Even more amazing, Nunavut represents a de facto ethnic state within Canada that 'fits comfortably within established traditions of mainstream Canadian governance' (Hicks and White, 2000: 31).

Vignette 9.1 The Road to Nunavut: A Chronological History	
Year	*Event*
1973	Inuit Tapirisat of Canada undertakes a study of Inuit land use and occupancy under the direction of Professor Milton Freeman.
1976	Inuit Tapirisat of Canada proposes the creation of a separate Arctic territory for the Inuit of the Northwest Territories.
1976	The Inuit of the western Arctic (the Inuvialuit) opt to undertake their own land claim, thus dividing the Inuit land claim and territory into two parts.
1990	Following years of negotiations, the Tungavik Federation of Nunavut, the Northwest Territories, and the federal government sign an agreement-in-principle that includes the formation of a separate territory for the Inuit of the central and eastern Arctic subject to the approval of the division of the Northwest Territories by means of a plebiscite.
1992	The residents of the Northwest Territories approve of its division into two separate territories.
1992	The Tungavik Federation of Nunavut and the federal government sign the Nunavut Political Accord.
1992	The Inuit of Nunavut ratify the Nunavut Land Claims Agreement.
1993	Parliament passes the Nunavut Land Claims Agreement Act and the Nunavut Act.
1993	Nunavut Tunngavik Inc. replaces the Tungavik Federation of Nunavut.
1997	The Office of the Interim Commissioner is established to help prepare for the creation of Nunavut.
1999	The residents of Nunavut elect the members of the Nunavut Legislative Assembly with Paul Okalik as the Premier.
1999	The Territory of Nunavut is formed, and its government begins to function.
1999	The Clyde River Protocol establishes the norms that will govern the relationship between Nunavut Tunngavik Inc.* and the new government of Nunavut.

*Nunavut Tunngavik Inc. receives and administers funds from the Nunavut land claim agreement. It is responsible for ensuring that the Nunavut government respects and follows the land claim, especially those aspects promoting Inuit culture. The Clyde River Protocol requires that the Nunavut government and Nunavut Tunngavik Inc. work together to ensure that legislation promotes Inuit culture. In 2002, for example, Nunavut's language commissioner proposed a Quebec-style commercial sign law to ensure that Inuktitut remains the dominant language used on business signs, posters, and commercial advertising. This proposal arose because most of Iqaluit's business signs are in English only.

How did this political breakthrough come about? In their land claims agreement the Inuit were able, through determined negotiation over some 20 years, to gain a commitment from Ottawa to form a new territory. Nunavut would accommodate the political aspirations of the Inuit of the central and eastern Arctic, and provide them with the power to promote both economic and cultural development. In 1992, this commitment took the legal form of the Nunavut Political Accord, which was signed by the governments of Canada and the Northwest Territories and the Inuit negotiating body, Tungavik Federation of Nunavut. In 1993, Ottawa passed the Nunavut Land Claims Agreement, and the government of Nunavut took charge of governing the new territory on 1 April 1999.

Vignette 9.2 Power-Sharing: Protecting Inuktitut or Attacking Canadian Unity?

Iqaluit, the capital of Nunavut, has drawn Canadians from across the country with the promise of high-paying jobs and business opportunities. While about 60 per cent of Iqaluit's population speak Inuktitut, most business signs are in English. Nunavut legislators are considering a sign law that they hope will recapture the cityscape for Inuktitut and thereby ensure that Inuktitut remains the dominant language in the capital city. Under this proposal, all business signs and commercial advertising must favour the use of the Inuktitut language. English and French would be permitted as long as their lettering was not more prominent. This proposal is similar to existing language laws in Quebec where French must be more prominent on outdoor signs. The negative reaction from one of Canada's national newspapers indicates the difficulty of power-sharing—in this case, the acceptance by the Canadian majority of special protection for a small minority whose language is under stress in its capital. The *National Post* (14 Feb. 2002: A15) took the view that:

> The government of Nunavut functions because taxpayers in the rest of the country pay its bills. More than 92 per cent of its budget comes straight from Ottawa. A government that could not function more than one day out of 12 without federal financial support is considering restricting the rights of those who prefer to communicate in one of our two official languages. This is as insulting to Canada as is the fact that Quebec receives the greatest share of federal equalization funds and yet its government still holds the rest of the country in contempt. But in Nunavut, it is not just a case of the seal biting the hand that feeds it. The proposed new law will also do real [economic] damage to the region. But if the territory hopes to become even modestly self-sufficient or prosperous, it should leave the language issue alone.

Except for Cree, Ojibwa, and Inuktitut, indigenous languages are disappearing. Since language is a critical element of culture, the proposed Inuktitut sign legislation seems appropriate. Dahl, Hicks, and Jull (2000: 12) observed:

Within Canada the Inuit have found themselves opposed by groups with very widely different agendas but a common misunderstanding of—or simple opposition to—the creation of Nunavut. Those groups have been a rich source of misinformation and, often, disinformation. Right-wing politicians oppose *all* indigenous rights and self-determination, and pretend that Nunavut is a threat to the unity of Canada.

Needless to say, the *National Post* consistently represents and supports right-wing business and political interests.

SOURCES: *National Post* (2002); Dahl, Hicks, and Jull (2000: 12).

Political and economic consequences of Nunavut affect other northern regions with an Aboriginal majority. Already, the Quebec Inuit have reached an advanced stage of negotiations with the Quebec government for a similar political arrangement for Nunavik (the Arctic territory in northern Quebec). Since these discussions are taking place in a province, both parties are breaking new political ground. The central question is, how can a province create a territory-like region within its boundaries? If this question can be answered, then other Provincial Norths with a majority of Aboriginal residents may wish to follow the same political path. In this way, the political map of the Canadian North could be radically altered.

DIRECTIONS FOR THE FUTURE

Solutions do not come easily or cheaply. Since the market economy alone is unlikely to create a more diversified economy and a more equitable society in the North, commitments and investments by both multinational corporations and governments are required. Two types of solutions are proposed—facilitating and breakthrough solutions.

Facilitating solutions include extending education opportunities, experimenting with on-the-job training programs, expanding the geographic range of fly-in/fly-out commuting to include all communities, revisiting the concept of a hunting subsidy, and enlarging the dual resource management system that flows out of comprehensive land claim agreements to other areas. Each approach, in its own way, is providing direction for the future. For example, those Aboriginal groups that have negotiated comprehensive agreements have several advantages, including a substantial cash settlement and a dual administrative structure that allows a foot in the new world of commerce and another in the old world of hunting and trapping. In fact, this dual structure serves as a balance between the new ventures and the traditional lifestyle in two ways. First, the dual structure allows participation in the market economy and the traditional one. Second, the very nature of this form of dualism allows those involved in the traditional economy associated with the environment and wildlife to confront those in the capitalist resource extraction economy to ensure that the environment is protected and that renewable resources are managed properly.

Breakthrough solutions require a vision and a long-term commitment by governments and industry. Recognizing that the North has limited opportunities for economic diversification compared to other regions of Canada, how can its small population and the great distance to markets work to its advantage? One way is to make more use of resources within the North while another is to harness unused resources. One example takes advantage of wind power. Each community and remote mine must import diesel fuel at great cost to produce electricity. Wind power, as a supplementary source of energy to reduce dependency on fossil fuels, could utilize the extensive wind energy found in the North, but it requires organization—perhaps an innovative combination of private industry, governments, and Aboriginal organizations. The wind energy exists but it needs to be harnessed. Canada's Arctic coast, for instance, registers some of the highest average annual wind speeds in North America. Producing electricity from wind energy has several advantages. First, it is a renewable resource. Second, it has a stable cost that is not subject to the same volatility as diesel fuel prices. Third, it would require the training of local utility workers. Fourth, it could be the basis of a new scientific industry in Canada where a wind turbine technology centre could undertake research design and product development for small northern communities and isolated industrial sites; offer advanced training in the operation and maintenance of this technology to northerners; and, with the help of northern leaders, government officials, and company officials, sell this technology to similar communities and industrial sites around the circumpolar world. Fifth, substituting wind energy for fossil fuel energy could help Canada meet its Kyoto Protocol commitments.[5] Sixth, as a joint venture led by resource companies but supported by governments and Aboriginal organizations, such a project could serve as a model for other joint efforts to search for breakthrough solutions to northern problems (Vignette 6.1). Resource companies operating in a hinterland will find it to their advantage to go beyond their narrow economic goal of profit-making and harness their vast power to tackle social and environmental issues of concern to northerners.

NOTES

1. In the 1990s, impacts and benefits agreements between Aboriginal groups and resource companies became mandatory. These agreements have the potential to increase Aboriginal employment, but low education levels, lack of job experience in the resource industry, and limited technical skills have so far prevented Aboriginal workers from realizing this potential. As well, the problem of hiring Aboriginal workers becomes even more complex on union jobs for two reasons: (1) very few Aboriginal workers hold union cards; and (2) union hiring halls are located in southern cities.
2. Coates (1988: 86) described the evolution of the mixed economy in Yukon up to the 1980s in the following terms: 'The Natives' reliance on a mixed economy represented a combination of Indian preferences and economic realism. The Yukon Indians, like all harvesting peoples, placed particular importance on their hunting and gathering activities. It provided an "affluent" lifestyle, formed the basis of their spirituality, and determined much of the nature of their social organization.' The mixed economy was best suited for living on the land. Once in settlements, the cost of living rose sharply as new needs and wants surfaced. The cash generated by the mixed economy was often insufficient, creating a greater need for wage employment and a greater dependency on social welfare.

3. Watkins (1977: 87) sees the staple trap as a consequence of resource development. When the non-renewable resources are depleted and renewable resources exhausted, the region will be stripped of its natural wealth and abandoned by the resource companies. The trap, then, in this Marxist interpretation is one of 'damned if you do, damned if you don't' exploitation of resources, and leads to a state of underdevelopment.

4. The annual budget for the Nunavut Hunter Support Program is generated primarily by the interest on a $30 million fund, and, to a much lesser degree, by drawing down the principal. In 1994, the government of the Northwest Territories and the Nunavut Tunngavik Inc. contributed $15 million each to this fund. According to Légaré (2000), additional contribution will be necessary by 2010 to keep this program functioning.

5. Canada produces 830 megatonnes of greenhouse gases a year and, according to the Kyoto Protocol, must reduce this figure by 30 per cent within 10 years. The Alberta oil sands developments are a major contributor of greenhouse gases.

REFERENCES AND SELECTED READINGS

Abele, Francis, Katherine A. Graham, and Allan M. Maslove. 1999. 'Negotiating Canada: Changes in Aboriginal Policy over the Last Thirty Years', in Leslie A. Pal, ed., *How Ottawa Spends 1999–2000*. Toronto: Oxford University Press, 251–92.

Berger, Thomas R. 1977. *Northern Frontier, Northern Homeland: The Report of the Mackenzie Valley Pipeline Inquiry*. Ottawa: Department of Supply and Services.

Coates, Kenneth. 1988. 'On the Outside in Their Homeland: Native People and the Evolution of the Yukon Economy', *Northern Review* 1: 73–89.

Dahl, Jens, Jack Hicks, and Peter Jull. 2000. *Inuit Regain Control of Their Lands and Their Lives*. Skive, Denmark: Centraltrykkeriet Skive A/S.

DiFrancesco, Richard J. 2000. 'A Diamond in the Rough?: An Examination of the Issues Surrounding the Development of the Northwest Territories', *The Canadian Geographer* 44, 2: 114–34.

Hicks, Jack, and Graham White. 2000. 'Nunavut: Inuit Self-Determination through a Land Claim and Public Government?', in Dahl, Hicks, and Jull (2000: 30–117).

Jull, Peter. 2000. 'A Different Place', in Dahl, Hicks, and Jull (2000: 118-36).

Légaré, André. 2000. 'La Nunavut Tunngavik Inc.: Un examen de ses activités et de sa structure administrative', *Études/Inuit/Studies* 24, 1: 97–124.

———. 2002. 'Collective Identity in the Canadian Eastern Arctic', *Review of Constitutional Studies* 1, 1/2: 55–78.

Nunavik Commission. 2001. *Amiqqaaluta—Let Us Share: Mapping the Road toward a Government for Nunavik*. Report of the Nunavik Commission. Quebec City: Nunavik Commission.

'Nunavut's Bill 101', 2002. *National Post*, 4 Feb., A15.

Perreaux, Les. 2002. 'Manitoba Hydro in deal with Xcel', *National Post*, 10 Aug., FP6.

Scott, Colin H., ed. 2001. *Aboriginal Autonomy and Development in Northern Quebec and Labrador*. Vancouver: University of British Columbia Press.

——— and Jeremy Webber. 2001. 'Conflicts between Cree Hunting and Sport Hunting', in Scott (2001: 149–74).

Usher, Peter J., Frank J. Tough, and Robert M. Galois. 1999. 'Reclaiming the land: Aboriginal title, treaty rights, and land claims in Canada', *Applied Geography* 12, 2: 109–32.

Watkins, Melville H. 1977. 'The Staple Theory Revisited', *Journal of Canadian Studies* 12: 3–10.

Wenzel, George. 2000. 'Inuit Subsistence and Hunter Support in Nunavut', in Dahl, Hicks, and Jull (2000: 180–93).

White, Graham. 2002. 'Politics and Government in the Territorial North: Familiar and Exotic', in *The Canadian North: Embracing Change*. Montreal: Centre for Research and Information on Canada, 16–23.

Willy, Doug. 2002. 'Integrated Land Management and Community Involvement at ALPac', paper presented to 'Search for Tomorrow: Aboriginal Community Growth in Natural Resource Development', 10th annual conference of the Canada Aboriginal Mineral Association, Fort McMurray, 19 Nov.

THE METHOD OF CALCULATING NORDICITY

While the division of the North into the Arctic and Subarctic demonstrates the existence of two physical environments, nordicity permits us to measure differences between places and to create human/physical regions. But what exactly does nordicity measure? A Canadian geographer, Louis-Edmond Hamelin, created this term to quantify 'northernness' into a single value measured as polar units. In sum, nordicity is a quantitative measure based on 10 variables found at a particular northern place. Nordicity is based on both physical elements, such as annual cold, permafrost, and ice cover of water bodies, and human elements such as population size, accessibility by land, sea, and air, and degree of economic activity. These 10 physical and human elements seek to represent all facets of the North. Hamelin set numeric values (polar units) for each variable. At a particular place, the sum of polar values for the 10 variables results in a single numeric value. This value represents the nordicity of that particular place. The North Pole, for example, has a nordicity of 1,000 polar units. Isachsen, the northern most weather station in Canada, has 925 polar units while Vancouver has only 35. Hamelin determined that the boundary between northern and southern Canada followed a line representing 200 polar units. Hamelin is describing the Canadian North from a southern perspective. Northerners may not have the same mental map of Canada. For them, southern Canada is a distant and different place while the terms Middle North, Far North, and Extreme North have no meaning for them.

The method of calculating the number of polar units for a place is summarized below. For example, the number of polar units assigned to varying degrees of latitude ranges from zero units for latitudes of 45°N or less to 100 units at the North Pole (90°N).

List of 10 Variables and Their Polar Units

Variable		Polar Units
1. Latitude	90°	100
	80°	77
	50°	33
	45°	0
2. Summer Heat	0 days above 5.6°C	100
	60 days above 5.6°C	70
	100 days above 5.6°C	30
	>150 days above 5.6°C	0
3. Annual Cold	6,650 degree days below 0°	100
	4,700 degree days below 0°	75
	1,950 degree days below 0°	30
	550 degree days below 0°	0

Variable			Polar Units
4. Types of Ice	Frozen ground	Continuous permafrost 457 m thick	100
		Continuous permafrost <457 m thick	80
		Discontinuous permafrost	60
		Ground frozen for less than 1 month	0
	Floating ice	Permanent pack ice	100
		Pack ice for 6 months	36
		Pack ice <1 month	0
	Glaciers	Ice sheet >1,523 m thick	100
		Ice cap 304 m thick	60
		Snow cover <2.5 cm	0
5. Annual Precipitation		100 mm	100
		300 mm	60
		500 mm	0
6. Natural Vegetation		Rocky desert	100
		50% tundra	90
		Open woodland	40
		Dense forest	0
7. Accessibility	Land or sea	No service	100
		For two months	60
		By both land and sea	15
		By either land or sea	0
8. Accessibility	Air	Charter only	100
		Weekly regular service	25
		Daily regular service	0
9. Population	Settlement size	None	100
		About 100	85
		About 1,000	60
		>5,000	0
	Population density	Uninhabited	100
		1 person per km^2	50
		4 persons per km^2	0
10. Economic Activity		No production	100
		Exploration	80
		20 hunters/trappers	75
		Interregional centre	0

SOURCE: Hamelin (1979: ch. 1).

ESTIMATED POPULATION GROWTH OF NORTHERN CANADA, 1871–2001

Year	Population Size
1871	60,000
1881	60,000
1891	80,000
1901	100,000
1911	130,000
1921	150,000
1931	250,000
1941	350,000
1951	600,000
1961	900,000
1971	1,200,000
1981	1,500,000
1991	1,500,000
2001	1,500,000

NOTE: Population totals are based on the decennial census figures. Except for the figures after 1971, these are estimates because strikingly different census divisions were used. In addition, historical population statistics are, at best, rough estimates. Prior to 1951, the census figures are best considered approximations.

POPULATION BY NORTHERN CENSUS DIVISIONS

Northern Census Divisions	1981	1996	2001	% Change 1996–2001
Newfoundland/Labrador	57,056	52,045	47,955	−7.9
Division 9	25,738	22,855	20,091	−12.1
Division 10	31,318	29,190	27,864	−4.5
Quebec	487,943	457,395	439,075	−3.9
Abitibi (84)	93,529	90,000	86,000	−4.4
Chicoutimi (94)	174,441	171,000	164,000	−4.1
Lac-Saint-Jean-Ouest (90)	62,952	60,000	57,000	−5.0
Saguenay (97)	115,881	98,000	94,000	−4.1
Territorie-du-Nouveau Quebec (98)	41,140	38,395	38,575	0.5
Ontario	443,826	439,674	416,476	−5.3
Algoma District (57)	133,533	125,455	118,567	−5.5
Cochrane District (56)	96,875	93,240	85,247	−8.6
Kenora District (60)	59,421	63,360	61,802	−2.5
Thunder Bay District (58)	153,997	157,619	150,860	−4.3
Manitoba	73,668	83,134	82,427	−0.9
Division 19	12,227	14,722	15,805	7.4
Division 21	24,714	23,150	22,556	−2.6
Division 22	26,673	35,584	35,077	−1.4
Division 23	10,004	9,678	8,989	−7.1
Saskatchewan	25,304	31,104	32,029	3.0
Division 18	25,304	31,104	32,029	3.0
Alberta	87,636	91,203	100,479	10.2
Division 16	43,573	36,494	42,971	17.7
Division 17	44,063	54,709	57,508	5.1

Northern Census Divisions	1981	1996	2001	% Change 1996–2001
British Columbia	227,556	242,104	233,445	−3.6
Bulkley-Nechanko District (51)	38,309	41,642	40,856	−1.9
Fraser-Fort George District (58)	89,431	98,974	95,317	−3.7
Kitimat-Stikine District (49)	42,400	43,618	40,876	−6.3
Peace River-Liard District (55)	55,463	56,477	55,080	−2.5
Stikine Region (57)	1,953	1,393	1,316	−5.5
Yukon (01)	23,153	30,766	28,674	−6.8
Northwest Territories	29,829	39,672	37,360	−5.8
Fort Smith Region (06)	22,344	30,225	28,824	−4.6
Inuvik Region (07)	7,485	9,447	8,536	−9.6
Nunavut	15,912	24,730	26,745	8.1
Baffin Region (04)	8,300	13,218	14,372	8.7
Keewatin Region (05)	4,327	6,868	7,557	10.0
Kitikmeot Region (08)	3,285	4,644	4,816	3.7
North	1,471,883	1,491,827	1,445,165	−3.1

SOURCES: Statistics Canada, *Population: Census Divisions and Subdivisions*. Catalogue no. 92–101 (Ottawa: Minister of Supply and Services, 1987); Statistics Canada, 'Population and Dwelling Counts, for Canada, Provinces and Territories, and Census Divisions, 2001 and 1996 Censuses', 2002, available at: <http://www12.statcan.ca/english/census01/products/standard/popdwell/Table-PR.cfm>.

Aboriginal peoples: Those Canadians of Indian, Inuit, and Métis ancestry.

Accessibility: The ease with which interchange can occur between two or more places. One measure of accessibility is the cost of travel or communications between places.

Acid rain: Popular term used to describe precipitation that has become acid through reactions between moisture and chemicals in the atmosphere; raindrops combined with gaseous pollutants, such as oxides of sulphur and nitrogen, to make falling rain acidic.

Arctic: A natural region of North America distinguished by either a tundra vegetation or a polar desert; the traditional homeland of the Inuit.

Air mass: A large body of air that has similar horizontal temperature and moisture characteristics.

Air pollutants: Airborne substances with concentrations high enough to cause harm to the health of people, animals, and vegetation. Air pollutants may also erode stone-faced buildings and statues as well as toxify an environment.

Animism: Belief that objects, such as animals, plants, and rocks, or natural events, like earthquakes, have a spirit and conscious life.

Annual range of temperature: The difference between the warmest and coldest months at any given geographic point.

Assimilation: The process of integrating one culture into another so that the former loses its distinctiveness.

Atmosphere: The layer of gases surrounding the earth. The three major divisions of the atmosphere are troposphere, stratosphere, and ionosphere. The earth's atmosphere is mainly nitrogen (78 per cent) and oxygen (21 per cent); water vapour (up to 4 per cent) and carbon dioxide (0.04 per cent) are the principal greenhouse gases.

Aurora borealis: Glowing and moving light, sometimes in many colours, displayed in the nighttime sky in northern latitudes and caused by the interaction of atmospheric gases and charged solar particles with the earth's magnetic field; also called northern lights.

Bioaccumulation: The buildup of contaminants in organisms. These toxic substances often take the form of chlorinated organic compounds such as DDT and PCBs. See *Biomagnification*.

Biodiversity: The number of species of plants, animals, and microorganisms in a geographic area.

Biomagnification: The concentration of toxic substances in organisms increases as the contaminants are passed up food chains, i.e., they accumulate in the fatty tissues of mammals such as seals.

Biome: Major geographic area of the earth marked by a distinct environment, especially natural vegetation.

Birth rate: The annual number of births per 1,000 individuals within a given population.

Blizzard: A severe weather condition characterized by low temperatures, strong winds, and blowing snow.

Boreal forest: The northern coniferous forest; also known as the taiga. Coniferous trees, especially black and white spruce, make up most of this forest.

Carbon dioxide (CO_2): An odourless and colourless gas comprising 0.035 per cent of the atmosphere; as a greenhouse gas, it absorbs infrared radiation.

Carrying capacity: The number of organisms an ecosystem can support while maintaining its productivity and capability for renewal. Application to human beings is more complicated but the concept remains valid.

Climate: Over a long period of time, weather conditions, but particularly temperature and precipitation, remain within a small daily and seasonal range.

Climatic controls: Permanent factors that govern the general nature of the climate of a region.

Circumpolar world: The parts of those countries in the northern hemisphere that contain either Arctic or Subarctic environments: Canada, Finland, Iceland, Greenland, Norway, Sweden, Russia, and United States of America.

Colonialism: The attempt by one country to establish its society in another territory and to impose its political, economic, and cultural values on the original inhabitants living in that territory.

Condensation: Water in a gaseous state changes into a liquid state.

Continental climate: The type of climate associated with the interior of continents that is characterized by wide seasonal temperature range and low annual precipitation.

Continental shelf: Submerged margin of continents; gently sloping land extending from the coast to the edge of the continental shelf, usually defined as depths less than 200 metres.

Core/periphery model (heartland/hinterland model): A general theory of polarized economic growth comprised of an industrial centre surrounded by a resource hinterland. This highly simplified and abstract model attempts to represent the geographic arrangement of economic activities in a capitalist system. A key element is that decisions affecting the hinterland are made by the elite business leaders in the industrial core who determine the nature and pace of resource development in the hinterland. This model has both Marxist and conventional economic interpretations. Marxists see the exploitation of the hinterland leading to a state of underdevelopment while others see the hinterland benefiting from resource development. It is applicable at all geographic scales: internationally, nationally, or regionally. In this book, the model is applied to the North as a resource periphery within the industrial world but especially within North America.

Country food: Food obtained by hunting, fishing, or gathering. While country food is no longer the chief source of food for many Native northerners, it remains important both nutritionally and culturally for Native families, particularly those in more remote communities.

Coureurs de bois: Unlicensed fur traders of New France who played an important role in the European exploration of Canada and in establishing trading contacts with the Indians.

Cryosoils: Thin soils formed in the continuous permafrost zone. These soils have active or thawed layers less than one metre thick.

Daily range of temperature: The difference between the maximum and minimum temperatures for any given day.

Death rate (crude death rate): The annual number of deaths per 1,000 population in a given population.

Demographic transition theory: A sequence of demographic changes in which populations progressively move over time from high birth and death rates to low birth and death rates.

Dene: Indian people of Canada's western Subarctic. Traditionally, the Dene lived by hunting, fishing, snaring wild animals, fish, and birds, and gathering berries.

Denendeh: The proposed Dene political state. Native self-determination in the Northwest Territories called for an autonomous state within Canada. The Dene Nation attempted to tie this political concept to its land claims settlement but the federal government, while later accepting the idea of dividing the Northwest Territories roughly along the treeline, did not allow this linkage.

Dependency: A corollary of dominance; a situation where a region or people must rely on other regions for their economic well-being. Dependency can also mean that external capital and technology play a paramount role in the regional economy and that local politicians have little power in the provincial and federal governments.

Development: The process by which people's standard of living, their quality of life, and their capacity to participate in the political, social, and economic systems and institutions improves.

Diffusion: The spread or movement of a concept, practice, article, or population from a point of origin to other areas.

Drift: Material laid down by glacial ice sheets.

Drumlin: Streamlined elongated hill composed of glacial deposits; its long axis parallels the direction of glacier flow.

Dual economy: Two types of social and economic systems existing simultaneously within the same territory; in the case of the Canadian North, the resource economy and the Native economy.

Ecological footprint: Impact of human activities on the land; a measure of regional sustainability by relating the region's population size to exploitation of natural resources necessary to support that population.

Ecology: The study of interactions of living organisms with each other and with their environments.

Economic growth: Rising levels of national output and income as a result of the increase in productive capacity of the economy over time.

Economic leakage: The loss of economic benefits from one region to another; often occurs when a large-scale construction project requires goods and labour not found in the region, thus forcing the company to purchase goods and hire workers in other regions.

Economic location: Firms attempt to locate in places where their costs of production and distribution are minimized. Accordingly, there are three possible economic locations—optimal location, where costs reach the lowest point and profits are highest; suboptimal locations, where costs are sufficiently low to result in a profitable situation; and marginal locations, where costs are so high that the firm is losing money and eventually ceases its operation.

Economies of scale: The cost advantage gained by large-scale production; these arise as the average per unit cost of production falls while output increases.

Ecosystem: A community of plants and animals and the environment in which they live and react with each other.

Ecumene: Permanently inhabited areas of the earth.

Empowerment: A process whereby marginalized groups gain power and become the agents of their own development.

Environmentalism: The ideas, language, and practices designed to promote the well-being of the natural world; often takes the form of identifying industrial activities that damage the environment and then calling for a halt to such practices.

Environmental impact assessment (EIA): The critical investigation of the likely environmental, social, economic, and cultural effects of proposed industrial projects.

Epidemiological transition: A sequence of health changes that progressively move over time from high infant mortality to low infant mortality and death coming at higher ages. Control of infectious diseases accounts for the decline in infant mortality rates while control of degenerative diseases has resulted in longer life spans.

Erosion: The loosening and removal of material by various geomorphic processes.

Erratic: A boulder that has been moved by glacial ice and deposited in another place.

Esker: Ridge of sand and gravel, sometimes many kilometres long, deposited by streams beneath or within a glacier.

Ethnocentrism: The perception that one's own ethnic group is superior to other ethnic groups.

Extended family: Social unit comprising parents, children, and other relatives.

Fast ice: An extensive, unbroken sheet of sea ice that is attached to the land.

Fault: Crack in the earth's crust; also known as fracture.

Fauna: Wildlife.

Fertility rate: The number of live births in a given year per 1,000 women aged 15–44.

Fjord: Steep-walled glacial trough that has been invaded by the sea, producing a deep inlet; found along mountainous coasts in high latitudes.

Flora: Natural vegetation.

Fourth World: Encapsulated indigenous societies in economically advanced countries. In this book, the term refers to the Canadian North as a place where the original inhabitants have become minorities and generally disadvantaged minorities within their 'own' lands. What defines Fourth World peoples, but especially those living in Canada, is their close relationship to the land, their use of land as a source of food, spiritual strength, and a common resource base, and their struggle to find a place within a modern industrial state.

Furan: Colourless, volatile, liquid hydrocarbon (C_4H_4O) used in the synthesis of organic compounds.

Gelifluction (solifluction): The movement of thawed, wet soil downslope in a series of distinct lobes; occurs in tundra regions.

General circulation of the atmosphere: Large-scale atmospheric motions over the entire earth.

Glacial till: Unsorted and unstratified material carried and laid down by glacial ice.

Glaciofluvial: Landforms associated with glacial meltwater streams.

Glaciolacustrine: Landforms associated with glacial lakes.

Global economy: With the decline in trade barriers, international trade has greatly increased, creating a highly integrated world economy.

Global warming: The apparent warming of the earth's surface as the concentration of greenhouse gases in the atmosphere has increased.

Globalization: Common processes of economic, political, cultural, and environmental change that are leading to increased connectedness of different parts of the world.

Greenhouse effect: Atmospheric warming by transmission of incoming short-wave solar radiation and trapping of outgoing long-wave terrestrial radiation.

Greenhouse gases: Gases in the atmosphere that partially absorb long-wave terrestrial radiation emitted by the warm surface of the earth. The main greenhouse gases are water vapour, carbon dioxide, methane, nitrous oxide, and ozone.

Gross domestic product (GDP): Total value of all goods and services produced in a country per year, excluding the value of income residents receive from abroad (less similar payments made to non-residents who contribute to the domestic economy).

Gross national product: The total value of all goods and services produced in a country per year.

Growth rate: The rate at which a population is increasing (or decreasing) in a given year due to natural increases and net migration; expressed as a percentage of the base population.

Hinterland: The market area or region served by an urban centre; see *Core/periphery model*.

Holocene: The most recent geological epoch that began some 10,000 years ago, marking the end of the last ice advance and the beginning of an interglacial phase.

Homeguard: Indian employed at or residing near a trading post.

Homeland: The place where inhabitants live and have a strong attachment; the image held by Native northerners of the North.

Human ecology: The application of ecological concepts to the study of the relations between people and their physical and social environment.

Ice fog: Smog-like feature found in larger urban centres in the North such as Whitehorse and Yellowknife. Ice fog occurs during prolonged cold spells and inversions.

Indian: The term 'Indian' is a legal one in Canada. A person whose name is on the band list of any Indian community in Canada, or on the central registry list in Ottawa, is an Indian. The main Indian linguistic groups in the Canadian North are Algonkian and Athapaskan.

Infant mortality rate: The number of deaths of infants under one year of age in a given year per 1,000 live births in that year.

Informal economy: That part of an economy performing productive, useful, and necessary labour without a formal system of control and remuneration and operating beyond official recognition.

Interglacial: An interglacial phase is a relatively short geological time between ice advances.

Inuit: Aboriginal people whose homeland is the Arctic and who, traditionally, were nomadic hunters, especially of sea mammals such as seal, whale, and walrus; they comprised about 85 per cent of the population of the recently created Territory of Nunavut.

Inversion: An atmospheric condition in which cold air underlies warm air; inversions are highly stable conditions and thus not conducive to atmospheric mixing.

Isoline: A map line connecting points of constant value, such as pressure (isobar) or temperature (isotherm).

Isostatic uplift: Isostacy is a state of balance maintained in the crust of the earth. Disturbance of the balance causes isostatic movements to act to restore the balance. The removal of an ice sheet triggers a rebound of the depressed earth's crust that was due to the weight of the ice sheet.

Labour force/workforce: The economically active population, consisting of productive employed and temporarily unemployed people.

Latitude: The numbering system used to indicate the location of parallels drawn on a globe and measuring distance north or south of the equator in degrees.

Life expectancy: The average number of additional years a person would live if current mortality trends were to continue. Most commonly cited as life expectancy at birth.

Little Ice Age: A period of cool temperatures that lasted some 400 years from around 1450 to 1850.

Longitude: The numbering system used to indicate the location of meridians drawn on a globe and measuring distance east or west from zero degrees, which is known as the prime meridian.

Maritime climate: An area close to the sea has a temperate climate because the sea heats and cools more slowly than the land.

Market economy: An economic system characterized by private ownership in which prices are driven by the forces of supply and demand. Also known as capitalism.

Megaprojects: Large-scale industrial undertakings, which, because of their enormous size, dominate the local and regional economy during the construction phase. Construction costs usually exceed $1 billion and the start-up phase can extend for several years.

Métis: During the early fur trade era many fur traders took Indian wives. Their offspring, the Métis, developed a separate culture and history. In 1982, the Métis gained official recognition as one of the three Aboriginal peoples of Canada.

Metropolis: A principal city of a country or region.

Modernization theory: A theory of development emphasizing a lineal progression of economic and social advances over time.

Moraine: Any of several types of landforms composed of debris transported and deposited by a glacier.

Morbidity: The frequency of disease and illness in a population.

Mortality: Refers to deaths as a component of population change. The rate depends on age, sex, race, occupation, and social class. Its incidence can reveal much about a population's standard of living and health care. There are several ways to measure mortality, such as death rate per 1,000 population, age-specific death rate per 1,000, and infant mortality rate per 1,000 live births.

Multinational (company or corporation): A business organization usually headquartered in one parent country but with established operations in several countries.

Muskeg: An Indian term for a sphagnum-moss-covered bog found primarily in the Subarctic.

Native peoples (Aboriginal peoples): Those Canadians of Indian, Inuit, and Métis ancestry.

Non-governmental organizations (NGOs): An umbrella term encompassing a range of diverse organizations that are fundamentally outside government and generally not-for-profit.

Non-renewable resource: A resource that does not have the capacity to replenish itself, such as oil, gas, and minerals.

Non-status Indians: Those Canadian Indians who by birth, marriage, or choice have no legal status, under the Indian Act, to benefit from reserve lands and special federal programs.

Nordicity: A measure of the degree of 'northernness' of a place. Concept created by Hamelin. Nordicity provides a quantitative definition of the southern boundary of the North. It also allows a composite measure of northernness for any place. Nordicity is based on 10 selected variables that are supposed to represent all facets of the North.

Nuclear family: Social unit comprising a man and a woman living together with their children.

Nunatak: A mountain peak that stood above the ice sheets.

Nunavut: Created in 1999, the Territory of Nunavut in the eastern Arctic was carved from the present Northwest Territories; means 'our land' in Inuktitut; represents a political expression of the vision of an indigenous homeland.

OPEC (Organization of Petroleum Exporting Countries): The 13 major oil-exporting countries of the Third World act as a cartel or oligopoly to promote their joint national interests. Members include Saudi Arabia, Nigeria, Algeria, Venezuela, Libya, Kuwait, United Arab Emirates, Iran, Iraq, Ecuador, Qatar, Gabon, and Indonesia.

Ozone depletion: Ozone is the main atmospheric gas that absorbs biologically damaging ultraviolet radiation; chlorofluorocarbons (CFCs) are depleting the ozone layer. In the Arctic, a crater-like hole in the ozone layer of the atmosphere was discovered in 1986 but does not appear to be increasing in size.

Pack ice: Floating sea ice beyond the fast ice that is not attached to the land.

Patterned ground: Stones and pebbles arranged in a geometric pattern, e.g., circles or polygons. It is widespread in Arctic environments where frost action is the dominant geomorphic force.

Pemmican: A food made by Plains Indians; dry meat (usually buffalo) pounded into a coarse powder and then mixed with melted fat and possibly dried Saskatoon berries. It was light for transport, high in protein, and did not spoil.

Permafrost: A ground condition in which the soil or subsoil is permanently frozen; long-term frozen ground in periglacial environments; ground remaining at or below the freezing point for at least two years.

Pingo: An ice-cored hill found in permafrost areas. Pingos range in height from a few metres to 50 metres. Pingos expand in size as water seeps into the core and freezes, causing the ice core to expand. Most pingos are found in the Mackenzie Delta.

Pleistocene: A geological epoch associated with the last ice age; included at least four major ice advances, including the Wisconsin; began some 1.6 million years ago and ended some 10,000 years ago when the Holocene epoch began.

Podsoil: A leached soil containing oxides of iron, formed mainly in cool, humid climates.

Polar world: Those lands with Arctic and Subarctic natural environments.

Polynya (north water): Large area of open water in the Arctic Ocean surrounded by sea ice.

Population pyramid: A diagrammatic representation of the age and sex structure of a population.

Population trap: Malthusian belief that populations, if unchecked, tend to increase at a geometric rate while subsistence increases at an arithmetic rate. The trap occurs when a country or region has a higher rate of population increase than its rate of economic growth.

Primary activities: Economic pursuits involving production of natural resources, such as agriculture, livestock raising, forestry, fishing, and mining.

Psychic income: Non-monetary rewards such as pleasure or satisfaction gained from choosing a less than optimum economic option.

Push-pull migration: A theory used to explain the movement of people from rural to urban centres. The migrants are forced out of one area by limited opportunity and attracted to cities by perceived advantages.

Quality-of-life index: A measure of social well-being.

Quaternary: The most recent period of the Cenozoic era; includes the Pleistocene and Holocene; began some 1.6 million years ago and has not yet ended.

Rain shadow: The precipitation is noticeably less on the lee side of a mountain than on the windward side.

Raised beaches: These are remnants of former coastlines, usually the result of isostatic uplift.

Region: A portion of the earth that has some internal feature of cohesion or uniformity; for example, the Arctic.

Relief: A description of the surface of the land in terms of the difference in elevation between high and low points in an area.

Renewable resource: A resource that has the capacity to replenish itself, such as forests.

Reserve: Lands assigned to Indian bands when treaties were signed between a band and Ottawa. The purpose was to provide an Indian homeland for each band and to protect them from settlers and prospectors. Ownership of land granted to the tribe or band was a communal arrangement and land could not be sold. There are over 2,200 reserves in Canada and title to the land is held by the Crown.

Resource: A substance in the environment that is useful to people.

Scrip: A promissory note given to the Métis people that could be converted into either cash or land. For the most part, Métis sold their scrip.

Society: A social community wherein the sum of human activity and conditions function interdependently as a whole.

Solifluctation/solifluction (gelifluction): The movement of thawed, wet soil downslope in a series of distinct lobes; occurs in areas of permafrost.

Sovereignty: The exercise of power by the state over the resources and people contained within national boundaries.

Status Indians: Canadian Indians who have 'status' fall under the Indian Act. They have rights to use reserve lands held by their band and access to federal funding for programs such as housing and education. Those status Indians whose ancestors signed a treaty also have treaty rights.

Stewardship: The concept that human beings have an ethical responsibility to care for the natural world due to their power to change it.

Subarctic: A natural region of North America distinguished by its cold, continental climate and its natural vegetation cover (northern coniferous forest). Also the traditional homeland of northern Indians.

Subsistence economy: An economic system of relatively simple technology in which people produce most or all of the goods to satisfy their own and their family's needs; little or no exchange occurs outside of the immediate or extended family.

Sustainable development: Development that meets the needs of the present without compromising the ability of future generations to meet their own needs, and that advocates movement towards local control of production for local needs.

Taiga: Russian name given to the northern coniferous forest belt that stretches around the world in the northern hemisphere; also called the boreal forest.

Technocentrism: A way of thinking about humanity's relationship with nature that sees, accepts, and even encourages the change of the natural environment by humans through the application of scientific innovations and techniques.

Tertiary activities: The service portion of an economy.

Thermokarst: Ground-surface depression created by the thawing of ground ice in the periglacial zone; describes landscape with irregular, hummocky terrain found in permafrost areas. This irregular terrain results from the melting of ice in the ground and the subsequent subsidence of the ground.

Threshold: The minimum market needed for a business to survive or to justify the establishment of a public agency in a community.

Till: Unsorted material deposited by glacial ice.

Tribal groups: Groups of Indians united by language and customs and belonging to the same band.

Tundra: The treeless land found in the Arctic regions; also a major type of natural vegetation consisting of grasses, mosses, sedges, and lichens.

Twilight: A faint light that occurs after the sun has set or just before sunrise. Twilight occurs when the sun is just below the horizon. At that point, the sun's rays can still reach the atmosphere but not the land. The faint light is generated by the reflection of the sun's ray from the atmosphere back to the earth's surface

Underemployment: Condition whereby part of the labour force is employable but is not looking for employment because of the lack of job opportunities in their community.

Unemployable: Describes that part of the labour force that is not employed because they lack basic education necessary for employment, have health problems, or are handicapped.

Urbanization: The process of becoming urban; city formation and expansion. Urbanization is associated with the concentration of population into towns and cities.

Urban primacy: Concentration of population and services in a region's largest city; cities of intermediate size are rare in the North, and there are many very small settlements.

Value added: The gross value of the product minus the costs of raw material and energy.

Wisconsin glacial period: The last glacial phase in North America; the last ice advance during the Wisconsin glacial period is known as the Late Wisconsin ice advance that began some 25,000 years ago.